sappi
tree

including the ... ...al Park

Silver Cluster-leaf
Terminalia sericea, p. 120

Rina Grant and Val Thomas
Illustrations by Joan van Gogh

Contents

Why Sappi Tree Spotting is different	12	**The Lowveld**	25
Trees Greet You	13	Ecozones and Habitats	27
You Find Trees	13	Ecozones A – P	34
Understand the Area	13	Ecozone Tree Lists	50
Create Search Images	14	You Find Trees by Ecozone or Habitat	59
You Find Trees Easily	20	A Six-step Guide	59
Visually summarised information - How to use the Book	20		

Trees Greet You

Distinctive Striking Features	61	**Unique**	83
Flowers	62	Kapok Family Bombacaceae	
Pods	64	**Baobab** *Adansonia digitata*	84
Fruit	66		
Leaves	68	Palm Family Arecaceae	
Albizias and others	71	**Lala-palm** *Hyphaene coriacea* and *Hyphaene petersiana*	86
Acacias	72	**Wild Date-palm** *Phoenix reclinata*	88
Bushwillows	74	Thorn-tree Sub-family of Pea Family Mimosoideae	
Cluster-leafs	75	**Fever-tree Acacia** *Acacia xanthophloea*	90
Bark	76	**Umbrella Acacia** *Acacia tortilis*	92

Quinine-tree
Rauvolfia caffra Tree no 647

This tall, high-branching tree is easiest to find along riverbanks of Malelane Mountain Bushveld (C). It has a spreading, dark green canopy which is shaped by the surrounding vegetation. The thinly corky **bark** has a wrinkled appearance. Branchlets are often ringed with numerous raised leaf-scars. Large, evergreen **leaves** (120 - 280 x 30 - 60 mm) are crowded in whorls of 3 - 6 at the end of twigs. They have a distinctive, pale yellow central vein and clearly visible herringbone lateral veins. **Flowers** are small (4 x 2 mm diam.), white, sweet-smelling, and grow in large dense heads (120 - 200 mm diam.) on long flower-stems above the leaf clusters (Jun - Oct). The almost spherical **fruit** is typically in two paired lobes, each lobe being on average 190 mm in diameter. The young fruit is shiny and dark green with white spots, maturing black and wrinkled.

Trees Greet You

Seasonally Striking 95

Bauhinia Sub-family of Pea Family   Caesalpinioideae
African Weeping-wattle   *Peltophorum africanum*   96
Long-tail Cassia   *Cassia abbreviata*   98
Pride-of-de-Kaap Bauhinia   *Bauhinia galpinii*   100

Bushwillow Family   Combretaceae
Flame Climbing Bushwillow
   Combretum microphyllum   102
Purple-pod Cluster-leaf   *Terminalia prunioides*   104

Spikethorn family   Celastraceae
Red Spikethorn   *Gymnosporia senegalensis*   106

Sweet-pea Sub-family of Pea Family   Papilionoideae
Tree Wistaria   *Bolusanthus speciosus*   108
Zebrawood Flat-bean   *Dalbergia melanoxylon*   110

Thorn-tree Sub-family of Pea Family   Mimosoideae
Broad-pod Albizia   *Albizia forbesii*   112

You Find trees by Ecozone and Habitat

Big Six 115

Bauhinia Sub-family of Pea Family   Caesalpinioideae
Mopane   *Colophospermum mopane*   116

Bushwillow Family   Combretaceae
Leadwood Bushwillow   *Combretum imberbe*   118
Silver Cluster-leaf   *Terminalia sericea*   120

Mango Family   Anacardiaceae
Marula   *Sclerocarya birrea*   122

Sweet-pea Sub-family of Pea Family   Papilionoideae
Apple-leaf   *Philenoptera violacea*   124

Thorn-tree Sub-family of Pea Family   Mimosoideae
Knob-thorn Acacia   *Acacia nigrescens*   126

Ecozone Specialists 129

Euphorbia Family   Euphorbiaceae
Lebombo-ironwood   *Androstachys johnsonii*   130

Monkey-orange Family   Strychnaceae
Black Monkey-orange   *Strychnos madagascariensis*   132

Mustard-tree Family   Salvadoraceae
Narrow-leaved Mustard-tree   *Salvadora australis*   134

Myrrh Family   Burseraceae
Tall Firethorn Corkwood   *Commiphora glandulosa*   136

Sweet-pea Sub-family of Pea Family   Papilionoideae
Kiaat Bloodwood   *Pterocarpus angolensis*   138

Thorn-tree Sub-family of Pea Family   Mimosoideae
Delagoa Acacia   *Acacia welwitschii*   140
Many-stemmed Albizia   *Albizia petersiana*   142
Red Acacia   *Acacia gerrardii*   144

Torchwood Family   Balanitaceae
Greenthorn Torchwood   *Balanites maughamii*   146

Quinine-tree
Rauvolfia caffra
Flowers, leaves, fruit and bark.
See tree on the opposite page.

FIND TREES BY EASY HABITAT

ROCKY FOUR 149

Bauhinia Sub-family of Pea Family   Caesalpinioideae
Pod-mahogany   *Afzelia quanzensis*   150

Euphorbia Family   Euphorbiaceae
Deadliest Euphorbia   *Euphorbia cooperi*   152

Fig and Mulberry Family   Moraceae
Large-leaved Rock Fig   *Ficus abutilifolia*   154

Kirkia Family   Kirkiaceae
White Kirkia   *Kirkia acuminata*   156

EASY RIVER TRUNKS 159

Ebony Family   Ebenaceae
Ebony Jackal-berry   *Diospyros mespiliformis*   160

Euphorbia Family   Euphorbiaceae
Tamboti   *Spirostachys africana*   162

Fig and Mulberry Family   Moraceae
Sycomore Fig   *Ficus sycomorus*   164

Sweet-pea Sub-family of Pea Family   Papilionoideae
Nyala-tree   *Xanthocercis zambesiaca*   166

EASY RIVER CANOPIES 169

Bauhinia Sub-family of Pea Family   Caesalpinioideae
Weeping Boer-bean   *Schotia brachypetala*   170

Buddleja Family   Buddlejaceae
Water Nuxia   *Nuxia oppositifolia*   172

Bushwillow Family   Combretaceae
River Bushwillow   *Combretum erythrophyllum*   174

Coffee and Gardenia Family   Rubiaceae
Matumi   *Breonadia salicina*   176

Jacaranda Family   Bignoniaceae
Sausage-tree   *Kigelia africana*   178

Mahogany Family   Meliaceae
Natal-mahogany   *Trichilia emetica*   180

Thorn-tree Sub-family of Pea Family   Mimosoideae
River Acacia   *Acacia robusta*   182

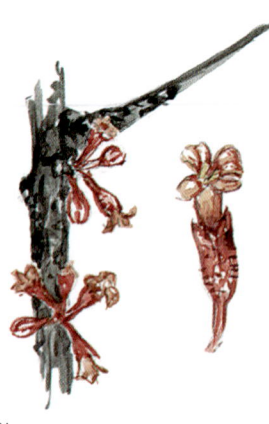

Firethorn Corkwood   Tree no 285
Commiphora pyracanthoides

This multi-stemmed shrub or small tree is common in drier areas, particularly where there are rocks, throughout the Lowveld. It is easiest to find in Ecozone P, Mopane Bushwillow Woodlands. The **bark** is grey to yellowish-green and flaky, peeling in layers to expose shiny underbark like other Corkwoods (See Corkwood GIFF p. 136). Simple, narrowly elliptic **leaves**, with toothed margins, are clustered on spine-tipped side-branches (38 x 25 – 30 mm). Small, bell-shaped pink or red **flowers** appear before the new leaves in spring (Sep – Oct). The **fruit** is an oval, fleshy berry (Nov – Feb) (10 mm). The botanical name *pyracanthoides* indicates that, like the *Pyrancantha* species, both thorny branches and red fruit are present.

FIND MORE DIFFICULT TREES

BRACK LOVERS 185

Buckthorn and Jujube Family   Rhamnaceae
Buffalo-thorn Jujube   *Ziziphus mucronata*   186

Coffee and Gardenia Family   Rubiaceae
Bushveld Gardenia   *Gardenia volkensii*   188

Ebony Family   Ebenaceae
Magic Guarri   *Euclea divinorum*   190

Litchi and Soapberry Family   Sapindaceae
Jacket-plum   *Pappea capensis*   192

Spikethorn Family   Celastraceae
Bushveld Saffron   *Elaeodendron transvaalense*   194

Thorn-tree Sub-family of Pea Family   Mimosoideae
Horned-thorn Acacia   *Acacia grandicornuta*   196
Scented-pod Acacia   *Acacia nilotica*   198

SMALLER TREES IN GROUPS 201

Bushwillow Family   Combretaceae
Large-fruited Bushwillow   *Combretum zeyheri*   202
Red Bushwillow   *Combretum apiculatum*   204
Russet Bushwillow   *Combretum hereroense*   206

Jute and Linden Family   Tiliaceae
Sandpaper Raisin   *Grewia flavescens*   208
White-leaved Raisin   *Grewia bicolor*   210

Sweet-pea Sub-family of Pea Family   Papilionoideae
Round-leaved Bloodwood
   Pterocarpus rotundifolius   212

Thorn-tree Sub-family of Pea Family   Mimosoideae
Flaky-bark Acacia   *Acacia exuvialis*   214
Sickle-bush   *Dichrostachys cinerea*   216

Family Features	220
Lowveld Maps	224
Tree Index	238
References	243

Large Sourplum Tree no 103
Ximenia caffra

This small, spiny tree or shrub grows in a variety of Habitats, but is easiest to find in granites on both crests and in valley bottoms as well as on termite mounds. It also occurs in the Lebombo Mountains, Ecozone I. It branches low down into numerous main branches. It then grows upwards to form a sparse, untidy, irregular canopy, with **spines** scattered on branches or at the end of twigs, but sometimes absent. **Leaves** are dull green and grow on the short, spine-tipped branchlets, and tend to fold inwards (30 - 80 x 20 - 40 mm). **Flowers** are sweet-scented, creamy-white, and star-shaped in the angle between spine or leaf (Aug - Oct) (12 mm). **Fruit** is oval, bright red when ripe, with pale spots and a thin skin. It is tasty, but very sour (Dec - Jan) (25 mm).

3

Acknowledgements

Sappi Tree Spotting Lowveld originally took two years of intensive research and testing to reach publication date. This has been followed by many months to update it with this revision. Jacana is grateful to all the people from many different fields who gave their time and commitment to produce this superb publication. We would like specifically to thank the following individuals and organisations sincerely for their dedication, their time and expertise during the project.

Acknowledgments

The research and development of **Sappi Tree Spotting** was carried out by Val Thomas and Rina Grant. This would not have been possible without the assistance of the following scientists: Nick Zambatis and Dr Freek Venter (National Parks Board), Mike Peel (Agricultural Research Council) and Dr Rina Grant.

Our special thanks and warmest congratulations to Joan van Gogh for the beautifully illustrated artwork which will assist tree spotters to discover and identify trees of the Lowveld. We would also like to acknowledge and thank Sally MacLarty for her contributions to the line-artwork, and Penny Noall for the cover artwork.

The book itself was designed by High Branching, and the cover by Hothouse Designs. The Desktop Publishing was done by Jacana and High Branching.

We thank the various companies and individuals who helped in the production of the Maps: CartoGraphics for layout and DTP, as well as Rizelle Stander, the South African National Biodiversity Institute (SANBI), Clive Webber and Barry Low for their expert help on the geology. The tree distribution maps of South Africa were supplied by Trevor Arnold and Mrs Hannelie Snyman (National Botanical Institute, Pretoria), and updated off maps by Rebelo and Low.

Many people gave generously of their time in order to test and check the book, and we thank them for their invaluable assistance: Sidney Miller, Nick Zambatis, Guin Zambatis, Dr Harry Biggs, Christo van der Linde and Robbie Clarke (National Parks Board); Honorary Rangers Corps; Penny and Gordon Brodie; John and Tish Payne; Shirley Clarke; BB Bengis; Duan Biggs; Sharon Pollard (Wits Rural Facility); Mike Peel (Agricultural Research Council), Johan Kluge (Lowveld Botanical Gardens, Nelspruit); Brandon Kemp and Debbie White. All the meanings of the names were taken from **Sappi Tree Spotting What's in a name?** by Dr Hugh Glen.

Sincere thanks to Peter Thomas and Ernst Schmidt for additional photographs; Anina Kruger and Rizelle Stander for design and DTP expertise; Rina Grant, Lorraine Doyle, Louis Barendse, Denise Raikin, Hazel Cuthbertson, and most particularly, Val Thomas, for a variety of contributions.

We are proud to acknowledge the work of both the Jacana and High Branching teams who have contributed in their specialised fields to produce **Sappi Tree Spotting, Lowveld.**

Finally, we would like to thank Sappi Limited for their vision and commitment in helping to fund the research and development of a book that we believe will add significantly towards helping South Africans and their visitors to be aware of, to care for, to protect and to enjoy our magnificent Lowveld trees.

Jacana Media
Johannesburg; August 2006

FOREWORD

The matured environment of Mpumalanga is mainly comprised of the following indigenous forest types: Lowveld of Mpumalanga mist belt and the Northern KwaZulu-Natal mist belt. The healthy functioning of the natured environment of the Lowveld is central to the success of the tourism industry in Mpumalanga. Of all South Africa's tourist destinations, the Lowveld has proved to be the most breathtaking adventure, with numerous scenic regions in the woodlands areas such as the Kruger National Park and other game parks.

There is so much to explore, and these easy-to-use guides make Tree Spotting much easier. Seeing these trees is one part of the pleasure. However, also knowing that there are about 18 000 plant species, in total, that occur in South Africa, makes us aware that we have a heritage that is worth our care. Our 1 300 indigenous tree species are more than just beautiful. They play an important part in the lives of our people. They have for centuries been significant in culture, in health preparations, and in providing food and materials for shelter and heating, especially for cooking.

Our indigenous trees need to be protected; unfortunately we have lost many trees in the past through the needs of modern industry and agriculture, as well as by the over-exploitation of these resources by impoverished communities. It is therefore important that in our efforts to protect trees we look at balancing the needs of industry with those of the environment; and create economic opportunities for our people, and support them with access to basic services such as housing, water, sanitation and electricity.

Global warming and climate change caused by increased emissions of carbon dioxide by industry is of great concern, and much is being done by governments across the world to reduce the damage to the environment. Trees help mitigate the effects of global warming by transforming the carbon dioxide into tree fibre and oxygen. The life cycle of trees is also important because the leaves and branches fall to the ground, and as they rot away, this restores nutrients to the soil to feed new growth.

It is pleasing that Sappi, and the timber industry in general, are concerned about preservation and conservation, for Government cannot preserve our heritage on its own. The private sector's involvement is essential. But we also need the local population to have a stake in these activities so that they share in all the benefits of the industry, and therefore come to willingly share in the conservation of our biological diversity.

Our Government is helping to conserve indigenous trees under the National Forests Act, 1998 (Act 84 of 1998), and has already published a list of 47 protected trees in the Government Gazette, and this list will be revised annually. This book will therefore assist in the identification of those protected trees and also in identifying trees that should be considered for inclusion on the list.

Trees are our heritage and we need to be able to identify them and enjoy the beauty and benefit they provide.

Mrs Lindiwe Hendricks, MP
Minister of Water Affairs and Forestry

Jacket-plum
Pappea capensis
p. 192

Sappi

South Africa has many beautiful landscapes, and the Lowveld ranks highly on this list. For the purpose of this book, the Lowveld stretches from the northern tip of KwaZulu-Natal upwards through Swaziland, Mpumalanga and Limpopo, all the way to Zimbabwe, taking in all of the Kruger National Park.

Sappi has a long involvement in the Lowveld. Indeed, the Lowveld has played a major role in the growth and global expansion of our company, housing as it does many of our plantation forest resources as well as our Ngodwana Kraft Mill. These assets enabled the company to enter global export markets in the 1980s, the first steps towards the creation of one of South Africa's first truly global companies, and today a leader in the pulp and paper industry worldwide.

Sappi is the largest corporate employer in the Lowveld and has made a lasting contribution, in particular to the towns of Nelspruit and Barberton and the surrounding communities. We have helped upgrade the Lowveld Botanical Gardens, including the building in 2006 of an aerial boardwalk. We are the founding sponsor of the largest teacher development programme on the African continent, Penreach at Penryn College, where we have impacted on the lives of more than 6 000 teachers and 300 000 scholars. We have also established the first multi-media resource centre for the community of Umjindi at the Barberton Town Library.

Our support for conservation and the environment includes tree plantings at local schools and libraries during Arbor Week each year, the Sappi Great Birding Adventure annual bird count on our plantations and the publication of various books on local fauna and flora. The Sappi Tree Spotting series was the first of its kind in South Africa, and we are pleased to see the interest it has generated in South Africa's rich collection of trees. We are sure this new edition will greatly add to your enjoyment and understanding of the natural wonders the Lowveld holds.

The first four books in the series (a fifth and final book on the Cape is in the process of being researched and written) are designed as an introduction and companions to exploring South Africa's rich tree heritage. Superbly illustrated and informative, they provide easy-to-access information for everyone from gardeners and hikers, to those with an interest in the medicinal properties of trees. A further enhancement is the recent publication, also by Jacana, of the *Sappi Lifer List*, which now enables both casual and ardent tree spotters to keep a lifelong record of their tree encounters, as well as *Sappi What's in a name?*, a fun publication explaining the meanings of the botanical names of trees.

South Africa is home to over 1 000 indigenous tree species, an extraordinary number when compared with the 100 indigenous species in Europe. Sappi does not harvest indigenous trees in South Africa for commercial purposes. We are committed to internationally certified forestry practices, and source wood fibre from independently audited and sustainably managed plantations everywhere in the world.

Please enjoy reading and using this and the other books in our Tree Spotting series. We hope you will share our commitment to protect and conserve South Africa's wonderfully diverse natural heritage.

Eugene van As
Chairman

The Mac Mac River on Sappi's Venus Tree Farm is an essential part of the unique ecosystem in this Lowveld region.

THE SOUTH AFRICAN NATIONAL BIODIVERSITY INSTITUTE (SANBI)

The mission of SANBI is to promote the sustainable use, conservation, appreciation and enjoyment of the exceptionally rich biodiversity of South Africa, for the benefit of all people. The vision of SANBI is to be the leading institution in biodiversity science in Africa, facilitating conservation, sustainable use of living resources, and human wellbeing.

SANBI
This is an autonomous, state-supported, statutory organisation. It has physical resources such as the eight National Botanical Gardens, three Herbaria and two Research Units. In addition, it boasts the human resources of many highly qualified scientists, horticulturists, academics and support staff.

NATIONAL BOTANICAL GARDENS
The eight National Botanical Gardens propagate and display the unique wealth and diversity of South African flora.

Free State National Botanical Garden	(051) 436-3530
Harold Porter National Botanical Garden	(028) 272-9311
Karoo National Botanical Garden	(023) 347-0785
Kirstenbosch National Botanical Garden	(021) 799-8800
KwaZulu-Natal National Botanical Garden	(033) 344-3585
Lowveld National Botanical Garden	(013) 752-5531
Pretoria National Botanical Garden	(012) 843-5000
Walter Sisulu National Botanical Garden	(011) 958-1750/1

HERBARIA
The combined collections of dried plant material of the three SANBI herbaria, in Durban, Cape Town and Pretoria, contain over 1,5 million specimens of mainly Southern African plant material. They are an invaluable resource to researchers throughout the African continent, as well as internationally.

EDUCATION
Environmental Education, both within the National Botanical Gardens and working with communities on greening projects country-wide, is a major priority of SANBI.

RESEARCH
Research efforts of SANBI Plant Scientists have been concentrated on issues that are important for the conservation and sustainable use of the Southern African flora and vegetation. The goal of Plant Systematics Research is to document plant diversity and this is achieved mainly through detailed studies of the natural affinities and phylogenetic relationships of plants. The goal of other biodiversity research is to understand biodiversity responses to land use, climate change and alien invasives and to study suitable ways to ameliorate these threats, as well as to undertake research on sustainable use of plant resources.

BOTANICAL SOCIETY MEMBERSHIP
Members of the public who are interested in the work of the SANBI can join their nearest branch of the Botanical Society, or can visit their local National Botanical Garden.

SANBI AND SAPPI TREE SPOTTING
By a sheer coincidence of positive energy, the early phase of planning the Tree Spotting series overlapped with the SANBI publication of the Low and Rebelo Vegetation Map of South Africa, p. 26.

Defining the boundaries of each Tree Spotting book, and the zones within each boundary, was automatically facilitated by this essential piece of scientific work. As part of the information about each tree, there are mini-maps of its South African distribution. The information for each of these maps was supplied by SANBI from data collected throughout the country. It is services and relationships such as these that make SANBI a unique and invaluable asset to South Africa.

Botanical Society of South Africa

The Botanical Society aims to support the South African National Biodiversity Institute (SANBI), and to promote the conservation, cultivation, study and wise use of the indigenous plants of Southern Africa for the benefit of all.

Botanical Society Membership

Information and application forms are obtainable from the various National Botanical Gardens, Botanical Society head office, or branches.

Head Office: Kirstenbosch

Tel: (021) 797-2090 Fax: (021) 797-2376
e-mail: info@botanicalsociety.org.za
Private Bag X10, Claremont, 7735
New members are welcome.
Members enjoy the following benefits:

- The privilege of visiting any of South Africa's National Botanical Gardens free of charge.
- First-hand experience of our magnificent indigenous plants can be gained on organised hikes and outings.
- The opportunity to increase their knowledge by attending demonstrations and lectures.
- The pleasure of receiving Veld & Flora, our quarterly magazine full of interesting articles, free of charge.
- A discount of 10% on books purchased at the bookshop at Kirstenbosch Gardens, Cape Town.
- The opportunity to support and participate in plant conservation and environmental education projects and to assist with development projects for SANBI.

Botanical Society Branches

Albany Branch	(046) 636-1370
Algoa Branch	(041) 372-1162
Bankenveld Branch	(011) 958-0529
Bredasdorp / Napier Branch	(028) 424-2082
Cederberg Branch	(027) 482-2763
Free State Branch	(051) 522-0590
Garden Route Branch	(044) 877-1360
Kirstenbosch Branch	(021) 671-5468
Kogelberg Branch	(028) 272-9311
KwaZulu-Natal Coastal Branch	(031) 201-5111
KwaZulu-Natal Inland Branch	(033) 396-9955
Limpopo Branch	(015) 299-0193
Lowveld Branch	(013) 744-0241
Pretoria Branch	(012) 333-4629
West Coast Branch	(022) 492-2750
Winelands Branch	076 672 3830

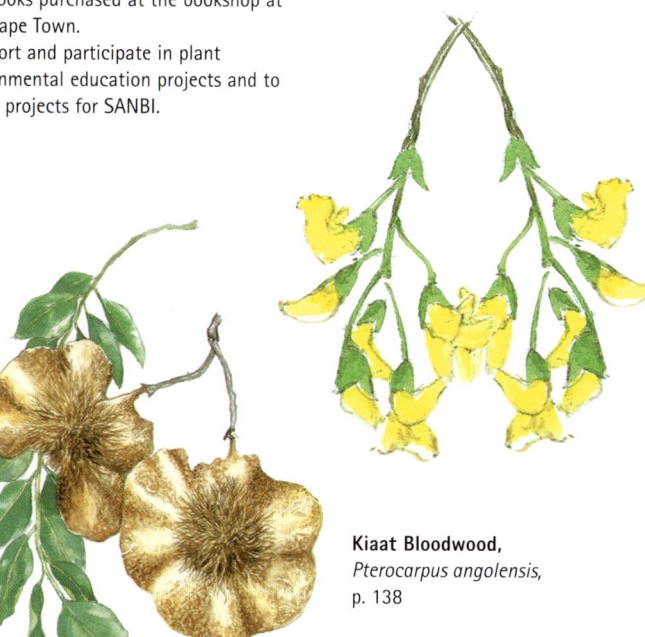

Kiaat Bloodwood,
Pterocarpus angolensis,
p. 138

Tree Society

The Tree Society of Southern Africa has been actively involved in promoting an interest in our natural heritage since 1946.

Outings, education and publications
Members are enthusiasts from all walks of life, including professional botanists, who will gladly assist in extending your knowledge of the environment.
- Enjoy visits to undisturbed areas not generally accessible to the public. Discussions on walks extend beyond trees to cover geology, general flora, fauna and history. Day outings, within reasonable driving distance of Johannesburg and Pretoria, as well as weekend and long-weekend visits, are organised to areas in neighbouring provinces.
- The Society collaborates with the C.E. Moss Herbarium offering courses on identifying trees.
- A prime objective is compiling vegetation checklists for landowners, and noting rare species and noxious invaders.
- The Society has been instrumental in establishing three prizes for excellence in the field of Plant Systematics at Wits University.
- Funds being available, the Society assists deserving students furthering studies in Botany.

- The Society journal, 'Trees in South Africa', has been published since 1949, and back numbers of many issues are still available. Articles are of general and botanical interest.
- 'Peltophorum' – The Society Newsletter is issued twice a year.

Membership
Details may be obtained from:
The Tree Society of Southern Africa
P.O. Box 70720, Bryanston, 2021
Walter Barker: Tel / Fax (011) 465-6045
e-mail: walterb@icon.co.za
Cheryl Dehning: Tel (011) 316-1426; 083 376 1734
Fax (011) 316-1095
e-mail: dehning@mweb.co.za

Wits courses
For information contact:
Reneé Reddy: Tel (011) 717-6467
e-mail: kevinb@gecko.biol.wits.ac.za: renee@gecko.biol.wits.ac.za

Dendrological Society

Arborum silvarumque conservatio salus mundi est.
The conservation of trees and forests is the salvation of the world.

Aims, activities and publications
The Dendrological Foundation, formed in 1979 by Dr F. von Breitenbach, was created as an independent, non-profit, non-racial association aimed at the promotion of the knowledge of trees. In 1980 the Dendrological Society was formed, with similar aims, focusing on conservation and education.
- Dendron is the Society magazine, and the Journal of Dendrology contains more scientific essays on all aspects of dendrology.

Branches
Branches around the country are named after a tree species, or a significant geographical feature.
- Head Office: Waterberg, Modimolle
  PO Box 2008, Modimolle, 0510
  Secretary: Erwin Grobbelaar
  Tel: 083 292 3165; Fax: (014) 717-1693
  e mail: dendrosoc@esnet.co.za

- 'Magalies' – Pretoria
  (012) 567-4009 Jutta von Breitenbach
- 'Atalaya' – Port Elizabeth
- 'Boekenhout' – Witbank
- 'Celtis' – Pietermaritzburg
- 'Erythrina' – Polokwane
- 'Kameeldoring' – Mokopane
- 'Kwambonambi' – Zululand
- 'Langeberg' – Swellendam
- 'Manketti' – Lephalale
- 'Olienhout' – Groot Marico
- 'Outeniqua' – Knysna
- 'Soutpansberg' – Makhado
- 'Tafelberg' – Cape Town
- 'Umdoni' – Durban
- 'Vaal' – Meyerton
- 'Witwatersrand' – Johannesburg
- 'Wolkberg' – Tzaneen

Food and Trees for Africa

Food and Trees for Africa's (FTFA) mission is to contribute to a healthy and sustainable quality of life for all through environmental awareness and greening programmes.

Objectives

FTFA, established in 1990, is the only national, non-governmental, non-profit organisation in South Africa addressing sustainable national resources management and food security through permaculture and urban greening. Its objectives are to create an awareness of the benefits of environmental upliftment activities amongst all communities of Southern Africa. It is currently involved in diverse projects ranging from urban greening, permaculture, environmental awareness and education to township nurseries.

- Over 1,7 million trees have been distributed to thousands of disadvantaged communities throughout the country.
- Three newsletters are produced and distributed annually, to over 4 500 organisations and individuals, locally and internationally. Five environmental education booklets have been published and are available at FTFA.
- Plant a tree to celebrate or honour someone you know and FTFA will send a personalised certificate to register this.
- FTFA encourages South Africans to celebrate trees, and anyone wishing to contribute to the greening of Southern Africa can assist by becoming a member of FTFA.

Membership

- R50 Individual membership per year - receive FTFA's newsletter, Newsleaf, quarterly.
- R150 Family membership per year - receive a certificate in the family name, three newsletters quarterly, and trees will be planted where they are really needed.
- All businesses that support FTFA receive a personalised certificate, coverage in FTFA's newsletters and Annual Review, and subscription to all three newsletters. FTFA links companies with meaningful community upliftment programmes.

For more information contact: Jeunesse Park (CEO) or Annun Zietta (Programme Manager): (011) 803-9750; fax: (011) 803-9604; web: www.trees.org.za; email: trees@cis.co.za; info@trees.org.za

Names of South African Trees

All trees that have been identified and 'listed' internationally have a botanical, bi-nomial name. This is invaluable in recognising families and their linkages all over the Earth.

In South Africa there are about 1 000 woody species that can grow tall enough to offer shade to sit under – a daunting number of Latin names to learn – especially for beginners. In addition our rainbow nation has eleven official languages; many of our trees have at least that many 'common' names, if not more. In early South African human history, names were given by Koi-San peoples, and later by black tribes moving southwards from central Africa. The arrival of settlers from Europe led to many trees being named by farmers, timber merchants, carpenters and builders, the majority of whom were of Dutch descent. English speakers were, in the main, not people of the land, and the vast majority of trees did not have English names until the mid 1950s, except as translations.

Since then various groups have attempted to 'co-ordinate' or 'improve' the early translations, and this has led to a series of changes in the literature. Currently there is a world-wide move towards international standardisation, accuracy and the 'marketing' of trees to make them accessible, interesting and exciting for members of the general public who want to tree spot for recreation. The final lists have not been written, and in the interim changes are inevitable!

The Sappi Tree Spotting series is committed to ease of identification, and our names too have changed over the series. Two new books in the series have been published to help you to become familiar with the current names. Look out for **Sappi Tree Spotting Lifer List** and **Sappi Tree Spotting What's in a Name?** In both these books our Sappi Tree Spotting *Bookworm, Ettie* and *Al* are a treat to entertain and enlighten you.

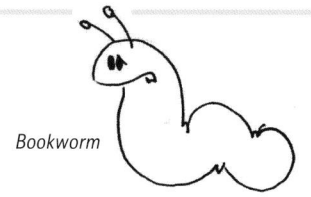

Bookworm

WHY SAPPI TREE SPOTTING IS DIFFERENT

Sappi Tree Spotting is a creative new way to make the most of the outdoors. It is hoped that it will increase the popularity of Tree Spotting as Roberts and Newman did for Bird Watching. Twelve years of intensive, scientific, field and market research have gone into fine-tuning a simple and innovative method of getting to know trees in their natural environments. Until recently, trees have remained inaccessible to all but the most devoted, botanically-minded, tree-key followers.

Sappi Tree Spotting changes this with innovative methods of linking real trees to book theory.
In most other field guides, for either animals or plants, the system is based on:
- seeing a species in the wild
- looking it up in the guidebook to identify it, and to gain further information

In **Sappi Tree Spotting** that system changes in four ways:

1 TREES GREET YOU
Identify a specific tree because it is spectacular (see opposite page).
This is similar to the traditional method described above, because these trees are spectacular enough to be recognised easily. Some feature of the tree is so Distinctively Striking, Unique, or Seasonally Striking that you cannot fail to identify it.

2 YOU FIND TREES
Understand the Lowveld area, to be able to look for the right trees in the right places (see opposite page).
This is a **Sappi Tree Spotting** innovation, and is based on your setting out to look for specific trees in specific places. In natural environments, most trees flourish and reach maturity in areas that suit them best. That is the right place for you to find and learn about them first. To approach it from the opposite angle, when you are in an area it makes sense first to find those trees that thrive there best. Much of the layout and philosophy of this book-series aims to make this identification of the right trees as easy as possible.

3 YOU FIND TREES
Create Search Images by using simple language p. 14.
This series highlights aspects of the chosen trees that are easiest to visualise. Whichever area you are in, you can work out which trees you are likely to find, and build up a mental picture of their most Striking Features. We have tried to make the text clear and easy-to-follow in non-botanical language. The average recreational Tree Spotter will never use 'pubescence' when 'hairy' will do! Learning to know and love trees need not only be for people who are scientifically trained.

4 YOU FIND TREES EASILY
Refer to the visually summarised information for easy access to information p. 20.
This series helps the Tree Spotter by means of accessible, easy-to-use information like: height and shade density icons, grids indicating seasonal changes, maps and information blocks. It also gives information on modern and traditional uses for trees, and their possible use in gardens.

Large-fruited Bushwillow,
Combretum zeyheri, p. 202

1   TREES GREET YOU – IDENTIFY A SPECIFIC TREE BECAUSE IT IS SO SPECTACULAR

Although there are literally hundreds of species of trees in the Lowveld, and many of these are difficult to identify, there are a number that are easily spotted. None of these needs a complex system of 'keying', because they are instantly recognisable, in many instances even from a distance. There are three ways of using this book to find the names of these distinctive trees.

DISTINCTIVE STRIKING FEATURES
On pages 62 - 81 you will find a series of visual summaries of striking leaves, flowers, fruit and bark, as well as comparisons. You could well come across a Distinctive Striking Feature on a tree in the wild, look it up in these pages, and be able to identify it immediately.

Long-tail Cassia flowers, p. 98

UNIQUE TREES
On pages 84 - 93 are the Unique Trees, so unusual in their growth form that after you have browsed through the book once or twice, you will not fail to recognise them if you see them in the wild.

Lala-palm leaves, p. 86

SEASONALLY STRIKING TREES
On pages 96 - 113 are the trees that have very striking flowers or fruit in certain seasons, and they may be difficult to identify without these features. The recommendation is that if you want instant recognition, you first look for these trees in the specified season. This is made easier by the Seasonal Grid on the first page of each tree's description.

Purple-pod Cluster-leaf pods, p. 104

2   YOU FIND TREES – UNDERSTAND THE AREA

LOOK FOR THE RIGHT TREES IN THE RIGHT PLACES
From pages 26 - 49 there are descriptions of the various Ecozones and Habitats of the Lowveld. There is always a strong correlation between any area and the trees you can look for there. It is worthwhile familiarising yourself with the area where you intend to go Tree Spotting. Use the maps on pages 224 - 237, and the cross-section diagram and Ecozone blocks shown below. A Six-step Guide is summarised on p. 59.

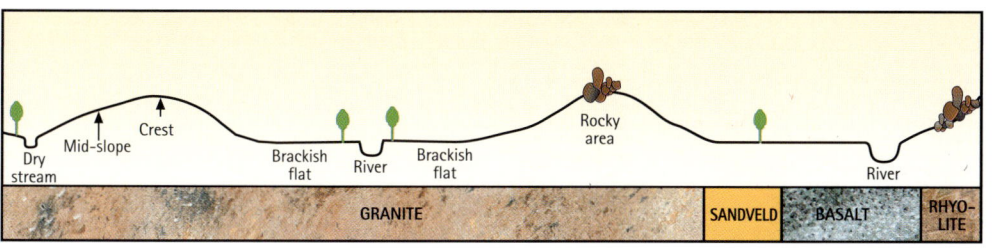

3 YOU FIND TREES – CREATE SEARCH IMAGES BY USING SIMPLE LANGUAGE

Finding a tree that you do not know is like looking for a stranger in a crowded room. You need to have a clear Search Image of certain Striking Features that you can visualise easily.

For example, when looking for a specific person, you may think of a tall, red-haired woman with glasses. In the same way, most trees covered in this book have a specific form and look about them that will help you find them.

Look at a number of different trees carefully and you will see many patterns. The fascinating part is that most species do have their own pattern so strongly encoded that it is repeated to a greater or lesser degree in each individual tree. As you learn these patterns of growth, you will learn to recognise many trees at a glance.

Sappi Tree Spotting describes these patterns in this order:
- Main branches splitting off the trunk/stem.
- Branchlets splitting off the branches, then dividing into twigs.
- Leaf-stalks attaching the leaves to the twigs, or in a few trees, the leaves to the branchlets.

Main branches always leave the main trunk (or stem) in a generally upward or horizontal direction. However, branchlets and twigs tend to grow in their own specific upward, horizontal or even downward pattern, or they can be a mixture.

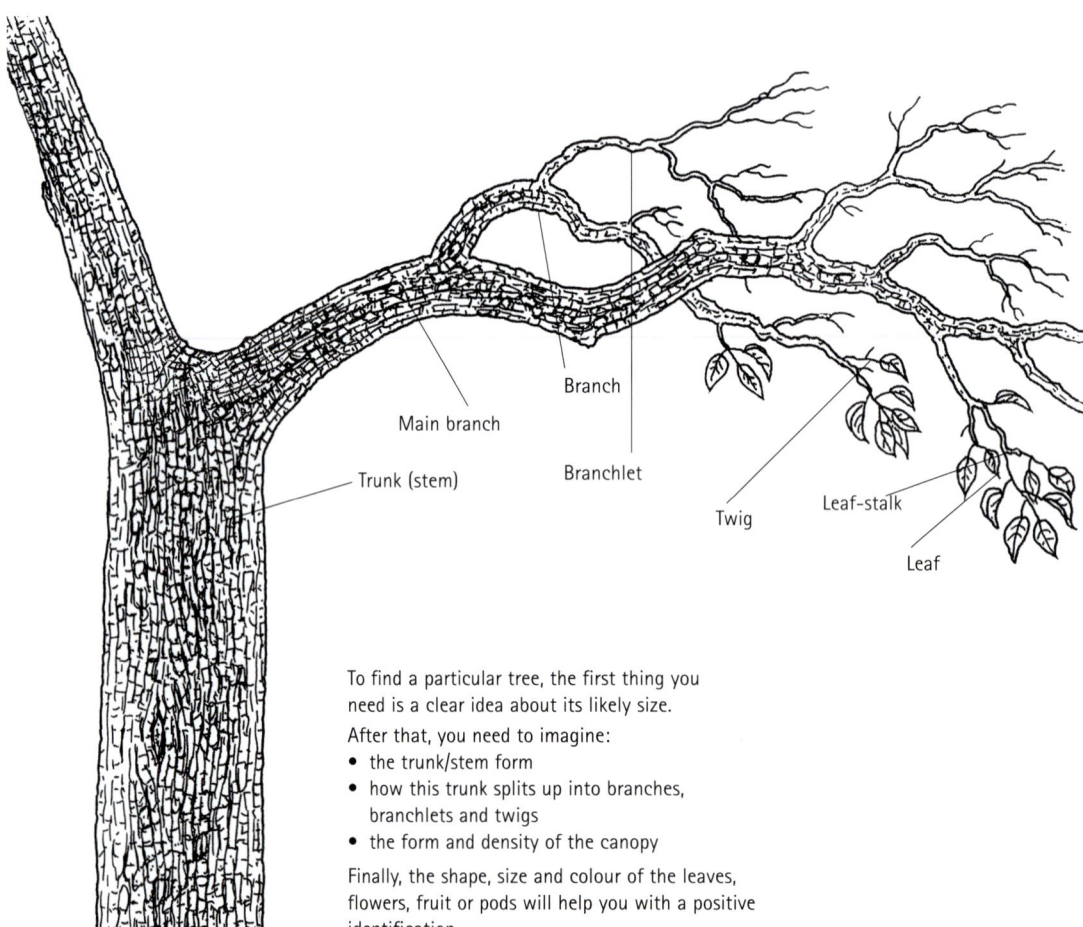

To find a particular tree, the first thing you need is a clear idea about its likely size.

After that, you need to imagine:
- the trunk/stem form
- how this trunk splits up into branches, branchlets and twigs
- the form and density of the canopy

Finally, the shape, size and colour of the leaves, flowers, fruit or pods will help you with a positive identification.

On the following pages, you will find the terms used in **Sappi Tree Spotting**. These will help you to create your Search Images.

TRUNKS AND STEMS

'Trunk' is used for larger trees and 'stems' for smaller and/or multi-stemmed trees.

Multi-stemmed
eg. Many-stemmed Albizia
p. 142

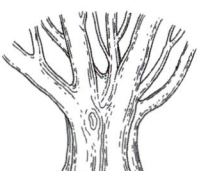

Single-trunked, low-branching
eg. Sycomore Fig
p. 164

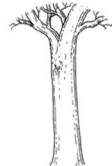

Straight, single-trunked, high-branching
eg. Leadwood Bushwillow
p. 118

Straight trunk
eg. Marula
p. 122

Crooked trunk
eg. Apple-leaf
p. 124

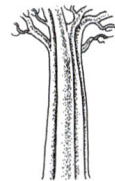

Fluted trunk
eg. Greenthorn Torchwood
p. 146

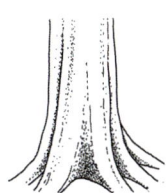

Buttressed trunk
eg. Sycomore Fig
p. 164

CANOPIES

The canopy is the upper area of a tree, formed by the branchlets/twigs and the leaves.

Round Canopy
eg. Natal-mahogany
p. 180

Semi-circular Canopy
eg. Marula
p. 122

Umbrella Canopy
eg. Umbrella Acacia
p. 92

Wide spreading Canopy
eg. Pod-mahogany
p. 150

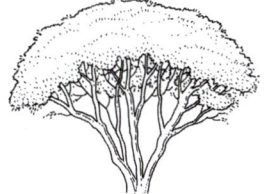

V-shaped Canopy
eg. Many-stemmed Albizia
p. 142

Narrow Canopy
eg. Tree Wistaria
p. 108

Irregular Canopy
eg. Apple-leaf
p. 124

LEAVES

A leaf usually grows on a leaf-stalk that attaches the leaf to the twig or branchlet.
It snaps off the twig or branchlet relatively easily at the leaf-bud (axillary bud). You can often see this bud as a swelling at the base of the leaf-stalk – it may be where a flower or twiglet comes from.

All leaves are described as Simple or Compound. Sometimes it is not easy to tell the difference between a simple and a compound leaf.

Some of the ways are:
- Look for the position of the leaf-bud.
- Compound leaves look organised on their leaf-stalk. Most simple leaves that are grouped close together look irregular on the twig.
- The leaflet of a compound leaf tends to tear off the leaf-stalk – it does not snap off neatly, the way the leaf itself usually snaps off the twig at the leaf-bud. Please note this is not true for all species, nor at all times of the year.

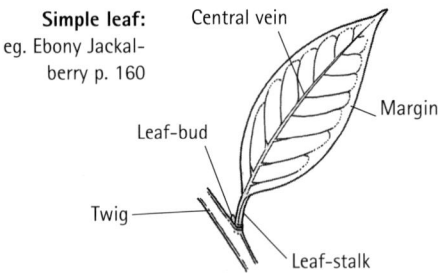

Simple leaf:
eg. Ebony Jackal-berry p. 160

Labels: Central vein, Margin, Leaf-bud, Twig, Leaf-stalk

Compound leaves:

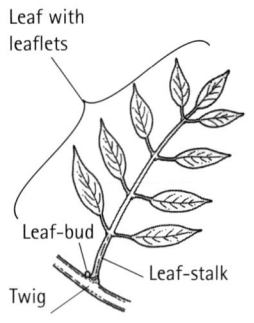

Once Compound
(Pinnate)
eg. Marula
p. 122

Leaf with leaflets. Labels: Leaf-bud, Leaf-stalk, Twig

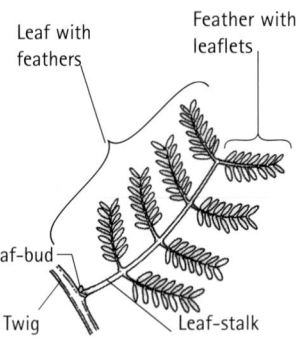

Twice Compound
(Bipinnate)
eg. Acacias
p. 74-76

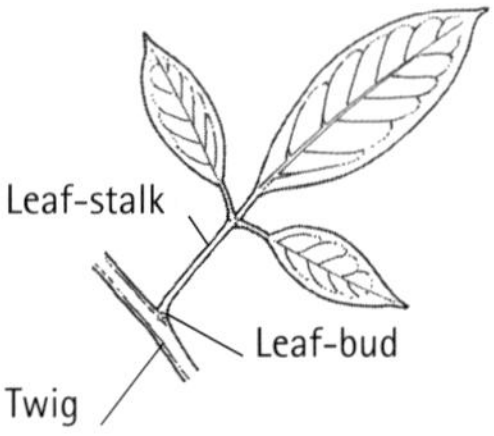

Leaf with feathers; Feather with leaflets. Labels: Leaf-bud, Twig, Leaf-stalk

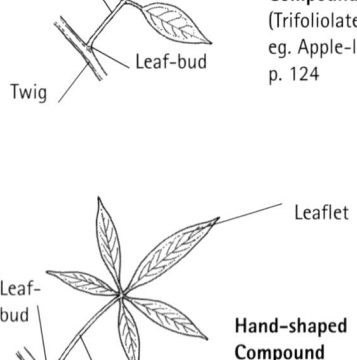

Three-leaflet Compound
(Trifoliolate)
eg. Apple-leaf
p. 124

Labels: Leaf-stalk, Leaf-bud, Twig

Hand-shaped Compound
(Digitate)
eg. Baobab
p. 84

Labels: Leaflet, Leaf-bud, Twig, Leaf-stalk

Once Compound leaves can end in two ways:

A pair of leaflets at the tip
(Paripinnate)
eg. Weeping Boer-bean p. 170

A single leaflet at the tip
(Imparipinnate)
eg. Sausage-tree
p. 178

Vein patterns on leaves vary a great deal.
Two distinctive patterns are:

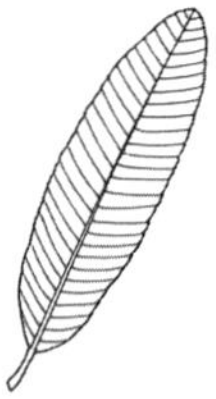

Herringbone
eg. Drooping Resin-tree
p. 40

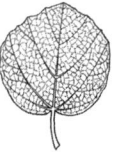

Net-veining
eg. Wild-pear Dombeya
p. 36

LEAF ATTACHMENTS TO TWIGS OR BRANCHLETS

Leaf-stalks can be attached to the twigs in a number of ways, and these tend to be predictable species by species. Sometimes, however, you will find a variety of attachments on a single tree – perhaps Nature is doing this simply to confuse you and to make traditional keying methods using vegetative (non-flowering) criteria difficult to follow! Attachments of the leaves to the twig or branchlet can be in any of the forms shown below.

    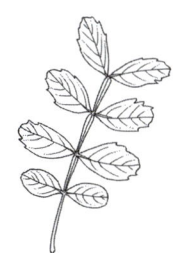

Opposite
eg. Water Nuxia
p. 172

Alternate
eg. Buffalo-thorn
Jujube p. 186

Spiralled
eg. Purple-pod
Cluster-leaf p. 104

Clustered
eg. Bushveld
Gardenia
p. 188

Winged
None in this
book

LEAF OR LEAFLET SHAPE

There are many varieties of leaf shape.
As a basis for all descriptions this book refers to them as:

 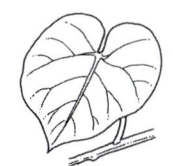

Round
eg. Round-leaved
Bloodwood p. 212

Heart-shaped
eg. Large-leaved
Rock Fig p. 154

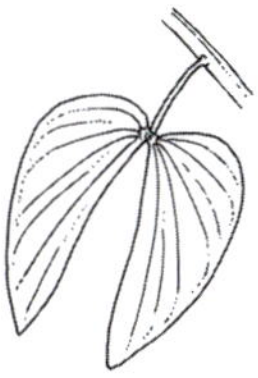

Butterfly
eg. Mopane
p. 116

Broad elliptic
eg. Ebony Jackal-berry
p. 160

Narrow elliptic
eg. Water Nuxia
p. 172

Triangular
eg. Feverberry
Croton p. 46

LEAF MARGINS

The edge of the leaf can be:

 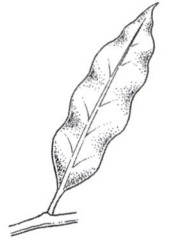

Smooth
eg. Sycamore Fig
p. 164

Wavy
eg. Magic Guarri
p. 190

Toothed
eg. Tamboti
p. 162

Deeply serrated
None in this
book

Lobed
None in this
book

BARK AND TRUNKS

The bark texture, and/or colour, is often characteristic of a tree.
However, it often differs between trunk and branches, older and younger trunks, and older and younger branches. Thinner and younger branches mostly have smoother and paler bark.

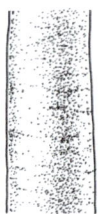

Smooth
eg. Fever-tree
Acacia
p. 90

Coarse
eg. Ebony
Jackal-berry
p. 160

Fissured or grooved
eg. Knob-thorn Acacia
p. 126

Blocky
eg. Tamboti
p. 162

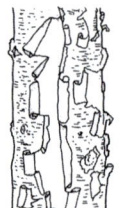

Flaking, peeling
eg. Flaky-bark
Acacia
p. 214

FLOWERS

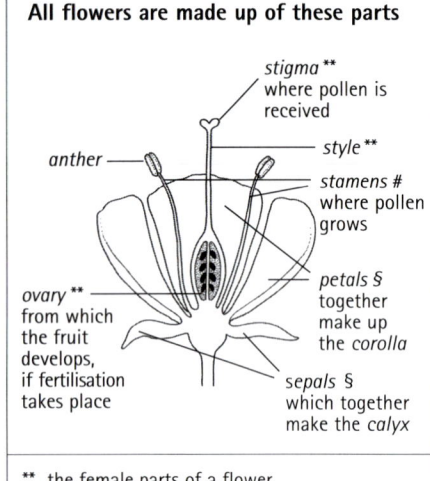

All flowers are made up of these parts

- *stigma* ** where pollen is received
- *style* **
- anther
- *stamens* # where pollen grows
- *ovary* ** from which the fruit develops, if fertilisation takes place
- *petals* § together make up the *corolla*
- *sepals* § which together make the *calyx*

** the female parts of a flower
\# the male part of a flower
§ asexual parts of the flower

Plants, including trees, are scientifically classified and named according to their flower-shape.
Looking carefully at flower-shapes can help with family identification, but this is often very technical or dependant on whether flowers are present. Most species within a family share general flower-shapes. Some flowers have a unique shape, eg. Baobab p. 84, or are inconspicuous, eg. Tall Firethorn Corkwood p. 136. These are described in detail in the specific texts.

Spike
eg. Knob-thorn
Acacia p. 126

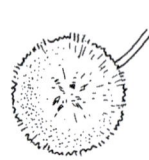

Ball
eg. Fever-tree Acacia
p. 90

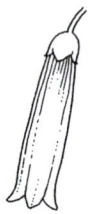

Trumpet
eg. Bushveld Gardenia
p. 188

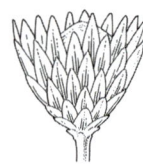

Protea
None in
this book

Star
eg. Raisins
p. 208 - 211

Pea-like
eg. Apple-leaf
p. 124

Pincushion-like
eg. Albizias
p. 77

Tree Section, Protuberances and Aerial Roots

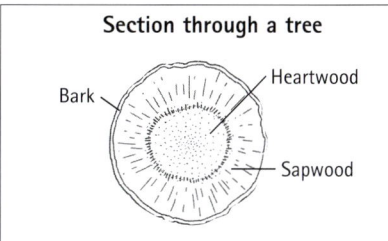
Section through a tree
Bark, Heartwood, Sapwood

Protuberances and Aerial Roots
Thorns, **spines** and **prickles** are all sharp.
Some plants have **spines**.
Thorns are independent protuberances with a vascular core.
Prickles are usually very small and may be easily removed (as they have no vascular core).
Aerial roots are found on Fig species and arise from branches or trunks, hanging free as they 'fall' towards the ground where they will take root and ultimately may prop up the tree.

Fleshy Fruit

Fruit has a fleshy pulp covering the seed/s.
The pulp may be oily, watery or dry, and must be removed before the seeds can germinate. Birds and animals are attracted to the fruit and help distribute the seeds.

Berry – small, single
eg. Ebony Jackal-berry
p. 160

Plum – larger, single
eg. Jacket-plum
p. 192

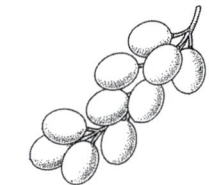
Grape – small, in bunches
eg. Wild Date-palm
p. 88

Pods (dry fruit)

Pods are hard envelopes covering a seed, or more often, several seeds.

Flat bean
eg. Knob-thorn
Acacia p. 126

Broad bean
eg. African Weeping-wattle p. 96

Bumpy bean
eg. Scented-pod
Acacia p. 198

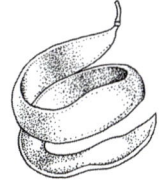
Coiled
eg. Umbrella Acacia
p. 92

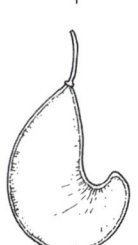
Sickle/kidney
eg. Mopane
p. 116

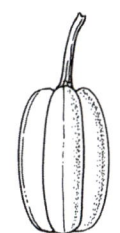
Capsule
eg. White Kirkia
p. 156

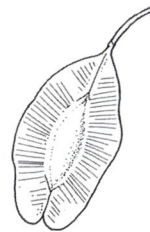
Two-winged
eg. Cluster-leafs
p. 73

Four-winged
eg. Bushwillows
p. 71-73

4 You Find Trees Easily
Visually summarised information – How to use the Book

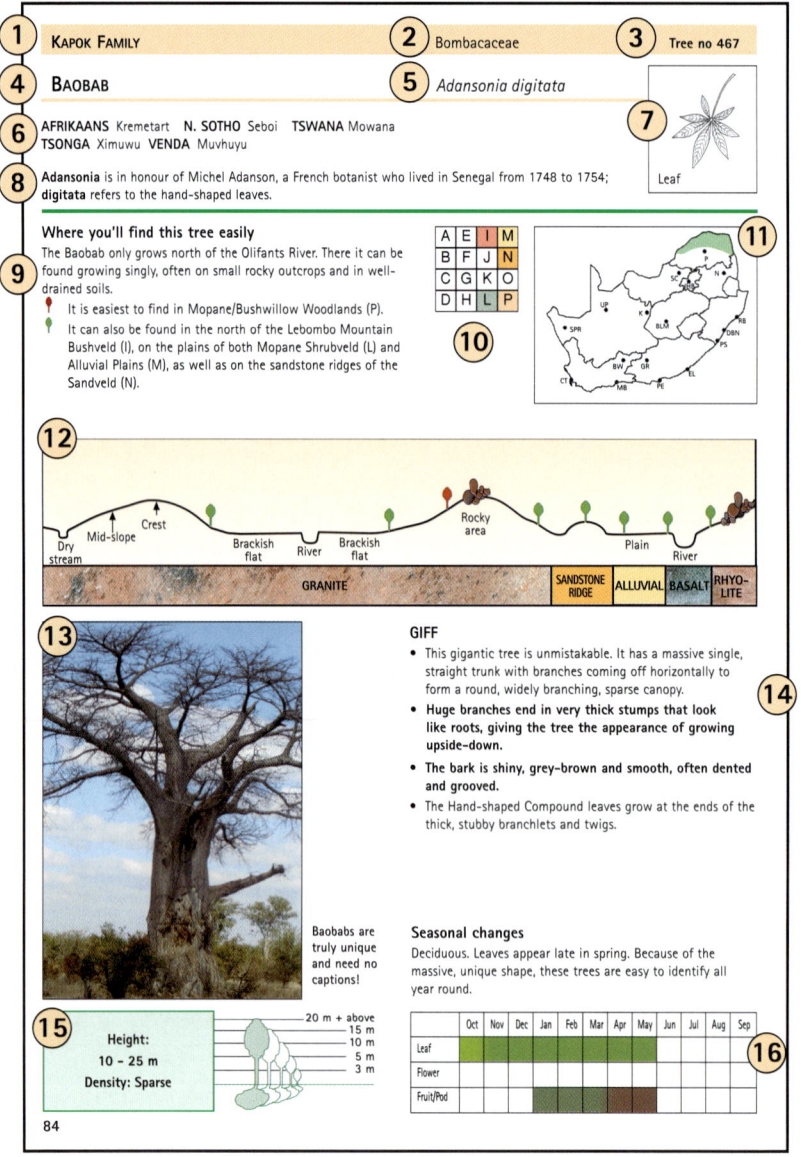

1. English family name that is used to alphabetise each section.

2. Scientific family name

3. South African tree number
The numbers are according to the National List of Indigenous Trees, compiled by the South African National Biodiversity Institute.

HOW TO USE THE BOOK (continued)

(4) English common name

(5) Species scientific name

(6) Other South African names (mostly compiled by the Dendrological Society)

(7) Line drawing
This drawing will indicate the most important GIFF, whether fruit, leaf, flower or bark that will help you to differentiate the tree from others that are similar.

(8) Meaning of species scientific name

(9) Where you'll find this tree easily
As with the cross-section diagram (No. 12), the red tree icon shows the easiest place to find the tree. The green tree icon shows the other Habitats where the tree is likely to be found.

(10) Ecozone blocks
The blocks that are coloured show the Ecozones in which you can find this tree easily. The colours and their letters are the same ones you will find on the Maps, pages 224 - 237, and on the Ecozone Tree Lists, pages 50 - 58. The Riverine block H has been coloured green. On the map keys, however, it its represented as a river 🌿 as no letter reference is indicated on the maps themselves.

(11) Map of South Africa
This is an adaptation from maps supplied by the National Botanical Institute in Pretoria.

Abbreviations:		GR:	Graaff Reinet	PE:	Port Elizabeth
BLM:	Bloemfontein	JHB:	Johannesburg	PS:	Port Shepstone
BW:	Beaufort West	K:	Kimberley	RB:	Richard's Bay
CT:	Cape Town	MB:	Mossel Bay	SC:	Sun City
DBN:	Durban	N:	Nelspruit	SPR:	Springbok
EL:	East London	P:	Polokwane	UP:	Upington

(12) Cross-section diagram of landscape profile
This is an easy visual impression of where it is easiest to find the species. The red tree icons show the Habitat where it is easiest to find the tree. The green tree icons show the Habitat where the tree may also be found. **Note that the tree icons are not to the same scale as the landscape profile.** Remember that this profile is only a diagram – but the main geology does run left to right (west to east).

(13) Photograph of tree or illustration of the most Striking Feature.

(14) GIFF of mature trees
The GIFF (pronounced JIFF) stands for General Information Form and Features, as a follow-on to the GISS of birds (General Information Size and Shape). These are features of mature trees to help you create a Search Image of the tree with the greatest ease. **The bold items are those features that are the most important in helping you with positive identification.**

(15) Density and height icon
This will help you form a more accurate Search Image. The tree which is coloured gives an idea of the average height of mature trees you will find easiest to identify, in comparison with other common trees, in this area. The height is given in metres. The density of the colour indicates the average summer density of the leaves and branches, as well as the resultant density of the shade.

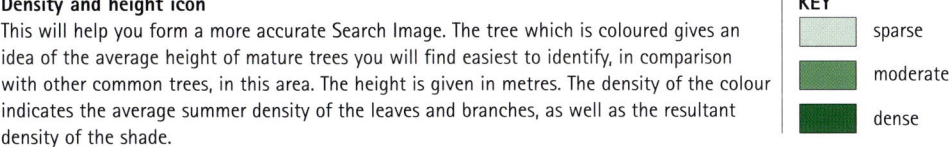

KEY
- sparse
- moderate
- dense

(16) Seasonal changes
This grid is to help you look out for specific features of trees at different times of the year. However, different Habitats in various parts of the area offer varying protection, so this is an average guide only.
- The information will vary from year to year depending on temperature and rainfall.
- The information also varies from one Ecozone to another, and within Habitats.
- The colours represent the months during which the leaves, flowers and fruit/pods are most likely to be seen.
- The colours themselves are a very rough guide only. You should refer to the artwork for more accurate colours.
- Pale grey is used for inconspicuous flowers or pods.
- Whether a fruit/pod is ripe or not, it is shown on the grid, while it is still visible on the tree, even after losing its seeds.

How to use the Book (continued)

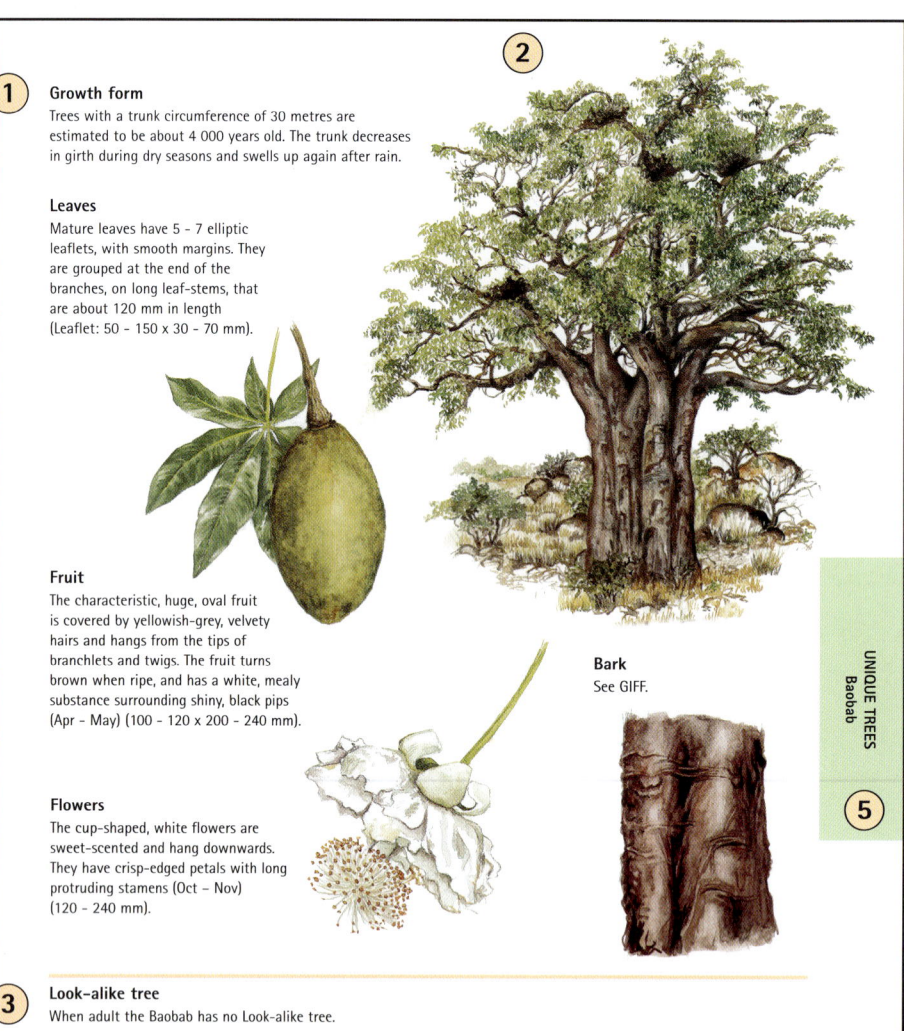

Growth form
Trees with a trunk circumference of 30 metres are estimated to be about 4 000 years old. The trunk decreases in girth during dry seasons and swells up again after rain.

Leaves
Mature leaves have 5 - 7 elliptic leaflets, with smooth margins. They are grouped at the end of the branches, on long leaf-stems, that are about 120 mm in length (Leaflet: 50 - 150 x 30 - 70 mm).

Fruit
The characteristic, huge, oval fruit is covered by yellowish-grey, velvety hairs and hangs from the tips of branchlets and twigs. The fruit turns brown when ripe, and has a white, mealy substance surrounding shiny, black pips (Apr - May) (100 - 120 x 200 - 240 mm).

Bark
See GIFF.

Flowers
The cup-shaped, white flowers are sweet-scented and hang downwards. They have crisp-edged petals with long protruding stamens (Oct – Nov) (120 - 240 mm).

UNIQUE TREES — Baobab

Look-alike tree
When adult the Baobab has no Look-alike tree.

Links with animals
The tree is partly pollinated by the Straw-coloured Fruitbat (*Eidolon helvum*). The fruit is eaten by baboon, and the bark by elephant. Cattle, elephants and antelope chew on the spongy wood to relieve thirst in times of drought.

Human uses
Fibre is made from the bark to weave baskets and hats. As the spongy wood contains a high proportion of water, humans chew on the wood to relieve thirst. The hollow trunks have been used as houses, prisons, storage barns and water tanks. Hollow branches catch rainwater and act as reservoirs. Bark and leaves have been used in treating malaria, dysentery, urinary disorders and diarrhoea. Flour is prepared from the roots, and fresh leaves are eaten as spinach. The fruit is also edible and is rich in Vitamin C.

Gardening
The Baobab can be very attractive in a large garden. It will grow best in warmer areas, on the majority of well-drained soils. It is susceptible to frost, but is fairly drought-resistant. It can be grown from seed and is fairly fast-growing under warm, well-watered conditions.

85

How to Use the Book (continued)

(1) Growth details
These details will help you to check your identification. They build up a wider Search Image so you can find the same tree elsewhere. For each specific tree, the sizes of the leaves, flowers, fruit and/or pods are shown in relation to one another. However, this size relationship does not carry through proportionately from one species to another.

(2) Artwork of the tree
Trees vary greatly and no single photograph or illustration can represent every tree you will find. However, this artwork gives an overall impression of the size and the common form of mature trees, which are easiest to find. It emphasises the GIFF of the species listed on the opposite page.

(3) Look-alike trees
Noted here are trees that can be confused with the featured tree. They are not necessarily in the same family or genus, but share a similar general GIFF, or one specific feature.

(4) General information and uses
Details of interest about the tree, in relation to people and to animals, as well as gardening, are given here.

(5) Easy-search Tabs
For easy reference the colour-coded tabs indicate the specific tree on that page, as well as its Ecozone. These same colour-codes are used in the Contents, p. 1.

Note on GIFF
The GIFF can contain information about any of the above features, for example growth form or leaf description. Always refer to the GIFF for the most important information.

Spiny Monkey-orange Tree no 629
Strychnos spinosa

This shrub or small tree is not common, but occurs along rivers and in sandy or rocky areas throughout the Lowveld. The **bark** is rough, peeling or flaking. The **leaves** are Simple, opposite and shiny, and, as with all Monkey-oranges, are 3–5 veined from the base of the leaf. As the leaves are in pairs, with each pair at right angles to the one above and below, they are easy to distinguish from the greener, softer, clustered leaves of the Black Monkey-orange, *Strychnos madagascariensis*, p.132 (15 – 90 x 10 – 75 mm). There are slender, paired, straight or slightly curved, woody **spines** at the base of the leaves.

The **flowers** are inconspicuous, creamy-green on short flower-stems, in tight clusters on short side shoots (Sep – Feb) (Cluster: 4 – 35 mm; individual: up to 6 mm). The **fruit** is large and turns yellowish-brown when ripe (Mar – Aug) (120 mm). Monkey-orange species are well-known for the medicinal properties resulting from the chemicals in the bark and unripe fruits. Many of these uses relate to snakebite and other infected, open wounds. Ripe fruit are prized as a food, and are sometimes picked green and then buried, to allow them to ripen without being taken by baboon!

23

LOWVELD

ECOZONES AND HABITATS

Understanding different areas of the Lowveld will help with tree identification. Trees have evolved and are adapted to specific soil, temperature and moisture conditions, as well as to specific patterns of animal utilisation and fire. In addition, a tree will only thrive and become part of the plant community when it is well enough adapted to also compete with the other trees and plants that grow in that area. Trees that are common in the Lowveld can withstand long seasonal droughts, many are susceptible to frost, and all are in some way protected against over-utilisation by browsing animals.

The following pages have information that describes the different areas of the Lowveld, and some of the trees you can expect to look for.

Ecozones and Habitats	26
Habitats	
Look for the Right Tree in the Right Place	27
Crests and Seeplines	28
Valleys and Plains	29
Riverine Habitat (also Ecozone H)	30
Brackish Flats	31
Rocky Outcrops	32
Pans	33
Ecozones	
You Find Trees by Ecozone	34
Ecozone A - Mixed Bushwillow Woodlands	35
Ecozone B - Pretoriuskop Sourveld	36
Ecozone C - Malelane Mountain Bushveld	37
Ecozone D - Sabie / Crocodile Thorn Thickets	38
Ecozone E - Thorn Veld	39
Ecozone F - Knob-thorn / Marula Savannah	40
Ecozone G - Delagoa Thorn Thickets	41
Ecozone I - Lebombo Mountain Bushveld	42
Ecozone J - Olifants Rugged Veld	43
Ecozone K - Stunted Knob-thorn Savannah	44
Ecozone L - Mopane Shrubveld	45
Ecozone M - Alluvial Plains	46
Ecozone N - Sandveld	47
Ecozone O - Tree Mopane Savannah	48
Ecozone P - Mopane / Bushwillow Woodlands	49
Ecozone Tree Lists	50
A Six-step Guide	59

In the Lebombo Mountain Bushveld, Ecozone I, you often see some interesting formations of reddish rhyolite rocks.

25

THE LOWVELD

ECOZONES AND HABITATS

The **Sappi Tree Spotting** series helps you find trees by Ecozone and Habitat. The fundamental definition of the Ecozones is based on the detailed vegetation map by Rebelo and Low published by the National Botanical Institute in 1996. This map was adapted by Jacana to create the five Ecozones that are one of the foundations of this book.

The Lowveld as defined for this book, is a low-lying area between two mountain ranges – the Drakensberg in the west and Lebombos in the east. A narrow tongue extends through Swaziland to northern KwaZulu-Natal. Northwards the Lowveld and its vegetation patterns are evident well into Zimbabwe. The altitude ranges from 150 to 600 metres above sea level.

The Lowveld is a summer rainfall area receiving between 200 and 600 mm per annum. This decreases from west to east, and from south to north. The summers are hot and humid with temperatures up to 44°C, while winters are mild, with frost occurring only rarely in most of the area.

About 130 million years ago the Lowveld was formed by massive movements of the continental plates. Due to tilting and subsequent erosion, different layers of underlying geology were exposed.

The diverse geology of the Lowveld is very important because it forms the basis of the Ecozones and Habitats which influence the distribution of different species of trees. In addition to the ranges in altitude, rainfall and geology the large geographic area ensures that you can look for a wide variety of trees.

Some of these trees are the common-place South African favourites, like Marula, *Sclerocarya birrea*, p. 122 and Tamboti, *Spirostachys africana*, p. 162. Others are truly unique, and even breathtaking, and are found only in very limited ranges. They obviously include the well-loved Baobab, *Adansonia digitata*, p. 84, as well as the lesser-known but equally magnificent Pod-mahogany, *Afzelia quanzensis*, p. 150. You are going to have fun Tree Spotting in the Lowveld!

The Lowveld of Southern Africa

In South Africa lions do not usually climb trees – but this Marula was simply too well designed as a sighting perch, to resist!

HABITATS – LOOK FOR THE RIGHT TREE IN THE RIGHT PLACE

On p. 12 there is an important concept that differentiates Sappi Tree Spotting from other field guides.
This is: **Look for the right tree in the right place.**

It is worth understanding this fully – or this book will simply frustrate you. The book is not designed for you to walk up to a tree, pick up a leaf and ask 'what tree is this'.

To help you to understand the process, imagine that a huge banquet has been prepared for 1 000 people.
- Think of this banquet laid out with literally hundreds of plates of food – over many tables. This is like the whole Lowveld over hundreds of square kilometres.

Look carefully at all the components
- The meal is made up into courses. These are all food obviously, but each course is actually very different in the way it looks. These are the equivalent to the Ecozones within the Lowveld. There are 16 of them covered in this book. It is possible to learn to recognise these with the same ease you can tell a starter from a dessert – once you read about their differences from page 34 to 49.
- Each course can consist of a number of platters, side dishes, sauce bowls and condiments. These are similar to the Habitats that make up each Ecozone. Don't be surprised to find that some Habitats keep appearing, like butter or salt, in different courses, in different Ecozones. These Habitats combine in different ways to make up the Ecozones, and they are described on pages 28 to 33.
- Now in terms of the banquet, go back a step to the day before – and think of the preparation. See a kitchen piled with literally hundreds of different ingredients – from pepper, coriander and curry, to legs of lamb and strawberries. And each and every ingredient is needed to make a dish. In this book these ingredients are the trees. As with the example used above, some trees re-appear in many different Habitats. Some others are very specific about their requirements, and are literally only found in one Ecozone! The trees in their Habitats are described from page 82 to 217.

This magnificent River Acacia, *Acacia robusta*, p. 182, is in a human-made Habitat, the golf course at Skukuza in Kruger Park, where it thrives with regular watering!

DIAGRAMMATIC CROSS-SECTIONS OF THE LOWVELD
In the text of each main tree there is a diagram showing visual data to help you with **'Where to find that tree easily'.**

- Across the bottom of the picture are the base rocks that create the 16 Ecozones – granite, basalt and rhyolite. Sometimes there is sandveld, Ecca shales and / or gabbro.
- Above these base rocks are the Habitats that occur with each rock type.
- And above that are trees placed to show you where to look for your tree. Red trees are marked as the places where it is easiest to find the tree. Green icons indicate trees that are still common but slighty less obvious in that Habitat.

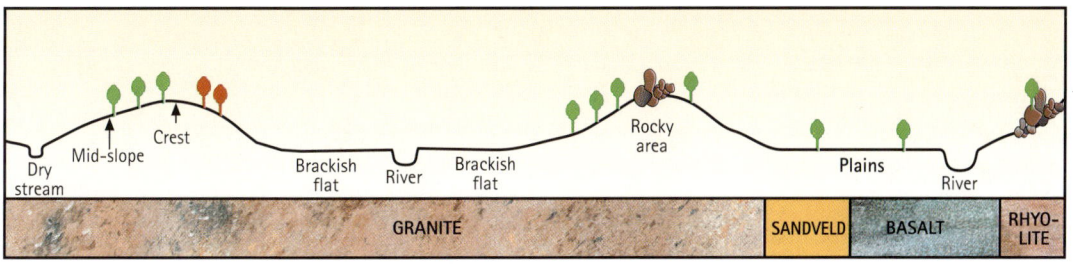

CRESTS AND SEEPLINES IN GRANITE

ECOZONES A, B, C, D AND P

CRESTS

The oldest, exposed layers of the Lowveld are the ancient granites in the west. These granites have eroded to form an undulating landscape, criss-crossed by many drainage lines, where rainwater flows, above or below ground level. The soils derived from the granites are coarse and sandy. They are low in nutrients and water drains easily into these soils. Water caught between the sandy grains can be readily absorbed by plant roots. These sandy soils are typically found on the crests of the granite hills, and between the rocks of granite rocky outcrops.

Trees that grow on sandy soils normally have large leaves, like Bushwillows, *Combretum* species. This is because the trees have to absorb large amounts of water to obtain enough nutrients for growth. They need to get rid of excess water, and larger leaves facilitate evaporation. These large leaves are very prone to insect attacks, and produce chemicals to protect themselves. These same chemicals make the leaves unpalatable to browsers. They tend to only eat these leaves when there is little else available. The most common tree on the crests in the granites in the south is the Red Bushwillow, *Combretum apiculatum*, p. 204. In the north in Mopane/Bushwillow Woodlands the dominant tree is Mopane, *Colophospermum mopane*, p. 116.

SEEPLINES

In the granite undulations, water flows downhill from the crests. Where the sand meets the hard rock on the midslope, water seepage into the soil is stopped. The water runs along the rock, and out onto the soil surface, to form a seepline. These seeplines are clearly visible in years of high rainfall. During these periods, soils here are very damp, and water can often be seen on the surface. These areas often have a dense grass cover, interspersed with the tall Silver Cluster-leaf, *Terminalia sericea*, p. 120. Lower down the slopes the crest evens out, with some clay being deposited. These areas generally have shallower soils, with more clay, than the crests, and both broad-leaved and fine-leaved trees are found here. (See explanation of fine-leaved trees, growing on clay, on opposite page).

Giraffe on the crest add excitement to your Tree Spotting!

VALLEYS IN GRANITE : PLAINS IN ECCA SHALE + GABBRO + BASALT

VALLEYS OF GRANITE ECOZONES A, B, C, D, AND P
PLAINS IN ECCA SHALE G AND O, GABBRO E, AND BASALT F, J, K AND L

Because granite Ecozones are hilly they naturally have slopes. Therefore, smaller sand particles, and animal and plant material are carried downhill, resulting in fine-grained, nutritious, clay soils in the valleys.

The other Ecozones, listed in the heading above, are naturally flat, with plains, and their soils are all essentially clay-like.

The clay soils of the basalts and Ecca shales support less varied vegetation than the granites, and are often dominated by a few tree species. Because of this it is easier for beginners to start identifying trees in these Ecozones – F, G, J, K and L.

Particles lie close together in clay, and water is held between them, like any liquid added to milled flour. Here water does not seep into the soils easily, but once held, gives rise to areas that become very muddy, and waterlogged in the rainy season. Clay soils are rich in nutrients, but water molecules are held tight, and plants have more difficulty extracting liquid from them.

Trees growing on clay soils can only absorb small amounts of liquid, and they therefore have to conserve water, and **not** lose too much through large-leaved evaporation. They tend to have smaller, finer leaves, that are less accessible to insects. The trees, however, do have to defend themselves against animals that find the small leaves very palatable. Most of them have thorns, such as the Acacia family. The Knob-thorn Acacia, *Acacia nigrescens*, p. 126, is one of the most common trees, both in granite valley bottoms and on the southern basalt plains. The Scented-pod Acacia, *Acacia nilotica*, p. 198, is common in brack areas and on gabbro plains.

Valleys in the granites tend to be dominated by various Acacias. They also have sweet grasses, and so attract both grazers and browsers. Impala eat both grass and trees.

RIVERINE HABITAT (ALSO ECOZONE H)

There is riverine vegetation along all of the large perennial rivers, as well as many smaller rivers and stream banks, throughout the Lowveld. The most magnificent, huge trees can be found here. This is because their root systems are able to access enough moisture all year round, often from underground water flow. In addition, the mean temperature in the Lowveld does not often drop to frost or freezing levels, giving year round warmth for some growth.

Water-loving trees such as the Water Nuxia, *Nuxia oppositifolia*, p. 172, and River Bushwillow, *Combretum erythrophyllum*, p. 174, occur on the banks of large perennial rivers near the water, while the Matumi, *Breonadia salicina*, p. 176, often grows in the rocky reaches of the same rivers.

Large evergreen trees such as the Sausage-tree, *Kigelia africana*, p. 178, and the Natal-mahogany, *Trichilia emetica*, p. 180, are found on the banks of almost all the larger rivers. The Nyala-tree, *Xanthocercis zambesiaca*, p. 166, however, is more common along the rivers from the Olifants northwards. During spring the red flowers of the Flame Climbing Bushwillow, *Combretum microphyllum*, p. 102, form a striking picture in the riverbeds.

Large rivers cut through the Lowveld, flowing from west to east, and finally reach the Indian Ocean in Mozambique. Along their banks in South Africa they are lined with magnificent trees of a wide variety of species.

Umdoni Waterberry Tree no 555
Syzygium cordatum

This tree occurs along the banks of permanent rivers and on the hills of the Pretoriuskop Sourveld, Ecozone B. It is a single-trunked, low-branching, evergreen tree and has a dense, semi-circul. canopy. The stemless **leaves** are round, Simple, blue-green, leathery, with a distinct, yellow central vein. Leaves grow at branchlet ends, forming rosettes. **Flowers** are sweet-smelling, creamy-white to pinkish, pincushion-like and grow in bunches in leaf rosettes (Oct - Jun). **Fruit** is fleshy, berry-like, deep purple when ripe, and grows in bunches in leaf rosettes (Nov -Jun).

BRACKISH FLATS

These areas tend to occur on the inner bends of rivers as they flow through the granites. These areas have a different salt composition. This is the result of the movement of salts down the crests and along the drainage lines, although there is no hard data as to why these areas occur on the bends.

The vegetation growing here is very palatable and often high in sodium. There are often large, open patches of short, very nutritious grasses that are usually heavily grazed, leaving bare, exposed soil. Some trees can tolerate these salty soils well, and they are often quite distinctive and easy to find. The most common is the Magic Guarri, *Euclea divinorum*, p. 190, which is one of the indicator trees of the sodic (salty) or brack patches. Because these areas are so open, animals like to rest here where they can see approaching predators. These are therefore always good areas to look for game.

Jacket-plum, *Pappea capensis*, p. 192, Bushveld Gardenia, *Gardenia volkensii*, p. 188, and Bushveld Saffron, *Elaeodendron transvaalense*, p. 194, are also common here.

An open area with short grass surrounded by Magic Guarri, *Euclea divinorum*, p. 190, often indicates a brackish flat.

Young Tamboti Tree no 341
Spirostachys africana

Large stands of young, pale-barked, spiny Tamboti trees can most easily be identified on clay soils that form near drainage lines in the granite Ecozones. They can also be found in Ecozone G, Delagoa Thorn Thickets on Ecca shale, further from water. The grass cover in these areas is mostly sparse, and animals tend to congregate here to rest in the shade.

During the dry months, the fallen Tamboti **leaves** are eaten by smaller browsers such as impala. These patches differ from the sodic patches where the Magic Guarri grows. They are not open, as are the brack areas discussed above. Tambotis are described in detail on page 162.

ROCKY OUTCROPS

Rocky outcrops are most commonly formed by granite boulders in the granite Ecozones, A, B, C, D and P. Rocky outcrops are also found in the Sandveld (Ecozone N) where the boulders are formed by sandstone. This is softer than granite and is often covered in a wide variety of lichen species. The dark-coloured boulders of the gabbro in Thorn Veld, Ecozone E, also form some of the well-known landmarks of the Lowveld.

These rocky outcrops are well drained, and many of the drought-resistant species such as Euphorbias and Corkwoods, *Commiphora* species, are found there. White Kirkia, *Kirkia acuminata*, p.156, are a favourite of elephants, but escape from them in this less accessible Habitat.

The long roots of Large-leaved Rock Fig, *Ficus abutilifolia* p. 154, are a common sight on most rocky outcrops, and the new red leaves of the Red-leaved Fig, *Ficus ingens*, see below, are conspicuous on these outcrops in early spring.

Granites erode to leave magnificent rocky outcrops, forming a unique, protective Habitat.

Red-leaved Fig Tree no 55
Ficus ingens

This Fig can be found on rocky outcrops and mountains throughout the Lowveld. It branches low down, and spreads widely to form a semi-circular canopy, often with obvious white roots, or a fluted trunk if larger. Large, Simple **leaves** are long and narrowly elliptic, with distinct, yellowish, indented central and side veins. In spring there is a spectacular flush of wine-red to coppery young leaves. Small berry-like **figs** are smooth, or slightly hairy, and dull-red to copper when ripe from June to December. All parts of the tree have some milky latex.

PANS

Pans are most common in Ecozones which are relatively flat, i.e. the basalt Ecozones F, K and L, as well as Ecca shale Ecozones G and O, where they form an important part of the drainage system. They are obviously also vital in the life of the animal populations living or moving nearby.

These pans usually form away from any drainage lines and are often very similar to brack areas, p. 31. They are relatively open areas which have palatable grasses, and animals often visit them. Many pans are actually maintained, and/or enlarged, by animals such as rhino and warthog.

The most common trees are Fever-tree Acacias, *Acacia xanthophloea*, p. 90, and Lala-palms. The Northern Lala-palm, *Hyphaene petersiana*, is the one illustrated on page 86. It grows into a tall tree, has more-or-less round fruit, and is more common in the north. The Southern Lala-palm, *Hyphaene coriacea*, is usually a shrub with pear-shaped fruit, and is more common in the south. The Red Spikethorn, *Gymnosporia senegalensis*, p. 106, often forms large stands near pans, while the Pioneer Spikethorn, *Gymnosporia buxifolia*, see below, may be found growing on the edges of the pan itself.

An added attraction of the pans is the bird life - here an Egret is fishing.

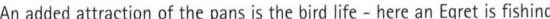

Pioneer Spikethorn   Tree no 399
Gymnosporia buxifolia

This evergreen, single-stemmed, low-branching tree has an untidy, angular outline formed by haphazardly upward-growing branchlets. Straight **spines** of variable lengths grow beneath the leaf-bud. The **bark** is pale to dark brown, maturing to deeply furrowed in regular, protruding blocks.

The Simple **leaves** are variable, mostly elliptic with a very short leaf-stem, broad tip and sharp base. They are clustered on ends of short, stubby twigs, forming a sleeve around the branchlets. Conspicuous clusters of white star-shaped **flowers** smell offensive. The berry-like **fruit** is three-celled (May - Jan).

YOU FIND TREES BY ECOZONE

Lowveld Geology, Soils and Ecozones

As different rocks (geology) erode, soils form with different characteristics. An Ecozone is an area where there is relatively uniform geology and therefore landform (landshape), as well as uniform altitude, latitude, longitude and rainfall. Soils are all derived from the rocks, and therefore in any single Ecozone are from a similar base. However, the actual soils themselves change, according to the different slopes, the various heights and their exposure to water and heat. Different trees grow in different soils. As a result you can expect to find specific trees in each Ecozone, but subject to changes in Habitat.

As a sweeping overview, the Lowveld can be longitudinally divided into three main geological zones, each with very different main features. You can therefore see three long strips running roughly from north to south.

- Older, more resistant granites and gabbro are in a very broad band thoughout the west.
- Younger Ecca shales and basalts are in a fairly wide strip nearer the eastern side.
- Youngest rhyolite is in a narrow strip in the extreme east.

Ecozone number and colours

Each Ecozone has its own number and its own colour throughout the book.

	GRANITE AND GABBRO ECOZONES IN THE WEST THAT TOGETHER FORM ROLLING HILLS WITH SOME DOTTED PLAINS
	Granite Ecozones
A	Mixed Bushwillow Woodlands
B	Pretoriuskop Sourveld
C	Malelane Mountain Bushveld
D	Sabie / Crocodile Thorn Thickets
P	Mopane / Bushwillow Woodlands
	Gabbro Ecozone
E	Thorn Veld

	ECCA SHALE, BASALT, ALLUVIAL AND SANDVELD ECOZONES THAT FORM FLAT PLAINS
	Ecca shale Ecozones
G	Delagoa Thorn Thickets
O	Tree Mopane Savannah
	Basalt Ecozones
F	Knob-thorn / Marula Savannah
K	Stunted Knob-thorn Savannah
L	Mopane Shrubveld
	SPECIALIST NORTHERN ECOZONES
M	Alluvial Plains
N	Sandveld

	RHYOLITE ECOZONES THAT FORM ROCKY, LOW MOUNTAINS
	Rhyolite Ecozones
I	Lebombo Mountain Bushveld
J	Olifants Rugged Veld

You will find blocks like this next to every tree. The coloured blocks indicate the Ecozones where you will find each tree easily.

ECOZONE A – MIXED BUSHWILLOW WOODLANDS (ON GRANITE)

This Ecozone shares features with all the granite Ecozones, A, B, C, D and P, and occurs in the southern part of the Lowveld. The rainfall varies between 550 and 700 mm, and the altitude between 350 and 500 m. This landscape is large and occupies about 11% of the Kruger National Park.

These granitic areas consist of granite domes, intersected by drainage lines, creating undulating crests and valleys. These are discussed in detail on pages 28 - 29.

On the crests of the domes, boulders are often exposed by erosion to form rocky outcrops. The granite rocks weather to form sandy soils that vary in depth from deep to very shallow. The most common tree on these crests is the Red Bushwillow, *Combretum apiculatum*, p. 204. In the valleys where the soil is a heavier clay, the most common trees are the Acacias, particularly the Knob-thorn Acacia, *Acacia nigrescens*, p. 126.

Towards both the west and the south of this Ecozone the rainfall is slightly higher, and the Large-fruited Bushwillow, *Combretum zeyheri*, p. 202, and the Weeping Bushwillow, *Combretum collinum*, see below, are more common.

Although this Ecozone does not have any large perennial rivers, there are a number of larger streams, where typical riverine vegetation can be found. It is a good Ecozone to find kudu.

Bushwillows tend to be formless, but their sheer numbers make them easy to find.

Weeping Bushwillow   Tree no 541.2
Combretum collinum

This Bushwillow is more common in areas of higher rainfall including Pretoriuskop Sourveld, Ecozone B. In the past this tree has been called Variable Bushwillow for good reason! Large, broad, elliptic to oval **leaves** can be opposite or alternate, dark green above and paler green to silvery below. **Flowers** can be cream to yellow, and sweetly scented in spikes (Aug - Oct). **Pods** are characteristically four-winged, as in all Bushwillows, and are rosy-red, not rusty-red when young, and they dry to dark brown.

ECOZONE B – PRETORIUSKOP SOURVELD (ON GRANITE)

This Ecozone is located in the south-western corner of the Lowveld and is very similar to the Sour Bushveld discussed in **Sappi Tree Spotting – Bushveld.**

Ecozone B, like A, C, D and P, is a granite Ecozone with the typical undulating landscape of crests and valleys. This is more fully described on pages 28 - 29. The rainfall is higher than in most of the other granitic Ecozones, varying from 600 to 1 000 mm. The altitude varies from 550 to 600 m above sea level.

This Ecozone only covers about 3% of the Kruger National Park. However, many of the private game reserves along the Sabie and Sand rivers are also located in this Ecozone. Many areas of this Ecozone are characterised by long grass typical of Sour Bushveld, as well as extensive stands of Silver Cluster-leaf, *Terminalia sericea*, p. 120. Some trees, which prefer higher rainfall, are only found in the Lowveld in this Ecozone. These include the Kiaat Bloodwood, *Pterocarpus angolensis*, p. 138. The Black Monkey-orange, *Strychnos madagascariensis*, p. 132, is also more common here. Many trees such as the Sycomore Fig, *Ficus sycomorus*, p. 164, and Ebony Jackal-berry *Diospyros mespiliformis*, p. 160, that normally only occur along rivers in the rest of the Lowveld, are found here on the crests. Look for White Rhino and sable in the open, grassy areas.

Extensive stands of Silver Cluster-leaf, *Terminalia sericea*, are common in Ecozone B.

Wild-pear Dombeya Tree no 471
Dombeya rotundifolia

This deciduous, single-stemmed tree has an irregular, moderate canopy. **Leaves** are Simple, hairy, rough and parchment-like, and are conspicuously round. It is spectacular in early spring when covered in star-like, cream to pale brown **flowers** which appear before the leaves (Jul - Oct). **Seeds** grow in small capsules, surrounded by brownish, dry flower-petals (Oct - Dec).

ECOZONE C – MALELANE MOUNTAIN BUSHVELD (ON GRANITE)

This is the most mountainous of the Ecozones, with an altitude of 350 to 800 m. The undulating Malelane Mountains are formed by ancient granites, and the area has a high rainfall of 600 to 700 mm. Because of both its mountainous nature, and the higher rainfall, this area is not truly part of the 'Lowveld', but has been included here because it constitutes about 2.5% of the Kruger National Park.

Not unexpectedly many trees found here are unlike the rest of the Lowveld. These include the Mountain Kirkia, *Kirkia wilmsii*, see below, that can be seen on some of the higher rocky outcrops. This tree also forms a splendid autumn landscape along the main tar road between Nelspruit and Komatipoort where it runs along the Crocodile River. This is the only Ecozone where Mountain Reedbuck can be found.

There are many Tree Spotting treats, and panoramic views across the Malelane Mountains, on the Bushman's Trail in Kruger Park, with its camp and walks all in Ecozone C.

Mountain Kirkia Tree no 269
Kirkia wilmsii

This deciduous tree boasts spectacular autumn colours (Apr - May) on the northern slopes of the mountainous areas of Ecozones B and C. It is a multi-stemmed tree with a spreading, irregular canopy. Branchlets and twigs end bluntly with tightly clustered, slender, Once Compound leaves at the tips of the branchlets. **Leaves** have 10 to 20 opposite pairs of tiny leaflets and a leaflet at the tip. **Flowers** grow in yellow-green, small, inconspicuous sprays (Sep - Dec). **Fruit** is brown and woody, and when mature splits into four sections joined at the apex (Feb - Mar).

ECOZONE D – SABIE / CROCODILE THORN THICKETS (ON GRANITE)

This is the least undulating of the granite Ecozones. It is a low-lying landscape between the Crocodile and Sabie rivers, and is characterised by dense stands of Acacia species. The rainfall varies between 500 and 550 mm per year, and the altitude between 200 and 350 m above sea level. The soils of this landscape have more clay than any of the other granite landscapes, which is why it has such dense Acacia stands – a good Ecozone to get to know the common Acacias.

Many riverine trees, p. 30, and brack areas, p. 31, can be found along the banks of the two large rivers, as well as along the numerous other large streams. This Ecozone comprises about 6% of the Kruger National Park, and for reasons which are not fully understood seems to be an Ecozone of the Kruger National Park only.

There are two tree species that are easier to find in this Ecozone than in any other in the Lowveld. The False-marula Lannea, *Lannea schweinfurthii*, see below, is common, as is the Greenthorn Torchwood, *Balanites maughamii*, p. 146. The Greenthorn is easy to identify in all phases of its growth as it often creates colonies of various ages, fairly close together. Because of the permanent water and riverine vegetation, bushbuck are fairly common along the major riverbanks.

Scented-pod Acacia, *Acacia nilotica*, are common in this Ecozone.

False-marula Lannea Tree no 363
Lannea schweinfurthii

This deciduous tree has a single, bare, relatively straight stem and a spreading canopy. It is found throughout the Lowveld, but is not as common as its look-alike the Marula, *Sclerocarya birrea*, p. 122. The bark peels in large, irregular flakes, that are not the same shape as the round, whitish, golf-ball patches unique to Marula. The Once Compound **leaves** are smooth, shiny, fresh-green. There is a terminal leaflet, plus 1 – 3 pairs, the lateral pairs having leaflet stems of only 1.5 mm. This feature is a strong GIFF to differentiate the tree from the Marula. The **flowers** are unisexual and are found on separate trees. Male flowers are yellow-green, while female flowers are pale yellow and slightly smaller, both appearing November to December. The small, berry-like **fruit** grows in long bunches, is pale red while swelling, but turns dark wine-red when ripe (Jan - Feb).

Ecozone E – Thorn Veld (on Gabbro)

This Ecozone occurs wherever gabbro has intruded into the granite of Ecozones A, B, D and P. Gabbro is a volcanic rock that was formed millions of years ago, when lava flowed out between the granite sheets.

Because the parent rock is not the same as the surrounding granite, the resultant soils and landscape are noticeably different, even to the amateur eye. As a consequence, the Ecozone not only has its own unique landform, but it also has very different trees from those in the nearby Ecozones. Ecozone E is generally flat with dark boulders strewn over the plains, or 'heaped' in blocky hillsides or small 'mountains'. Ship Mountain in Kruger is an example of this.

Knob-thorn Acacia, *Acacia nigrescens*, p. 126, and Marula *Sclerocarya birrea*, p. 122, are common, and it is also a good Ecozone to find the Long-tail Cassia, *Cassia abbreviata*, p. 98. The long, finger-like branchlets and twigs of the Rubber-hedge Euphorbia, *Euphorbia tirucalli*, see below, can be seen on some of the rocky outcrops.

The rainfall average is 500 to 600 mm. The soils are rich and the vegetation very palatable, and it is therefore a good Ecozone to find large numbers of browsers such as kudu and giraffe, and grazers such as zebra and wildebeest.

This Ecozone, covers about 3.5% of the Kruger National Park and is dotted throughout the south. It also occurs west of Kruger in the private Game Reserves.

Open Woodland with tall trees and short grass attracts grazers.

Rubber-hedge Euphorbia Tree no 355
Euphorbia tirucalli

This tree is so unusual in growth form that it is unique, and very easy to identify. It is most easily found on rocky outcrops, but also grows in most other Habitats. All parts have toxic, milky latex. Cylindrical, smooth, leafless, green branchlets and twigs are succulent, forming a rounded canopy usually on a single trunk. Inconspicuous yellowish-green **flowers** cluster at the tips of twigs (Oct - Dec). **Fruit** is a rounded, 3-lobed capsule (Nov - Jan).

Ecozone F – Knob-thorn / Marula Savannah (on basalt)

This Ecozone is found in the southern part of the Lowveld in areas that have volcanic basalts as their parent rock. Basalts erode to form flat, rich clay soils that support open, grassy plains – home to large numbers of zebra and wildebeest. The rainfall varies from 550 to 600 mm, and the area is about 250 m above sea level.

This very flat Ecozone does not develop distinct streamlets, streams and rivers. Rainwater drains into shallow drainage lines, depressions and pans where it collects. The water, however, does not run off easily, as it does in the undulating granites.

Larger drainage lines form alluvial-like plains, where Fever-tree Acacias, *Acacia xanthophloea*, p. 90, flourish.

The main vegetation of the plains of Ecozone F consists of large Marulas, *Sclerocarya birrea*, p. 122, and Knob-thorn Acacias, *Acacia nigrescens*, p. 126, with large stands of the smaller Round-leaved Bloodwood, *Pterocarpus rotundifolius*, p. 212, and Sickle-bush, *Dichrostachys cinerea*, p. 216. Near the drainage lines, Red Spikethorn, *Gymnosporia senegalensis*, p. 106, thrive. The Drooping Resin-tree, *Ozoroa engleri*, see below, although not common, is found south of the Olifants River, and is conspicuous in Ecozone F.

The basalt plains of Knob-thorn / Marula Savannah stretch westward from Nkumbe.

Bushveld and Drooping Resin-trees Tree no 375 and 371
Ozoroa paniculosa and *Ozoroa engleri*

These trees are conspicuous in specific areas in the Lowveld. The Bushveld Resin-tree is more common in the basalt Ecozones and the Lebombos north of the Olifants River. The Drooping Resin-tree can be found south of the Olifants River. Resin-trees can be identifed by their long, narrow, peach-like **leaves**, clustered in whorls of three, with distinct herringbone veins. Bushveld Resin-trees have a silvery tint in the canopy, while Drooping Resin-trees are bluish. Both have milky, resinous sap, and dark brown to grey rough **bark**, flaking in small, square segments. White to creamy small **flowers** occur in sprays (Oct - Feb), and kidney-shaped **fruit** grows in loose clusters.

ECOZONE G – DELAGOA THORN THICKETS (ON ECCA SHALE)

This flat Ecozone occurs on Ecca shales, which are a strip of Karoo sediment with some sandstone ridges. The Ecozone runs north-south between the undulating granites in the west, and the flat basalts in the east.

Because the soft shales weather so easily, and the Ecozone is bounded on both east and west by harder-wearing rocks, a number of drainage lines 'find it easier' to run from north to south. There are also many small pans that are rich in birdlife. The soils are nutrient-rich, and the grasses very palatable.

The fact that Delagoa Acacia, *Acacia welwitschii*, p. 140, and Many-stemmed Albizia, *Albizia petersiana*, p. 142, dominate this Ecozone, makes it one of the most unique, vegetation-wise, in the Lowveld. It is very easy to find both these species once you are in the Ecozone. Some other Acacia species, however, are also found here, that can be confused with the Delagoa Acacia, particularly Black-monkey Acacia, *Acacia burkei*, see below. Giraffe like the flowers and pods of the Delagoa Acacia, and are often found browsing from November through to July.

Ecozone G covers about 3% of the Kruger National Park. Rainfall is between 500 and 600 mm per year, and the altitude is between 260 and 320 m above sea level.

This flat Ecozone is dominated by Delagoa Acacia, *Acacia welwitschii*, the large tree on the right.

Black-monkey Acacia   Tree no 161
Acacia burkei

This Acacia is most common in Ecozone G and in the granites south of the Olifants River. It is tall, single-trunked and deciduous, and is often high-branching, with a dense, dark green, semi-circular to thick-umbrella canopy. The **bark** is dark, rough and deeply fissured lengthways, exposing yellowish underbark. Alternate, Twice Compound **leaves** are short and stiff, and stand upright, hardly moving in the wind. The leaflets are relatively large (4-20 x 2-12 mm). **Thorns** are short, dark, and sharply hooked, in pairs far apart below leaf-buds. White **flower-spikes** bloom after new leaves appear (Oct - Jan). Flat bean **pods** are dark brown when ripe, with a pointed tip. This tree is favoured by elephants, and is less common where elephant densities are high.

ECOZONE I – LEBOMBO MOUNTAIN BUSHVELD (ON RHYOLITE)

The Lebombo Mountains form the eastern boundary of the Kruger National Park, from as far north as Shingwedzi. They then continue southwards through Swaziland, well into northern KwaZulu-Natal. The rainfall increases southwards from 400 mm in the north, to 700 mm near Crocodile Bridge. The average altitude varies between 300 and 400 m. This Ecozone covers about 8% of the Kruger National Park.

Volcanic rhyolite rocks form these mountains, and many of the large west-east rivers cut through them forming deep gorges. A wide variety of Euphorbias contrast with the red rhyolite rocks, and the Lebombo Euphorbia, *Euphorbia confinalis*, see below, is one of the more unique species found here. Surprisingly, waterbuck are often found on the rocky slopes. It is also a good place to look for klipspringer.

The Lebombo Euphorbia, *Euphorbia confinalis*, is prominent on the reddish rhyolite rocks of Ecozone I.

Lebombo Euphorbia Tree no 345
Euphorbia confinalis

This leafless tree grows only in Ecozone I, on the Lebombo Mountains, and in Ecozone J where it prefers rocky terrain. It is a single-trunked Euphorbia with a candelabra-like canopy of upward-growing branches. Individual branches form many side branchlets originating at the same level. The Deadliest Euphorbia, *Euphorbia cooperi*, p. 152, that also grows in Ecozone I, has branches that do not split. Its branches are square and form long rectangular segments. **Flowers** are small and pale yellow (Jun - Aug). Capsule-like **fruit** has three parts which ripen to red (Jul - Oct).

Ecozone J – Olifants Rugged Veld (on rhyolite / basalt)

This rugged Ecozone occurs on a mixture of volcanics. The rhyolite of the Lebombos means many red rhyolite boulders are strewn across the landscape. The basalt forms dark clays with dark basalt boulders. The altitude varies between 180 and 300 m above sea level, and the rainfall ranges between 450 and 500 mm per annum.

The Timbavati and Olifants rivers cross this Ecozone, and the dense, green riverine belts contrast with the sparser vegetation of the Ecozone generally. The Purple-pod Cluster-leaf, *Terminalia prunioides*, p. 104, is very common in rocky areas while the Shepherds-tree, *Boscia albitrunca*, see below, can be found in the hills around the Olifants River. This Ecozone occurs only within the Kruger National Park, and covers about 1.5% of the Park. Steenbuck are often seen in open areas.

Deadliest Euphorbia, *Euphorbia cooperi*, p. 152, and White Kirkia, *Kirkia acuminata*, p. 156, are both striking trees in Ecozone J.

Shepherds-tree Tree no 122
Boscia albitrunca

This evergreen tree is associated with hot, dry areas, and prefers well-drained soils, such as the sandy or rocky areas around the Olifants River in Ecozone J. It is single-trunked, branching into a few large branches that divide profusely to form a rounded, dense canopy. **Bark** is noticeably pale grey with white, yellowish or black patches. Young, dull-green twigs stand out among the spirally-arranged, Simple, elliptic, tough, leathery **leaves**. Yellow star-shaped **flowers**, with no individual petals, are inconspicuous, in bunches of 4 to 5 (Jul - Nov, depending on rain). **Fruit** is yellow and berry-like when ripe (Dec - Mar).

ECOZONE K – STUNTED KNOB-THORN SAVANNAH (ON BASALT)

Small Knob-thorn Acacias, *Acacia nigrescens*, dominate this slightly undulating Ecozone with underlying basalt rocks. The rainfall varies between 500 and 550 mm, and the altitude between 250 and 500 m above sea level. These soils are high in clay content, and are shallow and dark, and erode easily.

The rainfall here is too low for the clay soils to provide the trees with enough water to grow tall. This fact, combined with the dense grass layer, and resulting hot veld fires, keep the trees small.

This area has one of the highest kudu populations in the Kruger National Park. Giraffe are also very fond of Knob-thorn Acacias, and because these trees are small here, their leaves are easier to reach than in the other Ecozones. Due to the heavy utilisation by giraffe, the small Knob-thorns have a regular cone shape like a Christmas-tree, with only the highest branches escaping to form a more irregular canopy, see below.

This Ecozone occurs only within the Kruger National Park and covers about 2% of the Park.

Stunted Knob-thorn Acacias, *Acacia nigrescens*, green in early spring, dominate this relatively flat Ecozone.

Small Knob-thorn Acacia Tree no 178
Acacia nigrescens

The Knob-thorn in this Ecozone looks very different from the same tree in the other Ecozones. Here the trees are kept small by the low available soil moisture, hot fires and particularly by the heavy browsing of giraffe and kudu. Even in this Ecozone, when a tree grows tall enough to be beyond the effect of the browsers, there is enough soil moisture to allow it to reach the full mature height of Knob-thorns in other Ecozones. See page 126 for a full description of the Knob-thorn Acacia. Everything that applies to the trees that are larger when they are mature, also applies to this stunted form, except the height, and overall browsed shape.

Ecozone L – Mopane Shrubveld (on basalt)

This Ecozone is based on flat, volcanic basalt that leads to very uniform vegetation, consisting mostly of dense Mopane shrubs, *Colophospermum mopane*, p. 116. Mopane stay small here, because the dense clay soils dry out, and as they do so, they tend to break the roots of the trees. Regular fires also keep the trees low, as they have to resprout from the bottom after every hot fire.

The altitude varies between 300 and 400 m above sea level, and the rainfall ranges between 450 and 500 mm per annum. This Ecozone covers about 15% of the Kruger National Park, and is also found north of the Limpopo in the Lowveld of Zimbabwe.

Ecozone L is traversed by many broad, grass-covered drainage lines with Lala-palms, *Hyphaene coriacea*, p. 86, along the banks. This is also where the small Acacia-like Bushveld Albizia, *Albizia harveyi*, see below, is common. Open vleis along the drainage line have very few trees, making this Ecozone suitable for rare game such as roan and tsessebe. However, generally on the uplands, spotting game is not easy in the dense Mopane vegetation.

Shrub Mopane, *Colophospermum mopane*, p. 116, dominate Ecozone L, looking eastward towards the Lebombo Mountains in this photograph.

Bushveld Albizia   Tree no 155
Albizia harveyi

This slender tree is deciduous. It is widely distributed in the Lowveld, and is also common on brackish flats. Large trees are found along the alluvial plains. The **bark** of large trees sub-divides into prominent vertical ridges. The feathery **leaves** are Twice Compound with up to 16 feathers, with a large number of tiny, sickle-shaped leaflets per feather. White, powder-puff **flowers** are grouped at the end of twigs; stamens up to 20 mm (Oct - Nov). The large **pods** (180 x 20 - 30 mm) are pale brown, thin and flat, split open readily, and ripen in late summer (Mar - Aug).

ECOZONE M – ALLUVIAL PLAINS

Ecozone M, Alluvial Plains, is found in the north. It occurs along the large rivers as they cross the basaltic plains, flowing west to east towards the Lebombo Mountains and Mozambique. The Ecozone is best developed along the Shingwedzi, Luvuvhu and Limpopo rivers. These rivers regularly flood during periods of high rainfall, depositing rich clays along their banks, which alters the type of vegetation that grows there.

Rainfall ranges between 400 and 550 mm per annum, and altitude between 200 and 300 m above sea level. The area covers a little more that 1% of the Kruger National Park. Nyalas are common along the Luvuvhu River.

The floodplains of the Shingwedzi and Luvuvhu are the best examples of these plains. Many interesting and unique trees can be found, including the very common Narrow-leaved Mustard-tree, *Salvadora australis*, p. 134. Also of interest are Fever-tree Acacia forests, *Acacia xanthophloea*, p. 90, and large stands of Sycomore Figs, *Ficus sycomorus*, p. 164. The heart-shaped leaves of the Feverberry Croton, *Croton megalobotrys*, see below, are also very striking and easy to recognise.

Narrow-leaved Mustard-trees, *Salvadora australis*, p. 134, are common around Shingwedzi, in Ecozone M.

Feverberry Croton Tree no 329
Croton megalobotrys

Common along large rivers such as the Limpopo, Olifants and Sand, it has slender, smooth, pale grey stems, and a dense, drooping canopy. Large Simple, alternate **leaves** are spirally arranged and triangular, with a toothed leaf-edge. The under-surface of young leaves has silvery-white hairs. Characteristic three-lobed, yellowish-brown **fruit** capsules look like small apples, and are covered by grey-white, woolly hairs when young (Dec - Mar).

Ecozone N – Sandveld

The Sandveld Ecozone has unique geology. It has rugged sandstone hills in the north-west, and is flat with deep sands in the north-east. The sandstone mountains form the lowest foothills of the Soutpansberg in the west. The deep Sandveld continues both eastward, across the Mozambique boundary, and northwards, over the Limpopo into Zimbabwe. This Ecozone covers about 2% of the Kruger National Park.

The rainfall varies from 600 mm near Punda Maria in the west, to 450 mm per annum in the east. These sandy soils are well drained and support drought-resistant trees such as the Corkwoods, *Commiphora* species, a wide variety of which are found in this Ecozone. (See Zebra-bark Corkwood, *Commiphora viminea*, below). Pod-mahogany, *Afzelia quanzensis*, p. 150, and White Kirkia, *Kirkia acuminata*, p. 156, are also fairly common.

Dramatic autumn leaves of White Kirkia, *Kirkia acuminata*, and Baobab, *Adansonia digitata*, decorate the sandstone hills near Punda Maria.

Zebra-bark Corkwood Tree no 279
Commiphora viminea

This is an exceptionally twiggy, deciduous tree. It is characterised by its yellow-white **bark** that peels in horizontal, dark bands to form the distinctive zebra-striped bark. It grows in low altitudes in hot, dry areas. It prefers well-drained sandy soils, but can also be found on the basalts of Ecozone L, east of Punda Maria. The Simple **leaves** are bluish-green with a distinct, greyish bloom and are clustered in rosettes on dwarf, spine-tipped side shoots. They are oval, often narrowly so. Pale yellow **flowers** grow in inconspicuous clusters from November to December. The **fruit** has no stalk, and is oblong and red when ripe, in late summer.

ECOZONE O – TREE MOPANE SAVANNAH (ON ECCA SHALE)

Ecca shales, with deep soil that can support large trees, form this flat Ecozone. This is the same underlying geological shale as in Ecozone G, further south. The altitude varies between 360 and 420 m above sea-level, and the rainfall between 500 and 550 mm per annum.

Mopane, *Colophospermum mopane*, p. 116, that grow here, are unlike those found in Ecozones P and L. These reach a substantial height, between 10 and 15 m tall.

The rare Arnot's Chat, which only occurs in tall woodland, is sought after by serious birders adding it to their life list. Although not common, the Bushveld Bead-bean, *Maerua angolensis*, see below, is conspicuous, both when it flowers, and when it bears its bean-like pods, in early spring and summer.

The impressive, tall Mopanes, *Colophospermum mopane*, create a woodland, very different from the shrub-form in other Ecozones.

Bushveld Bead-bean Tree no 132
Maerua angolensis

This tree can be found on rocky outcrops and termite mounds, and is usually evergreen. It has a single, pale grey trunk that branches high up to form a moderate, semi-circular canopy. Simple, broad, elliptic, dark green **leaves** spiral in clusters, and have a small, but distinct, hard, hair-like tip. Masses of sweet-scented, creamy-white, pin-cushion **flowers** with very long stamens cover the tree from July to October. Characteristic, long, slender, yellow-green, bumpy bean **pods** resemble a chain of unequal-sized beads from September to April.

Ecozone P – Mopane / Bushwillow Woodlands (on granite)

This granite Ecozone covers 15% of the Kruger National Park. It is also the basic Ecozone of many farms and reserves still in the Lowveld (to the west and north-west of the Park). It is also the base of a great deal of the land in Zimbabwe, across the Limpopo where Lowveld altitudes dominate the landscape. The altitude throughout varies between 250 and 400 m above sea level. The rainfall is variable between 450 and 500 mm per year.

As with the other granite Ecozones, this is an undulating landscape with many dissecting streams and rivers. This vegetation is more variable than on the basalts, and the crests of the granite are dominated by the Red Bushwillow, *Combretum apiculatum*, p. 204. Although Mopane, *Colophospermum mopane*, p. 116, are also found on the crests, they are more common in the midslopes and valleys, where some Acacia species will also be found.

The Small False Mopane, *Guibourtia conjugata*, see below, is fairly common in the northern part of this Ecozone, and it can be confused with Mopane because of its similar butterfly-leaf. It is, however, easy to distinguish by its bark and closer inspection of its leaves. This is an important Ecozone for sable, as are Ecozones A, B and C, because sable prefer the more undulating granites to the flatter basalts. The reason for this is that mammal, and therefore predator densities, are generally lower in undulations. Large breeding herds of elephants are also common.

The undulating granite hills of this Ecozone are dominated by Shrub Mopane and Bushwillows.

Small False Mopane Tree no 200
Guibourtia conjugata

This deciduous, upright tree has heavy wood and grows slowly. It is found in deep, sandy soils in low altitude, open woodland and bush, often along rivers. It is more common in the far north of this Ecozone, and in Ecozone N. Butterfly Compound **leaves**, with 1 pair of leaflets, are oval, with a curved leaf-edge. They look very similar to Mopane. The star-shaped sprays of **flowers** appear from November to January. They have long stamens, and are creamy-yellow, while Mopane are greenish. The **fruit** is a thin, flat, circular pod which ripens in winter while the Mopane pod is kidney-shaped.

ECOZONE TREE LISTS

Sappi Tree Spotting is based on two fundamental concepts – Look for the right trees in the right place, and create Search Images of the trees you are looking for. On the following pages are the trees you are most likely to find in each Ecozone, and in each Habitat.

The trees you should look for first are shown at the top of the list in the darker colour. The trees in the paler colour are the next 'easiest' to look for. The rest of the list consists of the other trees that you could find, less easily, in each Habitat. Each list does also include Look-alike trees, and trees described in the introductory section, pages ii - 49.

ECOZONE A – MIXED BUSHWILLOW WOODLANDS

CREST		SEEPLINE		VALLEY BOTTOM		RIVER/DRAINAGE LINE	
Flaky-bark Acacia *Acacia exuvialis*	214	Silver Cluster-leaf *Terminalia sericea*	120	Apple-leaf *Philenoptera violacea*	124	Apple-leaf *Philenoptera violacea*	124
Marula *Sclerocarya birrea*	122	African Weeping-wattle *Peltophorum africanum*	96	Flaky-bark Acacia *Acacia exuvialis*	214	Ebony Jackal-berry *Diospyros mespiliformis*	160
Red Bushwillow *Combretum apiculatum*	204	Marula *Sclerocarya birrea*	122	Knob-thorn Acacia *Acacia nigrescens*	126	Matumi *Breonadia salicina*	176
Russet Bushwillow *Combretum hereroense*	206	Red Acacia *Acacia gerrardii*	144	Russet Bushwillow *Combretum hereroense*	206	River Acacia *Acacia robusta*	182
African Weeping-wattle *Peltophorum africanum*	96	Tree Wistaria *Bolusanthus speciosus*	108	Greenthorn Torchwood *Balanites maughamii*	146	Tamboti *Spirostachys africana*	162
Black Monkey-orange *Strychnos madagascariensis*	132	Bushveld Albizia *Albizia harveyi*	45	Large Sourplum *Ximenia caffra*	3	Weeping Boer-bean *Schotia brachypetala*	170
Large-fruited Bushwillow *Combretum zeyheri*	202	Red Bushwillow *Combretum apiculatum*	204	Long-tail Cassia *Cassia abbreviata*	98	Knob-thorn Acacia *Acacia nigrescens*	126
Large Sourplum *Ximenia caffra*	3	Red Spikethorn *Gymnosporia senegalensis*	106	Red Acacia *Acacia gerrardii*	144	Leadwood Bushwillow *Combretum imberbe*	118
Sickle-bush *Dichrostachys cinerea*	216			Round-leaved Bloodwood *Pterocarpus rotundifolius*	212	Marula *Sclerocarya birrea*	122
Silver Cluster-leaf *Terminalia sericea*	120	**MIDSLOPE**		Scented-pod Acacia *Acacia nilotica*	198	Sausage-tree *Kigelia africana*	178
Weeping Boer-bean *Schotia brachypetala*	170	African Weeping-wattle *Peltophorum africanum*	96	Zebrawood Flat-bean *Dalbergia melanoxylon*	110	Umbrella Acacia *Acacia tortilis*	92
Weeping Bushwillow *Combretum collinum*	35	Black Monkey-orange *Strychnos madagascariensis*	132	African Weeping-wattle *Peltophorum africanum*	96	Umdoni Waterberry *Syzygium cordatum*	30
Zebrawood Flat-bean *Dalbergia melanoxylon*	110	Black-monkey Acacia *Acacia burkei*	41	Black-monkey Acacia *Acacia burkei*	41	Zebrawood Flat-bean *Dalbergia melanoxylon*	110
Black-monkey Acacia *Acacia burkei*	41	Marula *Sclerocarya birrea*	122	False-marula Lannea *Lannea schweinfurthii*	38	Broad-pod Albizia *Albizia forbesii*	112
Buffalo-thorn Jujube *Ziziphus mucronata*	186	Red Acacia *Acacia gerrardii*	144	Horned-thorn Acacia *Acacia grandicornuta*	196	Flame Climbing Bushwillow *Combretum microphyllum*	102
False-marula Lannea *Lannea schweinfurthii*	38	Russet Bushwillow *Combretum hereroense*	206	Tall Firethorn Corkwood *Commiphora glandulosa*	136	Natal-mahogany *Trichilia emetica*	180
Naboom Euphorbia *Euphorbia ingens*	152	Sickle-bush *Dichrostachys cinerea*	216	Umbrella Acacia *Acacia tortilis*	92	Pioneer Spikethorn *Gymnosporia buxifolia*	33
Tall Firethorn Corkwood *Commiphora glandulosa*	136	White-leaved Raisin *Grewia bicolor*	210	Weeping Boer-bean *Schotia brachypetala*	170	Red Bushwillow *Combretum apiculatum*	204
Wild-pear Dombeya *Dombeya rotundifolia*	36	Bushveld Albizia *Albizia harveyi*	45			River Bushwillow *Combretum erythrophyllum*	174
		Flaky-bark Acacia *Acacia exuvialis*	214			Russet Bushwillow *Combretum hereroense*	206
		Umbrella Acacia *Acacia tortilis*	92			Water Nuxia *Nuxia oppositifolia*	172
						Wild Date-palm *Phoenix reclinata*	88

Red Bushwillow
Combretum apiculatum
p. 204

50

ECOZONE B – PRETORIUSKOP SOURVELD

CREST

African Weeping-wattle *Peltophorum africanum*	96
Black Monkey-orange *Strychnos madagascariensis*	132
Kiaat Bloodwood *Pterocarpus angolensis*	138
Large-fruited Bushwillow *Combretum zeyheri*	202
Marula *Sclerocarya birrea*	122
Red Bushwillow *Combretum apiculatum*	204
Ebony Jackal-berry *Diospyros mespiliformis*	160
Naboom Euphorbia *Euphorbia ingens*	152
Sycomore Fig *Ficus sycomorus*	164
Weeping Boer-bean *Schotia brachypetala*	170
Deadliest Euphorbia *Euphorbia cooperi*	152
Large-leaved Rock Fig *Ficus abutilifolia*	154
Red-leaved Fig *Ficus ingens*	32
Sickle-bush *Dichrostachys cinerea*	216
Spiny Monkey-orange *Strychnos spinosa*	23
Weeping Bushwillow *Combretum collinum*	35
Wild-pear Dombeya *Dombeya rotundifolia*	36

SEEPLINE

Silver Cluster-leaf *Terminalia sericea*	120
African Weeping-wattle *Peltophorum africanum*	96
Black Monkey-orange *Strychnos madagascariensis*	132
Marula *Sclerocarya birrea*	122
Tree Wistaria *Bolusanthus speciosus*	108
Buffalo-thorn Jujube *Ziziphus mucronata*	186
False-marula Lannea *Lannea schweinfurthii*	38
Red Spikethorn *Gymnosporia senegalensis*	106
Umdoni Waterberry *Syzygium cordatum*	30

ROCKY AREAS

Large-leaved Rock Fig *Ficus abutilifolia*	154
Bushveld Saffron *Elaeodendron transvaalense*	194
Deadliest Euphorbia *Euphorbia cooperi*	152
Mountain Kirkia *Kirkia wilmsii*	37
Red Bushwillow *Combretum apiculatum*	204
Red-leaved Fig *Ficus ingens*	32
Wild-pear Dombeya *Dombeya rotundifolia*	36

VALLEY BOTTOM

Apple-leaf *Philenoptera violacea*	124
Knob-thorn Acacia *Acacia nigrescens*	126
Umbrella Acacia *Acacia tortilis*	92
African Weeping-wattle *Peltophorum africanum*	96
Leadwood Bushwillow *Combretum imberbe*	118
Long-tail Cassia *Cassia abbreviata*	98
Marula *Sclerocarya birrea*	122
Red Acacia *Acacia gerrardii*	144
Russet Bushwillow *Combretum hereroense*	206
Scented-pod Acacia *Acacia nilotica*	198
Sickle-bush *Dichrostachys cinerea*	216
Buffalo-thorn Jujube *Ziziphus mucronata*	186
Ebony Jackal-berry *Diospyros mespiliformis*	160
False-marula Lannea *Lannea schweinfurthii*	38
Red Bushwillow *Combretum apiculatum*	204
Weeping Boer-bean *Schotia brachypetala*	170
White-leaved Raisin *Grewia bicolor*	210
Wild-pear Dombeya *Dombeya rotundifolia*	36

DRAINAGE LINE

Ebony Jackal-berry *Diospyros mespiliformis*	160
Knob-thorn Acacia *Acacia nigrescens*	126
River Acacia *Acacia robusta*	182
Weeping Boer-bean *Schotia brachypetala*	170
Flame Climbing Bushwillow *Combretum microphyllum*	102
Marula *Sclerocarya birrea*	122
Pride-of-de-Kaap Bauhinia *Bauhinia galpinii*	100
Sausage-tree *Kigelia africana*	178
Sycomore Fig *Ficus sycomorus*	164
Tamboti *Spirostachys africana*	162
Umbrella Acacia *Acacia tortilis*	92
Buffalo-thorn Jujube *Ziziphus mucronata*	186
Large-leaved Albizia *Albizia versicolor*	77
Red Spikethorn *Gymnosporia senegalensis*	106
Umdoni Waterberry *Syzygium cordatum*	30
Wild Date-palm *Phoenix reclinata*	88

BRACK

Magic Guarri *Euclea divinorum*	190
Tamboti *Spirostachys africana*	162
Buffalo-thorn Jujube *Ziziphus mucronata*	186
Bushveld Saffron *Elaeodendron transvaalense*	194
Jacket-plum *Pappea capensis*	192
Scented-pod Acacia *Acacia nilotica*	198
Umbrella Acacia *Acacia tortilis*	92

ECOZONE A – MIXED BUSHWILLOW WOODLANDS – Continued

ROCKY AREAS

Large-leaved Rock Fig *Ficus abutilifolia*	154
Bushveld Gardenia *Gardenia volkensii*	188
Bushveld Saffron *Elaeodendron transvaalense*	194
Pod-mahogany *Afzelia quanzensis*	150
Red Bushwillow *Combretum apiculatum*	204
Deadliest Euphorbia *Euphorbia cooperi*	152
Purple-pod Cluster-leaf *Terminalia prunioides*	104
Red-leaved Fig *Ficus ingens*	32
Russet Bushwillow *Combretum hereroense*	206

BRACK

Horned-thorn Acacia *Acacia grandicornuta*	196
Magic Guarri *Euclea divinorum*	190
Buffalo-thorn Jujube *Ziziphus mucronata*	186
Bushveld Gardenia *Gardenia volkensii*	188
Bushveld Saffron *Elaeodendron transvaalense*	194
Jacket-plum *Pappea capensis*	192
Scented-pod Acacia *Acacia nilotica*	198
Tamboti *Spirostachys africana*	162
Bushveld Albizia *Albizia harveyi*	45
Russet Bushwillow *Combretum hereroense*	206
Umbrella Acacia *Acacia tortilis*	92

ECOZONE C – MALELANE MOUNTAIN BUSHVELD

CREST

Large-fruited Bushwillow *Combretum zeyheri*	202
African Weeping-wattle *Peltophorum africanum*	96
Black Monkey-orange *Strychnos madagascariensis*	132
Kiaat Bloodwood *Pterocarpus angolensis*	138
Red Bushwillow *Combretum apiculatum*	204
Silver Cluster-leaf *Terminalia sericea*	120
Weeping Boer-bean *Schotia brachypetala*	170
Weeping Bushwillow *Combretum collinum*	35
Flaky-bark Acacia *Acacia exuvialis*	214
Marula *Sclerocarya birrea*	122
Red Spikethorn *Gymnosporia senegalensis*	106
Round-leaved Bloodwood *Pterocarpus rotundifolius*	212
Sickle-bush *Dichrostachys cinerea*	216
Zebrawood Flat-bean *Dalbergia melanoxylon*	110

SEEPLINE

Silver Cluster-leaf *Terminalia sericea*	120
African Weeping-wattle *Peltophorum africanum*	96
Black Monkey-orange *Strychnos madagascariensis*	132
Red Bushwillow *Combretum apiculatum*	204
Weeping Bushwillow *Combretum collinum*	35

ROCKY AREAS

Large-leaved Rock Fig *Ficus abutilifolia*	154
Red-leaved Fig *Ficus ingens*	32
Deadliest Euphorbia *Euphorbia cooperi*	152
Large-fruited Bushwillow *Combretum zeyheri*	202
Mountain Kirkia *Kirkia wilmsii*	37
Naboom Euphorbia *Euphorbia ingens*	152
Purple-pod Cluster-leaf *Terminalia prunioides*	104
Red Bushwillow *Combretum apiculatum*	204

VALLEY BOTTOM

Knob-thorn Acacia *Acacia nigrescens*	126
Bushveld Albizia *Albizia harveyi*	45
Flaky-bark Acacia *Acacia exuvialis*	214
Leadwood Bushwillow *Combretum imberbe*	118
Red Acacia *Acacia gerrardii*	144
Russet Bushwillow *Combretum hereroense*	206
Scented-pod Acacia *Acacia nilotica*	198
Umbrella Acacia *Acacia tortilis*	92
White-leaved Raisin *Grewia bicolor*	210
Magic Guarri *Euclea divinorum*	190
Jacket-plum *Pappea capensis*	192
Wild-pear Dombeya *Dombeya rotundifolia*	36

BRACK

Magic Guarri *Euclea divinorum*	190
Tamboti *Spirostachys africana*	162
Buffalo-thorn Jujube *Ziziphus mucronata*	186
Bushveld Albizia *Albizia harveyi*	45
Jacket-plum *Pappea capensis*	192
Scented-pod Acacia *Acacia nilotica*	198

DRAINAGE LINE

Ebony Jackal-berry *Diospyros mespiliformis*	160
Knob-thorn Acacia *Acacia nigrescens*	126
River Acacia *Acacia robusta*	182
Weeping Boer-bean *Schotia brachypetala*	170
Apple-leaf *Philenoptera violacea*	124
Flaky-bark Acacia *Acacia exuvialis*	214
Forest Bushwillow *Combretum kraussi*	71
Large-leaved Albizia *Albizia versicolor*	77
Magic Guarri *Euclea divinorum*	190
Quinine-tree *Rauvolfia caffra*	ii
Tamboti *Spirostachys africana*	162

Buffalo-thorn Jujube
Ziziphus mucronata
p. 186

ECOZONE D – SABIE / CROCODILE THORN THICKETS

CREST

False-marula Lannea *Lannea schweinfurthii*	38
Flaky-bark Acacia *Acacia exuvialis*	214
Sickle-bush *Dichrostachys cinerea*	216
African Weeping-wattle *Peltophorum africanum*	96
Knob-thorn Acacia *Acacia nigrescens*	126
Large Sourplum *Ximenia caffra*	3
Marula *Sclerocarya birrea*	122
Red Bushwillow *Combretum apiculatum*	204
Sandpaper Raisin *Grewia flavescens*	208
Purple-pod Cluster-leaf *Terminalia prunioides*	104
Umbrella Acacia *Acacia tortilis*	92
Weeping Boer-bean *Schotia brachypetala*	170

ROCKY HILL

Large-leaved Rock Fig *Ficus abutilifolia*	154
Red-leaved Fig *Ficus ingens*	32
Deadliest Euphorbia *Euphorbia cooperi*	152
Purple-pod Cluster-leaf *Terminalia prunioides*	104
Red Bushwillow *Combretum apiculatum*	204
Naboom Euphorbia *Euphorbia ingens*	152
Rubber-hedge Euphorbia *Euphorbia tirucalli*	39

SEEPLINE

African Weeping-wattle *Peltophorum africanum*	96
Silver Cluster-leaf *Terminalia sericea*	120

VALLEY BOTTOM

Greenthorn Torchwood *Balanites maughamii*	146
Knob-thorn Acacia *Acacia nigrescens*	126
Long-tail Cassia *Cassia abbreviata*	98
Apple-leaf *Philenoptera violacea*	124
Flaky-bark Acacia *Acacia exuvialis*	214
Large Sourplum *Ximenia caffra*	3
Marula *Sclerocarya birrea*	122
Red Acacia *Acacia gerrardii*	144
Red Spikethorn *Gymnosporia senegalensis*	106
Russet Bushwillow *Combretum hereroense*	206
Scented-pod Acacia *Acacia nilotica*	198
Tamboti *Spirostachys africana*	162
Umbrella Acacia *Acacia tortilis*	92
Leadwood Bushwillow *Combretum imberbe*	118
Sickle-bush *Dichrostachys cinerea*	216

BRACK

Buffalo-thorn Jujube *Ziziphus mucronata*	186
Bushveld Gardenia *Gardenia volkensii*	188
Bushveld Saffron *Elaeodendron transvaalense*	194
Horned-thorn Acacia *Acacia grandicornuta*	196
Jacket-plum *Pappea capensis*	192
Magic Guarri *Euclea divinorum*	190
Scented-pod Acacia *Acacia nilotica*	198
Umbrella Acacia *Acacia tortilis*	92
False-marula Lannea *Lannea schweinfurthii*	38
Knob-thorn Acacia *Acacia nigrescens*	126
Marula *Sclerocarya birrea*	122
Round-leaved Bloodwood *Pterocarpus rotundifolius*	212
Sandpaper Raisin *Grewia flavescens*	208
Tamboti *Spirostachys africana*	162
Bushveld Resin-tree *Ozoroa paniculosa*	40
Ebony Jackal-berry *Diospyros mespiliformis*	160
Flaky-bark Acacia *Acacia exuvialis*	214
Greenthorn Torchwood *Balanites maughamii*	146
Nyala-tree *Xanthocercis zambesiaca*	166
Russet Bushwillow *Combretum hereroense*	206
Weeping Boer-bean *Schotia brachypetala*	170

MIDSLOPE

Red Bushwillow *Combretum apiculatum*	204
African Weeping-wattle *Peltophorum africanum*	96

RIVER/DRAINAGE LINE

Ebony Jackal-berry *Diospyros mespiliformis*	160
Flame Climbing Bushwillow *Combretum microphyllum*	102
River Acacia *Acacia robusta*	182
Water Nuxia *Nuxia oppositifolia*	172
Weeping Boer-bean *Schotia brachypetala*	170
White-leaved Raisin *Grewia bicolor*	210
Apple-leaf *Philenoptera violacea*	124
Broad-pod Albizia *Albizia forbesii*	112
Buffalo-thorn Jujube *Ziziphus mucronata*	186
Knob-thorn Acacia *Acacia nigrescens*	126
Marula *Sclerocarya birrea*	122
Matumi *Breonadia salicina*	176
Natal-mahogany *Trichilia emetica*	180
Nyala-tree *Xanthocercis zambesiaca*	166
Red Spikethorn *Gymnosporia senegalensis*	106
River Bushwillow *Combretum erythrophyllum*	174
Russet Bushwillow *Combretum hereroense*	206
Sausage-tree *Kigelia africana*	178
Sycomore Fig *Ficus sycomorus*	164
Tamboti *Spirostachys africana*	162
Pride-of-de-Kaap Bauhinia *Bauhinia galpinii*	100
Umdoni Waterberry *Syzygium cordatum*	30
Wild Date-palm *Phoenix reclinata*	88

Purple-pod Cluster-leaf
Terminalia prunioides
p. 104

Ecozone E – Thorn Veld

PLAINS

Round-leaved Bloodwood *Pterocarpus rotundifolius*	212
Tree Wistaria *Bolusanthus speciosus*	108
Zebrawood Flat-bean *Dalbergia melanoxylon*	110
African Weeping-wattle *Peltophorum africanum*	96
Bushveld Saffron *Elaeodendron transvaalense*	194
Jacket-plum *Pappea capensis*	192
Knob-thorn Acacia *Acacia nigrescens*	126
Marula *Sclerocarya birrea*	122
Red Bushwillow *Combretum apiculatum*	204
Russet Bushwillow *Combretum hereroense*	206
Tamboti *Spirostachys africana*	162
Umbrella Acacia *Acacia tortilis*	92
Apple-leaf *Philenoptera violacea*	124
Buffalo-thorn Jujube *Ziziphus mucronata*	186
Bushveld Albizia *Albizia harveyi*	45
False-marula Lannea *Lannea schweinfurthii*	38
Leadwood Bushwillow *Combretum imberbe*	118
Sickle-bush *Dichrostachys cinerea*	216
Weeping Boer-bean *Schotia brachypetala*	170

ROCKY HILL

Red Acacia *Acacia gerrardii*	144
Red Bushwillow *Combretum apiculatum*	204
Bushveld Saffron *Elaeodendron transvaalense*	194
Greenthorn Torchwood *Balanites maughamii*	146
Knob-thorn Acacia *Acacia nigrescens*	126
Large-leaved Rock Fig *Ficus abutilifolia*	154
Rubber-hedge Euphorbia *Euphorbia tirucalli*	39

Ecozone F – Knob-thorn / Marula Savannah

SOUTH

Knob-thorn Acacia *Acacia nigrescens*	126
Leadwood Bushwillow *Combretum imberbe*	118
Marula *Sclerocarya birrea*	122
Red Acacia *Acacia gerrardii*	144
Red Spikethorn *Gymnosporia senegalensis*	106
Scented-pod Acacia *Acacia nilotica*	198
Zebrawood Flat-bean *Dalbergia melanoxylon*	110
Apple-leaf *Philenoptera violacea*	124
Long-tail Cassia *Cassia abbreviata*	98
Round-leaved Bloodwood *Pterocarpus rotundifolius*	212
Tree Wistaria *Bolusanthus speciosus*	108
Bushveld Albizia *Albizia harveyi*	45
Drooping Resin-tree *Ozoroa engleri*	40
False-marula Lannea *Lannea schweinfurthii*	38
Forest Bushwillow *Combretum kraussii*	71
Pioneer Spikethorn *Gymnosporia buxifolia*	33
Sickle-bush *Dichrostachys cinerea*	216

NORTH

Knob-thorn Acacia *Acacia nigrescens*	126
Leadwood Bushwillow *Combretum imberbe*	118
Marula *Sclerocarya birrea*	122
Red Acacia *Acacia gerrardii*	144
Zebrawood Flat-bean *Dalbergia melanoxylon*	110
African Weeping-wattle *Peltophorum africanum*	96
Buffalo-thorn Jujube *Ziziphus mucronata*	186
Long-tail Cassia *Cassia abbreviata*	98
Tall Firethorn Corkwood *Commiphora glandulosa*	136
Umbrella Acacia *Acacia tortilis*	92
White-leaved Raisin *Grewia bicolor*	210
Bushveld Albizia *Albizia harveyi*	45
Bushveld Bead-bean *Maerua angolensis*	48
Bushveld Resin-tree *Ozoroa paniculosa*	40
False-marula Lannea *Lannea schweinfurthii*	38
Russet Bushwillow *Combretum hereroense*	206
Sickle-bush *Dichrostachys cinerea*	216
Weeping Boer-bean *Schotia brachypetala*	170

DRAINAGE LINE

Knob-thorn Acacia *Acacia nigrescens*	126
Apple-leaf *Philenoptera violacea*	124
Broad-pod Albizia *Albizia forbesii*	112
Ebony Jackal-berry *Diospyros mespiliformis*	160
Fever-tree Acacia *Acacia xanthophloea*	90
Lala-palm *Hyphaene coriacea* and *petersiana*	86
Leadwood Bushwillow *Combretum imberbe*	118
Magic Guarri *Euclea divinorum*	190
Natal-mahogany *Trichilia emetica*	180
Red Spikethorn *Gymnosporia senegalensis*	106
River Acacia *Acacia robusta*	182
Russet Bushwillow *Combretum hereroense*	206
Sausage-tree *Kigelia africana*	178
Sycomore Fig *Ficus sycomorus*	164
Umbrella Acacia *Acacia tortilis*	92
Feverberry Croton *Croton megalobotrys*	46
Wild Date-palm *Phoenix reclinata*	88

Round-leaved Bloodwood
Pterocarpus rotundifolius
p. 212

Ecozone G – Delagoa Thorn Thickets

PLAINS

Delagoa Acacia *Acacia welwitschii*	140
Many-stemmed Albizia *Albizia petersiana*	142
Apple-leaf *Philenoptera violacea*	124
Black-monkey Acacia *Acacia burkei*	41
Knob-thorn Acacia *Acacia nigrescens*	126
Magic Guarri *Euclea divinorum*	190
Red Acacia *Acacia gerrardii*	144
Sickle-bush *Dichrostachys cinerea*	216
Tamboti *Spirostachys africana*	162
Tree Wistaria *Bolusanthus speciosus*	108
Umbrella Acacia *Acacia tortilis*	92
Bushveld Bead-bean *Maerua angolensis*	48
Forest Bushwillow *Combretum kraussii*	71
Weeping Boer-bean *Schotia brachypetala*	170
White-leaved Raisin *Grewia bicolor*	210

Ecozone H – Riverine Habitat

River Banks

Common Name	Page
Apple-leaf *Philenoptera violacea*	124
Ebony Jackal-berry *Diospyros mespiliformis*	160
Knob-thorn Acacia *Acacia nigrescens*	126
Lala-palm *Hyphaene coriacea* and *Hyphaene petersiana*	86
Leadwood Bushwillow *Combretum imberbe*	118
Natal-mahogany *Trichilia emetica*	180
Pride-of-de-Kaap Bauhinia *Bauhinia galpinii*	100
River Acacia *Acacia robusta*	182
Sausage-tree *Kigelia africana*	178
Sycomore Fig *Ficus sycomorus*	164
Tamboti *Spirostachys africana*	162
Wild Date-palm *Phoenix reclinata*	88
Broad-pod Albizia *Albizia forbesii*	112
Feverberry Croton *Croton megalobotrys*	46
Magic Guarri *Euclea divinorum*	190
Marula *Sclerocarya birrea*	122
Nyala-tree *Xanthocercis zambesiaca*	166
Red Spikethorn *Gymnosporia senegalensis*	106
Umdoni Waterberry *Syzygium cordatum*	30
Weeping Boer-bean *Schotia brachypetala*	170
Black-monkey Acacia *Acacia burkei*	41
False-marula Lannea *Lannea schweinfurthii*	38
Fever-tree Acacia *Acacia xanthophloea*	90
Mopane *Colophospermum mopane*	116
Narrow-leaved Mustard-tree *Salvadora australis*	134
Pioneer Spikethorn *Gymnosporia buxifolia*	33
River Bushwillow *Combretum erythrophyllum*	174
Umdoni Waterberry *Syzygium cordatum*	30
White-leaved Raisin *Grewia bicolor*	210

In Rivers

Common Name	Page
Matumi *Breonadia salicina*	176
Water Nuxia *Nuxia oppositifolia*	172
Wild Date-palm *Phoenix reclinata*	88
Flame Climbing Bushwillow *Combretum microphyllum*	102

Ecozone I – Lebombo Mountain Bushveld

South

Common Name	Page
Deadliest Euphorbia *Euphorbia cooperi*	150
Lebombo Euphorbia *Euphorbia confinalis*	42
African Weeping-wattle *Peltophorum africanum*	94
Flaky-bark Acacia *Acacia exuvialis*	214
Jacket-plum *Pappea capensis*	192
Large-fruited Bushwillow *Combretum zeyheri*	202
Large-leaved Rock Fig *Ficus abutilifolia*	154
Long-tail Cassia *Cassia abbreviata*	98
Naboom Euphorbia *Euphorbia ingens*	152
Pod-mahogany *Afzelia quanzensis*	150
Red Acacia *Acacia gerrardii*	144
Red Bushwillow *Combretum apiculatum*	204
Round-leaved Bloodwood *Pterocarpus rotundifolius*	212
Sandpaper Raisin *Grewia flavescens*	208
Shepherds-tree *Boscia albitrunca*	43
Tall Firethorn Corkwood *Commiphora glandulosa*	136
White Kirkia *Kirkia acuminata*	156
White-leaved Raisin *Grewia bicolor*	210
Black-monkey Acacia *Acacia burkei*	41
Bushveld Albizia *Albizia harveyi*	45
Drooping Resin-tree *Ozoroa engleri*	40
False-marula Lannea *Lannea schweinfurthii*	38
Forest Bushwillow *Combretum kraussii*	71
Kiaat Bloodwood *Pterocarpus angolensis*	138
Purple-pod Cluster-leaf *Terminalia prunioides*	104
Red-leaved Fig *Ficus ingens*	32
Russet Bushwillow *Combretum hereroense*	206
Sickle-bush *Dichrostachys cinerea*	216
Velvet Bushwillow *Combretum molle*	72
Weeping Boer-bean *Schotia brachypetala*	170

North

Common Name	Page
Baobab *Adansonia digitata*	84
Deadliest Euphorbia *Euphorbia cooperi*	152
Lebombo Euphorbia *Euphorbia confinalis*	42
Lebombo-ironwood *Androstachys johnsonii*	130
Marula *Sclerocarya birrea*	122
Mopane *Colophospermum mopane*	116
Pod-mahogany *Afzelia quanzensis*	150
Purple-pod Cluster-leaf *Terminalia prunioides*	104
Red Bushwillow *Combretum apiculatum*	204
Shepherds-tree *Boscia albitrunca*	43
Tall Firethorn Corkwood *Commiphora glandulosa*	136
White Kirkia *Kirkia acuminata*	156
False-marula Lannea *Lannea schweinfurthii*	38
Red-leaved Fig *Ficus ingens*	32
Sandpaper Raisin *Grewia flavescens*	208
Weeping Boer-bean *Schotia brachypetala*	170
Zebra-bark Corkwood *Commiphora viminea*	47

Wild Date-palm
Phoenix reclinata
p. 88

Ecozone J – Olifants Rugged Veld

Rocky Hill

Purple-pod Cluster-leaf *Terminalia prunioides*	104
Shepherds-tree *Boscia albitrunca*	43
Tall Firethorn Corkwood *Commiphora glandulosa*	136
Bushveld Gardenia *Gardenia volkensii*	188
Jacket-plum *Pappea capensis*	192
Large-leaved Rock Fig *Ficus abutilifolia*	154
Leadwood Bushwillow *Combretum imberbe*	118
Red Bushwillow *Combretum apiculatum*	204
Russet Bushwillow *Combretum hereroense*	206
Sandpaper Raisin *Grewia flavescens*	208
White Kirkia *Kirkia acuminata*	156
Tamboti *Spirostachys africana*	162
Weeping Bushwillow *Combretum collinum*	35

Plains

Purple-pod Cluster-leaf *Terminalia prunioides*	104
Red Bushwillow *Combretum apiculatum*	204
Tall Firethorn Corkwood *Commiphora glandulosa*	136
African Weeping-wattle *Peltophorum africanum*	96
Apple-leaf *Philenoptera violacea*	124
Flaky-bark Acacia *Acacia exuvialis*	214
Red Spikethorn *Gymnosporia senegalensis*	106
Scented-pod Acacia *Acacia nilotica*	198
Weeping Boer-bean *Schotia brachypetala*	170
Bushveld Bead-bean *Maerua angolensis*	48
Knob-thorn Acacia *Acacia nigrescens*	126
Russet Bushwillow *Combretum hereroense*	206
Sickle-bush *Dichrostachys cinerea*	216
Velvet Bushwillow *Combretum molle*	72
White-leaved Raisin *Grewia bicolor*	210

Riverine

Apple-leaf *Philenoptera violacea*	124
Ebony Jackal-berry *Diospyros mespiliformis*	160
Flame Climbing Bushwillow *Combretum microphyllum*	102
Marula *Sclerocarya birrea*	122
Matumi *Breonadia salicina*	176
Natal-mahogany *Trichilia emetica*	180
Nyala-tree *Xanthocercis zambesiaca*	166
River Acacia *Acacia robusta*	182
Sandpaper Raisin *Grewia flavescens*	208
Sycomore Fig *Ficus sycomorus*	164

Ecozone K – Stunted Knob-thorn Savannah

Plains

Knob-thorn Acacia *Acacia nigrescens*	126
Sickle-bush *Dichrostachys cinerea*	216
African Weeping-wattle *Peltophorum africanum*	96
Buffalo-thorn Jujube *Ziziphus mucronata*	186
Umbrella Acacia *Acacia tortilis*	92
Bushveld Bead-bean *Maerua angolensis*	48
Velvet Bushwillow *Combretum molle*	72
Weeping Boer-bean *Schotia brachypetala*	170
White-leaved Raisin *Grewia bicolor*	210

Ecozone L – Mopane Shrubveld

Plains

Baobab *Adansonia digitata*	84
Flaky-bark Acacia *Acacia exuvialis*	214
Jacket-plum *Pappea capensis*	192
Mopane *Colophospermum mopane*	116
Round-leaved Bloodwood *Pterocarpus rotundifolius*	212
African Weeping-wattle *Peltophorum africanum*	96
Apple-leaf *Philenoptera violacea*	124
Knob-thorn Acacia *Acacia nigrescens*	126
Purple-pod Cluster-leaf *Terminalia prunioides*	104
Red Spikethorn *Gymnosporia senegalensis*	106
Tall Firethorn Corkwood *Commiphora glandulosa*	136
Bushveld Albizia *Albizia harveyi*	45
Bushveld Bead-bean *Maerua angolensis*	48
Drooping Resin-tree *Ozoroa engleri*	40
Marula *Sclerocarya birrea*	122
Sickle-bush *Dichrostachys cinerea*	216
Velvet Bushwillow *Combretum molle*	72
Zebrawood Flat-bean *Dalbergia melanoxylon*	110

Drainage Line

Mopane *Colophospermum mopane*	116
Russet Bushwillow *Combretum hereroense*	206
Apple-leaf *Philenoptera violacea*	124
Bushveld Albizia *Albizia harveyi*	45
Feverberry Croton *Croton megalobotrys*	46
Fever-tree Acacia *Acacia xanthophloea*	90
Knob-thorn Acacia *Acacia nigrescens*	126
Umbrella Acacia *Acacia tortilis*	92
White-leaved Raisin *Grewia bicolor*	210
False-marula Lannea *Lannea schweinfurthii*	38
Lala-palm *Hyphaene coriacea* and *petersiana*	86
Leadwood Bushwillow *Combretum imberbe*	118
Marula *Sclerocarya birrea*	122
Tamboti *Spirostachys africana*	162
Wild Date-palm *Phoenix reclinata*	88

Lebombo-ironwood
Androstachys johnsonii
p.130

ECOZONE M – ALLUVIAL PLAINS   ECOZONE N – SANDVELD

FLOOD PLAINS

Magic Guarri *Euclea divinorum*	190
Narrow-leaved Mustard-tree *Salvadora australis*	134
Apple-leaf *Philenoptera violacea*	124
Baobab *Adansonia digitata*	84
Bushveld Albizia *Albizia harveyi*	45
Bushveld Gardenia *Gardenia volkensii*	188
Leadwood Bushwillow *Combretum imberbe*	118
Mopane *Colophospermum mopane*	116
Red Spikethorn *Gymnosporia senegalensis*	106
Shepherds-tree *Boscia albitrunca*	43
Tall Firethorn Corkwood *Commiphora glandulosa*	136
Tamboti *Spirostachys africana*	162
Umbrella Acacia *Acacia tortilis*	92
Zebrawood Flat-bean *Dalbergia melanoxylon*	110
Fever-tree Acacia *Acacia xanthophloea*	90
Russet Bushwillow *Combretum hereroense*	206
Sickle-bush *Dichrostachys cinerea*	216
Weeping Boer-bean *Schotia brachypetala*	170

RIVER BANKS

Fever-tree Acacia *Acacia xanthophloea*	90
Nyala-tree *Xanthocercis zambesiaca*	166
Ebony Jackal-berry *Diospyros mespiliformis*	160
Feverberry Croton *Croton megalobotrys*	46
Flame Climbing Bushwillow *Combretum microphyllum*	102
Lala-palm *Hyphaene coriacea* and *petersiana*	86
Leadwood Bushwillow *Combretum imberbe*	118
Matumi *Breonadia salicina*	176
Mopane *Colophospermum mopane*	116
Natal-mahogany *Trichilia emetica*	180
River Acacia *Acacia robusta*	182
Russet Bushwillow *Combretum hereroense*	206
Sausage-tree *Kigelia africana*	178
Tamboti *Spirostachys africana*	162
Umbrella Acacia *Acacia tortilis*	92
Water Nuxia *Nuxia oppositifolia*	172
Magic Guarri *Euclea divinorum*	190
Sickle-bush *Dichrostachys cinerea*	216
Sycomore Fig *Ficus sycomorus*	164
Weeping Boer-bean *Schotia brachypetala*	170
White-leaved Raisin *Grewia bicolor*	210

SANDSTONE RIDGES

Large-fruited Bushwillow *Combretum zeyheri*	202
Pod-mahogany *Afzelia quanzensis*	150
Red Bushwillow *Combretum apiculatum*	204
Silver Cluster-leaf *Terminalia sericea*	120
Tall Firethorn Corkwood *Commiphora glandulosa*	136
White Kirkia *Kirkia acuminata*	156
Baobab *Adansonia digitata*	84
Large-leaved Rock Fig *Ficus abutilifolia*	154
Lebombo-ironwood *Androstachys johnsonii*	130
Zebra-bark Corkwood *Commiphora viminea*	47
Black Monkey-orange *Strychnos madagascariensis*	132
Small False Mopane *Guibourtia conjugata*	49
Weeping Bushwillow *Combretum collinum*	35
Zebrawood Flat-bean *Dalbergia melanoxylon*	110

SLOPES

Silver Cluster-leaf *Terminalia sericea*	120
Magic Guarri *Euclea divinorum*	190
Pride-of-de-Kaap Bauhinia *Bauhinia galpinii*	100
African Weeping-wattle *Peltophorum africanum*	96
Apple-leaf *Philenoptera violacea*	124
Large-leaved Albizia *Albizia versicolor*	77
Leadwood Bushwillow *Combretum imberbe*	118
Quinine-tree *Rauvolfia caffra*	ii
Red Acacia *Acacia gerrardii*	144
Round-leaved Bloodwood *Pterocarpus rotundifolius*	212
Russet Bushwillow *Combretum hereroense*	206
Sickle-bush *Dichrostachys cinerea*	216
Small False Mopane *Guibourtia conjugata*	49
Stink-bushwillow *Pteleopis myrtifolia*	73
Velvet Bushwillow *Combretum molle*	72
Weeping Boer-bean *Schotia brachypetala*	170
Weeping Bushwillow *Combretum collinum*	35
Wild-pear Dombeya *Dombeya rotundifolia*	36
Zebrawood Flat-bean *Dalbergia melanoxylon*	110

Baobab
Adansonia digitata
p. 84

Ecozone O – Tree Mopane Savannah

FOREST

Horned-thorn Acacia *Acacia grandicornuta*	196
Mopane *Colophospermum mopane*	116
Bushveld Bead-bean *Maerua angolensis*	48
Knob-thorn Acacia *Acacia nigrescens*	126
Leadwood Bushwillow *Combretum imberbe*	118
Shepherds-tree *Boscia albitrunca*	43
Tamboti *Spirostachys africana*	162
Umbrella Acacia *Acacia tortilis*	92
Zebrawood Flat-bean *Dalbergia melanoxylon*	110
White-leaved Raisin *Grewia bicolor*	210

RIVERS/DRAINAGE LINES

Magic Guarri *Euclea divinorum*	190
Russet Bushwillow *Combretum hereroense*	206
Sickle-bush *Dichrostachys cinerea*	216
Weeping Boer-bean *Schotia brachypetala*	170

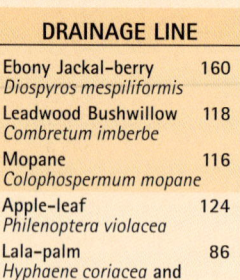

Ecozone P – Mopane / Bushwillow Woodlands

CREST

Red Bushwillow *Combretum apiculatum*	204
Mopane *Colophospermum mopane*	116
Zebrawood Flat-bean *Dalbergia melanoxylon*	110
African Weeping-wattle *Peltophorum africanum*	96
Black Monkey-orange *Strychnos madagascariensis*	132
Buffalo-thorn Jujube *Ziziphus mucronata*	186
Bushveld Albizia *Albizia harveyi*	45
Large Sourplum *Ximenia caffra*	3
Marula *Sclerocarya birrea*	122
Purple-pod Cluster-leaf *Terminalia prunioides*	104
Silver Cluster-leaf *Terminalia sericea*	120
Small False Mopane *Guibourtia conjugata*	49
White-leaved Raisin *Grewia bicolor*	210

VALLEY BOTTOM

Knob-thorn Acacia *Acacia nigrescens*	126
Leadwood Bushwillow *Combretum imberbe*	118
Mopane *Colophospermum mopane*	116
Apple-leaf *Philenoptera violacea*	124
Flaky-bark Acacia *Acacia exuvialis*	214
Large Sourplum *Ximenia caffra*	3
Long-tail Cassia *Cassia abbreviata*	98
Red Acacia *Acacia gerrardii*	144
Russet Bushwillow *Combretum hereroense*	206
Sandpaper Raisin *Grewia flavescens*	208
Umbrella Acacia *Acacia tortilis*	92
Bushveld Albizia *Albizia harveyi*	45
Sickle-bush *Dichrostachys cinerea*	216
Weeping Boer-bean *Schotia brachypetala*	170

SEEPLINE/MIDSLOPE

Apple-leaf *Philenoptera violacea*	124
Mopane *Colophospermum mopane*	116
Silver Cluster-leaf *Terminalia sericea*	120
African Weeping-wattle *Peltophorum africanum*	96
Red Bushwillow *Combretum apiculatum*	204

ROCKY AREAS

Baobab *Adansonia digitata*	84
Deadliest Euphorbia *Euphorbia cooperi*	152
Flaky-bark Acacia *Acacia exuvialis*	214
Large-leaved Rock Fig *Ficus abutilifolia*	154
Purple-pod Cluster-leaf *Terminalia prunioides*	104
Red Bushwillow *Combretum apiculatum*	204
Shepherds-tree *Boscia albitrunca*	43
Tall Firethorn Corkwood *Commiphora glandulosa*	136
White Kirkia *Kirkia acuminata*	156

BRACK

Magic Guarri *Euclea divinorum*	190
Buffalo-thorn Jujube *Ziziphus mucronata*	186
Bushveld Albizia *Albizia harveyi*	45
Sandpaper Raisin *Grewia flavescens*	208

DRAINAGE LINE

Ebony Jackal-berry *Diospyros mespiliformis*	160
Leadwood Bushwillow *Combretum imberbe*	118
Mopane *Colophospermum mopane*	116
Apple-leaf *Philenoptera violacea*	124
Lala-palm *Hyphaene coriacea* and *petersiana*	86
Russet Bushwillow *Combretum hereroense*	206
Tamboti *Spirostachys africana*	162
Zebrawood Flat-bean *Dalbergia melanoxylon*	110
Feverberry Croton *Croton megalobotrys*	46
Marula *Sclerocarya birrea*	122
Nyala-tree *Xanthocercis zambesiaca*	166
Wild Date-palm *Phoenix reclinata*	88

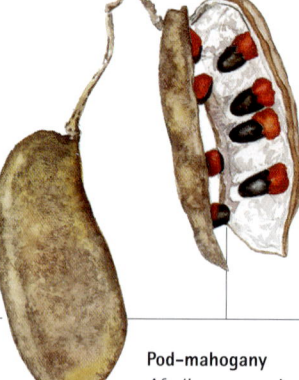

Pod-mahogany
Afzelia quanzensis
p. 150

YOU FIND TREES BY ECOZONE OR HABITAT – A SIX-STEP GUIDE

On pages 34-49, there is a full description of the 16 Ecozones (A - P), and their major Habitats, that occur throughout the Lowveld. Below are the steps you should follow every time you want to find a tree. It will soon become second nature.

1 Decide where you are.
In which Ecozone are you?
To identify specific trees you must first work out where you are. Turn to the Maps on pages 224-237, and note the Ecozone you are in. Example: Ecozone N - Sandveld.

2 In which Habitat are you?
The descriptions on pages 26-49 give details of the Ecozones and their Habitats. Decide which of these applies to you. Example: Sandstone Ridge of Ecozone N.

3 Which trees can you find in your Ecozone and Habitat?
On pages 50-58 you will find the Tree List for your Ecozone. Read this and make a note of the three or four trees you are most likely to find, and mark their pages. Example: White Kirkia, p. 156.

ECOZONE N – SANDVELD

SANDSTONE RIDGES		SLOPES	
Large-fruited Bushwillow *Combretum zeyheri*	202	Silver Cluster-leaf *Terminalia sericea*	120
Pod-mahogany *Afzelia quanzensis*	150	Magic Guarri *Euclea divinorum*	190
White Kirkia *Kirkia acuminata*	156	Pride-of-de-Kaap Bauhinia *Bauhinia galpinii*	100

GIFF
- It has a tall, straight, single trunk and is often a handsome, well-proportioned tree, standing out proudly, on the crest of a rocky outcrop or ridge.
- The bark is pale grey and smooth when young, and becomes flaky with corky knobs in older trees.

4 Create Search Images for these trees
Look at the pictures and read the GIFFs of each of these trees. In the same way as you would create a mental picture of a blonde child, with a green shirt eating an ice-cream, imagine the striking features of the trees you are hoping to find.

5 Match your Search Images to nearby trees
Look at the larger, mature trees nearby, and see if you can find one that has a similar GIFF to any of your Search Images.

6 Check the details
When you find a tree, check the details more carefully. Check all the GIFF information, then read the details about the leaf, flower, pod and bark. If you have any problems with any of the terms in the text, read the section on Simple Language, pages 14-19.

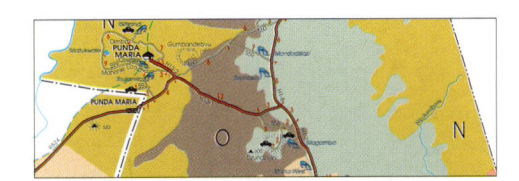

Flowers
The greenish-cream to creamy-white flowers have long stems (up to 110 mm). They grow in branched sprays at the ends of branchlets or in the angle formed by the leaves

Fruit
The small, pale brown, woody capsule is divided into four sections (valves) and grows in bunches.

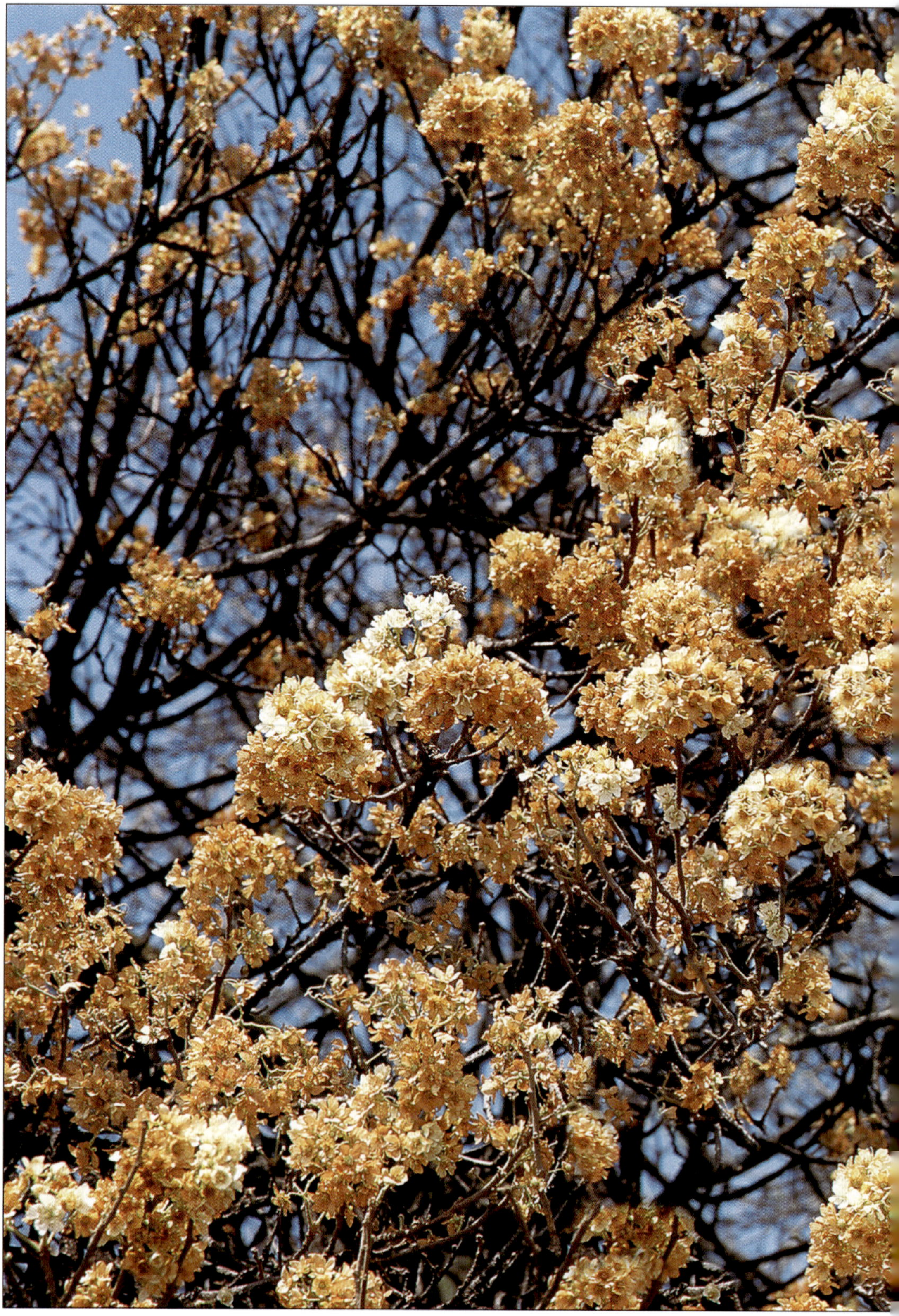

Trees Greet You

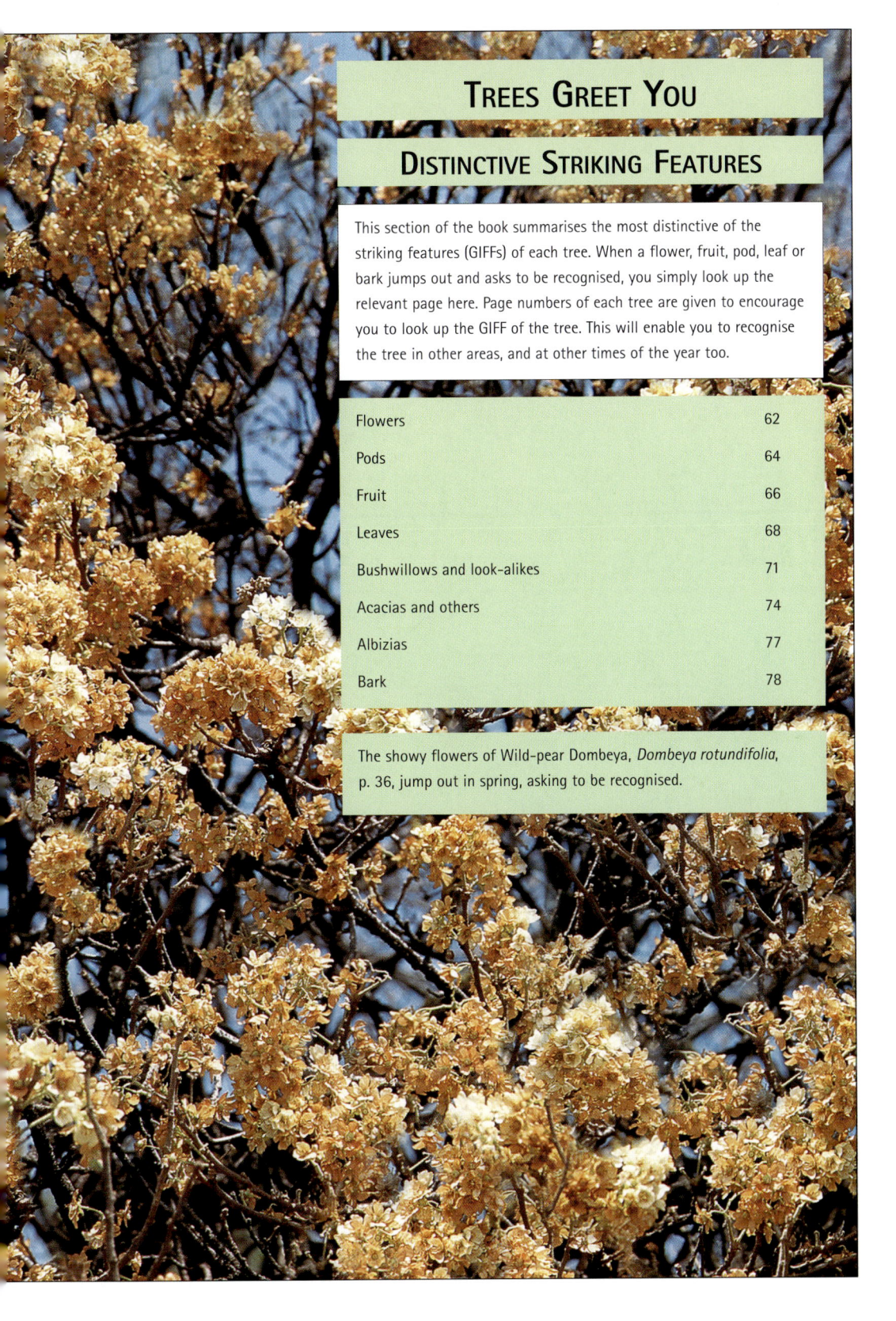

Distinctive Striking Features

This section of the book summarises the most distinctive of the striking features (GIFFs) of each tree. When a flower, fruit, pod, leaf or bark jumps out and asks to be recognised, you simply look up the relevant page here. Page numbers of each tree are given to encourage you to look up the GIFF of the tree. This will enable you to recognise the tree in other areas, and at other times of the year too.

Flowers	62
Pods	64
Fruit	66
Leaves	68
Bushwillows and look-alikes	71
Acacias and others	74
Albizias	77
Bark	78

The showy flowers of Wild-pear Dombeya, *Dombeya rotundifolia*, p. 36, jump out in spring, asking to be recognised.

61

DISTINCTIVE STRIKING FEATURES

The following pages show flowers, fruit, pods and leaves that are all very striking, or that are so distinctive you can often identify the trees on this information alone. You can use these pages as a quick reference – but it is wise to turn to the full tree description to be sure.

UNUSUAL FLOWERS

Baobab
Adansonia digitata
p. 84

Bushveld Gardenia
Gardenia volkensii
p. 188

Wild-pear Dombeya
Dombeya rotundifolia
p. 36

Natal-mahogany
Trichilia emetica
p. 180

Typical Spikethorn flowers

Pod-mahogany
Afzelia quanzensis
p. 150

Long-tail Cassia
Cassia abbreviata
p. 98

Pioneer Spikethorn
Gymnosporia buxifolia p. 33

Weeping Boer-bean
Schotia brachypetala
p. 170

Pride-of-de-Kaap Bauhinia
Bauhinia galpinii
p. 100

Sausage-tree
Kigelia africana
p. 178

White-leaved Raisin
Grewia bicolor
p. 210

62

Spikes, Sprays, Balls and Powder Puffs

Apple-leaf
Philenoptera violacea
p. 124

Zebrawood Flat-bean
Dalbergia melanoxylon
p. 110

Purple-pod Cluster-leaf
Terminalia prunioides
p. 104

Sickle-bush
Dichrostachys cinerea
p. 216

Tamboti
Spirostachys africana
p. 162

Round-leaved Bloodwood
Pterocarpus rotundifolius
p. 212

Typical Acacia spikes

Knob-thorn Acacia
Acacia nigrescens
p. 126

Tree Wistaria
Bolusanthus speciosus
p. 108

African Weeping-wattle
Peltophorum africanum
p. 96

Kiaat Bloodwood
Pterocarpus angolensis
p. 138

Umdoni Waterberry
Syzygium cordatum
p. 30

Typical Acacia balls

ed Acacia
cacia errardii
144

Broad-pod Albizia
Albizia forbesii
p. 112

Bushveld Bead-bean
Maerua angolensis
p. 48

Scented-pod Acacia
Acacia nilotica
p. 198

Flame Climbing Bushwillow
Combretum microphyllum
p. 102

UNUSUAL PODS

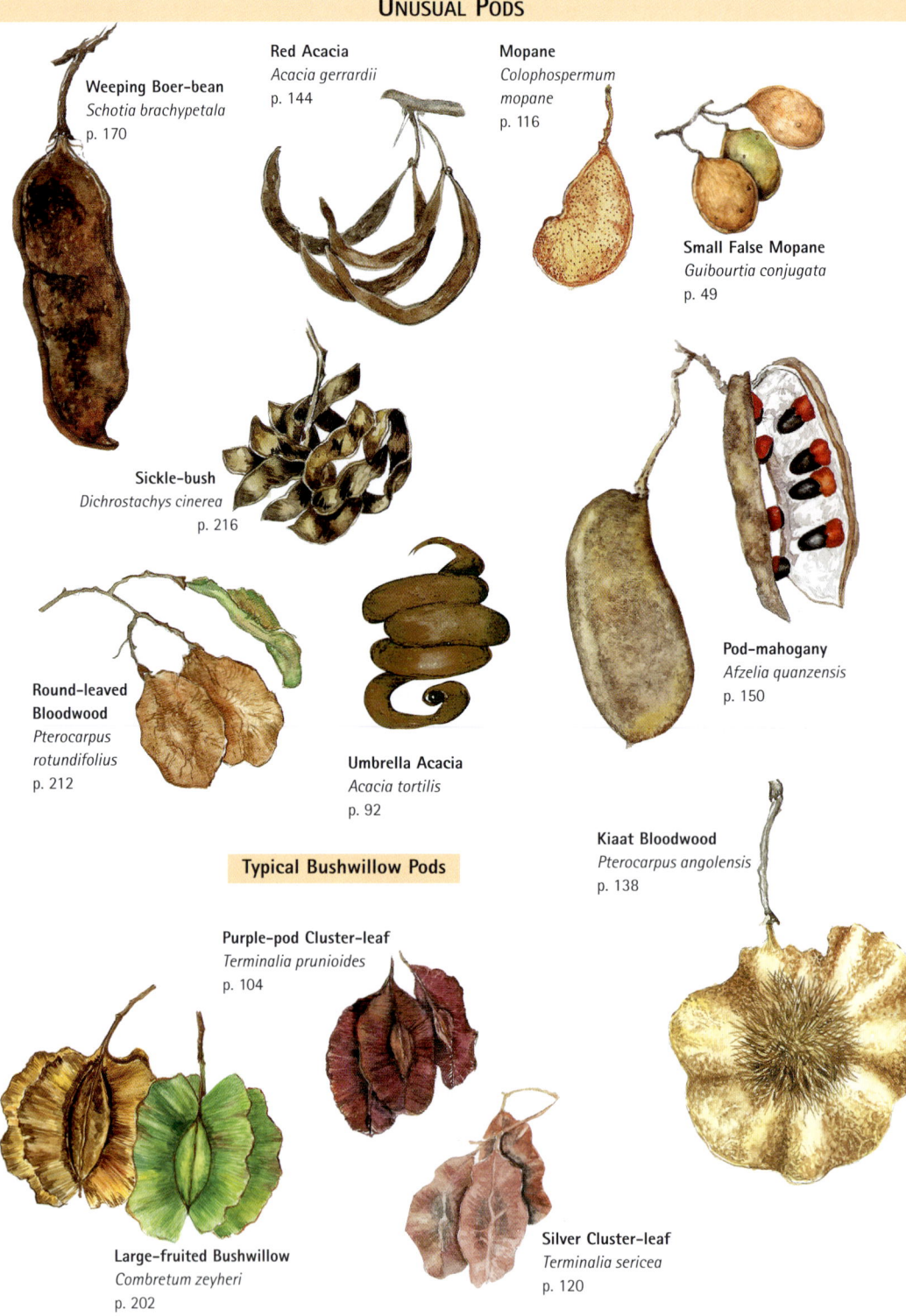

Weeping Boer-bean
Schotia brachypetala
p. 170

Red Acacia
Acacia gerrardii
p. 144

Mopane
Colophospermum mopane
p. 116

Small False Mopane
Guibourtia conjugata
p. 49

Sickle-bush
Dichrostachys cinerea
p. 216

Pod-mahogany
Afzelia quanzensis
p. 150

Round-leaved Bloodwood
Pterocarpus rotundifolius
p. 212

Umbrella Acacia
Acacia tortilis
p. 92

Kiaat Bloodwood
Pterocarpus angolensis
p. 138

Typical Bushwillow Pods

Purple-pod Cluster-leaf
Terminalia prunioides
p. 104

Large-fruited Bushwillow
Combretum zeyheri
p. 202

Silver Cluster-leaf
Terminalia sericea
p. 120

BEAN PODS

Bumpy bean pods

Bushveld Bead-bean
Maerua angolensis
p. 48

Scented-pod Acacia
Acacia nilotica
p. 198

Knob-thorn Acacia
Acacia nigrescens
p. 126

Broad-pod Albizia
Albizia forbesii
p. 112

Long-tail Cassia
Cassia abbreviata
p. 98

Pride-of-de-Kaap Bauhinia
Bauhinia galpinii
p. 100

Typical Acacia bean pods

River Acacia
Acacia robusta
p. 182

African Weeping-wattle
Peltophorum africanum
p. 96

Tree Wistaria
Bolusanthus speciosus
p. 108

Zebrawood Flat-bean
Dalbergia melanoxylon
p. 110

Apple-leaf
Philenoptera violacea
p. 124

UNUSUAL FRUIT

Natal-mahogany
Trichilia emetica
p. 180

Sausage-tree
Kigelia africana
p. 178

Jacket-plum
Pappea capensis
p. 192

Wild Date-palm
Phoenix reclinata
p. 88

Baobab
Adansonia digitata
p. 84

Wild-pear Dombeya
Dombeya rotundifolia
p. 36

Tall Firethorn Corkwood
Commiphora glandulosa
p. 136

Umdoni Waterberry
Syzygium cordatum
p. 30

Black Monkey-orange
Strychnos madagascariensis
p. 132

Lala-palm
Hyphaene coriacea
and *petersiana*
p. 86

Bushveld Gardenia
Gardenia volkensii
p. 188

66

ROUND AND OVAL FRUIT

Larger: Plum-shape

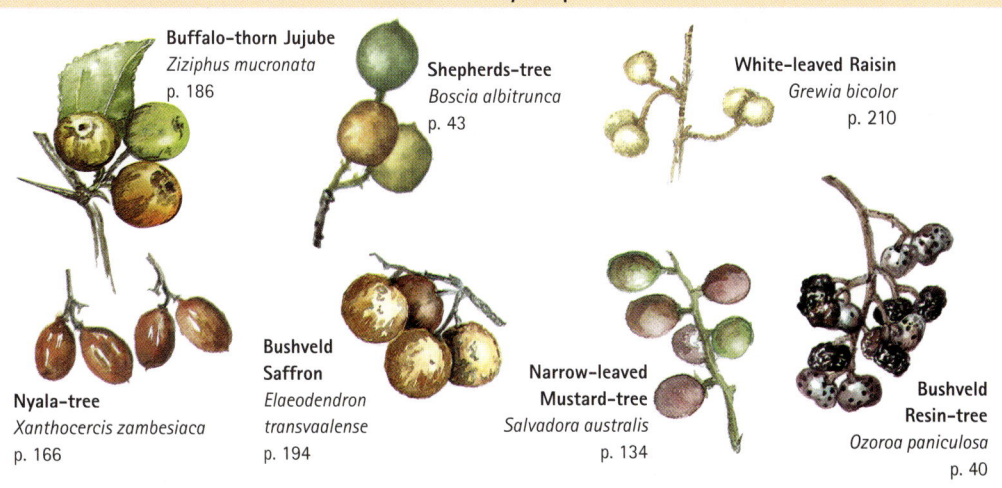

Feverberry Croton
Croton megalobotrys
p. 46

Marula
Sclerocarya birrea
p. 122

False-marula Lannea
Lannea schweinfurthii
p. 38

Greenthorn Torchwood
Balanites maughamii
p. 146

Smaller: Berry-shape

Buffalo-thorn Jujube
Ziziphus mucronata
p. 186

Shepherds-tree
Boscia albitrunca
p. 43

White-leaved Raisin
Grewia bicolor
p. 210

Nyala-tree
Xanthocercis zambesiaca
p. 166

Bushveld Saffron
Elaeodendron transvaalense
p. 194

Narrow-leaved Mustard-tree
Salvadora australis
p. 134

Bushveld Resin-tree
Ozoroa paniculosa
p. 40

Ebony Family: Leaves & Fruit

Ebony Jackal-berry
Diospyros mespiliformis
p. 160

Magic Guarri
Euclea divinorum
p. 190

Figs: Leaves & Fruit

Large-leaved Rock Fig
Ficus abutilifolia
p. 154

Red-leaved Fig
Ficus ingens
p. 32

Sycomore Fig
Ficus sycomorus
p. 164

67

SIMPLE LEAVES

Clustered

Corkwood species
Commiphora sp.
p. 136

Bushveld Gardenia
Gardenia volkensii
p. 188

Umdoni Waterberry
Syzygium cordatum
p. 30

Spiny Monkey-orange
Strychnos spinosa
p. 23

Silver Cluster-leaf
Terminalia sericea
p. 120

Bushveld Saffron
Elaeodendron transvaalense
p. 194

Jacket-plum
Pappea capensis
p. 192

Three-veined from the base

White-leaved and Sandpaper Raisins
Grewia bicolor and *Grewia flavescens*
p. 210, 208

Black Monkey-orange
Strychnos madagascariensis
p. 132

Feverberry Croton
Croton megalobotrys
p. 46

Buffalo-thorn Jujube
Ziziphus mucronata
p. 186

Wild-pear Dombeya
Dombeya rotundifolia
p. 36

Riverine

Matumi
Breonadia salicina
p. 176

River Bushwillow
Combretum erythrophyllum
p. 174

Water Nuxia
Nuxia oppositifolia
p. 172

Tamboti
Spirostachys africana
p. 162

SIMPLE AND COMPOUND LEAVES

Simple butterfly

Pride-of-de-Kaap Bauhinia
Bauhinia galpinii
p. 100

Once Compound butterfly

Mopane
Colophospermum mopane
p. 116

Small False Mopane
Guibourtia conjugata
p. 49

Greenthorn Torchwood
Balanites maughamii
p. 146

ONCE COMPOUND LEAVES

Huge

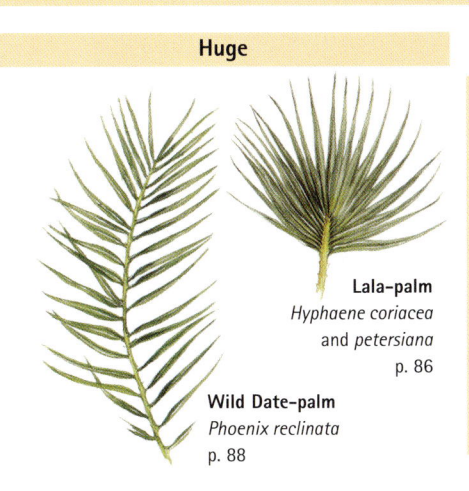

Lala-palm
Hyphaene coriacea and *petersiana*
p. 86

Wild Date-palm
Phoenix reclinata
p. 88

A pair of leaves at the tip

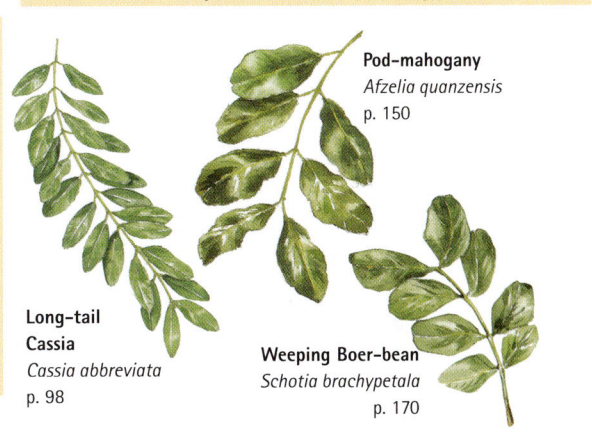

Pod-mahogany
Afzelia quanzensis
p. 150

Long-tail Cassia
Cassia abbreviata
p. 98

Weeping Boer-bean
Schotia brachypetala
p. 170

A single leaf at the tip

Kiaat Bloodwood
Pterocarpus angolensis
p. 138

Round-leaved Bloodwood
Pterocarpus rotundifolius
p. 212

Tree Wistaria
Bolusanthus speciosus
p. 108

Zebrawood Flat-bean
Dalbergia melanoxylon
p. 110

COMPOUND LEAVES

Once Compound Riverine

Nyala-tree
Xanthocercis zambesiaca
p. 166

Natal-mahogany
Trichilia emetica
p. 180

Sausage-tree
Kigelia africana
p. 178

Weeping Boer-bean
Schotia brachypetala
p. 170

Once Compound spiralling around twig tip

False-marula Lannea
Lannea schweinfurthii
p. 38

Mountain Kirkia
Kirkia wilmsii
p. 37

Marula
Sclerocarya birrea
p. 122

White Kirkia
Kirkia acuminata
p. 156

Three-leaflet Compound

Apple-leaf
Philenoptera violacea
p. 124

Hand-shaped Compound

Baobab
Adansonia digitata
p. 84

Simple Leaves – Bushwillows

Flame Climbing Bushwillow
Combretum microphyllum - p. 102
This riverine creeper grows on trees and shrubs along drainage lines in B, D, H, J, and Alluvial plains M. The **bark** is brown and flaking on older plants. Simple, alternate or opposite, elliptic to round **leaves** occur on new growth (40 - 100 x 30 - 50 mm). The small brilliant red **flowers** have prominent stamens (Aug - Nov). The **fruit** is small pink-green, four-winged, pods which grow in abundance (Sep - Jan) (20 x 20 mm).

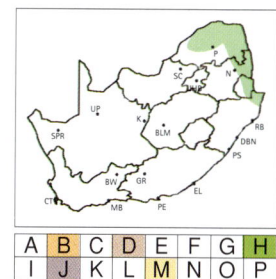

Forest Bushwillow
Combretum kraussii
Found as a magnificent tall tree in densely vegetated ravines in C, or as a shrub in forest margins. Also in G, F, and I. It has rough, dark grey, furrowed, flaking **bark** on older trunks. In spring, a spectacular flush of new silver-white **leaves** stick out above the flowers in a cluster. Older, opposite leaves are shiny dark green above, and paler below, turning bright red to purple in winter (50 - 120 x 20 - 40 mm). **Flowers** are creamy-white in dense heads in the leaf axils (Aug - Nov) (25 -60 mm). **Fruit** is 4-winged, pale pink to dark red pods, which cover the tree and turn brownish-red when dry (Feb - Jun) (16 x 15 mm).

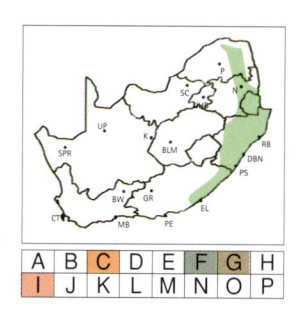

Large-fruited Bushwillow
Combretum zeyheri - p. 202
This tree is often found on crests in A, B, C, I and N. The **bark** is greyish-brown with rough patches that peel in small blocks. **Leaves** are opposite, leathery, yellow-green to dark green above and paler below, with prominent veins and wavy margins (25 - 140 x 30 - 85 mm). The small, yellow-green to yellow **flowers** grow singly in dense spikes (Flower-spike: up to 75 x 25 mm) (Aug - Nov). **Fruit** is very large, conspicuous, four-winged pods, initially green, ripening to brown (Feb - Oct) (50 - 100 mm).

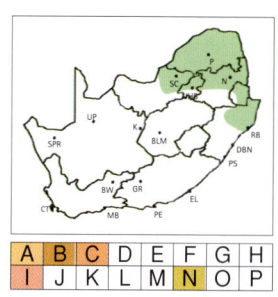

Leadwood Bushwillow
Combretum imberbe - p. 118
These majestic trees have sparse foliage and are found on plains and along rivers and drainage lines in A, B, C, F, H, J, M, O, and P. Pale grey **bark** breaks up into small, regular blocks, like snakeskin. The small Simple, opposite **leaves** are characteristically grey-green to yellow-green, with wavy margins (25 - 80 x 10 - 30 mm). The small, creamy to creamy-yellow **flowers** are sweet-smelling (Nov - Dec) (Flower-spikes: 40 - 80 x up to 15 mm). The **fruit** is a typical, but small, four-winged Bushwillow pod that matures from pale lime-green to straw-coloured (Feb – Jun) (15 - 19 mm diam.).

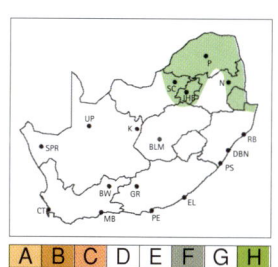

The art on this page is not to scale. Please refer to the text for sizes.

SIMPLE LEAVES – BUSHWILLOWS

Red Bushwillow
Combretum apiculatum - p. 204
This is the most common Bushwillow occurring in groups on the granites A, B, C, D and P, and is in rocky areas of E, I, J and N. The **bark** is grey to red-brown and breaks in flat, uneven pieces. Simple, broadly elliptic **leaves** are shiny green with smooth margins and a characteristically twisted tip (65 x 35 mm). The sweet-smelling, cylindrical **flower-spikes** are not very conspicuous and arise from red buds with the new leaves (Sep - Nov) (Spike: 70 x 20 mm). The **fruit** is a medium-sized, red-brown, four-winged Bushwillow pod with a smooth, slightly shiny centre (Dec - Aug) (25 x 20 mm).

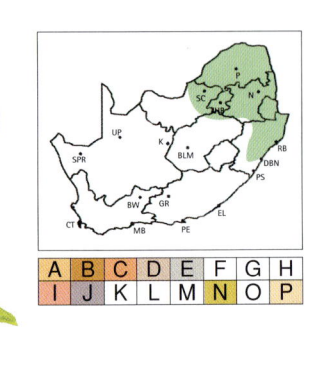

River Bushwillow
Combretum erythrophyllum - p. 174
This tree is easily found in the riverine areas, particularly of D. The **bark** is smooth, pale yellowish and grey-brown, flaking in irregular patches. Simple, opposite, narrow, elliptic **leaves** have smooth margins and a sharp tip (50 - 100 x 20 - 50 mm). Spikes of small, inconspicuous, cream to yellow-green, sweet-scented **flowers** appear just after the new leaves (Aug - Nov) (20 x 10 mm). The **fruit** is a typical, four-winged, Bushwillow pod which ripens to pale brown. (Jan - Aug) (10 - 15 mm).

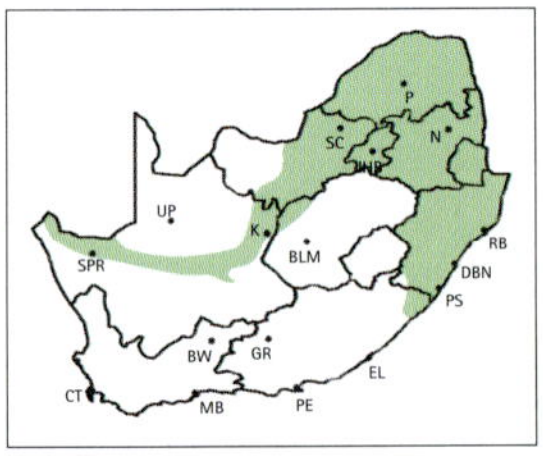

Russet Bushwillow
Combretum hereroense - p. 206
This tree grows in loose groups in the granites A, B, C, D and P as well as on the plains of E, F, J, L, M, and O. Older **bark** is pale grey to dark grey-brown, rough and fissured lengthways. Simple **leaves** are small, opposite, with smooth margins. They are dark green above, with rusty-brown hairs below (20 - 70 x 10 - 45 mm). The sweet-smelling **flowers** are white to cream-coloured to yellow (Aug - Nov) (Flower spike: up to 60 x 15 mm). The **fruit** is a small, dark, red-brown, characteristic four-winged Bushwillow pod, present in large numbers (Jan - Jul) (23 x 20 mm).

Velvet Bushwillow
Combretum molle
This single-trunked, fairly high-branching tree has an irregular, dark green canopy and is found in I, J, K, L and N. The **bark** is grey-brown to black in regular, small blocks with reddish under-bark. **Leaves** are Simple, opposite, oval to rounded, and covered in velvety hairs. There is a distinct herringbone pattern of veins, and a fine, hair-like tip (60 - 100 x 40 - 60 mm). **Flowers** grow in conspicuous, yellow-green, sweet-scented spikes (Sep - Nov) (Spike: 40 - 90 mm). **Fruit** grows in abundant, 4-winged pods turning from yellow-green to golden red-brown when mature (Jan - Jun) (13 - 23 mm).

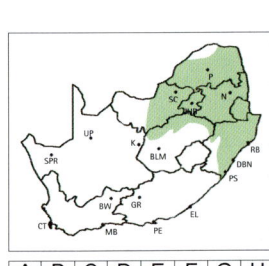

72

Simple Leaves – Bushwillows

Weeping Bushwillow
Combretum collinum - p. 35
This tree is found on granite crests in A, B, C, and the plains of J and N. The **bark** is greyish-brown, rough and peels off in irregular patches. Large, broad, elliptic to oval Simple **leaves** can be opposite or alternate, dark green above and paler green to silvery below (7 - 120 x 30 - 45 mm). **Flower-spikes** are cream to yellow and sweetly scented (Aug - Oct) (50 - 100 mm). The **fruit** is a characteristic four-winged Bushwillow pod, rosy-red, not rusty-red, maturing to dark brown. (Jan - Apr) (30 - 50 x 45 mm).

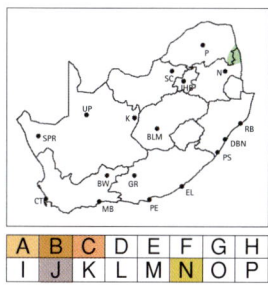

Simple Leaves – Bushwillow Look-alikes

Purple-pod Cluster-leaf
Terminalia prunioides - p. 104
This tree has a drooping, spiky appearance and is found in loose groups on rocky soils and alluvial sands in C, D, I, J, L, and P. The **bark** is dark brown and deeply grooved. The dull, dark green, heart-shaped, Simple **leaves** have smooth margins and are clustered at the ends of branchlets (35 x 15 mm). The white, cylindrical **flower-spikes** have a strong smell like dirty socks (Sep - Feb) (Single flower: 4 mm; spike: 65 x 20 mm). The **fruit** is a purple to wine-red, oval, flat, two-winged pod, thickened over a central seed (Feb - Sep) (40 x 30 mm).

Silver Cluster-leaf
Terminalia sericea - p. 120
Sandveld slopes and granite crests and seeplines are the easiest places to find loose groups of this silvery-blue tree. The rough, dark brown or purplish **bark** is deeply fissured lengthways. **Leaves** are pale green to grey-silvery-green and leathery, with smooth margins. Young leaves have silver hairs (55 - 120 x 13 - 45 mm). The inconspicuous, cream to yellow **flowers** have a pungent 'dirty sock' smell (Sep – Jan) (Spike: up to 70 mm; individual flower: 4 mm diam.). The **fruit** is a two-winged, pinky-purple pod, which dries to brown (Jan - Jun) (60 x 15 mm).

Stink-bushwillow
Pteleopsis myrtifolia
This specialised bushy tree is only found in the Lowveld around Punda Maria, in Sandveld N. It has numerous, thin, upright but meandering stems, growing from a small base into a wide-spread, V-shaped form. The **bark** is very pale grey, smooth to slighty fissured. The **leaves** are elliptic, shiny green above, and silvery with hairs, when young (20 - 50 x 10 - 23 mm). **Flowers** often appear before, or with new leaves, and are creamy-white to yellow with an unpleasant scent (Nov - Apr) (Spike: 10 - 25 mm). **Fruit** has 2 or 3 wings (very rarely 4), and is greenish-yellow, drying to pale brown (Feb - Jun) (15 mm long).

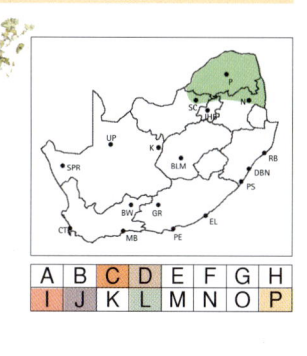

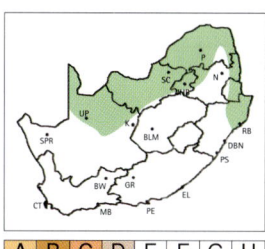

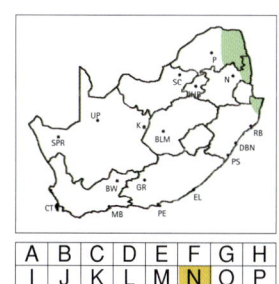

The art on these pages is not to scale. Please refer to the text for sizes.

73

Twice Compound Leaves: with thorns – Acacias

Black-monkey Acacia
Acacia burkei - p. 41
A tall, single-trunked, often high-branching tree, most common in Ecozone G and in the granites south of the Olifants River. The **bark** is dark, rough and deeply fissured lengthways. Twice Compound alternate **leaves** are short and stiff with relatively large leaflets (Leaf 25 - 70 mm; leaflet 4-20 x 2-12 mm). Short, dark, sharply-hooked **thorns** grow in pairs (3 - 9 mm). White **flower-spikes** bloom in small groups (Oct - Jan) (50 - 100 x 10 - 20 mm). The **fruit** is a flat, dark brown bean pod with a pointed tip (Dec - May) (90 - 160 x 12 - 25 mm).

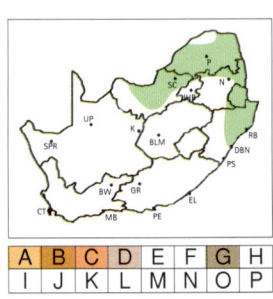

A	B	C	D	E	F	G	H
I	J	K	L	M	N	O	P

Delagoa Acacia
Acacia welwitschii - p. 140
It is a low-branching tree, usually with a single crooked trunk, which occurs only in Ecozone G. The **bark** is coarse, fissured and pale grey. Twice Compound **leaves** have relatively large leaflets for an Acacia (Leaves 40 mm; leaflet 7 x 4 mm). Paired, hooked, dark **thorns** are fairly close together (5 mm). White **flowers-spikes** are visible at the top of the canopy (Nov - Jan) (70 x 10 mm). The **fruit** is a long, narrow, flat bean pod, brown-black when ripe. (Mar - Jul) (80 - 110 mm).

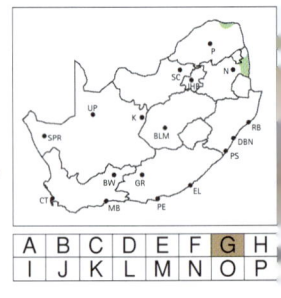

A	B	C	D	E	F	G	H
I	J	K	L	M	N	O	P

Fever-tree Acacia
Acacia xanthophloea - p. 90
This tree is easily found along rivers in F, L, and M. The straight single trunk has yellow-green **bark**, covered in yellow powder. The trunk and branches 'peel' in paper-thin layers. Feathery Twice Compound **leaves** are opposite and elliptic with smooth margins (Leaf 100 mm; leaflet 7 x 1 mm). The straight, paired **thorns** are white (80 mm). Round, golden **flower-balls** occur in the axil of the thorns (Sep - Nov) (10 mm). The **fruit** is a flat, papery bean pod which grows in clusters (Jan - Apr) (100 x 15 mm).

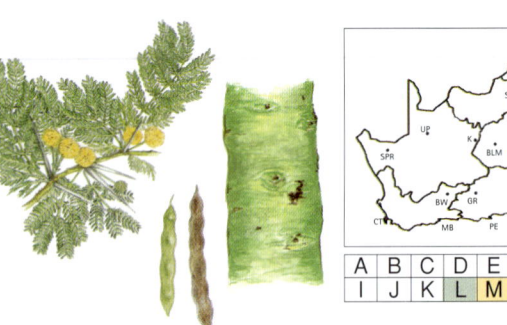

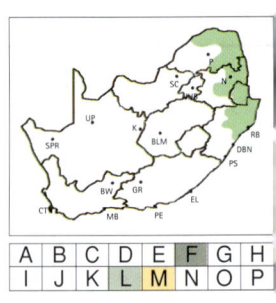

A	B	C	D	E	F	G	H
I	J	K	L	M	N	O	P

Flaky-bark Acacia
Acacia exuvialis - p. 214
Growing in groups, this often multi-stemmed, low-branching tree is found in rocky areas and on sandy soils in A, C, D, I, J, L and P. The **bark** is smooth and peels in large, orange-brown flakes. The Twice Compound **leaves** are fine and feathery, with elliptic leaflets having a rounded end, sharp tip and smooth margin (Leaflet: 3 - 10 x 1,5 - 4,5 mm). The straight, white, paired **thorns** can be very long, and are thickened at the base (70 - 100 mm). Yellow **flower-balls** are never abundant, but remain on the tree for long periods (Sep - Feb) (10 mm). The fruit is a sickle-shaped, segmented, brown to reddish-brown pod, covered by glands that secrete a sticky fluid (Feb - May) (10 x 65 mm).

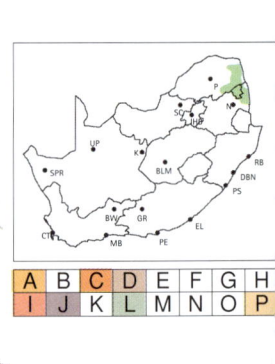

A	B	C	D	E	F	G	H
I	J	K	L	M	N	O	P

The art on these pages is not to scale. Please refer to the text for sizes

TWICE COMPOUND LEAVES: WITH THORNS – ACACIAS

Horned-thorn Acacia
Acacia grandicornuta - p. 196
This small tree, or shrub is easiest to find in clay soils and the brack areas of A, D and O. The **bark** is dark grey to black and rough with grooves. Twice Compound **leaves** grow in bunches at the base of the thorns. Leaflets are elliptic with smooth margins (Leaf: 70 mm; leaflet: 3 x 9 mm). Huge, white, spiny **thorns** are paired, and often thickened and fused at their bases (90mm). Sweet-scented white **flower-balls** grow in tufts throughout the summer. The **fruit** is a thin, woody brown pod, flat and sickle-shaped (Apr - Jul) (70 x 130 mm).

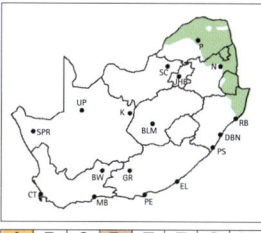

Knob-thorn Acacia
Acacia nigrescens - p. 126
This upright Acacia has a straight, single trunk that branches high up. It occurs in most Ecozones. The **bark** ages to dark brown, becoming rough and deeply fissured lengthwise. There are woody knobs with **thorns** on the trunks or branches. Twice Compound, opposite **leaves** are unusually shaped, with only 1 or 2 pairs of large butterfly-shaped leaflets in each feather (Leaf: 35 x 80 mm; leaflet: 10 - 30 x 8 - 25 mm). Plum-coloured buds open in a mass of sweet-scented, creamy-white **flower-spikes** (Jun - Jul) (80 - 100 mm). The **fruit** is a brown, flat, bean pod hanging down in clusters (Dec - Jun) (110 - 140 x 20 mm).

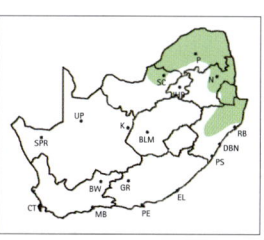

Red Acacia
Acacia gerrardii - p. 144
This single-stemmed, slender tree occurs in the granites A, B, C, D and P as well as in F, G, and I, in groups. The **bark** is dark grey to reddish and wrinkled, exposing a rusty under-layer. Twice Compound, dark green **leaves** appear to form a green 'sleeve' on branches. Leaflets are elliptic with fine hairs on the margin (Leaf: 90 mm; leaflet: 3,0 - 7,5 x 1 - 2 mm). The paired **thorns** are shortish, straight or slightly curved, and very stout (25 - 100 mm). Creamy-white, sweet-scented **flower-balls** on long stalks are crowded on the twigs (Oct - Feb) (10 - 20 mm). The **fruit** is a sickle-shaped, flat pod covered by fine, grey hair (Dec - May) (80 - 160 x 6 - 16 mm).

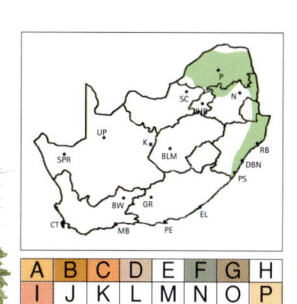

River Acacia
Acacia robusta - p. 182
A large, upright Acacia, with a dense, dark green canopy, this tree is found along rivers in A, B, C, D, F, H, J, and M. The **bark** is dark grey and grooved lengthways and the branches look thick even towards the ends. Tight clumps of relatively long and droopy Twice Compound **leaves** grow on dark, prickly 'cushions' (Leaf: 130 mm x 70 mm; leaflet: 12 x 3 mm). The straight, white, paired **thorns** also grow on 'cushions' (70 - 110 mm). Creamy-white **flower-balls** can be seen early in spring (Aug to Sep) (20 mm). The **fruit** is a slender, slightly sickle-shaped pod which hangs from the tree in prominent bunches (Oct - Feb) (130 x 20 mm).

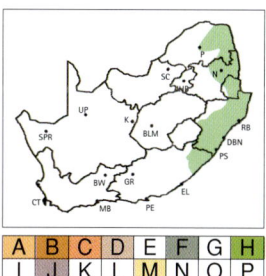

Twice Compound Leaves: with thorns – Acacias

Scented-pod Acacia
Acacia nilotica - p. 198
This small Acacia tree or shrub, has a V-shaped, irregular canopy, and grows in brack area and valley bottoms of the granites A, B, C, and D, as well as in F and J. The **bark** is dark grey to black and rough with grooves. Twice Compound **leaves** with elliptic leaflets grow in bunches at the base of the thorns. Margins are smooth (Leaf: 40 mm; leaflet: 1 x 4 mm). Scented yellow **flower-balls** are visible all summer (Oct - Feb) (12 mm). The variable white to red-brown, paired **thorns** are usually slightly furry (50 - 90 mm). The **fruit** is a pod, swollen and enlarged over the seeds, which looks like a string of beads (Mar - Aug) (15 x 120 mm).

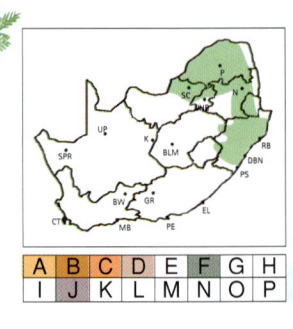

Umbrella Acacia
Acacia tortilis - p. 92
These trees are found singly or in groups in D and most other Ecozones. The **bark** is grey, and deeply fissured in older trees. Twice Compound **leaves** are tiny, among the tiniest of the Acacias (Leaf 25 mm; leaflet 1 - 2 mm). Paired, straight, white **thorns**, as well as hooked thorns, occur (Straight: 50 mm; hooked: 3 - 5 mm) Large numbers of sweet-scented, small, white **flower-balls** appear after rain (7mm) (Nov - Dec). The **fruit** is bunches of flat, spiralled bean pods (125 x 8 mm) (May - Jun).

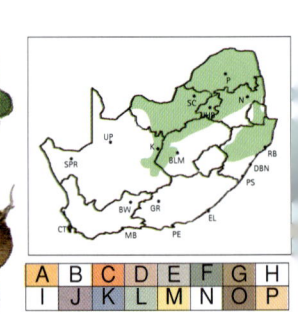

Twice Compound Leaves: with thorns – Other

Sickle-bush
Dichrostachys cinerea - p. 216
This multi-stemmed tree or shrub is easily found in dense groups in D, K, and most other Ecozones. The **bark** is pale brown to ash-grey with shallow lengthways grooves. Branches and twigs have long, straight, pale brown **spines** (20 - 40 mm). The long, Twice Compound, olive-green **leaves** stand out against pale bark (30 - 200 mm). Mauve-pink and yellow **flower-spikes** are distinctive (40 - 60 mm) (Oct - Jan). The **fruit** is clusters of tightly coiled, dark brown pods (70 mm diam.) (May - Sep).

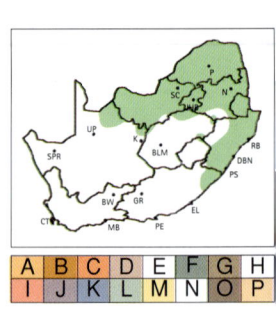

Twice Compound Leaves: without thorns – Other

African Weeping-wattle
Peltophorum africanum - p. 96
This single-stemmed, low branching tree has drooping branches. It is found on crests, seeplines and plains of A, C, D, and P, as well as plains in E, F, J, K and L. The **bark** is brown to dark grey and fissured lengthways. The large, soft, feathery **leaves** have rounded leaflets (Leaf: up to 180 x 901 mm; leaflet: 5 - 9 x 1,5 - 3 mm). There are no **thorns**. Abundant yellow **flowers** appear in sprays (Nov - Feb). The **fruit** is bunches of dark brown to black pods on the tree throughout the year (100 x 20 mm).

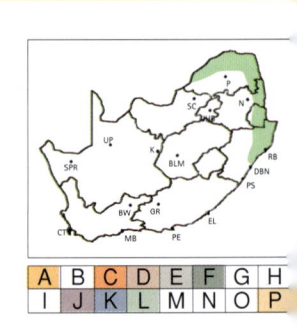

TWICE COMPOUND LEAVES: WITHOUT THORNS – ALBIZIAS

Broad-pod Albizia
Albizia forbesii - p. 112
This tall, single-trunked, low-branching tree grows along rivers, H and on drainage lines in D and F. Smooth, pale grey **bark** flakes in blocks. The Twice Compound **leaves** have opposite feathers which increase in size towards tip (Leaf: 90 mm; leaflet: 9 x 2 mm). There are no **thorns**. The **flowers** are white-yellow pincushions (Oct - Dec) (30 mm). **Fruit** is a flat, fibrous, russet pod, marked cross-wise with fine lines (Mar - Aug) (50 x 150 mm).

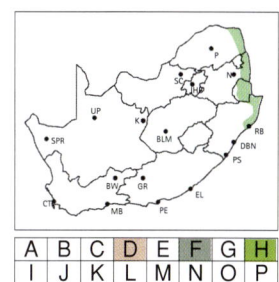

Bushveld Albizia
Albizia harveyi - p. 45
This slender tree occurs in the valley bottoms, crests and brackish flats of Ecozones A, P, E, F and M, and is easiest to find as a shrub in Mopane Shrubveld, L. The grey to dark brown **bark** divides into vertical ridges. **Leaves** are Twice Compound and feathery with sickle-shaped leaflets (4-6 mm). There are no **thorns**. **Flowers** are white powder-puffs grouped at the end of twigs (Stamens up to 20mm) (Oct - Nov). **Fruit** is a pale brown, thin, flat pod (Mar - Aug).

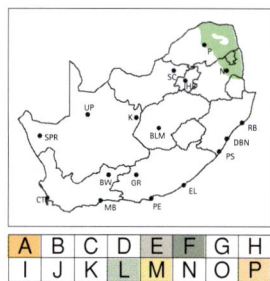

Large-leaved Albizia
Albizia versicolor
A single-trunked tree with a wide, moderate V-shaped canopy, it is found on the plains or near rivers in B, C, and N. The **bark** is dark grey, rough and corky. Alternate, Twice Compound **leaves** have distinctive large, rounded leaflets that are olive-green above and paler below (Leaf: 100 - 350 mm; leaflet: 25 - 50 x 20 - 35 mm). Large, conspicuous, sweet-scented **flowers** are creamy-white balls (Aug - Jan) (Stamens: 35mm). The **fruit** is a flat, woody pod which matures from green to red and pale brown (Jul - Sep the following year) (100 - 300 x 30 - 50 mm).

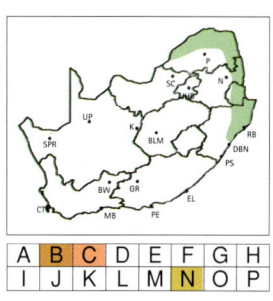

Many-stemmed Albizia
Albizia petersiana - p. 142
Found only in Ecozone G, this multi-stemmed, V-shaped tree, has smooth grey **bark** which peels in narrow, flat strips. The Twice Compound **leaves** are larger than most Acacia species (Leaf: 60 mm; leaflet: 10 x 6 mm). There are no **thorns**. The inconspicuous, white **flowers** have prominent red stamens (Oct - Dec) (30 mm diam.). **Fruit** is bunches of long flat, green bean pods (Mar - Jun) (120 x 16 mm).

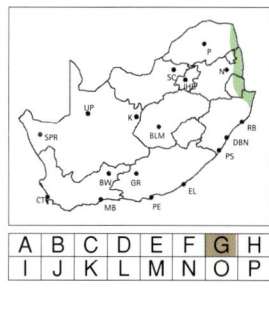

The art on these pages is not to scale. Please refer to the text for sizes.

Bark

Relatively smooth

Fever-tree Acacia
Acacia xanthophloea
p. 90

Natal-mahogany
Trichilia emetica
p. 180

Sycomore Fig
Ficus sycomorus
p. 164

Apple-leaf
Philenoptera violacea
p. 124

Black Monkey-orange
Strychnos madagascariensis
p. 132

Rough with knobs & thorns

Young Knob-thorn Acacia
Acacia nigrescens
p. 126

Older Knob-thorn Acacia
Acacia nigrescens
p. 126

Smooth & flaking / peeling

Sausage-tree
Kigelia africana
p. 178

Bushveld Gardenia
Gardenia volkensii
p. 188

Large-fruited Bushwillow
Combretum zeyheri
p. 202

White Kirkia
Kirkia acuminata
p. 156

Smooth & flaky with spines or thorns

Flaky-bark Acacia
Acacia exuvialis
p. 214

Tall Firethorn Corkwood
Commiphora glandulosa
p. 136

Zebra-bark Corkwood
Commiphora viminea
p. 47

BARK

Smooth with bumps and / or fissures

Jacket-plum
Pappea capensis
p. 192

Shepherds-tree
Boscia albitrunca
p. 43

Bushveld Saffron
Elaeodendron transvaalense
p. 194

River Bushwillow
Combretum erythrophyllum
p. 174

Rough & peeling / flaking

Marula
Sclerocarya birrea
p. 122

False-marula Lannea
Lannea schweinfurthii
p. 38

Red Bushwillow
Combretum apiculatum
p. 204

Spiny Monkey-orange
Strychnos spinosa
p. 23

Zebrawood Flat-bean
Dalbergia melanoxylon
p. 110

Coarse; looks burnt

Ebony Jackal-berry
Diospyros mespiliformis
p. 160

Coarse; blocky

Magic Guarri
Euclea divinorum
p. 190

79

BARK

Coarse & fissured or ropy

Black-monkey Acacia
Acacia burkei
p. 41

River Acacia
Acacia robusta
p. 182

Silver Cluster-leaf
Terminalia sericea
p. 120

Wild-pear Dombeya
Dombeya rotundifolia
p. 36

Buffalo-thorn Jujube
Ziziphus mucronata
p. 186

Umbrella Acacia
Acacia tortilis
p. 92

Horned-thorn Acacia
Acacia grandicornuta
p. 196

Sickle-bush
Dichrostachys cinerea
p. 216

African Weeping-wattle
Peltophorum africanum
p. 96

Red Acacia
Acacia gerrardii
p. 144

Pioneer Spikethorn
Gymnosporia buxifolia
p. 33

Tree Wistaria
Bolusanthus speciosus
p. 108

Scented-pod Acacia
Acacia nilotica
p. 198

BARK

Rough & blocky

Leadwood Bushwillow
Combretum imberbe
p. 118

Tamboti
Spirostachys africana
p. 162

Kiaat Bloodwood
Pterocarpus angolensis
p. 138

Umdoni Waterberry
Syzygium cordatum
p. 30

Weeping Boer-bean
Schotia brachypetala
p. 170

Nyala-tree
Xanthocercis zambesiaca
p. 166

Fluted / folded

Greenthorn Torchwood
Balanites maughamii
p. 146

Baobab
Adansonia digitata
p. 84

Large-leaved Rock Fig
Ficus abutilifolia
p. 154

81

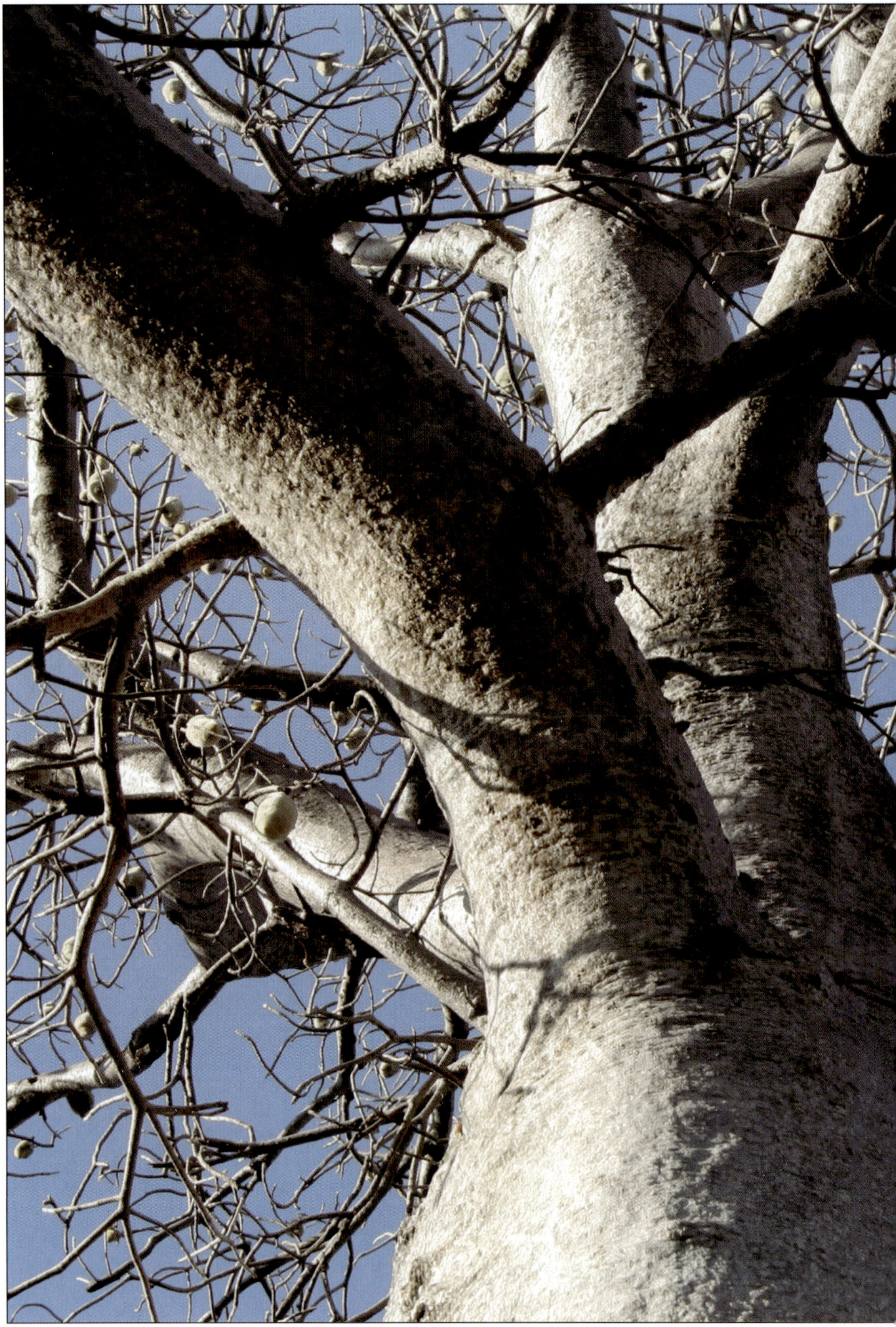

TREES GREET YOU

UNIQUE TREES

The trees in this section have such unique forms that you do not need to spend time developing comprehensive Search Images of them. It is helpful to page through this section and look at **'Where to find this tree easily'**, for each tree, to see if it is likely to occur in the area where you are Tree Spotting. Once you know the tree is there, you are going to find that it greets you!

Kapok Family   Bombacaceae
Baobab   *Adansonia digitata*   84

Palm Family   Arecaceae
Lala-palm   *Hyphaene coriacea* and *Hyphaene petersiana*   86
Wild Date-palm   *Phoenix reclinata*   88

Thorn-tree Sub-family of Pea Family   Mimosoideae
Fever-tree Acacia   *Acacia xanthophloea*   90
Umbrella Acacia   *Acacia tortilis*   92

The GIFF of any Baobab, *Adansonia digitata*, p. 84, includes its varying, unusual shape and bark. When there are pods as well this is a bonus!

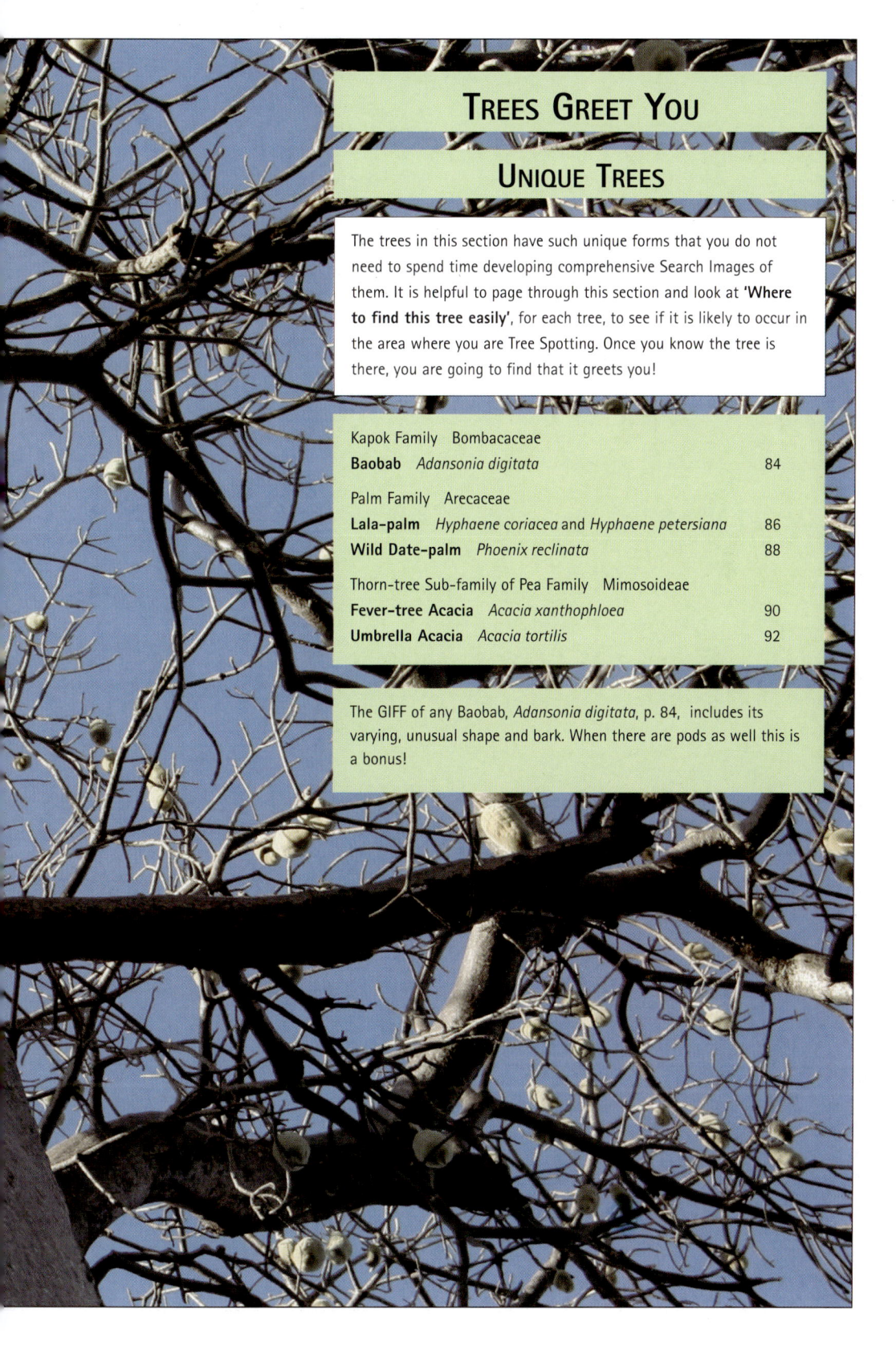

| KAPOK FAMILY | Bombacaceae | Tree no 467 |

BAOBAB
Adansonia digitata

AFRIKAANS Kremetart **N. SOTHO** Seboi **TSWANA** Mowana
TSONGA Ximuwu **VENDA** Muvhuyu

Adansonia is in honour of Michel Adanson, a French botanist who lived in Senegal from 1748 to 1754; **digitata** refers to the hand-shaped leaves.

Leaf

Where you'll find this tree easily
The Baobab only grows north of the Olifants River. There it can be found growing singly, often on small rocky outcrops and in well-drained soils.

A	E	I	M
B	F	J	N
C	G	K	O
D	H	L	P

- It is easiest to find in Mopane/Bushwillow Woodlands (P).
- It can also be found in the north of the Lebombo Mountain Bushveld (I), on the plains of both Mopane Shrubveld (L) and Alluvial Plains (M), as well as on the sandstone ridges of the Sandveld (N).

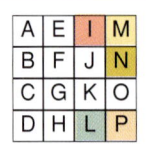

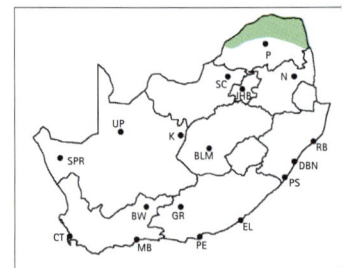

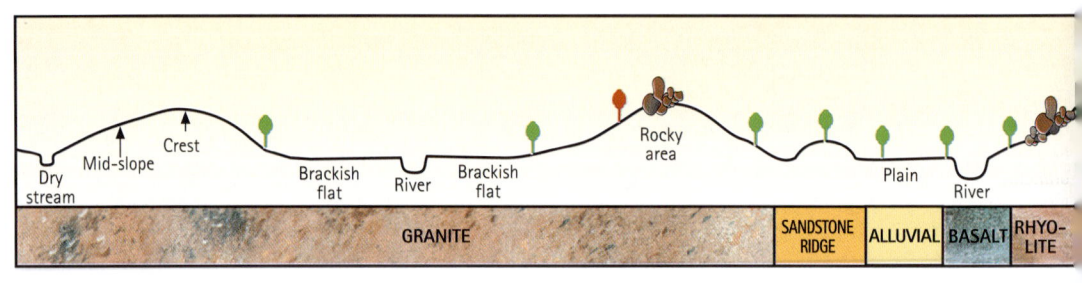

Dry stream · Mid-slope · Crest · Brackish flat · River · Brackish flat · Rocky area · Plain · River

GRANITE | SANDSTONE RIDGE | ALLUVIAL | BASALT | RHYOLITE

GIFF
- This gigantic tree is unmistakable. It has a massive single, straight trunk with branches coming off horizontally to form a round, widely branching, sparse canopy.
- **Huge branches end in very thick stumps that look like roots, giving the tree the appearance of growing upside-down.**
- The bark is shiny, grey-brown and smooth, often dented and grooved.
- The Hand-shaped Compound leaves grow at the ends of the thick, stubby branchlets and twigs.

Baobabs are truly unique and need no captions!

Seasonal changes
Deciduous. Leaves appear late in spring. Because of the massive, unique shape, these trees are easy to identify all year round.

Height:
10 - 25 m
Density: Sparse

20 m + above
15 m
10 m
5 m
3 m

	Oct	Nov	Dec	Jan	Feb	Mar	Apr	May	Jun	Jul	Aug	Sep
Leaf												
Flower												
Fruit/Pod												

Growth form
Trees with a trunk circumference of 30 metres are estimated to be about 4 000 years old. The trunk decreases in girth during dry seasons and swells up again after rain.

Leaves
Mature leaves have 5 - 7 elliptic leaflets, with smooth margins. They are grouped at the end of the branches, on long leaf-stems, that are about 120 mm in length (Leaflet: 50 - 150 x 30 - 70 mm).

Fruit
The characteristic, huge, oval fruit is covered by yellowish-grey, velvety hairs and hangs from the tips of branchlets and twigs. The fruit turns brown when ripe, and has a white, mealy substance surrounding shiny, black pips (Apr - May) (100 - 120 x 200 - 240 mm).

Flowers
The cup-shaped, white flowers are sweet-scented and hang downwards. They have crisp-edged petals with long protruding stamens (Oct – Nov) (120 - 240 mm).

Bark
See GIFF.

UNIQUE TREES
Baobab

Look-alike tree
When adult the Baobab has no Look-alike tree.

Links with animals
The tree is partly pollinated by the Straw-coloured Fruitbat (*Eidolon helvum*). The fruit is eaten by baboon, and the bark by elephant. Cattle, elephants and antelope chew on the spongy wood to relieve thirst in times of drought.

Gardening
The Baobab can be very attractive in a large garden. It will grow best in warmer areas, on the majority of well-drained soils. It is susceptible to frost, but is fairly drought-resistant. It can be grown from seed and is fairly fast-growing under warm, well-watered conditions.

Human uses
Fibre is made from the bark to weave baskets and hats. As the spongy wood contains a high proportion of water, humans chew on the wood to relieve thirst. The hollow trunks have been used as houses, prisons, storage barns and water tanks. Hollow branches catch rainwater and act as reservoirs. Bark and leaves have been used in treating malaria, dysentery, urinary disorders and diarrhoea. Flour is prepared from the roots, and fresh leaves are eaten as spinach. The fruit is also edible and is rich in Vitamin C.

85

| PALM FAMILY | Arecaceae | Tree nos 23/24 |

LALA-PALM   *Hyphaene coriacea* and *Hyphaene petersiana*

AFRIKAANS Lalapalm   **N. SOTHO** Mofaka, Mopalema   **SISWATI** iLala
TSONGA Nala   **VENDA** Mulala   **ZULU** iLala

Hyphaene is from the Greek *hyphaine* meaning to 'entwine', referring to the fibrous covering that enmeshes the seed; **coriacea** means 'thick and tough', or 'leathery'; **petersiana** is named after the German zoologist, Wilhelm Peters, who collected plants in the 19th Century.

Leaves

Where you'll find this tree easily
The Lala-palm grows in groups along the perennial rivers of the Lowveld.
- It is easiest to find this tree in Riverine areas (H), and it is more common north of the Sweni River.
- It can also be found in drainage lines and along river banks in Knob-thorn/Marula Savannah (F), Alluvial Plains (M) and Mopane/Bushwillow Woodlands (P).

A	E	I	M
B	F	J	N
C	G	K	O
D	H	L	P

GIFF
- This is a typical palm tree.
- In the south of the Lowveld the Southern Lala-palm has pear-shaped fruit, and is usually a shrub.
- In the north the Northern Lala-palm has rounder fruit, and often grows into a tall single-trunked tree.
- It has huge, Hand-shaped Compound leaves on a tall, bare, cylindrical trunk.
- The fruit is a large, dark, shiny ball.

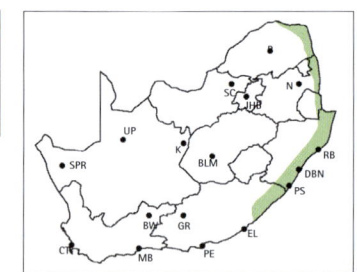

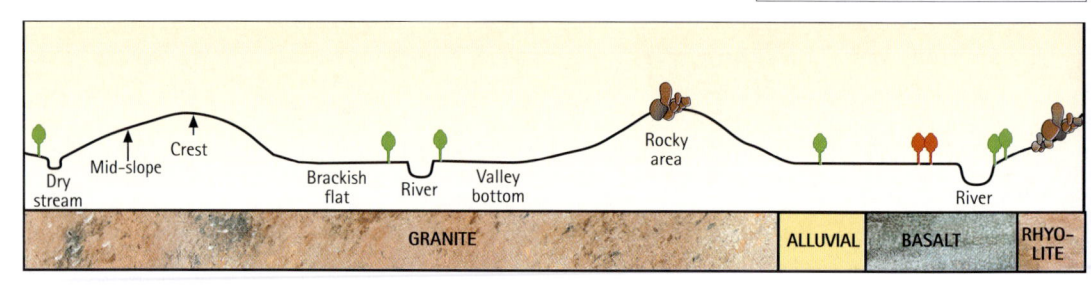

The Hand-shaped, Compound leaves of the Lala-palm are distinctive.

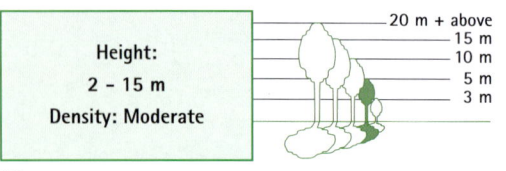

Seasonal changes
Evergreen. This tree is easy to identify throughout the year owing to its unique shape.

	Oct	Nov	Dec	Jan	Feb	Mar	Apr	May	Jun	Jul	Aug	Sep
Leaf												
Flower												
Fruit/Pod												

Height: 2 - 15 m
Density: Moderate

20 m + above
15 m
10 m
5 m
3 m

Growth form
It has a single, straight trunk, with leaves growing directly from it, to form a typical palm shape of moderate density.

Leaves
The leaves are bluish-green (1 300 mm).

Thorns
There are hooked thorns on the leaf-stems.

Flowers
Tiny flowers are tightly packed in long, drooping sprays. Growing on separate trees, the male flowers are in pairs, and the female flowers are single (Nov - Feb) (Male spray: 2 000 mm; Female spray: 3 000 mm).

(F) (M)

Fruit
The fruit hangs in long bunches below the leaves and is present throughout the year (60 mm).

Bark
Bark is fibrous and shows prominent leaf scars.

UNIQUE TREES
Lala-palm

Look-alike tree
The Wild Date-palm, *Phoenix reclinata*, p. 88, is also a Palm-tree, but is only common south of the Olifants River. It has fern-like leaves, while those of the Lala-palm are hand-shaped. It also has much smaller fruit that is more grape-like.

Gardening
This very attractive Palm-tree grows on most soil types, but requires plenty of water. It is not frost- or drought-resistant. It is slow-growing and cannot be grown from seed or cuttings.

Human uses
The white nut of the fruit is used as vegetable ivory for button-making and the carving of curios. The sap is brewed into beer and the leaves make mats, fibre, twine and thatching material.

Links with animals
The fruit is edible – the flesh is eaten by fruit bats and the nuts by baboon, elephant and monkey.

| PALM FAMILY | Arecaceae | Tree no 22 |

WILD DATE-PALM — *Phoenix reclinata*

AFRIKAANS Wildedadelpalm **N. SOTHO** Mopalema **SISWATI** liLala **TSONGA** Ncindzu, Xicindzu
VENDA Mutshema **ZULU** iSundu

Phoenix is the classical Greek name for the Date-palm; *reclinata* means 'bending down', and refers to the leaves.

Leaves

Where you'll find this tree easily
The Wild Date-palm grows in groups, only in riverbeds and on riverbanks along the larger rivers. It is more common south of the Olifants River.

❗ This tree is easily found in Riverine areas (H), throughout the Lowveld.

A	E	I	M
B	F	J	N
C	G	K	O
D	**H**	L	P

GIFF
- This is a reclining, multi-stemmed palm, often with no stems visible.
- **It is only found on riverbanks and in riverbeds.**
- It has large, Once Compound, fern-like leaves which come directly off the stems.
- Different male and female flowers grow on separate trees, in bunches, but both at the point where the young leaves join the branches.
- It has distinctive, grape-like fruit that grows in clustered bunches.

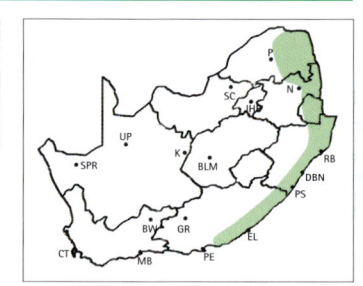

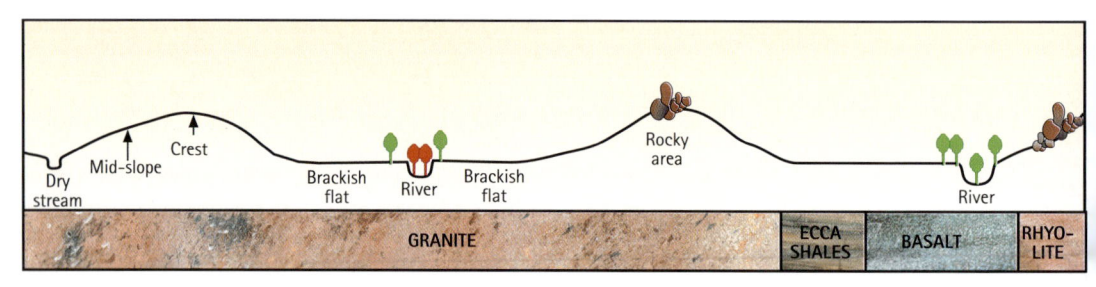

Wild Date-palms (in the foreground) follow the course of the riverbed. Here they grow near a Natal-mahogany, *Trichilia emetica*, p. 180.

Seasonal changes
Evergreen. This tree can be identified easily throughout the year owing to its unique shape.

	Oct	Nov	Dec	Jan	Feb	Mar	Apr	May	Jun	Jul	Aug	Sep
Leaf	■	■	■	■	■	■	■	■	■	■	■	■
Flower	■											■
Fruit/Pod			■	■	■	■	■					

Height: 3 – 6 m
Density: Moderate

88

Growth form
The leaves form an irregular, moderately dense, palm-like canopy. The trunk, when visible, displays old leaf scars.

(M)   (F)

Flowers
The female flowers are yellow-green and the males are yellow-cream. The male flowers have prominent stamens (Sep – Oct) (Single: 30 mm).

Leaves
The leaves come off at the end of the main trunk. There are up to 100 sharp, pointed leaflets. The lowest leaflets are reduced to spines (1 000 – 3 000 mm).

Fruit
Fruit grows from the point where the young leaves join the branches. It turns brown when ripe (Feb – Jun) (15 x 23 mm).

UNIQUE TREES — Wild Date-palm

Look-alike tree
The Lala-palm, *Hyphaene coriacea*, p. 86, grows south and north of the Olifants River, while the Wild Date-palm is more common south of the river. The Lala-palm has hand-shaped leaves, in comparison with the fern-like leaves of the Wild Date-palm. The fruit of the Lala-palm is much larger and hangs in long bunches, while the bunches of Wild Date-palm's fruit are clustered.

Gardening
This palm will grow well when generously watered in a warm garden, especially if the soil is rich. Once grown, it will produce palatable, edible fruits. It is not drought- or frost-resistant, and does not grow from seed. It is particularly slow-growing.

Links with animals
The fruit is eaten by mousebirds. The fruit, roots and leaves are eaten by elephant, and fruit and shoots by baboon and monkey. The caterpillars of the large brown butterfly, (Palm Tree Night Fighter, *Zaphotetes dysmephilai*) eat the leaves.

Human uses
The fruit is edible but has little flesh. The sap is brewed into beer and the leaves are woven into mats and hats. Fibres on the fruiting stems make good brushes and brooms.

THORN-TREE SUB-FAMILY OF PEA FAMILY — Mimosoideae — Tree no 189

FEVER-TREE ACACIA — *Acacia xanthophloea*

AFRIKAANS Koorsboom **N. SOTHO** Mmabane, Monang, Mohlaretodi **TSONGA** Nkelenga
ZULU imHlosinga, umHlofunga, umKhanyakude, umDlovume

Acacia is taken from the Greek *akis* meaning a 'sharp point'. It refers to the thorns that grow on all African Acacia species; **xanthophloea** refers to the yellow bark.

Flower/thorn

Where you'll find this tree easily
The Fever-tree Acacia grows in loose groups of large trees.
- This tree is easiest to find on Alluvial Plains (M).
- It can also be found near rivers and large streams in Knob-thorn/Marula Savannah (F) and in Mopane Shrubveld (L).

A	E	I	M
B	F	J	N
C	G	K	O
D	H	L	P

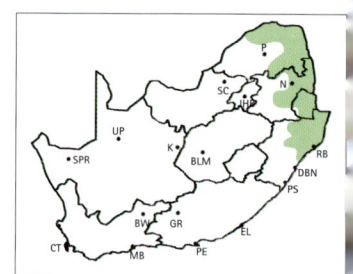

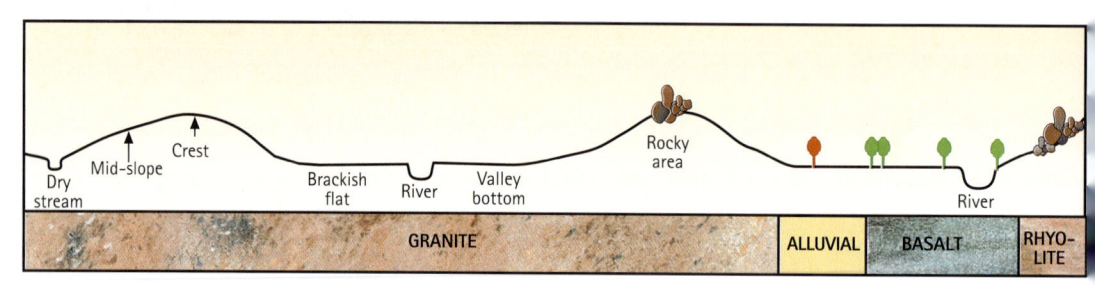

Crest — Mid-slope — Dry stream — Brackish flat — River — Valley bottom — Rocky area — River
GRANITE — ALLUVIAL — BASALT — RHYOLITE

GIFF
- No other tree in this area has a trunk and branches that are yellow-green and covered in yellow powder.
- It usually has a straight, smooth, single trunk.
- The trunk and branches 'peel' in paper-thin layers.
- It has a sparse, roundish, spreading canopy.
- Straight, white, paired thorns grow on a common base.
- The Twice Compound leaves are opposite and feathery.

Fever-trees lose leaves in winter, adding to their unique beauty.

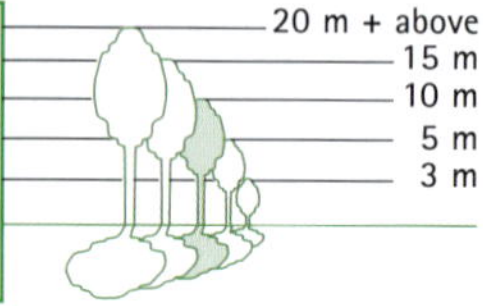

Seasonal changes
Deciduous. This tree is always easy to identify owing to the characteristic green bark and growth form.

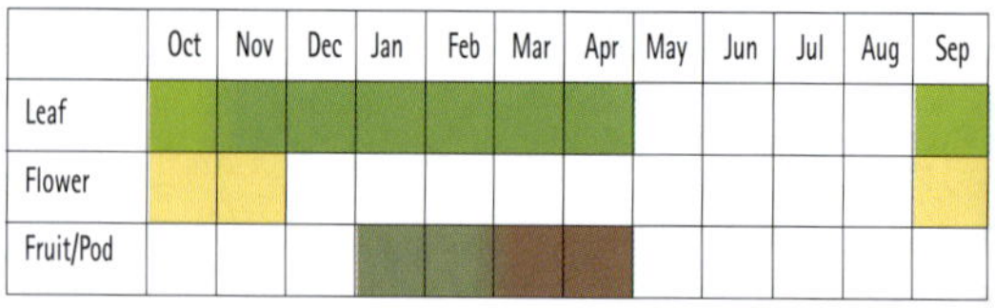

Height: 10 – 15 m
Density: Sparse

20 m + above / 15 m / 10 m / 5 m / 3 m

	Oct	Nov	Dec	Jan	Feb	Mar	Apr	May	Jun	Jul	Aug	Sep
Leaf												
Flower												
Fruit/Pod												

Growth form
The trunk is high-branching, with branches that come off horizontally.

Leaves
Leaves are smallish and feathery. They are opposite, and elliptic with a smooth margin. They have a pair of leaflets at the tip of the feather. (Average 7 feather pairs, 17 pairs of leaflets; leaf 100 mm; leaflet 7 x 1 mm).

Flowers
Round, golden balls on slender stalks are found in the axil of the thorns (Sep - Nov) (10 mm).

Thorns
On some trees, or branches, thorns may be under-developed or absent (80 mm).

Pods
The flat, bean pod is papery and grows in clusters. It is brown when ripe in late summer (Jan - Apr) (100 x 15 mm).

Bark
See GIFF.

UNIQUE TREES — Fever-tree Acacia

Look-alike tree
The Fever-tree Acacia has no Look-alike tree.

Gardening
This ornamental tree can be very attractive in indigenous gardens in warmer areas. It needs well-watered, clay soil and cannot take severe frost or drought. It can be grown from seed easily and, when well watered, is exceptionally fast-growing.

Human uses
The bark is used for treating fevers and eye complaints, and the wood for building.

Links with animals
The characteristic holes in the bark are caused by woodborers. Monkeys and baboons eat the flowers, young shoots and seeds, and elephants eat the pods, leaves and branches. Due to its proximity to permanent water, and the presence of thorns, this tree is often used by weavers to build their nests.

| THORN-TREE SUB-FAMILY OF PEA FAMILY | Mimosoideae | Tree no 188 |

UMBRELLA ACACIA
Acacia tortilis

AFRIKAANS Haak-en-steek, Haakdoring **N. SOTHO** Moswaana **SISWATI** isiThwethwe
TSONGA Nsasane **TSWANA** Moku, Mosu **ZULU** umSasane, isiThwethwe

Acacia is taken from the Greek *akis* meaning a 'sharp point', referring to the thorns that grow on all African Acacia species; **tortilis** refers to the twisted pods.

Leaf/pod

Where you'll find this tree easily
The Umbrella Acacia is often found in groups but larger trees also can be found growing singly.

- Umbrella Acacias are easiest to find growing in the brack areas of Sabie/Crocodile Thorn Thickets (D).
- They can also be found in most other Ecozones, often in brack areas and also along drainage lines, or in valley bottoms, as well as on plains.

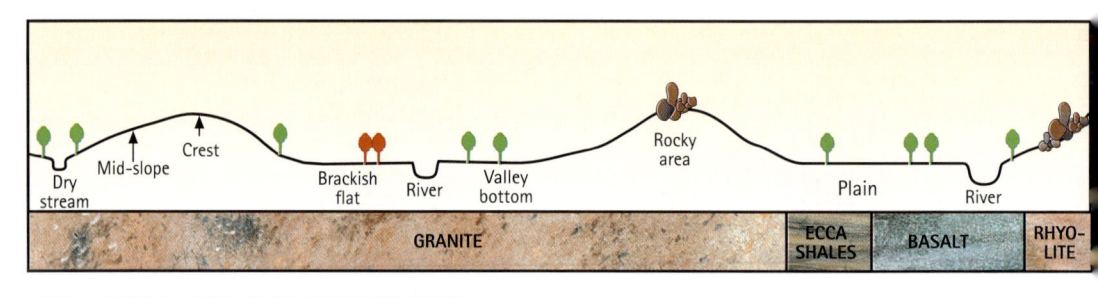

A	E	I	M
B	F	J	N
C	G	K	O
D	H	L	P

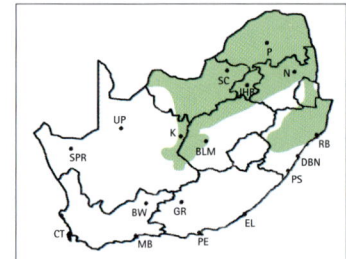

GIFF
- This is the most striking of the umbrella trees, with a particularly flat, thin-umbrella canopy of grey-green leaves.
- It is a fairly low-branching, usually single-stemmed, smallish tree.
- The Twice Compound leaves are tiny – among the tiniest of the Acacia leaves, giving the tree a fine, feathery appearance.
- The tightly curled pods are characteristic.
- This tree has both straight and hooked thorns which, although not always prominent, help with identification.

Young bark of the Umbrella Acacia with both straight and hooked thorns.

Height: 3 - 6 m
Density: Moderate

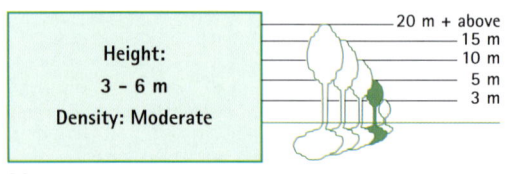

Seasonal changes
Deciduous. Because of the distinctive thorns, trees can often still be recognised in winter.

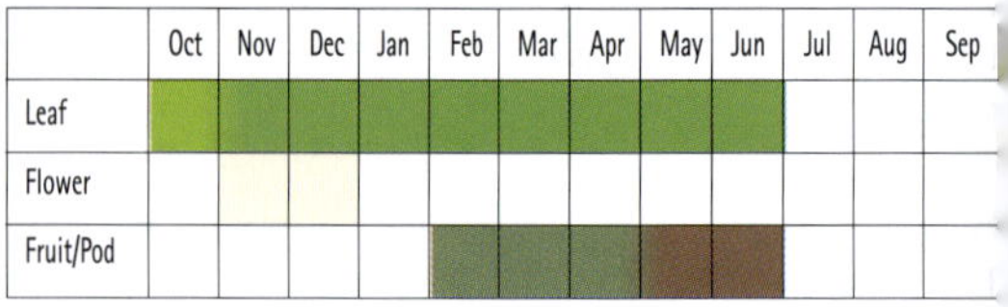

	Oct	Nov	Dec	Jan	Feb	Mar	Apr	May	Jun	Jul	Aug	Sep
Leaf												
Flower												
Fruit/Pod												

92

Growth form
The single, straight trunk is mostly high-branching, with branches coming off horizontally to form a moderately dense canopy. It does not always have the umbrella-like appearance, particularly when young, when it forms a dense, scrubby bush with an irregular canopy.

Leaves
Leaves are opposite and elliptic, with a smooth margin. They are grouped at nodes (Leaf: 25 mm; leaflet: 1 - 2 mm; feather: 13 with 19 leaflets).

Flowers
Large numbers of white, ball-like flowers grow on old twigs. Flowers are sweet-scented and normally appear just after rain (Nov - Dec) (7 mm).

Thorns
The white thorns, with a dark base and red tip, are usually in pairs, arranged spirally around the branchlets. Sometimes one hooked and one straight thorn may also form pairs on the same tree (Straight thorn: 50 mm; hooked thorn: 3 - 5 mm).

Pods
Flat, bean pods are curled up in a tight circle and hang in bunches. They ripen during May and June (Width: 8 mm; length: 125 mm).

Bark
The bark is grey and in older trees is deeply fissured. In young trees and on new branches it is coppery-gold with white markings.

UNIQUE TREES
Umbrella Acacia

Look-alike tree
See Acacia comparisons in Twice Compound leaves on pages 74-76.

Gardening
This tree will grow well in most of the warmer areas, in well-watered clay soils. It is a very attractive shade tree in the indigenous garden. It is drought-resistant and can be grown from seed.

Links with animals
The leaves are browsed by cattle, antelope and giraffe. The pods are high in protein and are a favourite with all antelope, giraffe, monkey and baboon.

Human uses
The wood was used as fuel.

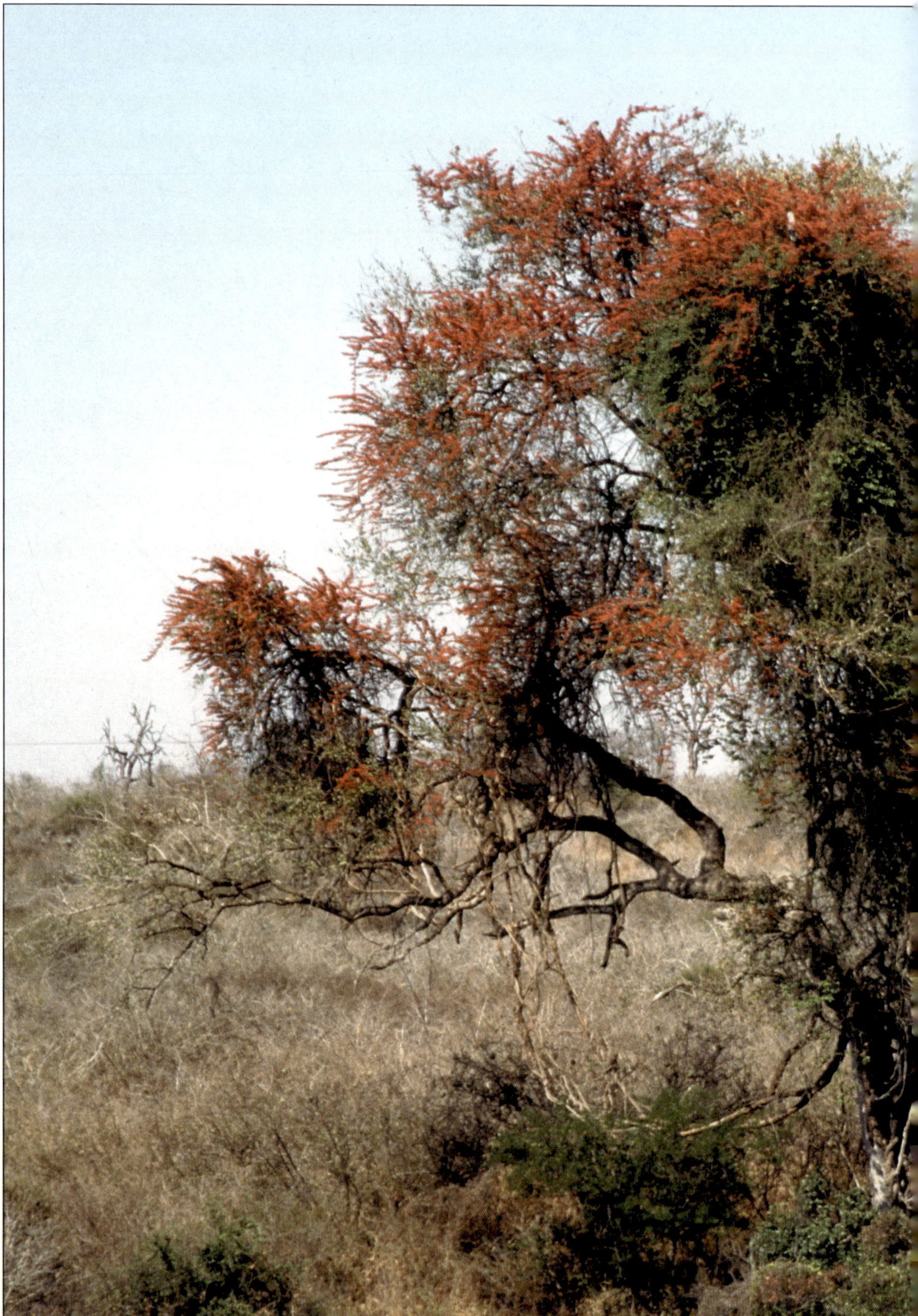

TREES GREET YOU

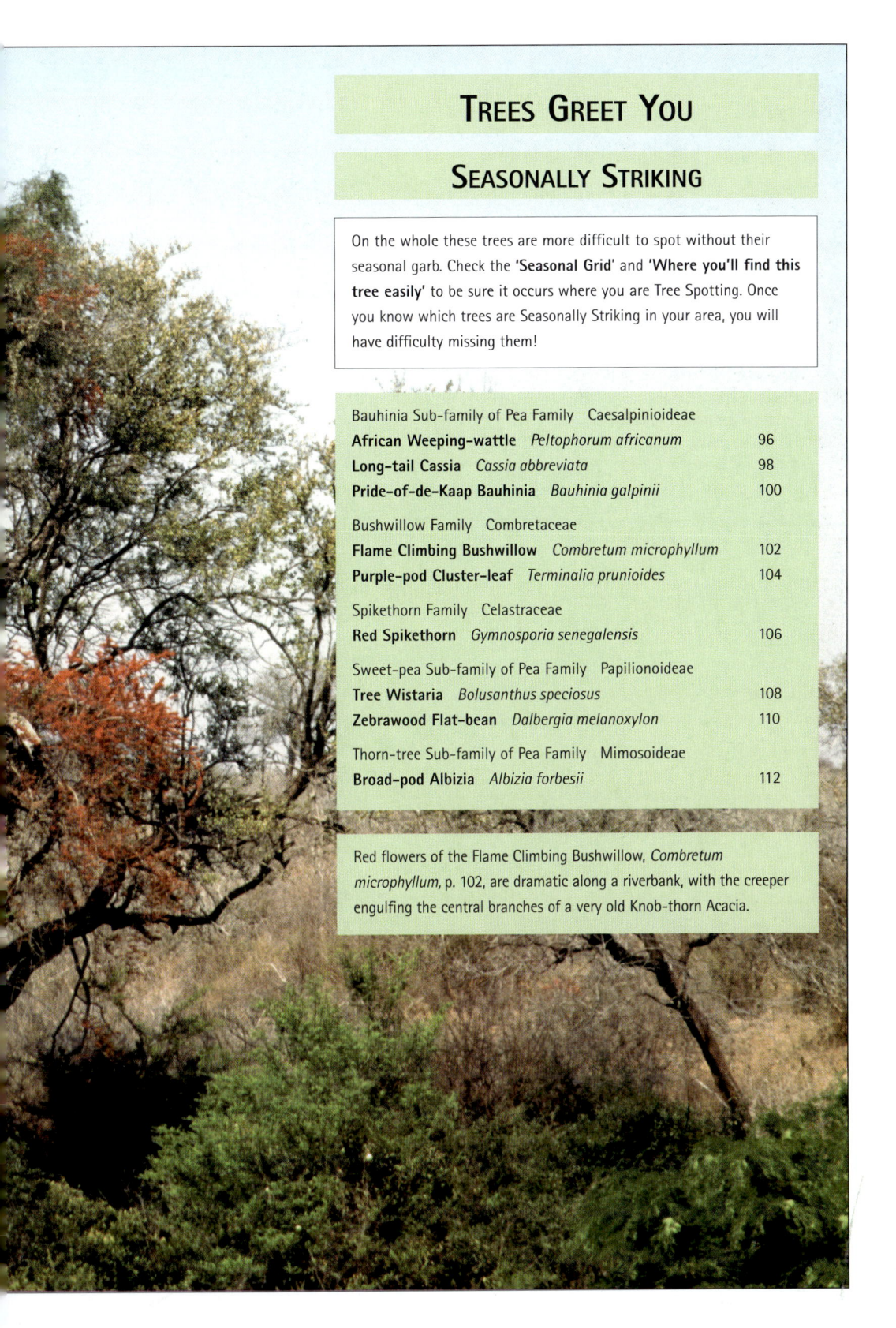

SEASONALLY STRIKING

On the whole these trees are more difficult to spot without their seasonal garb. Check the **'Seasonal Grid'** and **'Where you'll find this tree easily'** to be sure it occurs where you are Tree Spotting. Once you know which trees are Seasonally Striking in your area, you will have difficulty missing them!

Bauhinia Sub-family of Pea Family   Caesalpinioideae
African Weeping-wattle   *Peltophorum africanum*   96
Long-tail Cassia   *Cassia abbreviata*   98
Pride-of-de-Kaap Bauhinia   *Bauhinia galpinii*   100

Bushwillow Family   Combretaceae
Flame Climbing Bushwillow   *Combretum microphyllum*   102
Purple-pod Cluster-leaf   *Terminalia prunioides*   104

Spikethorn Family   Celastraceae
Red Spikethorn   *Gymnosporia senegalensis*   106

Sweet-pea Sub-family of Pea Family   Papilionoideae
Tree Wistaria   *Bolusanthus speciosus*   108
Zebrawood Flat-bean   *Dalbergia melanoxylon*   110

Thorn-tree Sub-family of Pea Family   Mimosoideae
Broad-pod Albizia   *Albizia forbesii*   112

Red flowers of the Flame Climbing Bushwillow, *Combretum microphyllum,* p. 102, are dramatic along a riverbank, with the creeper engulfing the central branches of a very old Knob-thorn Acacia.

| BAUHINIA SUB-FAMILY OF PEA FAMILY | Caesalpinioideae | Tree no 215 |

AFRICAN WEEPING-WATTLE
Peltophorum africanum

AFRIKAANS Huilboom **N. SOTHO** Mosehla **TSONGA** Ndedze **TSWANA** Mosêthla **VENDA** Musese **ZULU** umSehle

Peltophorum is from the Greek *pelte* + *phorein* meaning 'shield' + 'to bear', referring to the shape of the stigma in the flowers; *africanum* refers to Africa.

Leaves

Where you'll find this tree easily
The African Weeping-wattle grows singly, but where there is one tree there are usually others nearby. It is widespread in its Habitat choice.
- You can spot this tree throughout Pretoriuskop Sourveld (B), but it is easiest to recognise on the crests.
- It can be spotted in most other granite Ecozones on crests, seeplines and plains A, C, D and P.
- It can also easily be found on the plains in the clay Ecozones, E, F, J, K, and L, as well as in Lebombo Mountain Bushveld (I).

A	E	I	M
B	F	J	N
C	G	K	O
D	H	L	P

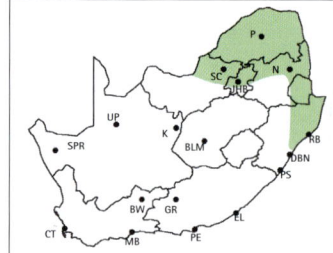

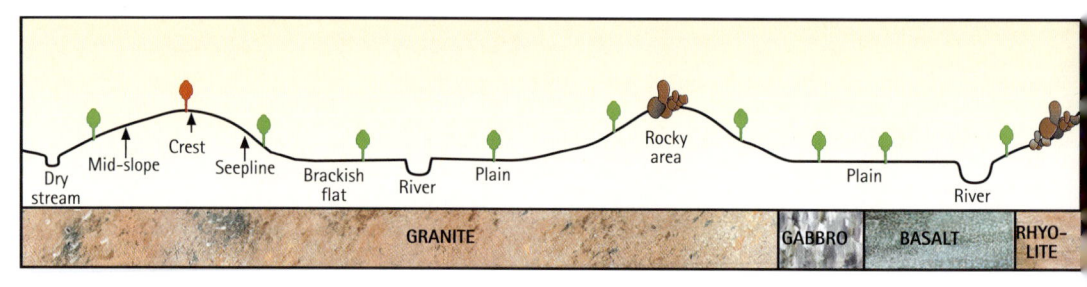

GIFF
- This tree branches low down from a stem that is often crooked, to form a spreading, irregular and untidy canopy.
- It has striking, dull green, large, Twice Compound, soft, feathery leaves, that are Acacia-like.
- The mature leaves, at the tips of the branches, are often yellowish.
- It does not have thorns.
- In summer, abundant yellow flowers, among the large, feathery leaves, are characteristic.
- The greyish-brown to dark brown pods grow in conspicuous hanging bunches, and remain on the tree for most of the year.

Pods and old leaves of the African Weeping-wattle stand out against a winter sky.

Seasonal changes
Deciduous. The leaves are lost late in the winter. They can be identified for most of the year, as either the leaves or pods are normally present.

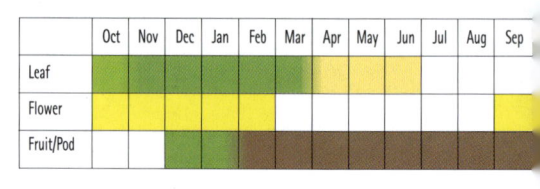

Height: 10 m
Density: Dense

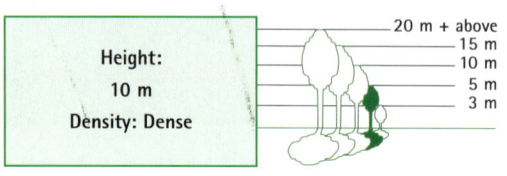

	Oct	Nov	Dec	Jan	Feb	Mar	Apr	May	Jun	Jul	Aug	Sep
Leaf												
Flower												
Fruit/Pod												

Growth form
There is usually a single stem with several downward curving branches. The trunk is often obscured by drooping branchlets and leaves.

Leaves
The alternate leaves have 4 - 9 pairs of feathers, and 10 - 23 pairs of leaflets. The small, soft, leaflets are silvery/dull-green above, and paler below. The leaflets are oblong to almost square. The feather-stalks and central vein, as well as the leaf-stalk, are covered in reddish-brown hairs (Leaf: up to 180 x 901 mm; leaflet: 5 - 9 x 1,5 - 3 mm).

Flowers
The conspicuous, sweet-scented flowers grow in sprays at the ends of twigs, or in the angles formed by the leaves. The flowers have crinkled petals that are up to 20 mm in diameter. The flower-stalks and the back of the petals are covered in reddish-brown hairs (Sep - Feb) (Spray: up to 150 x 80 mm; individual flower: up to 20 mm wide).

Pods
The pods are thinly woody and contain one or two seeds, which can be seen as bulges. They are found in much greater numbers from February to May (Pod: 40 - 100 x 12 - 20 mm).

Bark
The bark is grey and smooth on young branches, and young twigs are covered in reddish-brown hairs. The bark is brown to dark grey, to almost black, and fissured lengthways on older branches and stems.

Look-alike tree
In Malelane Mountain Bushveld, Ecozone C, this tree can be confused with the Mountain Kirkia, *Kirkia wilmsii*, p. 37. It can also be confused with the Acacias and Albizias listed on pages 74-77.

Gardening
This decorative tree will grow in most gardens. It is sensitive to severe frost, but drought-resistant once established. It can be grown from seed and is fast-growing when planted in fertile soils and watered well.

Links with animals
In summer the tree is often infested with the spittle bug, *Ptyelus grossus*. The bugs' secretions drip down, causing it to 'rain' under the tree. The tree is not browsed regularly, but young shoots may be eaten by Black Rhino, elephant, giraffe and kudu.

Human uses
The wood can be made into furniture, axe handles, buckets and ornaments, and was also used as fuel.

BAUHINIA SUB-FAMILY OF PEA FAMILY   Caesalpinioideae   Tree no 212

LONG-TAIL CASSIA (SJAMBOK POD)   *Cassia abbreviata*

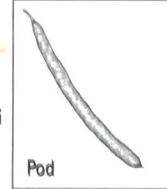

AFRIKAANS Sambokpeul, Kersboom **N. SOTHO** Dithetlwa, Mothetlwa (Mokgwankgusha) **TSONGA** Numanyama **TSWANA** Numanyama **VENDA** Muluma-nama, Munembe-nembe **ZULU** umHlambamanzi

Cassia is the Greek name for the genus; **abbreviata** means shortened.

Pod

Where you'll find this tree easily

The Long-tail Cassia grows singly in woodland and even savannah, in a wide variety of Habitats, including riverbanks, along drainage lines and valley bottoms, and on termite mounds.

A	E	I	M
B	F	J	N
C	G	K	O
D	H	L	P

- This tree is easiest to find in Sabie/Crocodile Thorn Thickets (D) along rivers, in valley bottoms and on termite mounds.
- It is also found growing in Mixed Bushwillow Woodlands (A), Pretoriuskop Sourveld (B), Knob-thorn/Marula Savannah (F), in the south of Lebombo Mountain Bushveld (I) and in Mopane/Bushwillow Woodlands (P).

Dry stream — Mid-slope — Crest — Brackish flat — River — Valley bottom — Rocky area — River
GRANITE   GABBRO   BASALT   RHYOLITE

GIFF

- This is a smallish tree with a slender stem and semi-circular canopy with drooping leaves.
- The drooping Once Compound leaves have a pair of leaflets at the tip.
- In early spring it is covered by masses of yellow flowers that appear before the new leaves.
- Exceptionally long pods, that stay on the tree for most of the year, are characteristic of this tree.

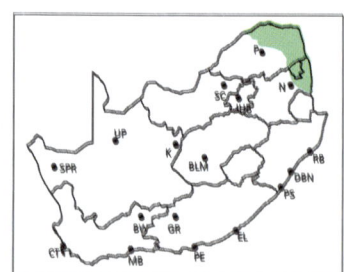

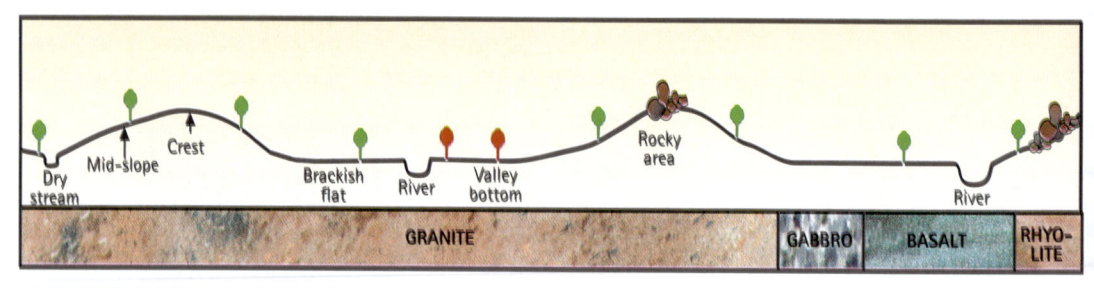

The canopy of magnificent yellow flowers on the Long-tail Cassia, in early spring, is in strong contrast to the winter colours that surround it.

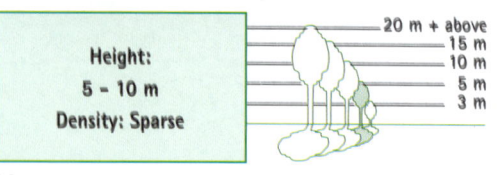

Seasonal changes

Deciduous. This tree is without leaves from early winter until it flowers in spring. It can be identified for most of the year by its characteristic pods.

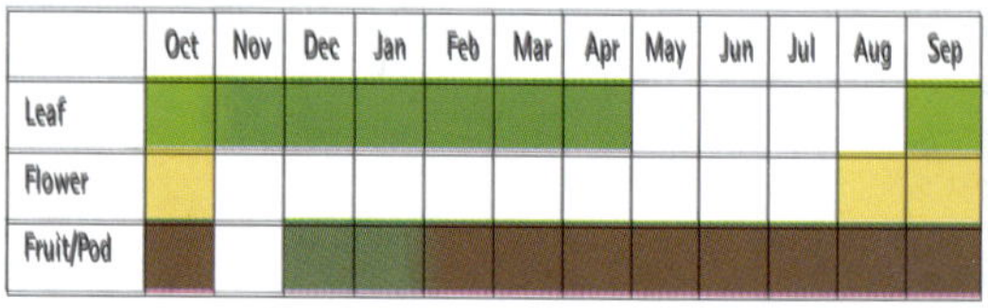

Height: 5 – 10 m
Density: Sparse

20 m + above / 15 m / 10 m / 5 m / 3 m

	Oct	Nov	Dec	Jan	Feb	Mar	Apr	May	Jun	Jul	Aug	Sep
Leaf												
Flower												
Fruit/Pod												

Growth form
The single, straight stem branches high up.

Flowers
Single flowers are clustered at the ends of the branches (Aug - Oct) (30 mm).

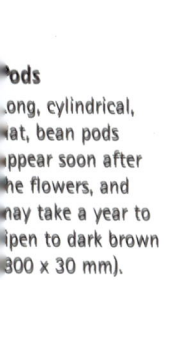

Pods
Long, cylindrical, flat, bean pods appear soon after the flowers, and may take a year to ripen to dark brown (300 x 30 mm).

Leaves
The leaves are elliptic with a smooth margin and are clustered along the ends of the branches. They are bright green when new in early summer, becoming darker and less striking as they mature (Leaf: 300 mm; 9 pairs of leaflets 45 x 20 mm).

Bark
The bark is dark, fissured and flaking.

Look-alike tree
The Tree Wistaria, *Bolusanthus speciosus*, p. 108, also has long, drooping Once Compound leaves, but they have a single leaflet at the tip.

Links with animals
The seeds are sought after by Brown-headed Parrots and Grey Turacos. Young leaves are eaten by kudu.

Human uses
Powdered bark has been successfully used for the treatment of bilharzia. The tree is believed to have some magical powers.

Gardening
This very attractive small tree will grow well in most gardens but will be damaged by severe frost, especially when still young. It is drought-resistant and slow-growing, and can be grown from seed easily.

SEASONALLY STRIKING — Long-tail Cassia

| BAUHINIA SUB-FAMILY OF PEA FAMILY | Caesalpinioideae | Tree no 208.2 |

PRIDE-OF-DE-KAAP BAUHINIA
Bauhinia galpinii

AFRIKAANS Vlam-van-die-Vlakte **TSONGA** Tswiriri **TSWANA** liSololo **VENDA** Mutswiriri
ZULU umVangatane, uiSololo, umDlondlovu

Bauhinia, with two lobes to its leaves, honours the brothers Johan and Caspar Bauhin, 16th Century Swiss Botanists; **galpinii** refers to the late 19th and early 20th Century botanical collector, EE Galpin.

Flower

Where you'll find this tree easily
The Pride-of-de-Kaap Bauhinia grows singly, often draped over other trees, or as a rambling shrub.
- It is easiest to find growing on riverbanks, in Riverine areas (H) of the granite Ecozones, that are all found on the western side of the Lowveld.
- It is also found in drainage lines in Pretoriuskop Sourveld (B) and on slopes of rocky hills in Sandveld (N).

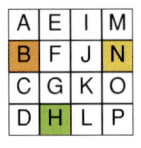

A	E	I	M
B	F	J	N
C	G	K	O
D	H	L	P

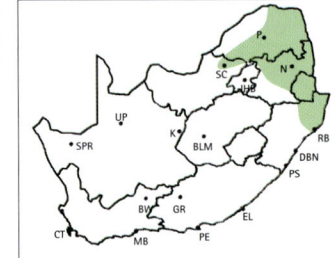

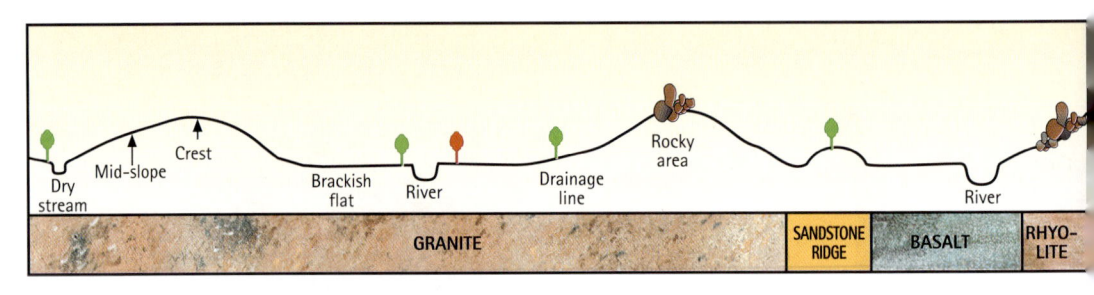

GIFF
- This is a vigorous, multi-stemmed climber/scrambler, covering trees and bushes.
- The Simple leaves are deeply lobed into a butterfly-shape.
- The abundance of large, brick-red flowers among the leaves is one of features of the Lowveld in summer.
- Bean-shaped, brown pods are also characteristic.

The red flowers of the Pride-of-de-Kaap Bauhinia are conspicuous against the butterfly-shaped leaves.

Seasonal changes
Deciduous to semi-deciduous. This climber is only conspicuous in summer when it is flowering.

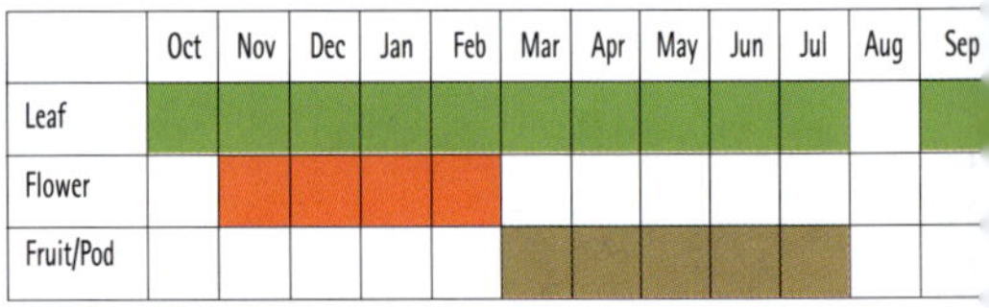

	Oct	Nov	Dec	Jan	Feb	Mar	Apr	May	Jun	Jul	Aug	Sep
Leaf												
Flower												
Fruit/Pod												

Growth form
This is a vigorous, multi-stemmed climber, occasionally seen as a lone-standing, multi-stemmed small tree. It tends to form long, drooping, whip-like branches.

Leaves
Alternate leaves have smooth margins. They are bright, pale green, with slightly yellow veins that are raised on the underside of the leaf (70 x 70 mm).

Flowers
The five petals are paddle-shaped and have wavy edges (Nov – Feb) (50 - 70 mm).

Pods
The long, flat, dark brown pods are pointed, slender, hard and woody. They split on the tree when ripe (Mar - Jul) (80 - 100 mm).

Bark
The bark is smooth and light brown.

SEASONALLY STRIKING — Pride-of-de-Kaap Bauhinia

Look-alike climber
The other red-flowered climber in damp places is the Flame Climbing Bushwillow, *Combretum microphyllum,* p. 102. It has brilliant scarlet flowers that appear before the Simple leaves. This robust climber has spines on its main branches, and occurs only along perennial rivers.

Human uses
Branchlets are used to make baskets. Various decoctions of seeds or roots are used in reproductive healing, such as venereal disease and amenorrhoea in women, as well as retained placenta in stock animals.

Gardening
This is a widely cultivated plant for larger gardens, particularly in rockeries or as screening. It grows easily from seed or cuttings, and prefers hot, frost-free areas. It will grow well in warm, sheltered positions in cooler gardens, if protected in winter.

Links with animals
The caterpillars of two butterflies of the genus *Deudorix,* the Brown Playboy and the Orange Barred Playboy, eat the leaves.

| BUSHWILLOW FAMILY | Combretaceae | Tree no 545 |

FLAME CLIMBING BUSHWILLOW — *Combretum microphyllum*

AFRIKAANS Vlamklimop   **TSONGA** Mpfunta   **VENDA** Murunda-gopokopo   **ZULU** iWapha

Combretum is derived from the classical Latin name for the genus used by Pliny, 23-79 AD; **microphyllum** refers to the small leaves.

Flowers

Where you'll find this tree easily
The Flame Climbing Bushwillow is a climber/scrambler that grows singly on trees in riverine vegetation.
- It is easiest to find growing in Riverine areas (H), throughout the granites in the west, and also along larger drainage lines in Sabie/Crocodile Thorn Thickets (D).
- It can be found on riverbanks in Olifants Rugged Veld (J) and Alluvial Plains (M), as well as along large drainage lines in Pretoriuskop Sourveld (B).

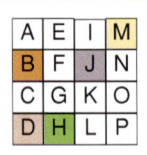

A	E	I	M
B	F	J	N
C	G	K	O
D	H	L	P

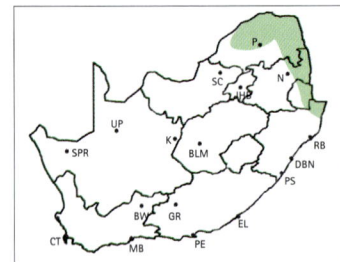

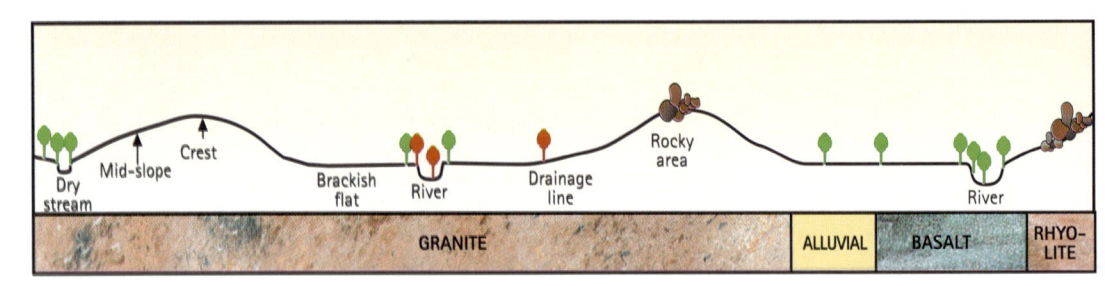

GIFF
- This is a climber/scrambler normally growing up trees and shrubs.
- Simple, alternate or opposite leaves occur on new growth, and are elliptic to round.
- **The very striking, large sprays of brilliant scarlet flowers with prominent stamens, stand out among the riverine vegetation.**
- The flowers appear in spring before the leaves.
- The pink-green, four-winged, Bushwillow pods grow in abundance early in summer.
- Long, often paired, curved, woody spines grow on main branches.

Robust stems of the Flame Climbing Bushwillow entwine together and use a large, strong, riverine tree for support.

Seasonal changes
Deciduous. This climber is only really easy to identify for the first time when the pods or flowers are present.

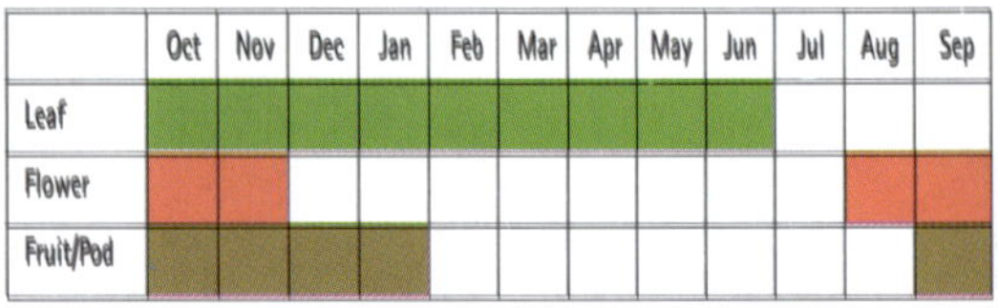

	Oct	Nov	Dec	Jan	Feb	Mar	Apr	May	Jun	Jul	Aug	Sep
Leaf												
Flower												
Fruit/Pod												

Growth form
This is a scrambling shrub or robust climber, and is often multi-stemmed.

Leaves
The leaf-tip is normally round but may have a short point. The leaf-base is round and hairy, especially on the underside, but becomes smoother with age. The margins are smooth and leaf-stalks are velvety (40 - 100 x 30 - 50 mm).

Flowers
The small flowers are clustered at the ends of the branches. Here they form spikes of up to 80 mm long that are held horizontally (Aug - Nov) (Stamen: 15 mm).

Pods
Large clusters of pods are greenish-pink when young and become straw-coloured when ripe. They develop quickly and may be found in among new flowers (Sep - Jan) (20 x 20 mm).

Bark
The bark is brown and flaking in older trees.

SEASONALLY STRIKING
Flame Climbing Bushwillow

Look-alike climber
The other red-flowered creeper in damp places is the Pride-of-de-Kaap Bauhinia, *Bauhinia galpinii*, p. 100. The flowers are brick-red, rather than brilliant scarlet, the leaves are noticeably butterfly-shaped and the main branches have spines. In addition, the pods are bean-shaped, not four-winged.

Gardening
This is a very attractive garden plant and can be decorative in a larger garden. It needs dry winters to grow well. It is a fast grower but sensitive to frost.

Links with animals
The leaves are browsed by a variety of animals. The flowers attract sunbirds.

Human uses
An extract of this plant is used to treat mentally disturbed people.

| BUSHWILLOW FAMILY | Combretaceae | Tree no 550 |

PURPLE-POD CLUSTER-LEAF
Terminalia prunioides

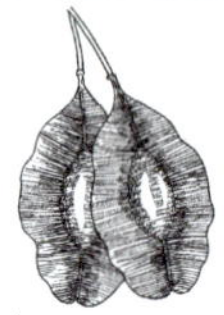

AFRIKAANS Sterkbos, Doringtrosblaar **TSONGA** Xaxandzawu **TSWANA** Mochiara, Motsiyara

Pods

Terminalia describes the way in which the leaves are clustered at the ends of the shoots; **prunioides** means plum-like, referring to the purple pods that are present for much of the year.

Where you'll find this tree easily
The Purple-pod Cluster-leaf grows in loose groups on rocky soils and in deep alluvial sand.
- It is easiest to find this tree in the rocky areas and plains of Olifants Rugged Veld (J).
- You can spot it in Malelane Mountain Bushveld (C), Sabie/Crocodile Thorn Thickets (D), Mopane Shrubveld (L) and in Mopane/Bushwillow Woodlands (P), as well as in the north of Lebombo Mountain Bushveld (I).

A	E	I	M
B	F	J	N
C	G	K	O
D	H	L	P

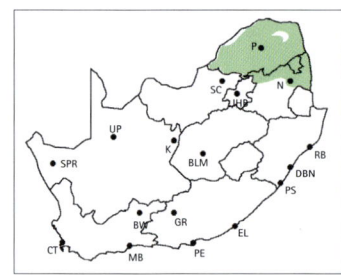

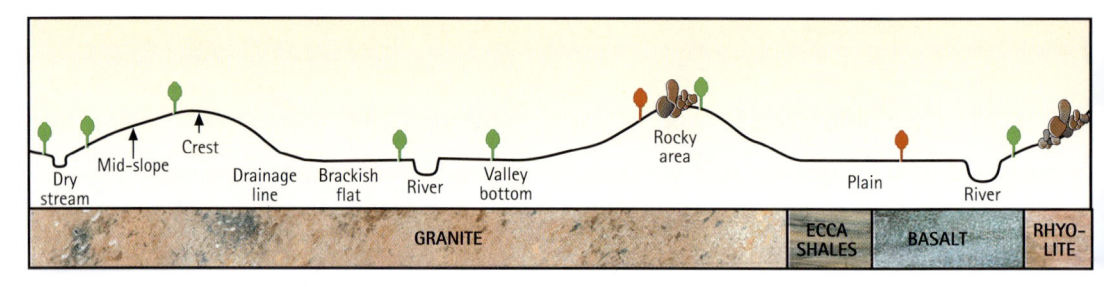

GIFF
- This is usually a single, but sometimes a multi-trunked, low-branching tree, with an irregular, sparse and tangled canopy.
- It has a drooping, spiky appearance owing to the downward-curving branchlets and side branches that end in spines.
- The clustered arrangement of the heart-shaped Simple leaves, at the end of branchlets, is characteristic.
- During spring and summer it can be identified by the pungent smell of the flowers.
- The conspicuous purple pods are present for most of the summer, autumn and winter, and are the main aid to identification.

The drooping, spiky appearance of the branchlets combined with the clustered leaves is distinctive.

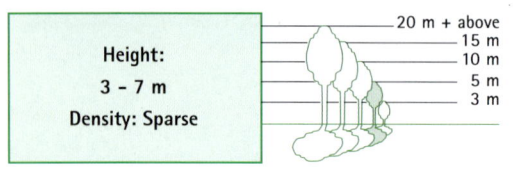

Seasonal changes
Deciduous to semi-deciduous. It can be identified most of the year by the wine-red/purple pods.

	Oct	Nov	Dec	Jan	Feb	Mar	Apr	May	Jun	Jul	Aug	Sep
Leaf												
Flower												
Fruit/Pod												

Height: 3 – 7 m
Density: Sparse

Growth form
See GIFF.

Leaves
The leaves are clustered, or in spirals. They are dull, dark green and have smooth margins (35 x 15 mm).

Pods
The oval, flat, two-winged pods are thickened over a central seed. They turn purple to wine-red when ripe (from Feb) (40 x 30 mm).

Flowers
The white, cylindrical flowers are widely spaced in spikes at the ends of the short branchlets. They often cover the whole tree (Sep - Feb) (Single flower: 4 mm; spike: 65 x 20 mm).

Bark
The dark brown, deeply grooved bark is often obscured by the drooping branches.

SEASONALLY STRIKING
Purple-pod Cluster-leaf

Look-alike tree
For Look-alike trees, see the Bushwillow comparisons on pages 71-73.

Gardening
This is a very attractive tree when covered in plum-coloured pods, but the strong smell of the flowers may be overwhelming in a small garden. It also has a tendency to shrubby growth. It will grow in most soils and is fairly drought-resistant, but sensitive to frost. It grows relatively fast from seed when well watered, but it is difficult to find healthy, viable seed.

Human uses
The hard wood is used in the building of huts and for making axe and pick handles. It was burnt as fuel.

Links with animals
The hard, green seeds are eaten by baboons, monkeys and Brown-headed Parrots. Young shoots and leaves are eaten by elephant, giraffe, kudu and impala.

105

| SPIKETHORN FAMILY | Celastraceae | Tree no 402 |

RED SPIKETHORN *Gymnosporia senegalensis (Maytenus senegalensis)*

AFRIKAANS Rooipendoring **ZULU** uBuhlangwe, isiHlangu, isiHlangwane

Gymnosporia is from the Greek *gymnos* + *spora* meaning 'naked' + 'seed', referring to the way in which the seeds remain attached and visible, once the fruit has opened; **senegalensis** means from Senegal.

Leaf / thorns

Where you'll find this tree easily
The Red Spikethorn is easiest to identify in winter, in basalt areas, as it is one of the few green trees away from the rivers. It is often in dry areas, and along roads.

- You will find this tree easily in the southern areas of Knobthorn/Marula Savannah (F).
- You will also find it growing in valley bottoms and riverine areas of Sabie/Crocodile Thorn Thickets (D), and in Riverine areas (H) throughout the Lowveld.
- It is also on the plains in Olifants Rugged Veld (J), in Mopane Shrubveld (L) and on Alluvial Plains (M).

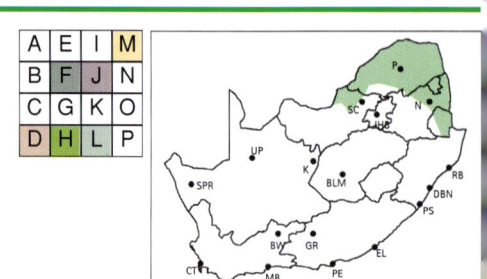

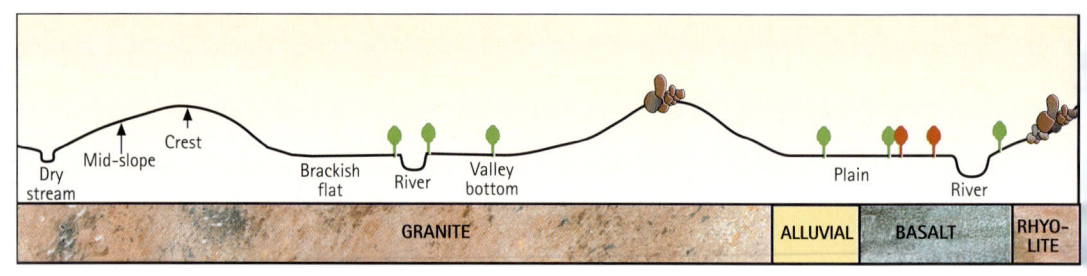

A	E	I	M
B	F	J	N
C	G	K	O
D	H	L	P

This coarse bark of the Pioneer Spikethorn, *Gymnosporia buxifolia*, p. 33, distinguishes it from the Red Spikethorn.

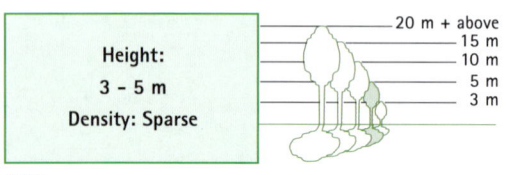

GIFF
- It is evergreen and very conspicuous in Ecozone F in winter.
- This is an untidy, sparse, multi-stemmed shrub.
- It branches into many long, thin, whitish-grey branchlets and twigs that curve downwards.
- **Young branches and twigs are red, and the central vein of the leaf may be pink-tinged – hence some common names.**
- Blue-grey-green, elliptic, Simple leaves are usually leathery with finely serrated margins.
- They grow towards the tips of twigs, and give the tree an overall pale grey appearance.
- **Long, thin spines may carry leaves.**
- **Abundant, small, white flowers have a sweet smell.**

Seasonal changes
Evergreen. They are easiest to identify in winter, being one of the few green trees away from the rivers, in basalt areas.

Height: 3 – 5 m
Density: Sparse

	Oct	Nov	Dec	Jan	Feb	Mar	Apr	May	Jun	Jul	Aug	Sep
Leaf												
Flower												
Fruit/Pod												

Growth form
This shrub seldom develops into a fully grown tree. The stems are short and crooked. Branches come off haphazardly to form a tangled, irregularly shaped canopy.

Leaves
Leaves are arranged alternately in clusters on short side branchlets or on the spines. They can be narrow or more oval, with a rounded or sometimes notched tip (20 - 120 x 40 - 60 mm).

Flowers
Conspicuous male and female flowers grow on separate trees. The star-shaped flowers grow in clusters at the base of the leaves (May - Sep) (4 - 6 mm; cluster 40 mm).

Spines
The spines may be absent on some branches (40 mm).

Fruit
The berry-like fruit is reddish when ripe. The fruit is a two-lobed capsule (Aug - Feb) (2 - 6 mm).

Bark
The bark is red and smooth when young, becoming grey-green with maturity. In really old trees the bark becomes greyer and blocky.

SEASONALLY STRIKING
Red Spikethorn

Look-alike tree
This tree can be confused with the Pioneer Spikethorn, *Gymnosporia buxifolia*, p. 33. It is normally single-stemmed with very coarse bark, with channelled ridges. This is shown in the photograph on the opposite page, while the Red Spikethorn is mostly multi-stemmed with smooth, reddish to grey bark becoming grey and blocky. The flowers of the Pioneer Spikethorn have an offensive smell, but those of the Red Spikethorn are sweet-smelling.

Human uses
The fruit is edible. Extracts of the roots and thorns are remedies for pneumonia, tuberculosis, colds and coughs. Root decoctions are used in human reproductive healing for menstrual problems, cramps and threatened abortion. Extracts of the tree can treat snakebite. The twigs were used to start fires by using friction.

Gardening
Trees can be grown easily from seed. They grow slowly and are drought-resistant but sensitive to frost.

Links with animals
The leaves are eaten by elephant, kudu, giraffe and impala, and the fruit by birds. The bark and leaves are browsed by Black Rhino.

SWEET-PEA SUB-FAMILY OF PEA FAMILY — Papilionoideae — Tree no 222

TREE WISTARIA — *Bolusanthus speciosus*

AFRIKAANS Vanwykshout **N. SOTHO** Mogohlo **SWAZI** umHohlo **TSONGA** Mpfimbahongonyi
VENDA Mukumba, Muswinga-phala **ZULU** umHonhlo

Bolusanthus is a combination of the Greek *anthos* meaning 'flower' and the name of the founder of the Bolus Herbarium, Harry Bolus; **speciosus** means beautiful.

Flowers

Where you'll find this tree easily
The Tree Wistaria grows singly, but other trees will be found in the vicinity. It is most often found on wooded plains.

- It is easiest to find growing on the plains in Thorn Veld (E).
- It is also found on the seeplines in the granite Ecozones, Mixed Bushwillow Woodlands (A) and Pretoriuskop Sourveld (B).
- It is also distinctive on the plains in the south of Knobthorn/Marula Savannah (F) and Delagoa Thorn Thickets (G).

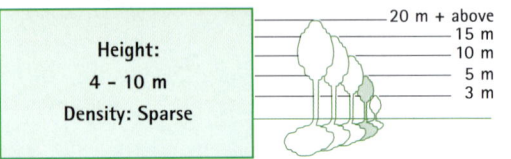

GIFF
- This tree is very upright and narrow, branching low down, but with the main branches growing upwards, almost parallel to one another.
- **Once Compound leaves have a single leaflet at the tip.**
- Branchlets and twigs are thin and the leaves grow towards their tips.
- The shiny leaves are light in weight, and grow on thin twigs.
- The leaves are tilted inwards, exposing both the bright green upper-surfaces and paler under-surfaces, creating a twinkling effect in the wind.
- The bark is deeply grooved and brown to dark brown.
- **It can be identified easily by bunches of violet and white, pea-like flowers in September and October.**
- Flat, narrow, papery pods are pale brown to black, and hang in clusters throughout the summer.

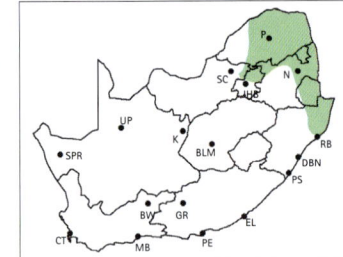

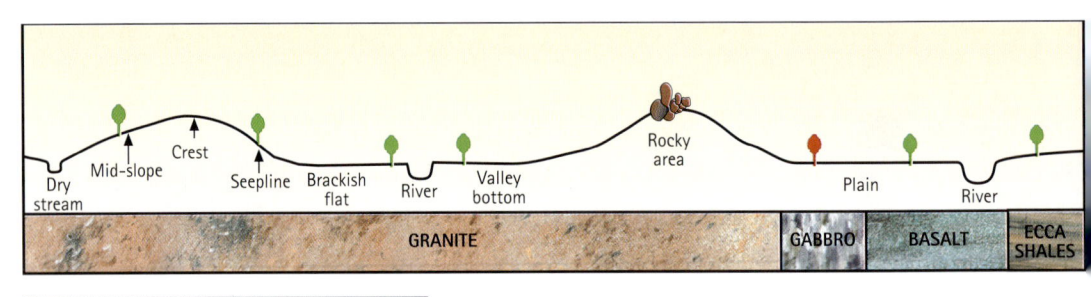

Baboons love to eat the flower-buds in late winter.

Seasonal changes
Deciduous. This tree can be identified even in the dry period by its spindly shape and deeply grooved bark.

Height: 4 – 10 m
Density: Sparse

	Oct	Nov	Dec	Jan	Feb	Mar	Apr	May	Jun	Jul	Aug	Sep
Leaf												
Flower												
Fruit/Pod												

108

Growth form
This is a fairly straight-stemmed tree with branchlets and twigs growing outwards to form a sparse, narrow canopy.

Leaves
The leaves have 5 - 6 pairs of opposite, or almost opposite, leaflets. Leaflets are narrowly elliptic to slightly sickle-shaped, with a smooth margin. The central vein is slightly off-centre and the tip is curled. The leaves are shiny, with an obvious yellow central vein. Young leaves are covered by fine hairs but older leaves are smooth (Leaf: 250 mm; leaflet: 70 x 10 mm).

Pods
Pods have sharp points at both ends, and they darken with age. They do not split open on the tree (Ripen Nov - Mar) (70 - 100 x 10 mm).

Flowers
Bunches of purple flowers appear with, or before, the new leaves (Sep - Oct) (Spray: 200 mm).

Bark
The bark is pale to warm-brown and deeply fissured lengthwise, almost ropey, in older trees.

SEASONALLY STRIKING
Tree Wistaria

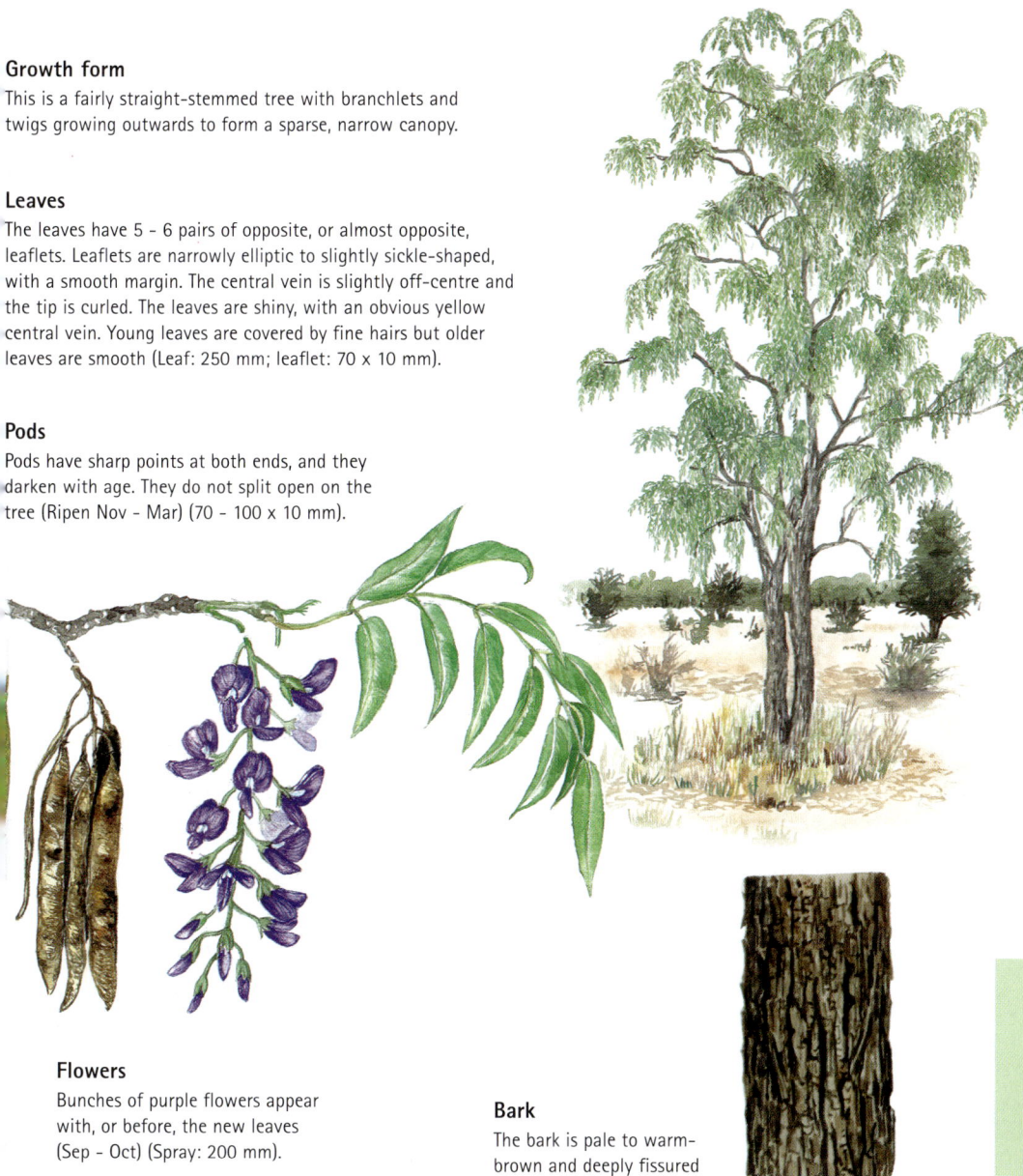

Look-alike tree
Long-tail Cassia, *Cassia abbreviata*, p. 98, also has long, drooping, Once Compound leaves, but they have a pair of leaflets at the tip. Its pods are strikingly longer and larger, and are not usually in bunches like the Tree Wistaria.

Human uses
The wood is termite-resistant, and has been used for wagons, yokes, axe handles, fence poles and furniture.

Links with animals
Baboons and monkeys eat the flower-buds, but otherwise the tree is seldom utilised.

Gardening
This is a very attractive garden tree and will grow well in most soil types. It grows fast in sandy soils, and can be grown easily from seed. Once established it is fairly drought- and frost-resistant.

SWEET-PEA SUB-FAMILY OF PEA FAMILY   Papilionoideae   Tree no 232

Zebrawood Flat-bean
Dalbergia melanoxylon

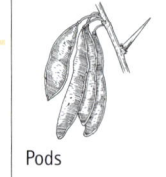

AFRIKAANS Sebrahout   **TSONGA** Shilutsi, Shipalatsi   **TSWANA** Mokelete   **VENDA** Muhuluri
ZULU umPhingo

Dalbergia honours the 18th Century Swedish Botanists Nils and Carl Dalberg; **melanoxylon** refers to the dark purple-black heartwood.

Pods

Where you'll find this tree easily
The Zebrawood Flat-bean grows in groups where there is increased moisture, in drainage lines, often on road verges and in rocky areas.
- It is easiest to find this tree on the plains in both the north and south Knob-thorn/Marula Savannah (F), in Thorn Veld (E) and in drainage lines in Mopane/Bushwillow Woodlands (P).
- It is also on crests and in drainage lines in Mixed Bushwillow Woodlands (A), and on Alluvial Plains (M).
- In the forests of Tree Mopane Savannah (O) it is easy to find among the uniform stands of Mopane.

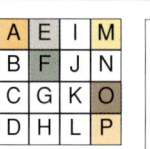

A	E	I	M
B	F	J	N
C	G	K	O
D	H	L	P

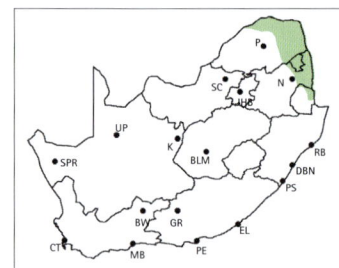

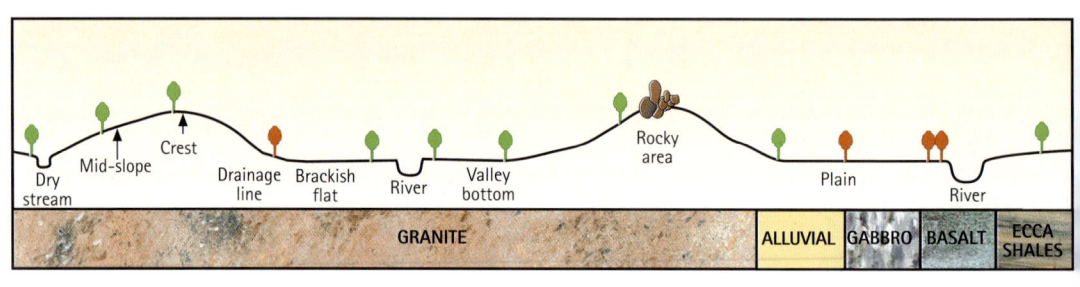

Dry stream — Mid-slope — Crest — Drainage line — Brackish flat — River — Valley bottom — Rocky area — Plain — River

GRANITE   ALLUVIAL   GABBRO   BASALT   ECCA SHALES

GIFF
- It is a multi-stemmed shrub or tree with a densely branched and intertwined, V-shaped canopy.
- Thick spines stand out at right angles from the branches, branchlets and younger stems.
- The spines are themselves modified branchlets, and often have leaves and flowers growing on them.
- The bark in young branches is pale grey, while the bark of older trees is rough and peels off in long strips.
- The Once Compound leaves are soft and droopy, and have a single leaf at the tip.
- Masses of tiny, greenish-white, scented, pea-shaped flowers cover these trees in summer.
- The papery bean pods can be seen on the tree for long periods from March to July.

The fine, Once Compound leaves and spines are distinctive.

Seasonal changes
Deciduous. The leaves turn yellow in autumn. The spines will help with identification even when no leaves are present.

Height: 2 - 4 m
Density: Sparse

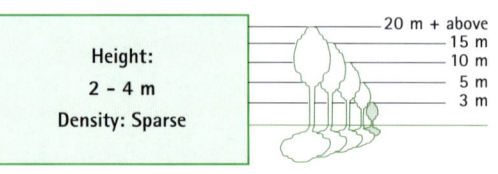

20 m + above / 15 m / 10 m / 5 m / 3 m

	Oct	Nov	Dec	Jan	Feb	Mar	Apr	May	Jun	Jul	Aug	Sep
Leaf												
Flower												
Fruit/Pod												

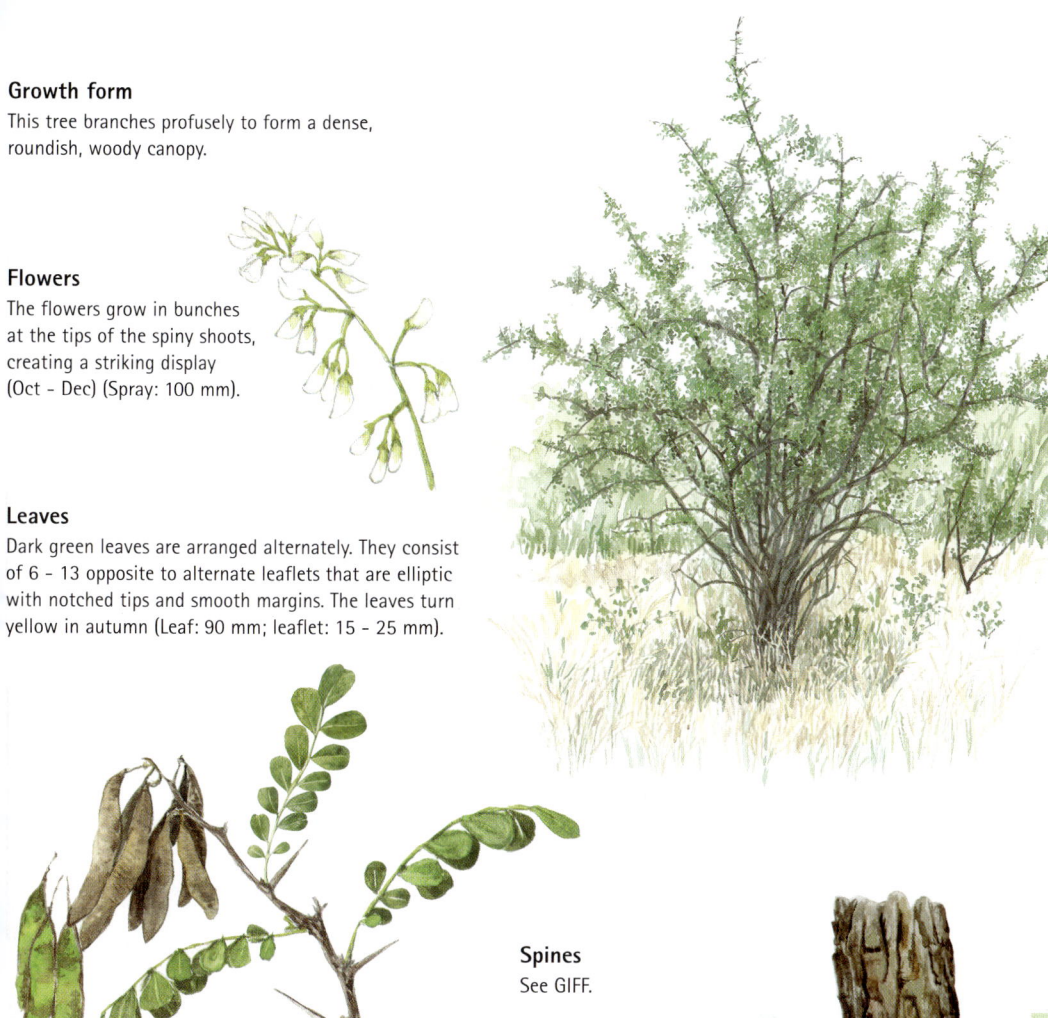

Growth form
This tree branches profusely to form a dense, roundish, woody canopy.

Flowers
The flowers grow in bunches at the tips of the spiny shoots, creating a striking display (Oct - Dec) (Spray: 100 mm).

Leaves
Dark green leaves are arranged alternately. They consist of 6 - 13 opposite to alternate leaflets that are elliptic with notched tips and smooth margins. The leaves turn yellow in autumn (Leaf: 90 mm; leaflet: 15 - 25 mm).

Spines
See GIFF.

Pods
The flat, oblong pods grow in bunches, are slightly swollen over the seeds, and are pointed at both ends. They are pale brown when young, but grey-brown to black when mature. They do not split open on the tree (Mar - Jul) (50 x 13 mm).

Bark
Mature bark is pale grey, relatively rough, and peels in flat, irregular-shaped strips. Younger bark is smoother with thick spines.

SEASONALLY STRIKING
Zebrawood Flat-bean

Look-alike tree
Because of its leaves, spines and pods, at first glance it can be confused with small Acacias. The leaves, however, are Once Compound, not Twice Compound, and each flower is pea-shaped not a fluffy ball or spike. These features distinguish Zebrawood from the Acacias and Albizias, compared on pages 74-77.

Links with animals
Elephant favour the roots. Leaves are eaten by giraffe, impala and kudu.

Human uses
The roots are used to treat headaches and toothache. Striking jewellery, such as earrings and brooches, is made out of the wood and the roots which both have very distinctive black and white colouring.

Gardening
This is not a particularly attractive garden plant except when flowering. It grows well from seed but grows slowly.

111

THORN-TREE SUB-FAMILY OF PEA FAMILY   Mimosoideae   Tree no 154

BROAD-POD ALBIZIA   *Albizia forbesii*

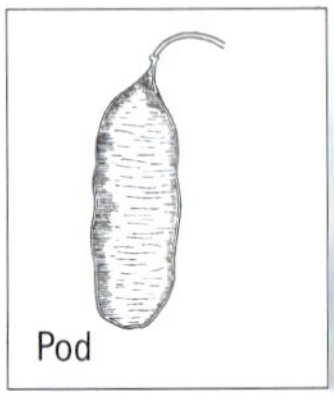

AFRIKAANS Breëpeulvalsdoring   **TSONGA** Rinyani   **ZULU** Umnala albizia, umNala

Albizia is named after Filippo degli Albizzi, an Italian nobleman who introduced the plant to European horticulture; **forbesii** is named after John Forbes (1798-1823).

Pod

Where you'll find this tree easily
The Broad-pod Albizia grows singly, alongside rivers in deep sandy soils.

A	E	I	M
B	F	J	N
C	G	K	O
D	H	L	P

- It is easiest to find this tree in Riverine areas (H) in the more southern parts of the Lowveld.
- It can be found in drainage lines of Sabie/Crocodile Thorn Thickets (D) and Knob-thorn/Marula Savannah (F).

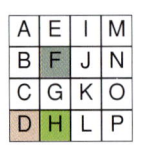

Dry stream — Mid-slope — Crest — Drainage line — Brackish flat — River — Valley bottom — Rocky area — River

GRANITE   ECCA SHALES   BASALT   RHYOLITE

GIFF
- This is a tall, single-trunked, low-branching tree with a few large branches forming a spreading canopy of feathery leaves.
- **Being an Albizia, it has no thorns, even though it looks very like an Acacia, with its Twice Compound leaves.**
- The bark is smooth and pale grey and may be broken into rectangular blocks that tend to flake.
- Both young leaves and branches have velvety, grey hairs.
- **The tree is covered by conspicuous, pincushion-like flowers in spring.**
- **The broad, flat, russet pods are marked cross-wise with fine lines and have thickened margins.**

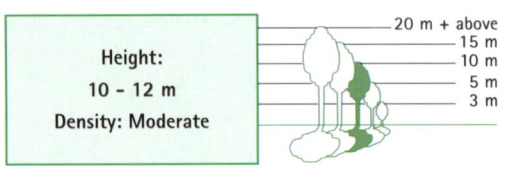

Seasonal changes
Deciduous. Recognisable for most of the year owing to the presence of the russet pods that stay on the tree for long periods.

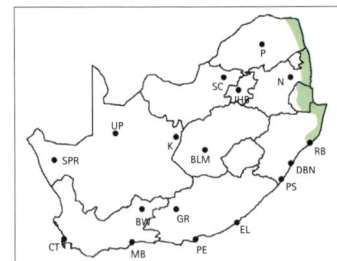

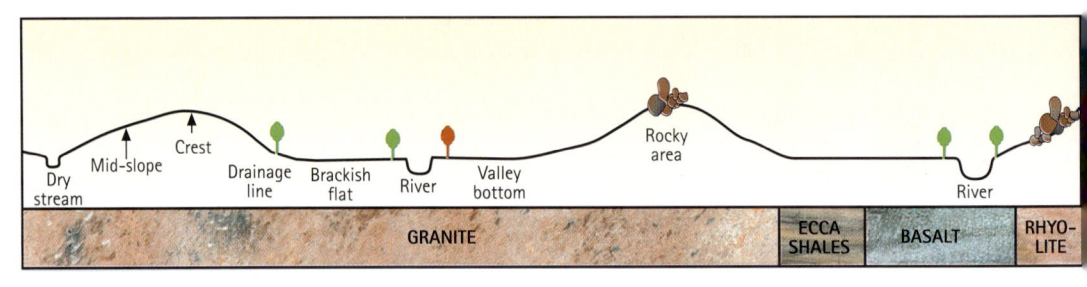

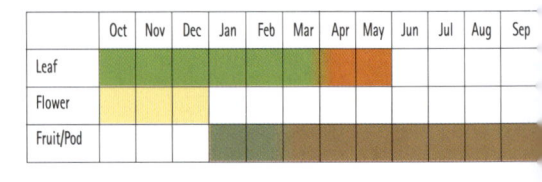

A distinctive Broad-pod Albizia grows on the Lower Sabie Road in Kruger, near the Sabie River bridge.

Height: 10 - 12 m
Density: Moderate

20 m + above
15 m
10 m
5 m
3 m

	Oct	Nov	Dec	Jan	Feb	Mar	Apr	May	Jun	Jul	Aug	Sep
Leaf												
Flower												
Fruit/Pod												

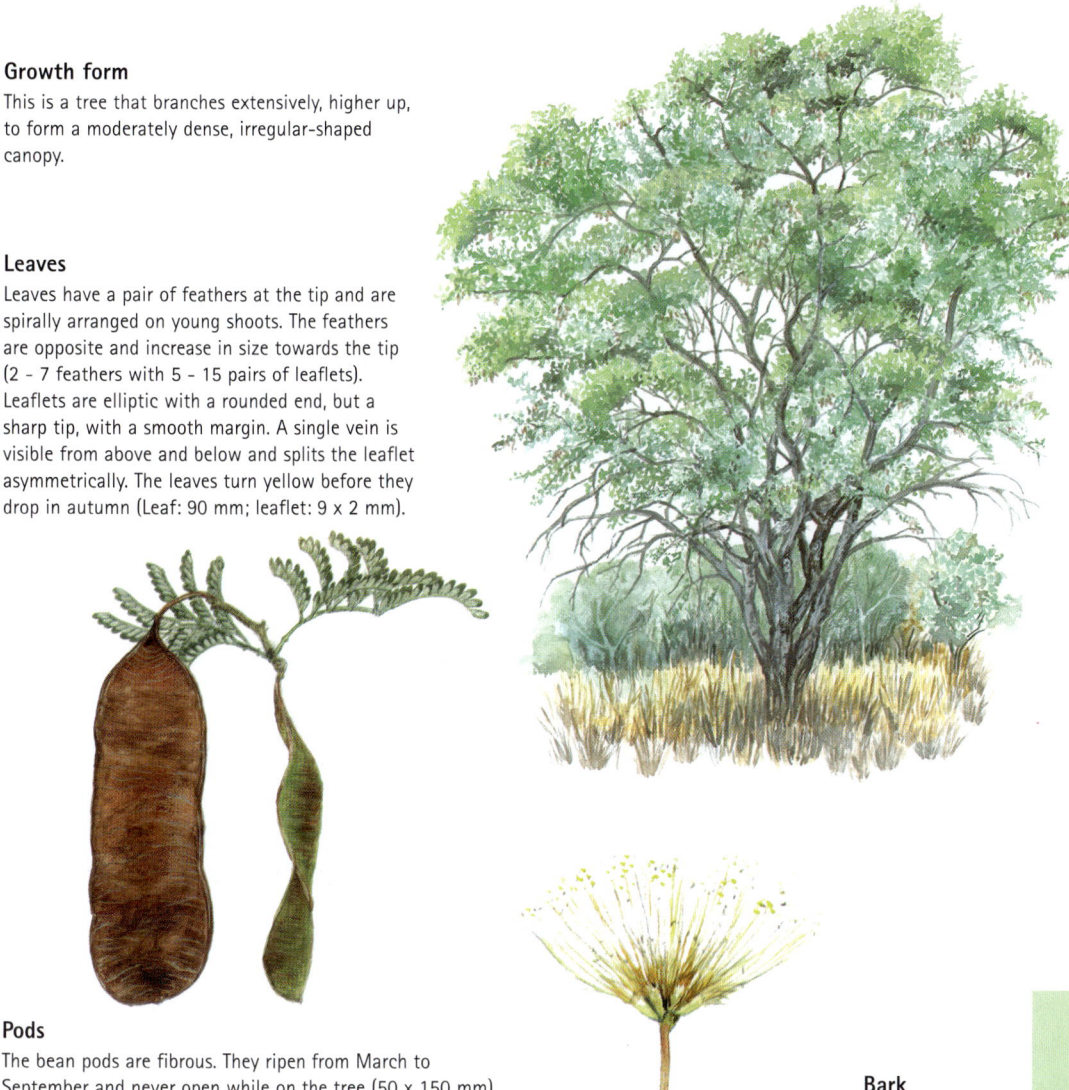

Growth form
This is a tree that branches extensively, higher up, to form a moderately dense, irregular-shaped canopy.

Leaves
Leaves have a pair of feathers at the tip and are spirally arranged on young shoots. The feathers are opposite and increase in size towards the tip (2 - 7 feathers with 5 - 15 pairs of leaflets). Leaflets are elliptic with a rounded end, but a sharp tip, with a smooth margin. A single vein is visible from above and below and splits the leaflet asymmetrically. The leaves turn yellow before they drop in autumn (Leaf: 90 mm; leaflet: 9 x 2 mm).

Pods
The bean pods are fibrous. They ripen from March to September and never open while on the tree (50 x 150 mm).

Flowers
Typical Albizia flowers appear with or after the leaves, and have prominent, white to yellow stamens (Oct - Dec) (30 mm).

Bark
See GIFF.

SEASONALLY STRIKING
Broad-pod Albizia

Look-alike tree
The Bushveld Albizia, *Albizia harveyi*, p. 45, is normally a smaller tree, and is more common on brackish flats. The leaves are longer (150 mm), with 18 pairs of feathers and 12 - 24 very small, sickle-shaped leaflets (4 - 6 mm). It has pods that are pale brown and papery, growing in bunches that burst open on the tree. See Albizia comparisons, p. 77.

Human uses
The wood is used for carving and as corner posts for huts. The roots were combined with other ingredients to create a potion to ward off evil spirits.

Gardening
This is a very attractive shade tree that grows well in most gardens. Seeds germinate easily, but the tree is not drought- or frost-resistant.

Links with animals
Leaves and twigs are heavily utilised by elephant and other browsing game.

113

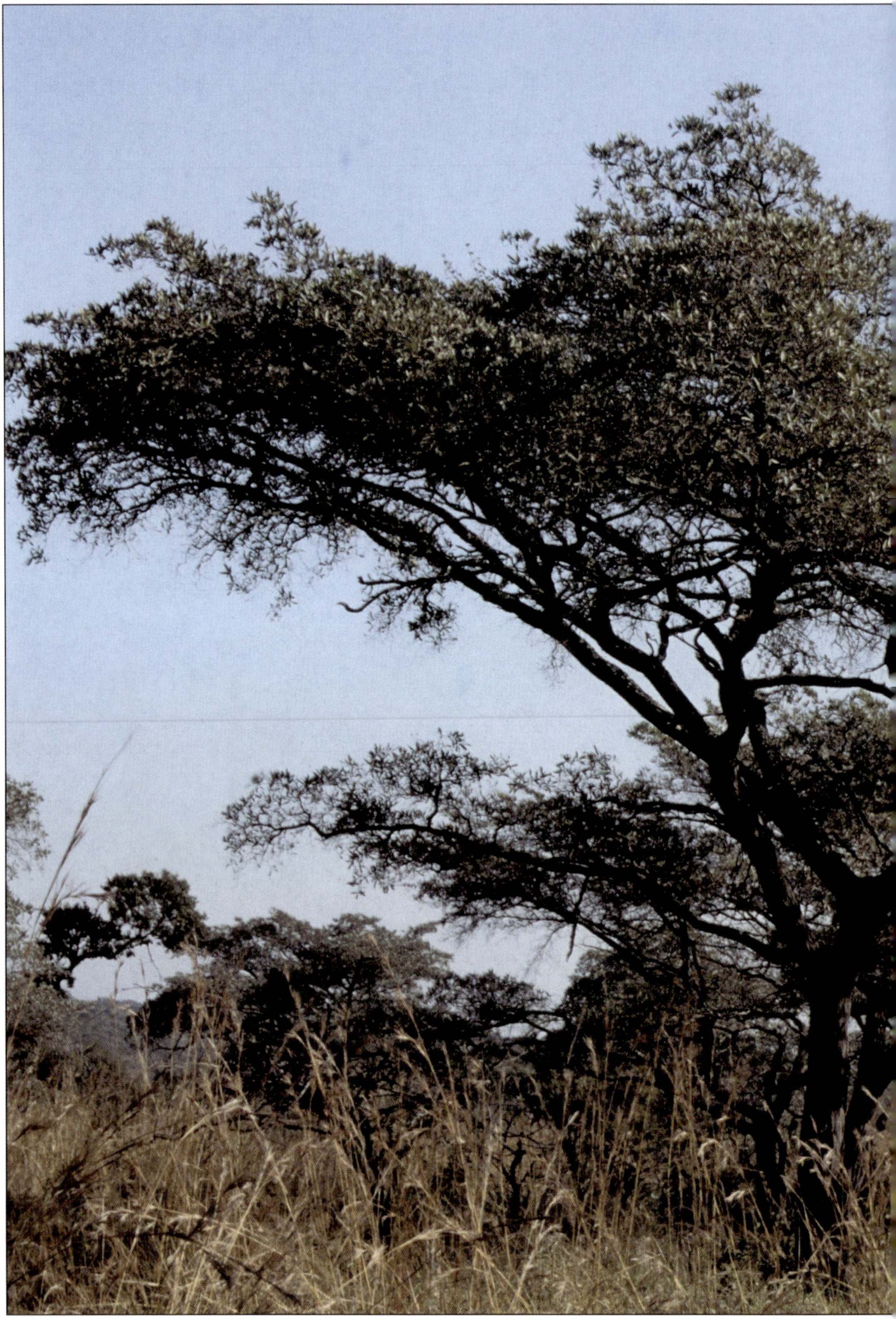

FIND TREES BY ECOZONE

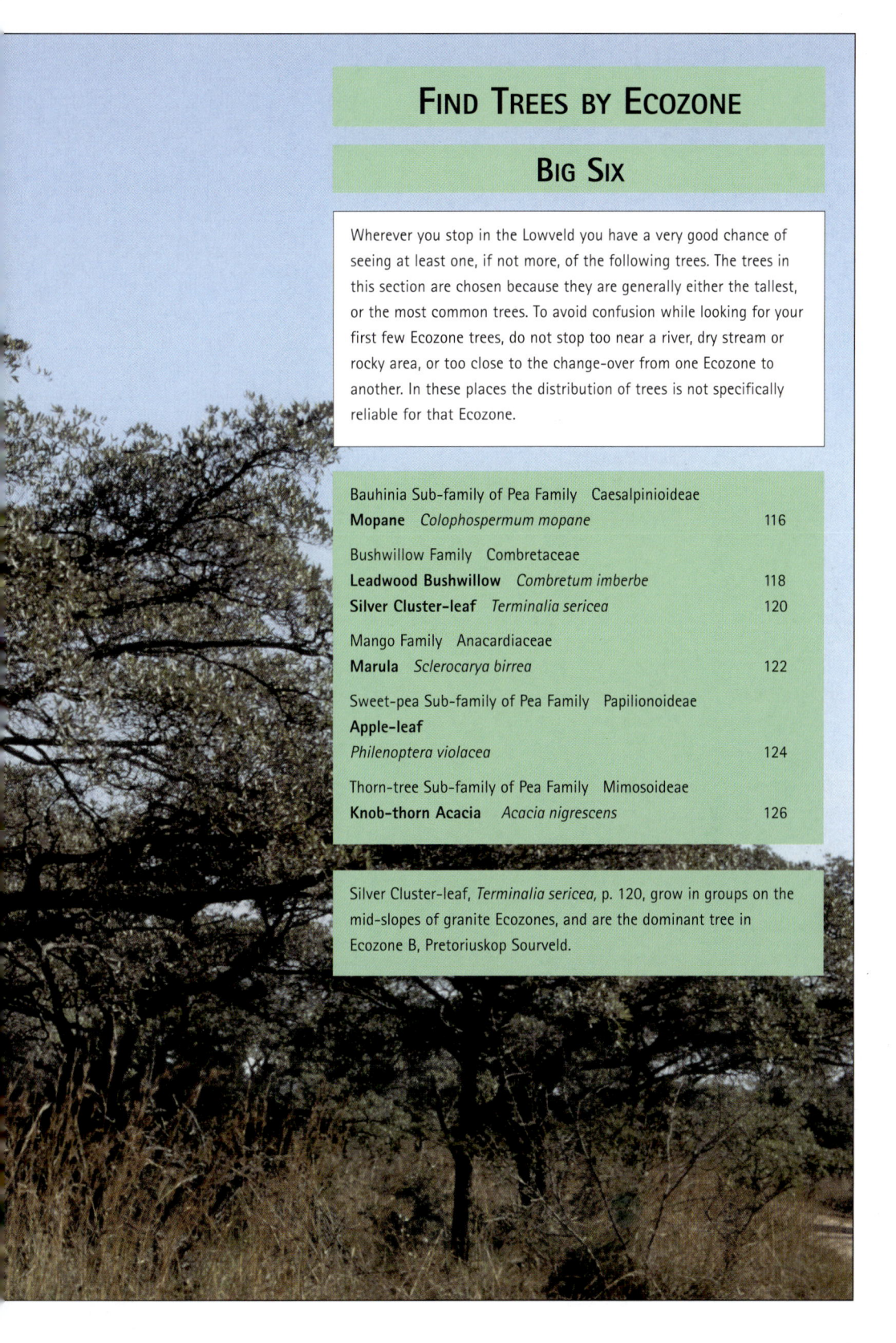

BIG SIX

Wherever you stop in the Lowveld you have a very good chance of seeing at least one, if not more, of the following trees. The trees in this section are chosen because they are generally either the tallest, or the most common trees. To avoid confusion while looking for your first few Ecozone trees, do not stop too near a river, dry stream or rocky area, or too close to the change-over from one Ecozone to another. In these places the distribution of trees is not specifically reliable for that Ecozone.

Bauhinia Sub-family of Pea Family   Caesalpinioideae
Mopane   *Colophospermum mopane*   116

Bushwillow Family   Combretaceae
Leadwood Bushwillow   *Combretum imberbe*   118
Silver Cluster-leaf   *Terminalia sericea*   120

Mango Family   Anacardiaceae
Marula   *Sclerocarya birrea*   122

Sweet-pea Sub-family of Pea Family   Papilionoideae
Apple-leaf
Philenoptera violacea   124

Thorn-tree Sub-family of Pea Family   Mimosoideae
Knob-thorn Acacia   *Acacia nigrescens*   126

Silver Cluster-leaf, *Terminalia sericea*, p. 120, grow in groups on the mid-slopes of granite Ecozones, and are the dominant tree in Ecozone B, Pretoriuskop Sourveld.

| BAUHINIA SUB-FAMILY OF PEA FAMILY | Caesalpinioideae | Tree no 198 |

MOPANE
Colophospermum mopane

AFRIKAANS Mopanie **N. SOTHO** Mopane **SISWATI** Mophne **TSONGA** Nxanatsi **VENDA** Mupani
ZULU umZololo

Colophospermum is from the Greek *kolophonios* + *sperma* meaning 'resin' + 'seed', referring to the resin glands on the seeds; **mopane** is derived from the local names for the tree, many of which refer to 'butterfly'.

Leaves

Where you'll find this tree easily
The Mopane tree grows in large, uniform groups north of the Olifants River. It survives in poorer soils than most other trees, and therefore tends to become dominant.
- The stunted tree is found in vast kilometre stands in Mopane Shrubveld (L) and in Mopane/Bushwillow Woodlands (P).
- The tall tree is dominant in Tree Mopane Savannah (O).
- It is also found in the northern parts of the Lebombo Mountain Bushveld (I), as well as in Alluvial Plains (M).

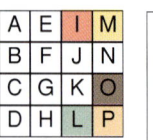

A	E	I	M
B	F	J	N
C	G	K	O
D	H	L	P

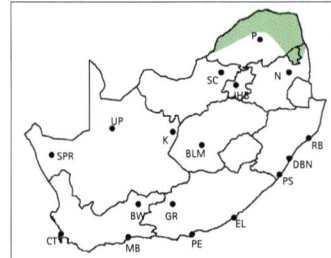

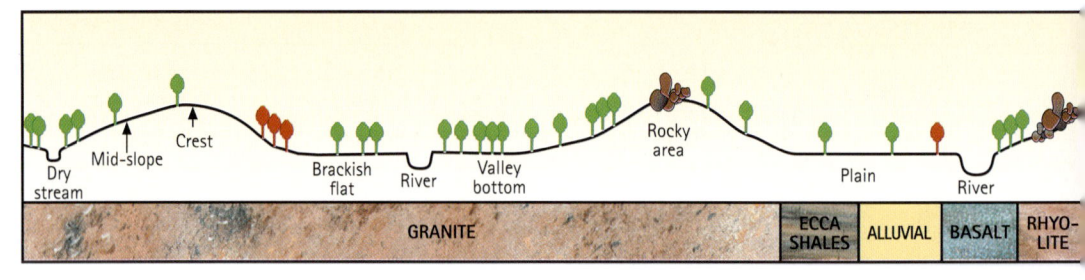

Dry stream — Mid-slope — Crest — Brackish flat — River — Valley bottom — Rocky area — Plain — River

GRANITE | ECCA SHALES | ALLUVIAL | BASALT | RHYOLITE

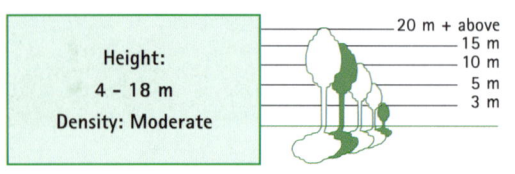

GIFF
- The Mopanes cover vast areas, as far as the eye can see, with few other shrubs or trees between them.
- It can be a small, stunted shrub or a tall, magnificent tree depending on both the Ecozone and soil where it grows. Both are illustrated on the opposite page.
- Shrubs are multi-stemmed with a V-form, and a round, poorly developed canopy.
- When large, the tree has a single, straight trunk and is high-branching, with a narrow canopy.
- **The Compound, butterfly leaf, with several veins radiating from the base, is characteristic; a number of local names imply 'butterfly'.**
- Flattened, oval, leathery, kidney-shaped pods are covered by glands that make them sticky, from April to June.

Seasonal changes
Deciduous. This tree has rich yellow and brown colours in autumn. It is bare throughout the winter. The new leaves that appear in early summer have a red tinge.

A tall Mopane tree shines in the sunlight, in bright autumn foliage.

Height: 4 - 18 m
Density: Moderate

20 m + above / 15 m / 10 m / 5 m / 3 m

	Oct	Nov	Dec	Jan	Feb	Mar	Apr	May	Jun	Jul	Aug	Sep
Leaf												
Flower												
Fruit/Pod												

Growth form
In large trees, the Mopane branches grow upwards, to form a moderately dense canopy. The shrub form is low-branching. One or other type tends to dominate an area, but both do often occur together.

Leaves
The leaves are opposite, with a smooth margin, and have an aromatic smell. A minute, third 'leaflet' can be seen between the butterfly wings. Veins radiate from the butterfly join. New leaves are reddish, and mature leaves turn yellow-gold during autumn (80 x 35 mm).

Tall tree

Pods
Pods turn pale brown when ripe from April to June (50 x 20 mm).

Flowers
Inconspicuous, greenish flowers grow in sprays at the ends of the branches (Dec - Jan).

Bark
The bark is fissured lengthways.

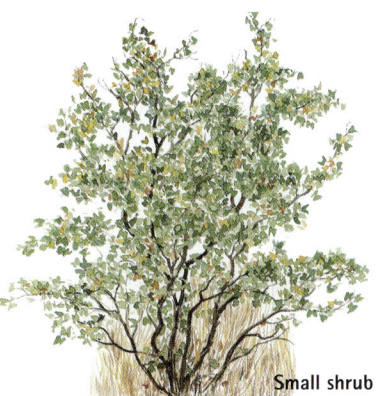

Small shrub

Look-alike tree
In the northern part of Kruger this tree can be confused with the Small False Mopane, *Guibourtia conjugata*, p. 49. It also has Compound butterfly leaves, with a pair of opposite leaflets, and has five veins from the base. Leaflets are smaller, and the margins are wavy, not smooth. The flowers are creamy, and the pods are close to being circular, not kidney-shaped.

Human uses
The wood produces good coals when burned. Venereal diseases are treated with extracts of the wood. The bark is used for tanning. Mopane worms that feed on the leaves are an important source of protein.

Gardening
Because of its predominance in certain areas, it has been largely ignored as a garden plant. However, where it is not too common, naturally, it could be an attractive tree in a larger garden, despite being deciduous, and slow-growing. It grows easily from seed, and is not frost-resistant.

Links with animals
The leaves are not very palatable but are eaten by elephant. Fallen leaves are eaten by almost all animals during drought periods. Scale-insects that infect the leaves are eaten by baboon. Holes in the trunk provide nesting sites for birds and small mammals.

BIG SIX
Mopane

| BUSHWILLOW FAMILY | Combretaceae | Tree no 539 |

LEADWOOD BUSHWILLOW *Combretum imberbe*

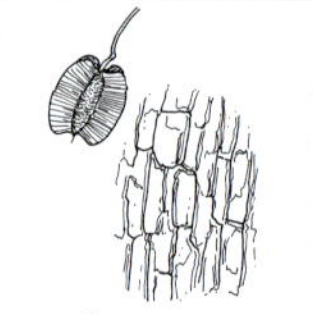

AFRIKAANS Hardekool **PEDI** Motswiri **SISWATI** umMono, imPondozendhlovu **TSONGA** Mondzo
TSWANA Motswere **VENDA** Muheri **ZULU** umBondwe omnyama

Combretum is derived from the classical Latin name for the genus used by Pliny, 23-79 AD; **i**mberbe refers to the hairless leaves.

Pod/bark

Where you'll find this tree easily
The Leadwood Bushwillow grows singly in the open on basalt plains, and in small groups along rivers and large drainage lines of granite Ecozones.
- It is easiest to find this tree along most major rivers (H).
- It is also easy to spot on the plains and along drainage lines of the Knob-thorn/Marula Savannah (F), and along larger drainage lines in Mopane/Bushwillow Woodlands (P).
- It is found in valley bottoms, or along drainage lines in granite Ecozones, Mixed Bushwillow Woodlands (A), Pretoriuskop Sourveld (B) and Malelane Mountain Bushveld (C).
- It is also easy to spot in Olifants Rugged Veld (J), in Alluvial Plains (M) and in Tree Mopane Savannah (O).

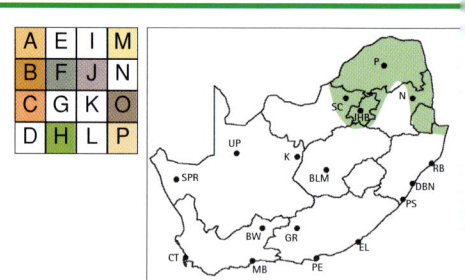

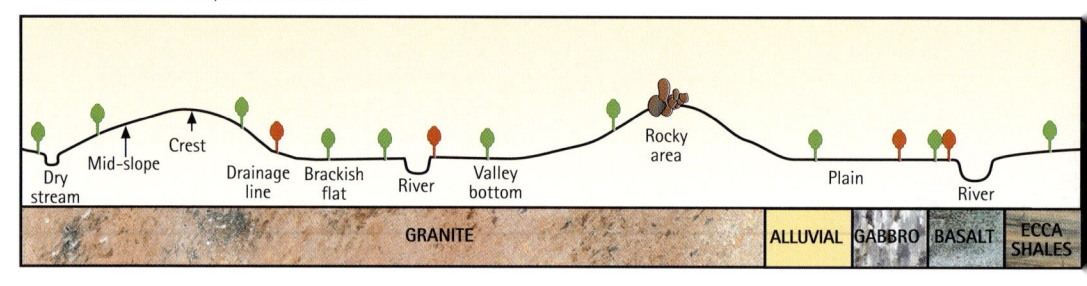

GIFF
- This is a very tall, high-branching, majestic tree.
- **The pale grey bark breaks up into small, regular blocks, like snakeskin, and is characteristic.**
- The Simple, opposite leaves are characteristically grey-green to yellow-green, with silvery scales.
- The sparse foliage therefore has a yellow tinge throughout the year.
- Mature trees often have dead, bare branches and twigs.
- **It has typical, but small, four-winged, Bushwillow pods, that are initially pale lime-green and darken to straw-coloured as they mature.**

An old Leadwood, on a riverbank, glows in the sunset as a breeding herd of elephant passes underneath. A land of giants!

Height: 15 m
Density: Sparse

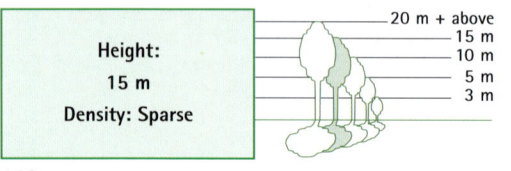

Seasonal changes
Deciduous. Leaves turn yellow-brown before falling in winter. The majestic growth form and characteristic pale grey, snake-skin bark make identification possible throughout the year.

	Oct	Nov	Dec	Jan	Feb	Mar	Apr	May	Jun	Jul	Aug	Sep
Leaf												
Flower												
Fruit/Pod												

Growth form
It has a single, straight trunk with branches growing both horizontally and upwards. The canopy is wide-spreading and sparse. Dead trees take a long time to decay, and some of these have been carbon-dated at over one thousand years old. Trees damaged by elephants or other animals usually recover well.

Leaves
The leaves are broadly elliptic to oval with a wavy margin. They are leathery and without hairs. The tip and the base of the leaf are rounded to broadly tapering (25 - 80 x 10 - 30 mm).

Pods
The pod is small for the size of the tree and often drops just after it has ripened in autumn (Feb – Jun) (15 - 19 mm diam.).

Flowers
The small, creamy to creamy-yellow flowers are sweet-smelling. The long, slender spikes grow in the angle formed by the leaf or at the ends of branches (Nov – Mar) (Flower-spikes: 40 - 80 x up to 15 mm).

Bark
See GIFF.

Look-alike tree
While young, this tree can be confused with other Bushwillows. See pages 71-73 for comparisons.

Gardening
The Leadwood Bushwillow will grow in most well-drained gardens. It is fairly drought-resistant, but could be damaged by frost. It can easily be grown from seed, but is extremely slow-growing forming exceptionally hard wood. The seeds are thought to be poisonous.

Human uses
As the wood burns slowly and forms good coals, it was highly sought-after as cooking fuel. However, to protect our trees, wood fires are discouraged. The calcium-rich ash is mixed with water as a whitewash on houses. The flowers are used in a cough mixture, and smoke from the burning leaf is inhaled to relieve coughs and colds.

Links with animals
The leaves are eaten by giraffe, kudu, elephant and impala.

BIG SIX
Leadwood Bushwillow

| BUSHWILLOW FAMILY | Combretaceae | Tree no 551 |

SILVER CLUSTER-LEAF — *Terminalia sericea*

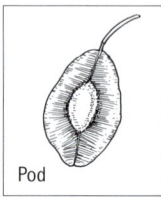

AFRIKAANS Vaalboom **N. SOTHO** Mogônônô, Moletsa-nakana **TSONGA** Nkonono
TSWANA Mogonono **VENDA** Mususu **ZULU** amaNgwe-amphlophe

Terminalia describes the way in which the leaves are clustered at the ends of the shoots; **sericea** refers to the soft, silky leaves.

Pod

Where you'll find this tree easily
The Silver Cluster-leaf grows in loose groups on the seeplines of granite crests, as well as in areas with deep sand.

- This tree is easiest to find on seeplines in Pretoriuskop Sourveld (B), as well as in Sandveld (N) on the slopes and ridges of sandstone hills.
- It can also be spotted on seeplines in Mixed Bushwillow Woodlands (A), in Malelane Mountain Bushveld (C), Sabie/Crocodile Thorn Thickets (D) and in Mopane/Bushwillow Woodlands (P).
- It can be found on crests of Ecozones A and C.

A	E	I	M
B	F	J	N
C	G	K	O
D	H	L	P

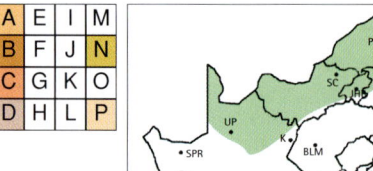

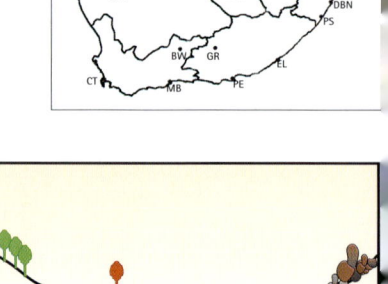

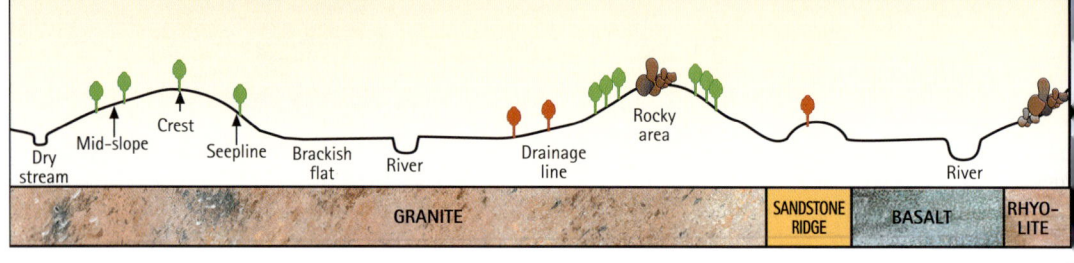

GIFF
- This is a silvery-blue, upright, single-trunked tree.
- **The branches leave the trunk at different levels to form distinct, horizontal layers.**
- The rough, dark bark is deeply fissured lengthways.
- The Simple leaves are clustered towards the tips of slender branchlets and twigs.
- **The young leaves have silver hairs, giving the tree a characteristic silver shine.**
- The two-winged pods are pinky-purple when mature, drying to brown, and remain on the tree for long periods.

Silver Cluster-leaf trees are most commonly single-trunked and relatively high-branching.

Seasonal changes
Deciduous. Although this tree is without leaves for most of the winter, the horizontal, branching growth form is characteristic and makes identification easy. In summer the new leaves with their silvery hairs further assist identification.

Height:
6 – 20 m
Density: Moderate

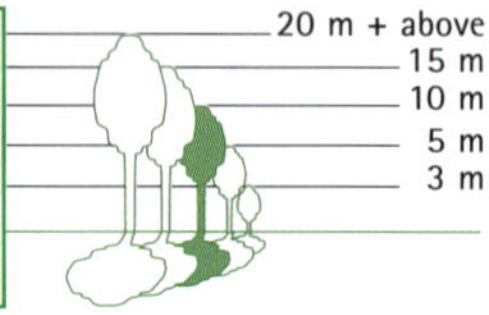

	Oct	Nov	Dec	Jan	Feb	Mar	Apr	May	Jun	Jul	Aug	Sep
Leaf												
Flower												
Fruit/Pod												

Growth form
This tree has a moderately dense, spreading canopy.

Leaves
The spirally arranged leaves are elliptic with a broadly tapering tip that tends to be pointed, and a narrowly tapering base. They are pale green to grey-silvery-green and leathery, and have a smooth margin (55 - 120 x 13 - 45 mm).

Pods
The pods grow in bunches at the ends of branchlets and twigs. They may remain on the tree until the next flowering season (Jan - Jun) (25 - 60 x 15 - 25 mm).

Flowers
The flowers are inconspicuous, very pungent, and cream to yellow. They grow in spikes in the angle made by the leaves (Sep – Jan) (Spike: up to 70 mm long; individual flower: 4 mm diam.).

Bark
The branchlets are dark brown or purplish. They flake in rings and strips, to reveal pale brown under-bark. Young twigs are covered in fine, silvery hairs.

Look-alike tree
The Silver Cluster-leaf has no Look-alike trees, but is shown in the Bushwillow Comparisons, pages 71-73.

Gardening
This tree grows well in deep, sandy soils and can be an attractive addition to gardens. It is fairly frost- and drought-resistant but is difficult to grow from the few undamaged seeds that may be found.

Human uses
Fence poles, household goods, firewood and axe handles are made from the wood. Extracts of the bark are used as an antidote to poisons, to treat diabetes and wounds, and for tanning. Root extracts are used as eye lotions and as remedies for stomach disorders, diarrhoea and pneumonia.

Links with animals
Although the nutritional value is low, leaves and young shoots are eaten by elephant, giraffe, kudu and impala. Dry leaves on the ground are eaten by wildebeest, and branches by elephant and giraffe.

BIG SIX
Silver Cluster-leaf

| MANGO FAMILY | Anacardiaceae | Tree no 360 |

MARULA *Sclerocarya birrea*

AFRIKAANS Maroela **N. SOTHO** Morula **SISWATI** umGana **TSONGA** Nkanyi **TSWANA** Morula
VENDA Mufula **ZULU** umGanu

Sclerocarya is from the Greek for a 'walnut', referring to the hard kernel inside the soft, fleshy fruit; **birrea** is based on the common name of the tree *'birr'* in Senegal and Gambia.

Leaves

Where you'll find this tree easily
The Marula tree grows singly throughout the Lowveld in a wide variety of Habitats, but often in open woodland or close to rivers.

A	E	I	M
B	F	J	N
C	G	K	O
D	H	L	P

- This tree is most common, and can most easily be found on the plains in both the north and south of Knob-thorn/Marula Savannah (F).
- It can be found in Riverine (H), and along the rivers and large streams in most other Ecozones. It is easiest to identify in A, B, D, E and J.
- It is striking in rocky areas in the north of Lebombo Mountain Bushveld (I).

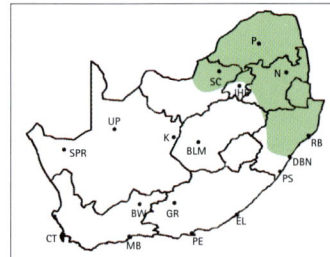

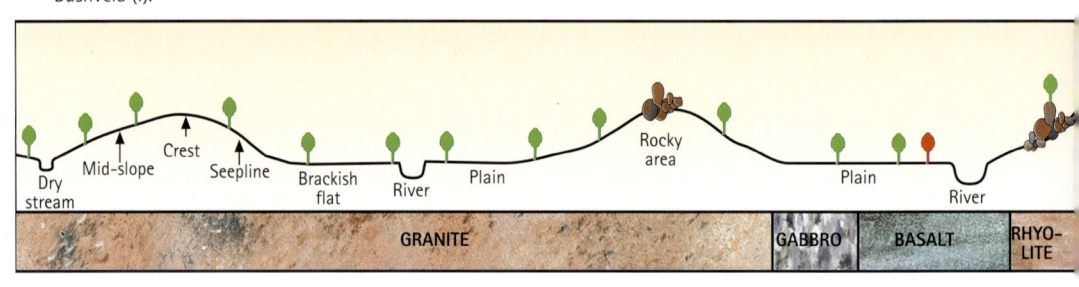

Dry stream — Mid-slope — Crest — Seepline — Brackish flat — River — Plain — Rocky area — Plain — River

GRANITE   GABBRO   BASALT   RHYO-LITE

GIFF
- This is a single-trunked, high-branching tree with a characteristic semi-circular canopy.
- **The bark often peels in conspicuous, characteristic, rounded depressions, exposing the smooth pink-brown under-bark.**
- The Once Compound blue-green leaves have long leaf and leaflet stems that are often tinged with pink.
- Leaves hang from the end of thickened twigs that stand out like stubby fingers, in winter.
- There are 3 to 7 pairs of opposite leaflets and a single leaflet at the tip.
- Marula fruit is often seen under the female trees during January and February.

Seasonal changes
Deciduous. The shiny leaves turn yellow-green before they drop, and the trees have long periods without leaves. However the characteristic bark and the stubby twigs are very striking, making identification very easy in winter.

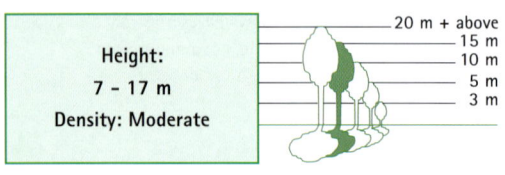

In the winter Marulas are very easy to identify with their bare, short, stubby twigs.

Height: 7 – 17 m
Density: Moderate

20 m + above
15 m
10 m
5 m
3 m

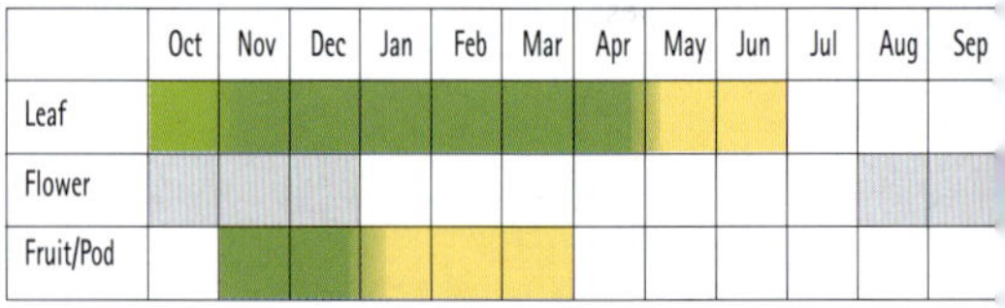

	Oct	Nov	Dec	Jan	Feb	Mar	Apr	May	Jun	Jul	Aug	Sep
Leaf												
Flower												
Fruit/Pod												

Growth form
It has a straight trunk that branches into a few bare, main branches. These grow slightly upwards and horizontally to form a moderately dense canopy.

Leaves
The leaves are alternate and leaflets are elliptic, with a smooth margin (Leaves: 150 - 300 mm; leaflets: 30 - 100 x 15 - 40 mm).

(M)

Flowers
The inconspicuous plum/pink and white flowers grow in sprays at the ends of branches and twigs. They appear with or before the new leaves in spring. Male and female flowers grow on separate trees (Male: spray 50 - 80 mm; female: 30 mm).

Fruit
The oval, plum-sized fruit ripens from January to March. The fruit drops when it is still green and ripens on the ground. Each fruit has two to three seeds, and their holes can be seen in the central woody stones (Visible Nov - Mar) (40 mm).

(F)

Bark
See GIFF.

Look-alike tree
The False-marula Lannea, *Lannea schweinfurthii*, p. 38, also has Once Compound leaves that are clustered on the ends of relatively thick branchlets. Its leaves usually consist of only 1 - 3 pairs of leaflets, with the terminal leaflet larger. In addition the leaflet-stems are noticeably short, being under 5 mm. Its leaflets are brighter green (not blue-green), and are slightly rounder than those of the Marula. The False-marula Lannea has bark that peels in large patches or strips, not like the small, round depressions of the Marula. See the comparisons of various Once Compound leaves in the Distinctive Striking Features, pages 69-70.

Gardening
This is a very attractive shade tree. Growing quickly and easily from seed, it is drought-resistant, but young trees are frost-sensitive.

Links with animals
The caterpillars of eight species of butterfly eat the leaves. Several types of parasitic plants grow on the Marula. The fruit is eaten by a wide variety of animals such as elephant, monkey, baboon, kudu, duiker, impala and zebra. The foliage and bark are eaten by elephant.

Human uses
Water that is stored in large quantities in the roots is tapped in times of drought. The fruit is very tasty and rich in Vitamin C. It is used to make beer, jelly and jam. Seed kernels are rich in oil and protein. The bark is traditionally used for the treatment of malaria. The tree plays an important part in marriage rituals, and has an integral role in fertility rites. The Marula is particularly sacred in the Lowveld.

BIG SIX
Marula

SWEET-PEA SUB-FAMILY OF PEA FAMILY — Papilionoideae — Tree no 238

APPLE-LEAF (RAIN TREE) — *Philenoptera violacea (Lonchocarpus capassa)*

AFRIKAANS Appelblaar **N. SOTHO** Lengana **SISWATI** isiHomuhomu **TSONGA** Mbhandzu, Mbandu
TSWANA Mohota **VENDA** Mufhanda **ZULU** umBandu, umPhandu, isiHomohomo

Philenoptera is from the Greek *philos* + *ptera* meaning 'manageable' + 'wing', referring to the wing on the pod that 'manages' seed dispersal; **violacea** refers to the violet-coloured flowers.

Leaves

Where you'll find this tree easily
The Apple-leaf grows singly along perennial rivers. Groups of smaller trees can also be found further from rivers in higher rainfall areas, or where the soil is waterlogged.
- It is easiest to find in Riverine areas (H) of granite Ecozones, and in moist areas in Mixed Bushwillow Woodlands (A), Pretoriuskop Sourveld (B), Malelane Mountain Bushveld (C), Sabie/Crocodile Thorn Thickets (D) and Mopane/Bushwillow Woodlands (P), as well as in Alluvial Plains (M).
- It is also found on moist plains and river areas of F, G, J and L.

Dry stream — Mid-slope — Crest — Drainage line — Brackish flat — River — Valley bottom — Rocky area — Plain — River
GRANITE — ALLUVIAL — GABBRO — BASALT — ECCA SHALES

GIFF
- The single, smooth, whitish-grey trunk meanders, and is high-branching.
- The tree has a sparse, irregularly shaped canopy with branches clearly visible between the leaves.
- Once Compound leaves have 1 to 2 pairs of opposite leaflets with a much larger leaflet at the tip.
- **The large, pale grey-green, leathery leaves are individually visible even from a distance of 30 metres.**
- **Bunches of pale lilac/purple flowers are conspicuous in late spring and early summer.**
- Pale green to pale brown, flat-winged bean pods grow in large, conspicuous bunches from January.

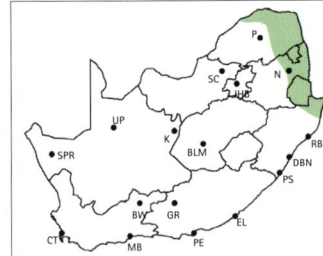

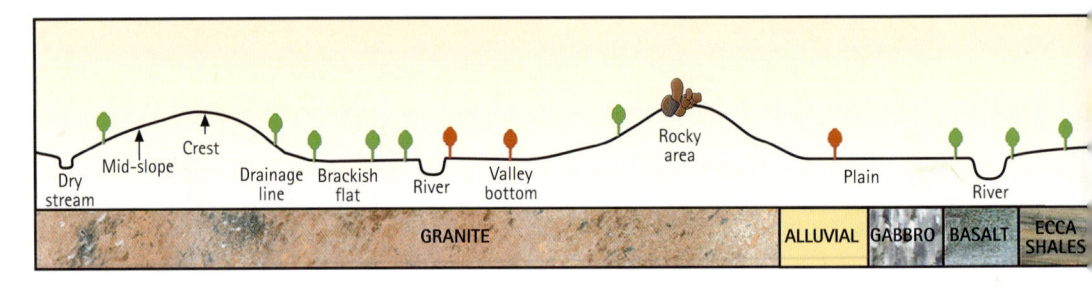

Apple-leaf trees have a distinctive meandering growth pattern.

Seasonal changes
Deciduous to semi-deciduous. This is one of the few trees that usually has some leaves in winter. Brown pods make identification easy in late summer and early winter.

Height: 5 - 18 m
Density: Sparse

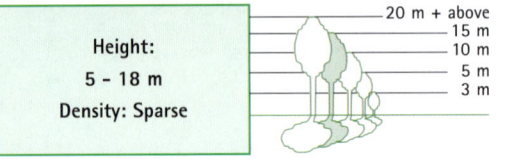

20 m + above / 15 m / 10 m / 5 m / 3 m

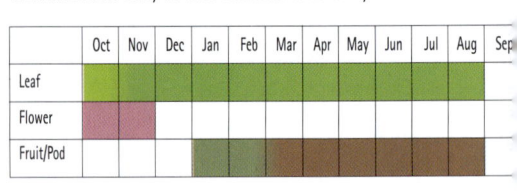

	Oct	Nov	Dec	Jan	Feb	Mar	Apr	May	Jun	Jul	Aug	Sep
Leaf												
Flower												
Fruit/Pod												

Growth form
The trunk divides into only a few main branches that tend to meander in various directions.

Flowers
Pea-like, fragrant flower bunches come out just before, or at the same time, as the new leaves in October and November. Dropped flowers are often seen as a carpet under the trees (Spray: 150 mm).

Pods
Pods stay on the tree long after they ripen in late summer (120 x 25 mm).

Leaves
The leaves are very hairy when young and become leathery when older. Except in early spring, they are often 'tatty' looking as if beaten brown by the wind, or partially eaten. They have a distinctive 'Granny Smith' apple smell when crushed (Leaf: 150 mm; leaflet: 60 x 35 mm).

Bark
The bark is smooth when young, and rougher when older.

Look-alike tree
When adult the Apple-leaf has no Look-alike trees.

Human uses
The wood provides poles for building, pestles for pounding grain, pots and axe handles.

Gardening
The unusual shape of this tree can make it an interesting addition to the garden. It will grow in most soil types, is fairly drought-resistant but not resistant to frost. Slow-growing, it can be grown easily from seed.

Links with animals
The tree may be infected with aphids (Froghopper, *Ptyelus grossus*) which excrete a sweet foam that drips down to form a wet patch on the ground. Hence the old name 'Rain Tree'. The leaves are not very palatable, but in the absence of other food young leaves are eaten by giraffe, eland, kudu, elephant, impala and steenbok. Elephants also eat the branches – in some areas this tree is known as the 'Elephant Tree'.

BIG SIX Apple-leaf

125

THORN-TREE SUB-FAMILY OF PEA FAMILY — Mimosoideae — Tree no 178

KNOB-THORN ACACIA — *Acacia nigrescens*

AFRIKAANS Knoppiesdoring **N. SOTHO** Mogaya **TSONGA** Nkaya **TSWANA** Mokala, Mokôba
VENDA Mukwalo **ZULU** umKhaya, umBhebe, isiBambapala

Acacia is taken from the Greek *akis* meaning a 'sharp point', referring to the thorns that grow on all African Acacia species; **nigrescens** means 'black' and probably refers to the pods.

Leaves

Where you'll find this tree easily

Larger Knob-thorn Acacias grow singly with many scattered trees in the area. They are often near drainage lines and rivers. Smaller, mature Knob-thorns grow in dense groups in clay soils.

- Large trees are easiest to find in Riverine areas (H), as well as on the plains of Knob-thorn/Marula Savannah (F).
- Smaller Knob-thorns are dominant on the plains of Stunted Knob-thorn Savannah (K).
- This tree can also be spotted easily in all the other granite, gabbro, Ecca shale and basalt Ecozones.

GIFF

- This is an upright Acacia, with a straight, single trunk that branches high up.
- It has a sparse, round, but relatively narrow canopy.
- **There are woody knobs with thorns on the trunks of young trees, and on large, young branches of older trees**
- The Twice Compound, opposite leaves are unusually shaped, with only 1 or 2 pairs of leaflets in each feather.
- Each leaflet is large for an Acacia, giving the impression of a butterfly-shaped leaf.
- **In spring and early summer, the Knob-thorn Acacia is the only tree to have no leaves and masses of white flower-spikes that age to creamy-brown.**

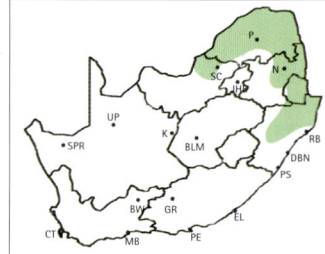

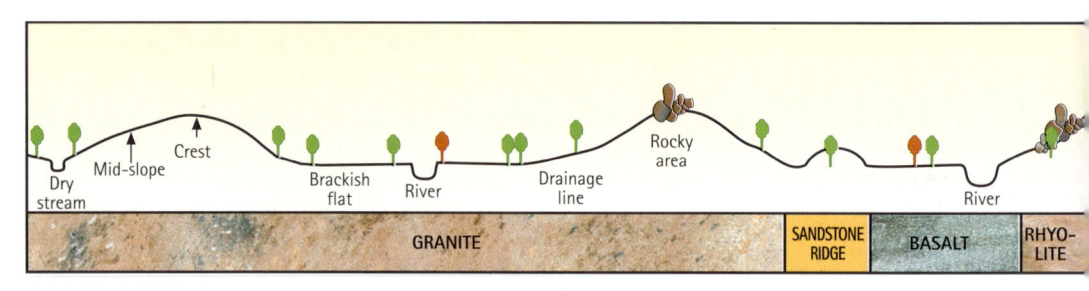

Knob-thorn Acacias dominate many Ecozones; they are at their most dramatic when in flower in early spring.

Seasonal changes

Deciduous. Leaves turn yellow before they fall in autumn. The knobs are still visible in winter making the tree easy to spot.

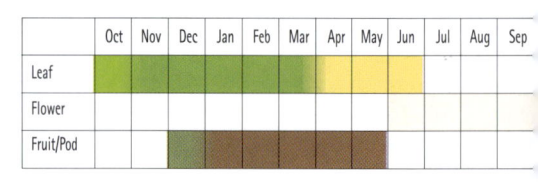

Height: 2 - 18 m
Density: Sparse

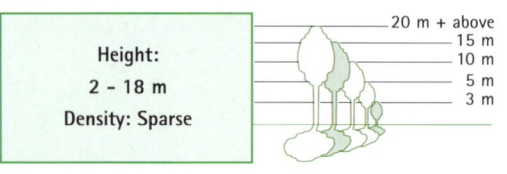

	Oct	Nov	Dec	Jan	Feb	Mar	Apr	May	Jun	Jul	Aug	Sep
Leaf												
Flower												
Fruit/Pod												

Growth form
See GIFF.

Leaves
The leaflets are pale green, almost round and have a smooth margin. There are 1 - 3 feather pairs, each feather consisting of 1 - 2 pairs of leaflets (Leaf: 35 x 80 mm; leaflet: 10 - 30 x 8 - 25 mm).

Flowers
From late June to early July, the tree has a plum-coloured sheen from the developing flower-buds. They open to form a spectacular, creamy-white display from July to September. The sweet-scented flower-spikes grow in clusters of 2 - 3 at the leaf-buds. Flowers are most abundant after good, late summer rains (30 - 100 mm).

Thorns
Downward-curving, hooked thorns grow on characteristic protruding knobs on the thicker branches and young trunks. Smaller, hooked thorns grow in pairs on branchlets and twigs (5 - 10 mm).

Pods
The flat bean pods hang down in clusters. They change from pale green to brown as they ripen. Pods never open on the trees but break up on the ground (Dec - Jun) (110 - 140 x 20 mm).

Bark
Younger branches and trees have pale bark that darkens with age to dark brown. It becomes rough and deeply fissured lengthwise, with yellowish under-bark.

Tall tree

Shrub

Look-alike tree
Can be confused with other Acacias. See pages 74-76 for comparisons.

Gardening
This tree will grow well in most gardens. It likes warm conditions, is susceptible to frost but is fairly drought-resistant. It can be grown from seed, but it tends to drop thorny twigs, which will be a disadvantage in family gardens.

Human uses
The wood is used for fence posts and also for walking sticks and knobkieries (fighting sticks). Poles are planted in the ground to act as lightning conductors. The bark is used for tanning.

Links with animals
This tree is vulnerable to animal damage. It is often attacked, and may even be killed, by woodborers. It seldom re-grows after being pushed over, or otherwise damaged, by elephants. The flowers are eaten by baboon, monkey and giraffe, and leaves and shoots by kudu, elephant and giraffe. Giraffe also enjoy the pods. Holes in the trunk and branches provide nesting sites for birds. White-backed Vultures often nest on top of these trees.

BIG SIX
Knob-thorn Acacia

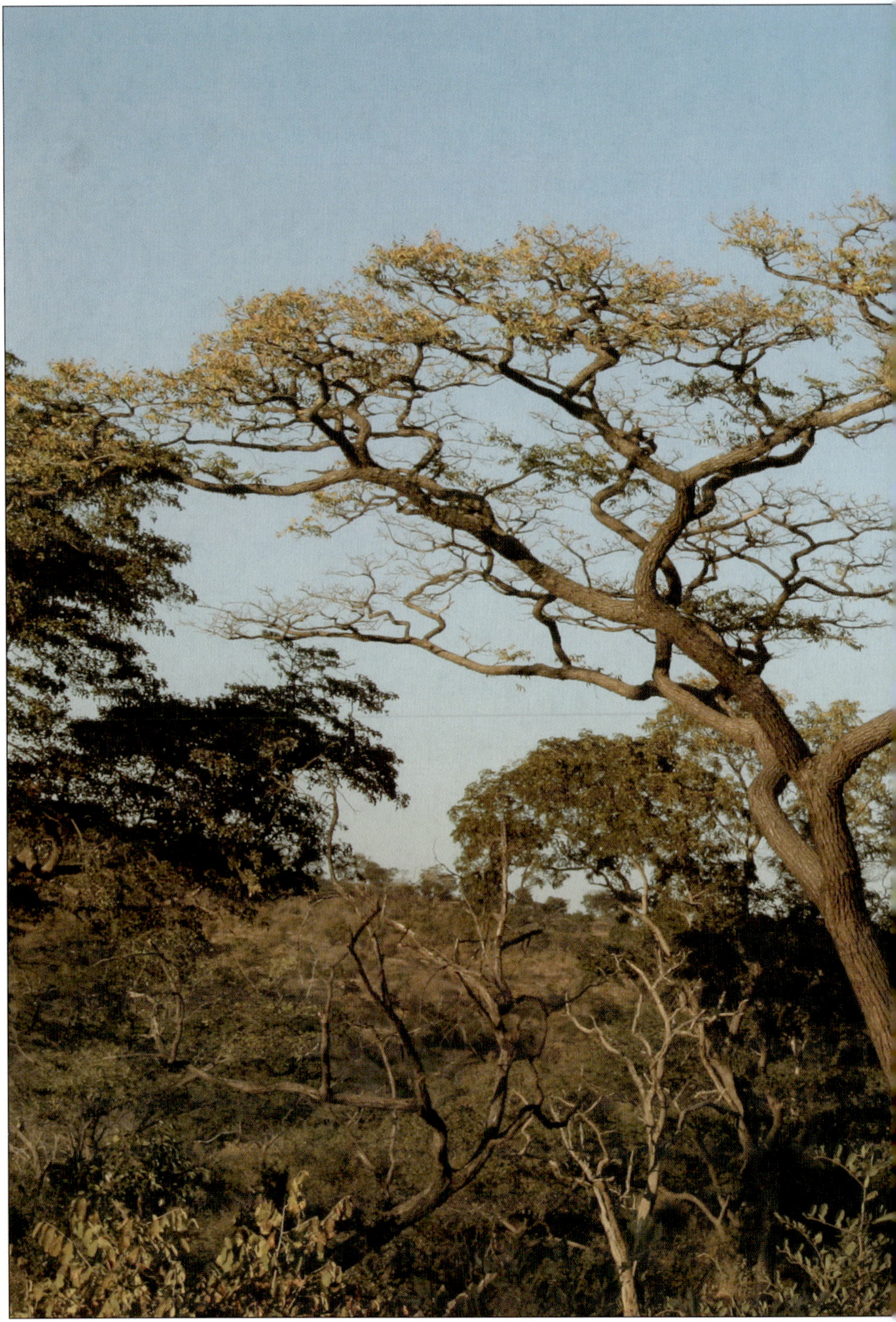

FIND TREES BY ECOZONE

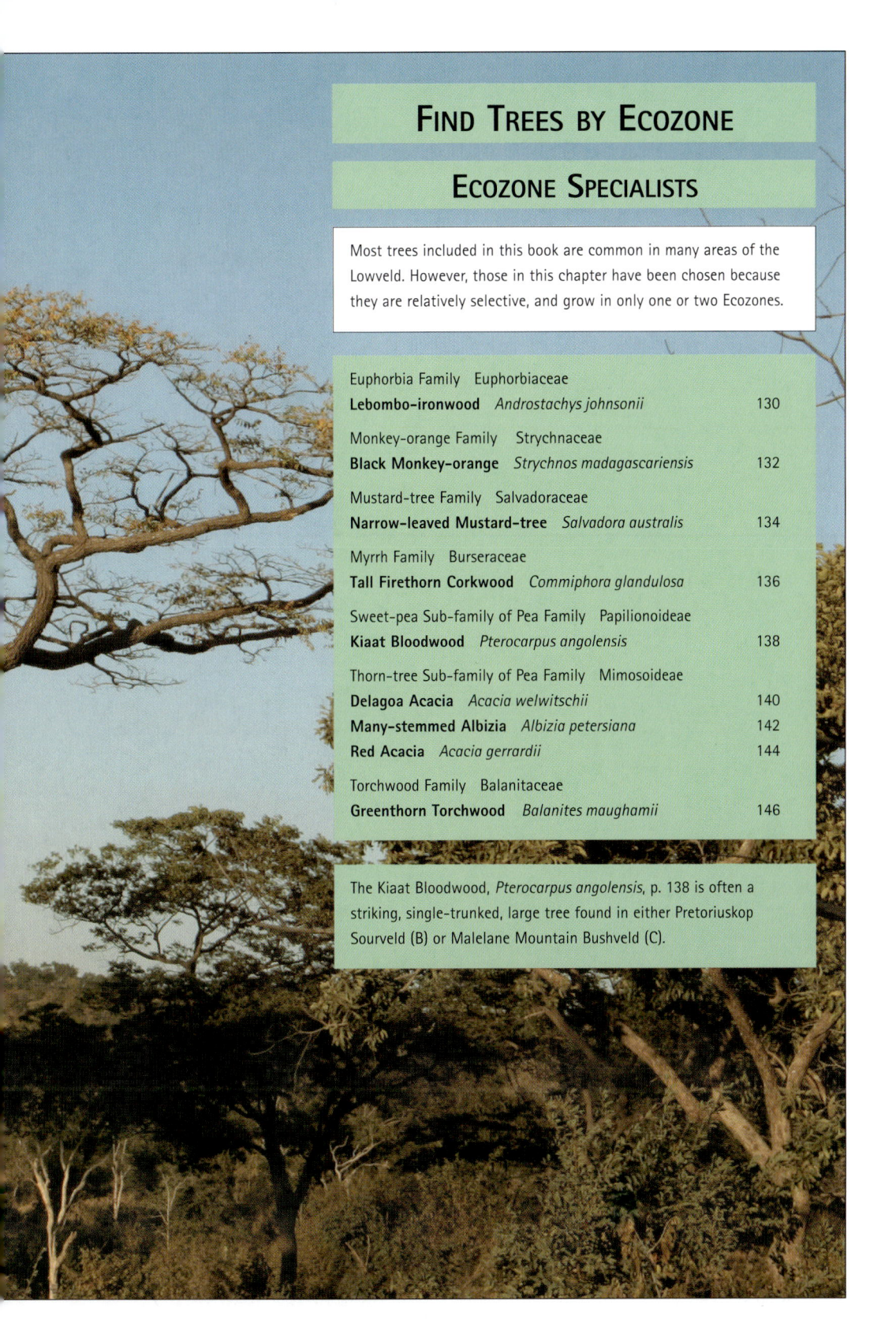

ECOZONE SPECIALISTS

Most trees included in this book are common in many areas of the Lowveld. However, those in this chapter have been chosen because they are relatively selective, and grow in only one or two Ecozones.

Euphorbia Family   Euphorbiaceae
Lebombo-ironwood   *Androstachys johnsonii*   130

Monkey-orange Family   Strychnaceae
Black Monkey-orange   *Strychnos madagascariensis*   132

Mustard-tree Family   Salvadoraceae
Narrow-leaved Mustard-tree   *Salvadora australis*   134

Myrrh Family   Burseraceae
Tall Firethorn Corkwood   *Commiphora glandulosa*   136

Sweet-pea Sub-family of Pea Family   Papilionoideae
Kiaat Bloodwood   *Pterocarpus angolensis*   138

Thorn-tree Sub-family of Pea Family   Mimosoideae
Delagoa Acacia   *Acacia welwitschii*   140
Many-stemmed Albizia   *Albizia petersiana*   142
Red Acacia   *Acacia gerrardii*   144

Torchwood Family   Balanitaceae
Greenthorn Torchwood   *Balanites maughamii*   146

The Kiaat Bloodwood, *Pterocarpus angolensis*, p. 138 is often a striking, single-trunked, large tree found in either Pretoriuskop Sourveld (B) or Malelane Mountain Bushveld (C).

| EUPHORBIA FAMILY | Euphorbiaceae | Tree no 327 |

LEBOMBO-IRONWOOD *Androstachys johnsonii*

AFRIKAANS Lebombo-ysterhout, Wildekweper **SWAZI** ubukhunku **TSONGA** Nsimbitsi
ZULU uBukhunku, umBitzani

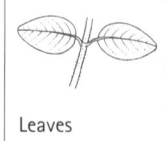

Androstachys is from the Greek *andros* + *stachys* meaning 'male' + 'spike', because the first recorded specimen at Kew was a male flower; **johnsonii** is for William Johnson (b.1875) who collected the type specimen.

Leaves

Where you'll find this tree easily
The Lebombo-ironwood grows only in the north, and is mostly found in loose groups, but larger trees may be found growing singly.
- It is easiest to find this tree in Lebombo Mountain Bushveld (I), in the north.
- It can also be found growing in Sandveld (N), on sandstone ridges.

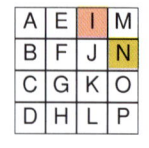

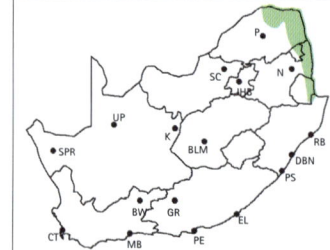

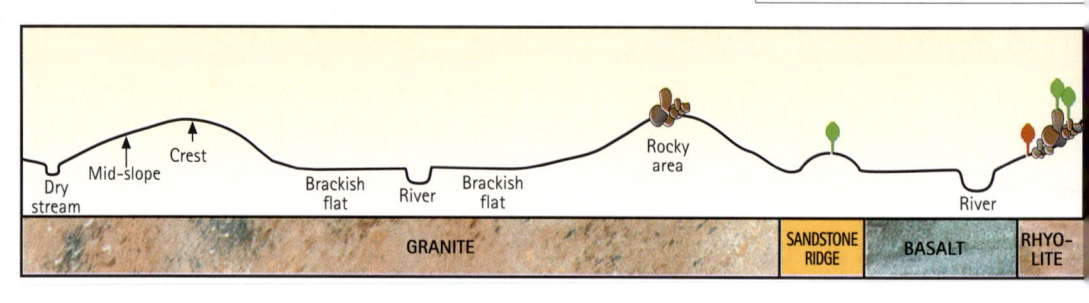

A	E	I	M
B	F	J	N
C	G	K	O
D	H	L	P

Lebombo-ironwoods on the Mahonie Loop in Kruger National Park can be spotted from a distance, because they form a uniform forest on a sandstone ridge.

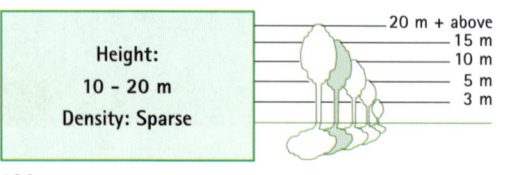

GIFF
- The specific distribution only in Ecozones I and N makes identification easy.
- This tree grows in large, uniform groups on the crests of hills and mountains.
- It is a single-stemmed, upright tree with a sparse, grey-green canopy.
- The canopy is narrow and almost pointed, especially from a distance.
- The young branches and twigs are angular.
- The Simple, heart-shaped leaves are arranged with each pair of opposite leaves at right angles to the pairs above and below. This is distinctive.
- The margins of the leaves curl under in dry conditions.

Seasonal changes
Evergreen. This tree may look very wilted in the dry season. It is possible to identify it throughout the year by its growth form and the presence of leaves.

Height: 10 - 20 m
Density: Sparse

	Oct	Nov	Dec	Jan	Feb	Mar	Apr	May	Jun	Jul	Aug	Sep
Leaf												
Flower												
Fruit/Pod												

Growth form
The stems of young branches and twigs are covered by dense, silvery-white hairs. Side branches are initially paired, but one of the pair may die off later.

Leaves
Leaves have a broad base and a round tip with a spiny end. They are dark green above and velvety-white underneath (40 x 30 mm).

Fruit
The three-lobed capsule turns red-brown before it ripens to pale brown. Capsules burst open on the trees with an audible crack (Ripen Jan - Mar) (12 mm).

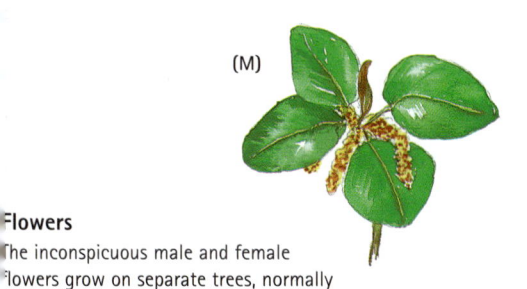

Flowers
The inconspicuous male and female flowers grow on separate trees, normally after the rains (Oct - Dec) (25 mm).

Bark
The bark is dark grey and grooved lengthways.

ECOZONE SPECIALISTS: Lebombo-ironwood

Look-alike tree
The Lebombo-ironwood has no Look-alike tree.

Links with animals
The leaves are eaten by a variety of game.

Human uses
The wood can be cut into sleepers and fence posts. It was made into flooring boards, and used in the construction of the first huts in Punda Maria and Shingwedzi rest camps.

Gardening
This is not a particularly attractive tree, unless well-watered. It will grow easily but slowly from seed. While it is drought-resistant, it not frost-resistant.

131

| MONKEY-ORANGE FAMILY | Strychnaceae | Tree no 626 |

BLACK MONKEY-ORANGE   *Strychnos madagascariensis*

AFRIKAANS Swartklapper, Botterklapper   **N. SOTHO** Mookwane   **TSONGA** Nkwakwa
ZULU umGuluguza

Strychnos is derived from the Greek word for deadly, referring to the poisonous properties of some plants; **madagascariensis** means from Madagascar.

Fruit

Where you'll find this tree easily
The Black Monkey-orange grows singly on well-drained soils.
- This tree can most easily be found in Pretoriuskop Sourveld (B). It is also found in Sandveld (N) on the sandstone ridges.
- It is can be spotted in Mixed Bushwillow Woodlands (A), in Malelane Mountain Bushveld (C), and in Mopane/Bushwillow Woodlands (P).

A	E	I	M
B	F	J	N
C	G	K	O
D	H	L	P

GIFF of Monkey-oranges in general
- Many of the species have spines.
- Leaves are Simple and opposite and do not have an obvious leaf-stem.
- Big, rounded, orange-like fruit characteristically have a very hard skin.

Specific GIFF of Black Monkey-orange
- It is a multi-stemmed shrub or short tree, with a heavily-branched, irregular, flattish canopy.
- The bark of the younger branches and trees is pale grey with white and dark grey patches, while the older branches are darker and rougher.
- **Knobbly side shoots resemble spines (10 - 30 mm).**
- Elliptic, shiny leaves cluster on ends of short, thick twigs.
- **The conspicuous, orange-sized, round fruit is blue-green for most of the year, becoming bright orange-yellow when ripe.**

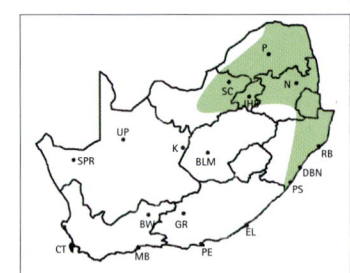

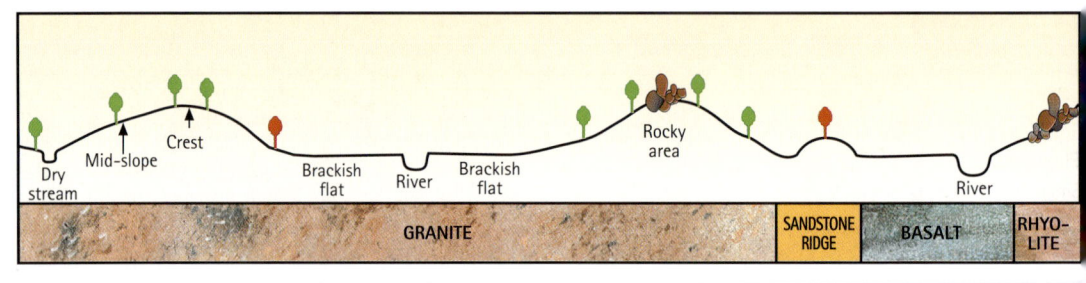

Black Monkey-orange fruit is distinctive in winter, often growing on knobbly branches with lichen.

Seasonal changes
Deciduous. The leaves turn yellow in autumn. It is possible to identify this tree all year round if fruit is present.

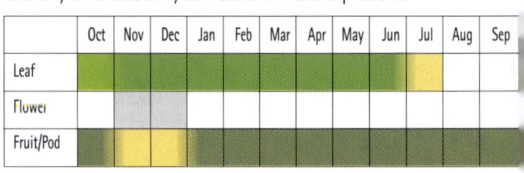

Height:
5 - 8 m
Density: Moderate

	Oct	Nov	Dec	Jan	Feb	Mar	Apr	May	Jun	Jul	Aug	Sep
Leaf												
Flower												
Fruit/Pod												

132

Growth form
This is a very variable tree. It may be single-stemmed with a grooved and dented stem, or (more often) multi-stemmed, branching low-down. Many thin branchlets and twigs come off the main branches irregularly, giving it a thick, matted appearance. Side branches tend to emerge at right angles.

Leaves
Broadly elliptic leaves are velvety, blue-green above and paler below. They have a round tip and wedge-shaped base, and the margins are smooth. 3 - 5 veins radiate from the base, with two secondary veins that run parallel to the margin (Leaf: 20 - 90 x 10 - 60 mm).

Flowers
Small, inconspicuous, greenish-yellow, trumpet-shaped flowers grow in small clusters at the base of the leaves on the old wood. Flowers tend to appear only after good rains (Nov - Dec) (8 - 10 mm diam.).

Fruit
The fruit may take a long time to ripen and may still be present into the next flowering season. Large seeds are tightly packed inside the shell, and each seed is covered by yellow pulp (Mar - Aug) (70 - 120 mm).

Bark
See GIFF.

ECOZONE SPECIALISTS
Black Monkey-orange

Look-alike tree
The Spiny Monkey-orange, *Strychnos spinosa*, p. 23, has slender, paired, slightly curved, woody spines at the base of the shiny, Simple, opposite leaves (15 - 90 x 12 - 75 mm). Bark is rough, peeling or flaking; the fruit is large (120 mm) and turns yellow-brown when ripe.

Gardening
This tree can be grown easily from seed, and will grow fairly fast when cultivated. It is sensitive to frost.

Links with animals
Leaves are eaten by duiker, kudu, impala, steenbok, nyala and elephant, and the fruit by baboon, monkey, bushpig, nyala and eland.

Human uses
The fruit pulp is edible but the seeds are avoided as they are a purgative. In India a *Strychnos* species is used to prepare strychnine.

133

| MUSTARD-TREE FAMILY | Salvadoraceae | Tree no 621 |

NARROW-LEAVED MUSTARD-TREE
Salvadora australis

AFRIKAANS Smalblaarmosterdboom, Leeubos **ZULU** umPheme, iChithamuzi

Salvadora is in honour of Juan Salvador y Bosca, a Spanish plant collector; **australis** means southern.

Leaves

Where you'll find this tree easily
The Narrow-leaved Mustard-tree grows in groups along the Shingwedzi and Luvuvhu rivers.
- This tree can be found growing on the floodplains along the rivers in the Alluvial Plains (M).

A	E	I	M
B	F	J	N
C	G	K	O
D	H	L	P

GIFF
- The specific distribution only in Ecozone M makes identification easy.
- This small tree or shrub is pale bluish-grey.
- It is multi-stemmed and sprawling, and grows in large groups.
- The branches often hang on the ground.
- The blue-grey leaves are Simple and opposite, and are thick and fleshy.
- Round to oval, berry-like fruit is pale greenish-pink, and grows in profusion in mid-summer.

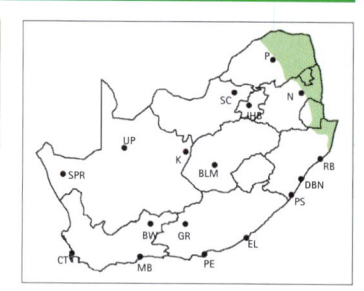

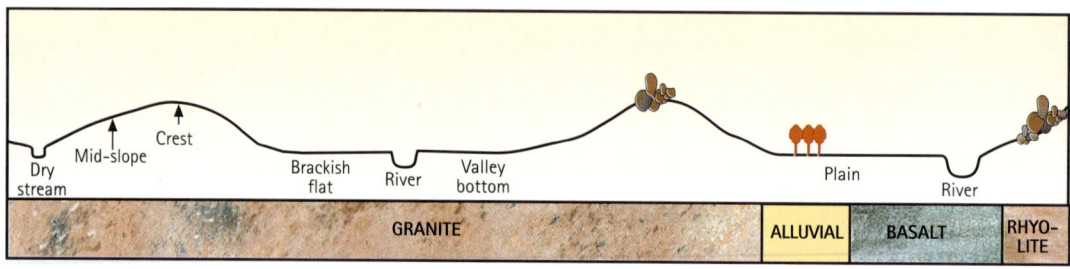

Although relatively low and bushy, these trees are so common that they are easy to recognise in Ecozone M.

Seasonal changes
Evergreen. This tree is therefore easy to identify throughout the year.

	Oct	Nov	Dec	Jan	Feb	Mar	Apr	May	Jun	Jul	Aug	Sep
Leaf												
Flower												
Fruit/Pod												

Height: 2 - 7 m
Density: Moderate

Growth form
This shrub has very short, grooved stems, that are often screened by the downward pattern of the branches. The branches form an irregular, moderately dense canopy and are covered with a pale green, furry layer.

Leaves
The leaves are usually narrowly elliptic, with a smooth margin. They are covered with fine, soft, blue-grey hairs, and are salty to taste (45 x 10 mm).

Fruit
The fruit is covered with fine hair, and ripens during November and December (5 mm).

Flowers
Sprays of inconspicuous, small, yellow-green flowers grow at the end of branches and at the base of the upper leaves (Aug - Sep) (2 mm).

Bark
The bark is pale grey, with darker flecks that may break up into irregular blocks.

ECOZONE SPECIALISTS: Narrow-leaved Mustard-tree

Look-alike tree
The Narrow-leaved Mustard-tree has no Look-alike tree in the Alluvial Plains of Ecozone M.

Links with animals
The fruit is readily eaten by impala, elephant and kudu. The leaves are utilised all year round, and are often heavily browsed in the dry season.

Gardening
This is not really a garden tree, but it is evergreen and will grow in clay soils. It is probably not frost-resistant, but is fairly drought-resistant. It is not known whether it can be grown from seed, and it appears to be slow-growing.

Human uses
Leaf extracts are used to treat eye ailments.

| Myrrh Family | Burseraceae | Tree no 285.1 |

Tall Firethorn Corkwood
Commiphora glandulosa

AFRIKAANS Grootdoringkanniedood **TSONGA** Xifati **TSWANA** Morôka **VENDA** Mutalu
ZULU iMinyela

Commiphora is from the Greek *kommi* + *phora* meaning 'gum bearing', as most species contain an aromatic resin; **glandulosa** refers to the glandular hairs on the flowers and flower-stalks.

Leaf/fruit

Where you'll find this tree easily
The Tall Firethorn Corkwood grows singly on well-drained soils and in rocky areas.

- This tree is easy to find on the rocky hills in Olifants Rugged Veld (J), as well as in the Sandveld (N) and Alluvial Plains (M).
- It can also be found on the more rocky areas in basalts, in the north of the Knob-thorn/Marula Savannah (F) and in Mopane Shrubveld (L).
- It can be spotted in both the north and south of Lebombo Mountain Bushveld (I) and in the rocky areas of Mopane/Bushwillow Woodlands (P).

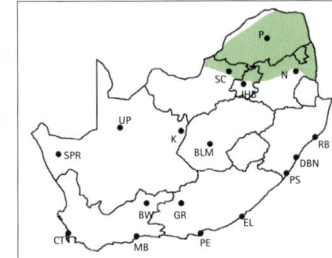

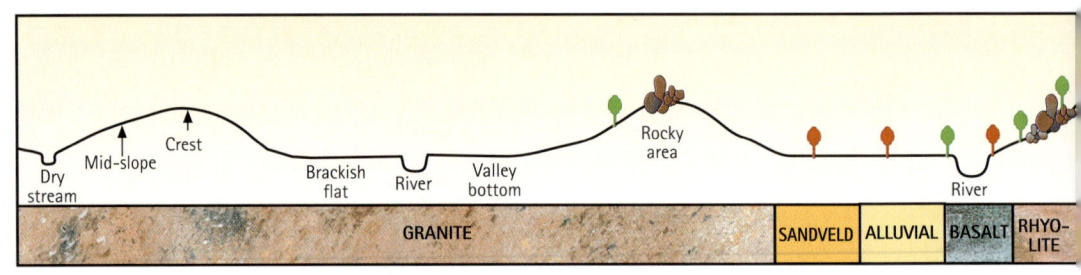

These are typical young leaves, spikes and bark of a Tall Firethorn Corkwood.

GIFF of Corkwoods in general
- All Corkwoods have robust, fleshy stems and branches.
- A conspicuous, often peeling, papery upper layer exposes shiny under-bark.
- Corkwoods vary, with Simple and/or Once Compound leaves.
- Many Corkwoods are spiny, with fruit that is berry-like.

Specific GIFF of Firethorn Corkwood
- This tree is single-stemmed, branching profusely to form a roundish canopy.
- The branchlets come off the main stem and branches at right angles and end in spines, giving the tree a spiky appearance.
- **The bark peels in small, straw-coloured, papery strips to expose shiny, green under-bark.**
- The Simple leaves are characteristically clustered at the base of the spines.

Seasonal changes
Deciduous. The characteristic bark and growth form of this tree makes identification possible throughout the year.

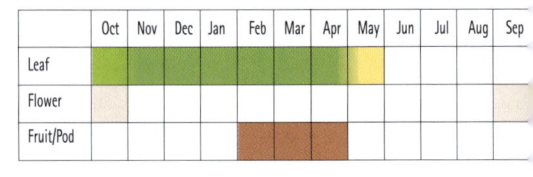

	Oct	Nov	Dec	Jan	Feb	Mar	Apr	May	Jun	Jul	Aug	Sep
Leaf												
Flower												
Fruit/Pod												

Height: 2 – 6 m
Density: Moderate

Growth form
The branches are stiff and arching and tend to hang down. The stem is obviously fleshy.

Leaves
Leaves are clustered in rosettes on short, spiny branchlets. They are elliptic to broadly elliptic with a broadly tapering tip that may be pointed, and a tapering base. They have a toothed margin and are bright green to grey-green above and paler green below. The central- and side-veins are yellow and clearly visible on the upper-surface. The young leaves are often 3-leaflet, with a larger terminal and two smaller leaflets (30 - 75 x 20 - 35 mm).

Fruit
The berry-like fruit is round to egg-shaped, and red-green to brown when ripe. The fruit splits open to expose black and red seeds (Feb - Apr) (13 x 10 mm).

Spines
Branchlets often end in hard spines, and there are sometimes single spines that grow on the main stem or branches.

Flowers
The small, inconspicuous, pink to reddish, slender, trumpet-shaped flowers grow in clustered groups on short side-branchlets. Similar female and male flowers are found on separate trees (Sep - Oct).

Bark
The bark is typical of many Corkwoods. It varies from grey to yellow, or is sometimes even reddish, but is usually yellow-green. Spines on the trunk and main branches are not always visible.

**ECOZONE SPECIALISTS
Tall Firethorn Corkwood**

Look-alike tree
Firethorn Corkwood, *Commiphora pyracanthoides*, p. 2, is very similar, but multi-stemmed with grey-green, flaky bark and clustered, spine-tipped side branches. It also usually has Simple leaves (75 x 32 mm), but may be Three-leaflet Compound. The Zebra-bark Corkwood, *Commiphora viminea*, p. 47, occurs in the far northern areas of Kruger. It has Simple leaves with a toothed edge in the top third (45 x 25 mm) and leaves clustered in rosettes. The bark of older trees peels in horizontal bands, with streaks, or stripes of grey, corky bark in-between, giving it its common English name.

Links with animals
The fruit is eaten by Southern Yellow-billed Hornbills. Young shoots and leaves are eaten by duiker and elephant.

Human uses
The wood is used to make cups and buckets, and is sometimes made into other household utensils. Most Corkwoods produce aromatic resins and gums.

Gardening
This tree can be planted to form a hedge. It grows fast from seed and easily from cuttings. It is fairly frost-resistant and very drought-resistant.

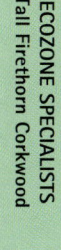

SWEET-PEA SUB-FAMILY OF PEA FAMILY | Papilionoideae | Tree no 236

Kiaat Bloodwood *Pterocarpus angolensis*

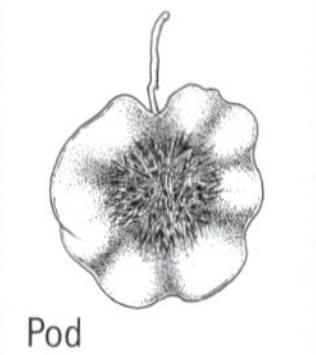

AFRIKAANS Kiaat **N. SOTHO** Morôtô **N. SOTHO** Mmilo (Morôtô) **TSONGA** Mvhangazi, Murotso
TSWANA Mokwa **VENDA** Mutondo **ZULU** umVangazi, umBilo

Pterocarpus is from the Greek *pteros + karpon* meaning 'wing' + 'fruit', referring to the conspicuously winged pod; *angolensis* refers to Angola.

Pod

Where you'll find this tree easily

The Kiaat Bloodwood grows singly on well-drained soils in areas with rainfall above 500 mm.
- It is easy to find this tree growing on the crests of hills in Pretoriuskop Sourveld (B).
- It can also be found growing on the crests in Malelane Mountain Bushveld (C).

A	E	I	M
B	F	J	N
C	G	K	O
D	H	L	P

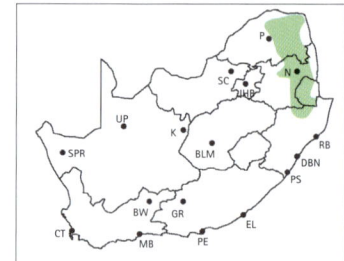

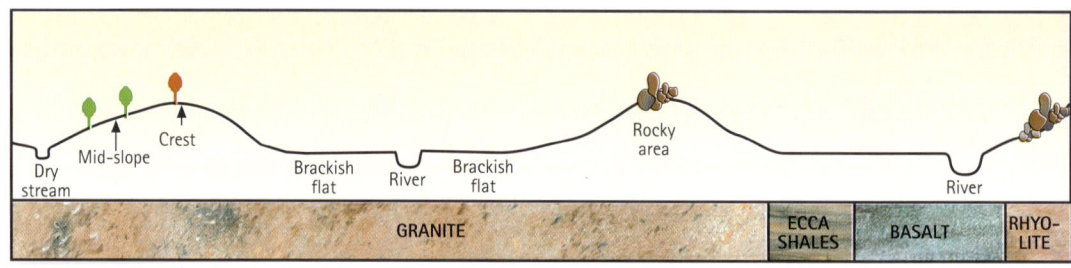

Dry stream — Mid-slope — Crest — Brackish flat — River — Brackish flat — Rocky area — River

GRANITE | ECCA SHALES | BASALT | RHYOLITE

GIFF

- This is a large, striking, single-trunked tree, with a few large branches growing upward and outward.
- Feathery, drooping leaves grow very high up, to form a soft umbrella-like canopy.
- The bark of the trunk and large branches is dark brown to black, and when sections flake off, there are paler patches in the under-bark.
- **The leaves are Once Compound with alternate leaflets and a single leaflet at the tip.**
- Striking, orange-yellow, pea-shaped flowers are abundant in branched sprays from spring to early summer.
- **The unusually shaped pods are characteristic and conspicuous, especially when the leaves have dropped.**

Visually the pods are a delight – and they serve as food for a number of primates and squirrels too.

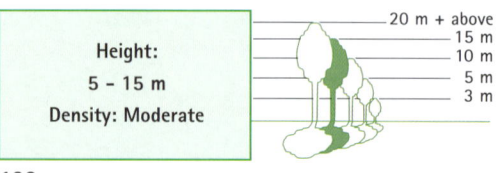

Seasonal changes

Deciduous. The tree can be identified easily in all seasons by its specific Ecozone preference, characteristic growth form and the presence of the pods for most of the year.

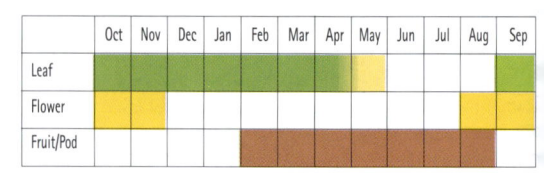

Height: 5 - 15 m
Density: Moderate

20 m + above
15 m
10 m
5 m
3 m

	Oct	Nov	Dec	Jan	Feb	Mar	Apr	May	Jun	Jul	Aug	Sep
Leaf												
Flower												
Fruit/Pod												

Growth form
See GIFF.

Leaves
The leaves are droopy, hang down, and turn yellow before dropping early in winter. There are 4 - 25 pairs of leaflets, that are elliptic with a prominent twisted tip and smooth margin. They are shiny, dark green above and have fine hairs below. Young leaflets are soft and covered in brown hairs (Leaf: up to 380 mm; leaflets: 20 - 70 x 25 - 45 mm).

Pods
The pods have a central seed-case covered by long, stiff bristles, surrounded by a single, round, flat but wavy, papery plate. They grow singly or in bunches on long twigs. The pods ripen in late summer (Feb - Aug), and remain on the tree long after the leaves have fallen (80 - 150 mm diam.).

Flowers
Flowers usually grow on the older, darker branches. They appear before, or with, the new leaves, and the flowering period lasts for 2 - 3 weeks during August and November (Spray: 100 - 200 mm long; individual flower: 10 - 20 mm long).

Bark
The bark is rough, and fissured or cracked into lengthways sections. Red sap oozes out when the bark is damaged, which gives the tree its English common name. Young twigs are smooth, grey and covered with hairs.

ECOZONE SPECIALISTS
Kiaat Bloodwood

Look-alike tree
See the comparisons of various Once Compound leaves in the Distinctive Striking Features, pages 69-70.

Gardening
This tree is extremely difficult to germinate from seed, but can be propagated from cuttings taken in spring. It grows slowly on most soil types, and is not frost-resistant.

Links with animals
The leaves are eaten by elephant and kudu, the young pods by baboon, and the seeds by baboon, monkey and tree squirrel. Elephant often push the trees over.

Human uses
The wood is excellent for making furniture and curios. It is also used for canoes and building. The red gum and sap make red dye, and the sap is painted onto cuts and sores.

139

THORN-TREE SUB-FAMILY OF PEA FAMILY | Mimosoideae | Tree no 163

Delagoa Acacia
Acacia welwitschii

AFRIKAANS Delagoa-doring

Flower-spike

Acacia is taken from the Greek *akis* meaning a 'sharp point', referring to the thorns that grow on all African Acacia species; **welwitschii** is named after Friedrich Welwitsch (1806-1872), pioneer botanical explorer.

Where you'll find this tree easily
The Delagoa Acacia can only be found growing in loose groups of large trees.
- It is easiest to find on the plains of Delagoa Thorn Thickets (G).

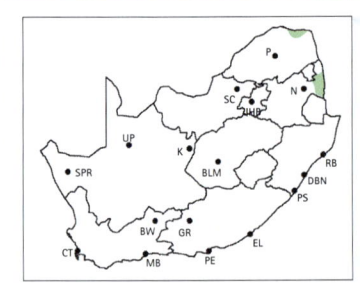

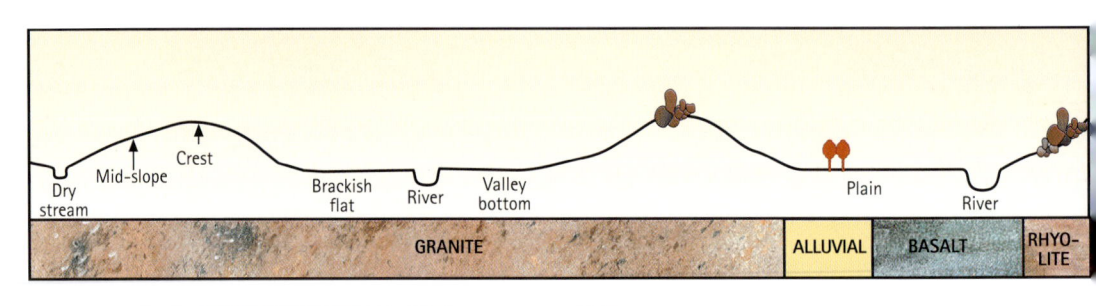

A	E	I	M
B	F	J	N
C	G	K	O
D	H	L	P

Crest
Mid-slope
Dry stream
Brackish flat
River
Valley bottom
Plain
River

GRANITE | ALLUVIAL | BASALT | RHYO-LITE

The typical layered shape of Delagoa Acacias is easily recognised in the Ecozone G.

GIFF
- Identification is primarily by Ecozone distribution – Ecozone G, where it cannot be mistaken.
- It is a low-branching tree, usually with a single, crooked trunk.
- It has a unusual 'layered' appearance as if sections of the tree are separate from one another.
- Prominent white twigs are visible as if they were thin 'spaghetti' in among the leaves.
- It has Twice Compound leaves with leaflets that are relatively large for an Acacia.
- White flower-spikes are unusual too, normally only being visible at the top of the canopy.
- Narrow, long, flat bean pods are deep wine-red, changing to purple-green, and finally to brown-black when ripe.

Seasonal changes
Deciduous. This tree may be recognised in winter by its Ecozone distribution, its growth form, and by the prominent white twigs.

Height:
10 – 15 m
Density: Moderate

20 m + above
15 m
10 m
5 m
3 m

	Oct	Nov	Dec	Jan	Feb	Mar	Apr	May	Jun	Jul	Aug	Sep
Leaf												
Flower												
Fruit/Pod												

Growth form
The trunk has branches leaving the main stem horizontally to form a wide-spreading canopy. Large branches are formed even high up in the canopy.

Leaves
Leaves have a pair of leaflets at the top of each feather. Leaflets are opposite and elliptic with a smooth margin (2 - 5 feather pairs, 40 mm; 8 pairs of leaflets, each 7 x 4 mm).

Flowers
See GIFF.
(Nov - Jan) (70 x 10 mm).

Pods
Pods are usually only visible at the top of the tree, as those lower down are eaten. They ripen late autumn and winter (Mar - Jul) (80 - 110 mm).

Thorns
Pairs of hooked, dark thorns are fairly close to one another (5 mm).

Bark
The bark is coarse, fissured and pale grey with yellow grooves that run lengthways.

ECOZONE SPECIALISTS
Delagoa Acacia

Look-alike tree
This can be confused with other Acacias. See pages 74-76 for comparisons. It is most easily confused with the Black-monkey Acacia, *Acacia burkei*, page 41, the bark of which is yellower.

Human uses
There are no recorded uses, probably because of its limited distribution.

Links with animals
This is a favourite food of giraffe.

Gardening
This is not an attractive garden plant and will need specific clay soils to flourish. It is fairly drought-resistant, but is sensitive to low temperatures. It is a slow-growing tree that can be grown from seed.

141

| THORN-TREE SUB-FAMILY OF PEA FAMILY | Mimosoideae | Tree no 153 |

MANY-STEMMED ALBIZIA
Albizia petersiana

AFRIKAANS Meerstamvalsdoring **TSONGA** Nnala **ZULU** umNala

Albizia is named after Filippo degli Albizzi, an Italian who introduced the plant to Europe; **petersiana** is named after Wilhelm Peters (1815-1883), the German zoologist who collected plants in Mozambique.

Trunk

Where you'll find this tree easily
The Many-stemmed Albizia grows in groups.
- It can only be found on the plains in Delagoa Thorn Thickets (G).

A	E	I	M
B	F	J	N
C	G	K	O
D	H	L	P

Dry stream — Mid-slope — Crest — Drainage line — Brackish flat — River — Valley bottom — Rocky area — Plain — River

GRANITE — ECCA SHALES — BASALT — RHYOLITE

GIFF
- **The specific distribution only in Ecozone G makes identification easy.**
- It is a moderately dense, multi-stemmed, V-shaped tree, with upward-growing branches.
- **In mature trees each stem is thick, like those of a single-trunked tree.**
- Twice Compound leaves form a dark green canopy, with reddish leaves in spring, and yellow leaves in autumn.
- The bark is smooth and grey with a yellow tinge, and peels in narrow, flat strips.
- Long flat, green bean pods hang in bunches and ripen in autumn to brown.

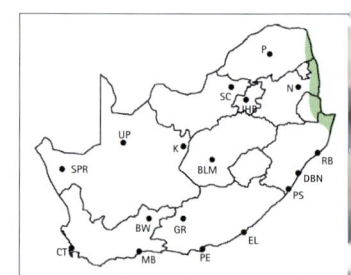

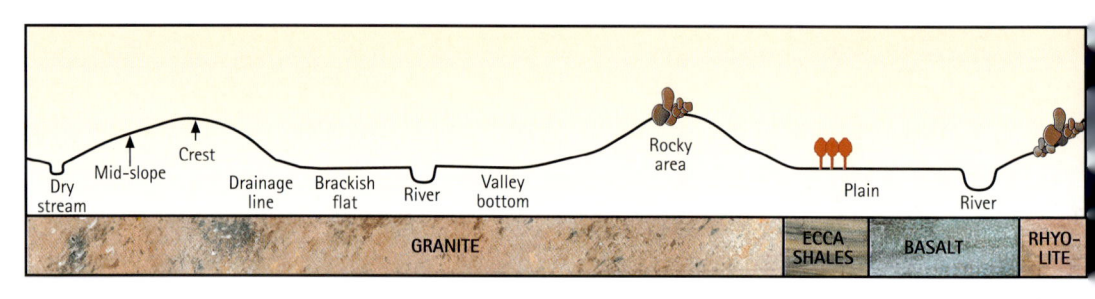

In early spring a Many-stemmed Albizia has pods, but is almost leafless. A Knob-thorn Acacia is nearby in flower.

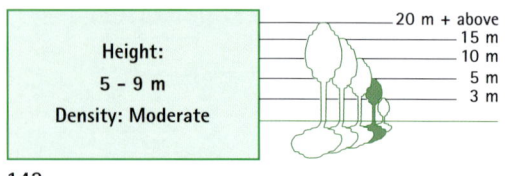

Seasonal changes
Deciduous. This tree is without leaves for most of the winter and spring. Owing to its very specific Ecozone distribution and characteristic shape, it is easily identified all year round.

Height: 5 - 9 m
Density: Moderate

20 m + above
15 m
10 m
5 m
3 m

	Oct	Nov	Dec	Jan	Feb	Mar	Apr	May	Jun	Jul	Aug	Sep
Leaf												
Flower												
Fruit/Pod												

Growth form
See GIFF.

Leaves
The leaves are larger than those of most common Acacia species. The leaves have a pair of leaflets at the tip of each feather, and a pair of feathers at each leaf tip. Leaflets are opposite, and broadly elliptic to heart-shaped (Leaf: 60 mm; leaflet: 10 x 6 mm).

Flowers
These are not the typical powder-puff flowers of most Albizias. They are inconspicuous, white with prominent red stamens, and they appear after the leaves (Oct - Dec) (30 mm diam.).

Pods
See GIFF.
(Mar - Jun) (120 x 16 mm).

Bark
See GIFF.

ECOZONE SPECIALISTS
Many-stemmed Albizia

Look-alike tree
This tree can be confused with other Albizias. See page 77 for comparisons.

Links with animals
The leaves are eaten by kudu, impala and elephant, the pods by giraffe, and the shoots by elephant.

Gardening
This is not a general garden tree, as it needs specific clay soils. It is fairly drought-resistant, but susceptible to frost. It can be grown from seed easily, but is slow-growing.

Human uses
The wood is generally not used because most trees are infected with woodborers.

THORN-TREE SUB-FAMILY OF PEA FAMILY — Mimosoideae — Tree no 167

RED ACACIA — *Acacia gerrardii*

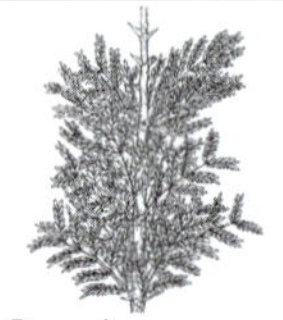

AFRIKAANS Rooidoring **N. SOTHO** Mooka **SWAZI** siNga **TSWANA** Moki **VENDA** Muunga
ZULU umPhuze, umNgampunzi

Acacia is taken from the Greek *akis* meaning a 'sharp point', referring to the thorns in all African species; *gerrardii* honours the English botanist, WT Gerrard, who collected the first specimen from KwaZulu-Natal.

Branches

Where you'll find this tree easily

In the granite Ecozones the Red Acacia often grows as a single tree. On the basalts it grows in groups of smaller trees.

- It is easiest to find in groups, in both the north and south, of basalt Knob-thorn/Marula Savannah (F).
- It can also be found in the valley bottoms of all the granite Ecozones A, B, C, D and P, as well as in Delagoa Thorn Thickets (G) and in the south of Lebombo Mountain Bushveld (I).

A	E	I	M
B	F	J	N
C	G	K	O
D	H	L	P

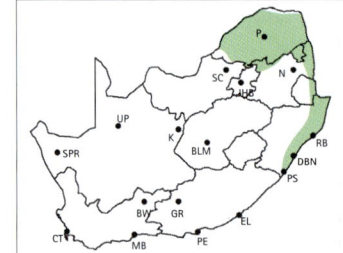

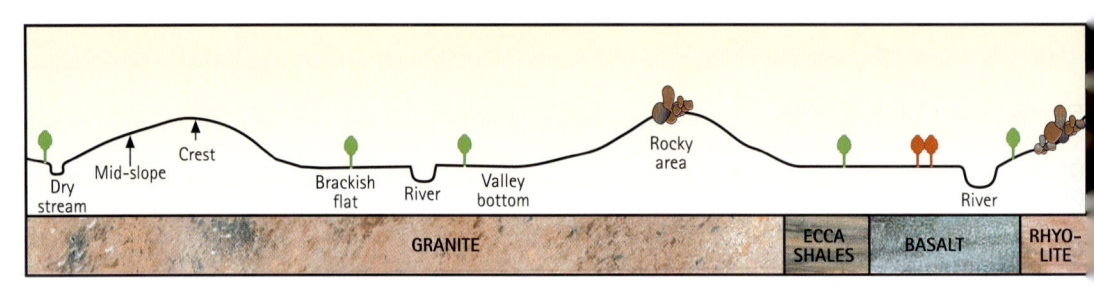

GIFF

- The specific distribution of this sparse Acacia makes identification easy in Ecozone F.
- It is a single-stemmed, slender tree, with reddish bark on younger branches and trees.
- Twice Compound, dark green leaves appear to be attached directly to the large branches, forming a continuous green sleeve that covers the entire length of most branches.
- The paired thorns are normally shortish, straight and very stout.
- Conspicuous, round, creamy-white, sweet-scented flower-balls are crowded on the twigs, next to the thorns, among the leaves.
- The sickle-shaped, flat pods are covered by fine, grey hairs and grow in bunches.

The leaves of the Red Acacia form a sleeve along the branches and branchlets.

Seasonal changes

Deciduous. The spindly form, bark colour and texture make identification possible even in winter.

Height: 5 - 10 m
Density: Very sparse

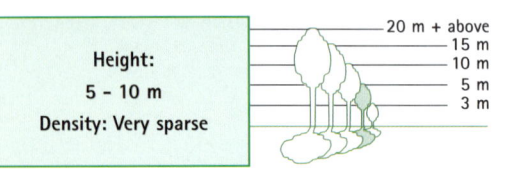

20 m + above / 15 m / 10 m / 5 m / 3 m

	Oct	Nov	Dec	Jan	Feb	Mar	Apr	May	Jun	Jul	Aug	Sep
Leaf												
Flower												
Fruit/Pod												

Growth form
This is a high-branching tree with an irregular canopy formed by a few upward-growing branches. The canopy is often flattened on one side.

Leaves
The leaf stalks and young twigs are covered with thick, grey hairs. The leaves consist of 5 - 10 pairs of feathers and 15 - 20 pairs of leaflets. Leaflets are elliptic with fine hairs fringing the margin (Leaf: 90 mm; leaflet: 3,0 - 7,5 x 1 - 2 mm).

Thorns
The thorns may be slightly curved or have swollen bases (25 - 100 mm).

Flowers
See GIFF. The flower-ball stalks are long (30 mm) and covered with hairs (Oct - Feb) (10 - 20 mm).

Pods
The pods ripen from December to May, and burst open while still on the tree (80 - 160 x 6 - 16 mm).

Bark
The bark of the trunk and branches in older trees is dark grey to reddish. It is smooth and seamed crosswise in young trees. In older trees and branches the bark is reddish and deeply fissured or wrinkled, exposing a rusty under-layer.

ECOZONE SPECIALISTS
Red Acacia

Look-alike tree
This tree can be confused with other Acacias. See pages 74-76 for comparisons.

Links with animals
The pods and young shoots are eaten by baboon. The bark and leaves are eaten by Black Rhino, and the foliage and pods by giraffe, duiker, kudu and steenbok.

Gardening
This can be an attractive addition to the indigenous garden and will grow in most climates. It grows well from seed but is slow-growing. The tree will take some frost, and is drought-resistant.

Human uses
The bark contains astringent chemicals called tannins. It is used for medicinal purposes because of this property. The inner bark peels in long strips to make twine.

| TORCHWOOD FAMILY | Balanitaceae | Tree no 251 |

GREENTHORN TORCHWOOD

Balanites maughamii

AFRIKAANS Groendoring **SWAZI** umNununu **TSONGA** Nnulu **ZULU** umNulu, uGobandlovu

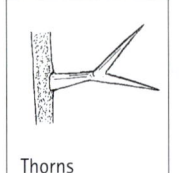

Balanites is from the Greek *balanos* meaning an 'acorn', referring to the acorn-shaped fruit; **maughamii** honours RCF Maugham, British Consul at Lourenço Marques (Maputo), who sent the type specimen to Kew.

Thorns

Where you'll find this tree easily

The Greenthorn Torchwood commonly grows singly, but large trees may be found surrounded by groups of smaller, young trees. It grows near water as well as in open, dry woodland.

A	E	I	M
B	F	J	N
C	G	K	O
D	H	L	P

- It is easiest to find in Sabie/Crocodile Thorn Thickets (D), near or in valley bottoms.
- It can also be found in valley bottoms in Mixed Bushwillow Woodland (A) and in rocky areas in Thorn Veld (E).

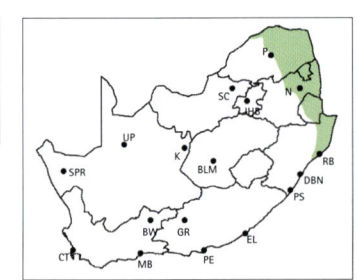

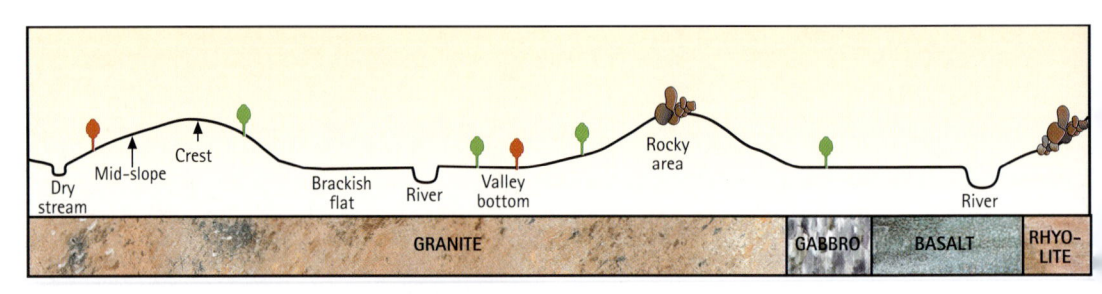

Dry stream | Mid-slope | Crest | Brackish flat | River | Valley bottom | Rocky area | River
GRANITE | GABBRO | BASALT | RHYO-LITE

Newly fallen fruit can be found beneath Greenthorn Torchwoods for several months of the year.

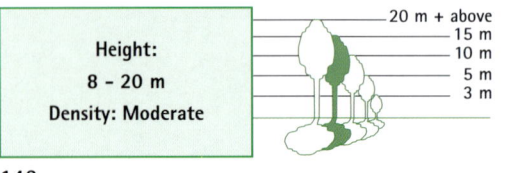

GIFF
- The specific distribution in Ecozone D makes identification much simpler.
- It is a very high-branching tree with a deeply multi-fluted trunk and smooth, grey bark.
- It has zigzag twigs and branchlets that grow outwards to give it an overall thorny look.
- Young trees often surround mature trees very closely, giving the trunk a multi-stemmed, untidy, thorny appearance.
- The canopy in very old trees is umbrella-like. It remains V-shaped in some quite large, mature trees.
- **The forked spines are green with brown tips.**
- The green to buff-green Two-leaflet Compound leaves are characteristic.

Seasonal changes

Evergreen or deciduous, depending on its locality. Trees near rivers tend to be evergreen. Owing to the presence of leaves most of the year, and the unique growth form, particularly of the trunk, it can be identified throughout the year.

Height: 8 – 20 m
Density: Moderate

20 m + above
15 m
10 m
5 m
3 m

	Oct	Nov	Dec	Jan	Feb	Mar	Apr	May	Jun	Jul	Aug	Sep
Leaf												
Flower												
Fruit/Pod												

Growth form
See GIFF.

Flowers
Small, inconspicuous, scented, star-shaped flowers are covered by velvety hairs. The tree only flowers every second or third year (Jul - Oct) (20 mm).

Fruit
The big, oval, plum-like fruit is pale brown and covered with fine hairs. The flesh is thin and bitter. It appears from November to January, and is yellowish when ripe from May. Ripe fruit is dropped with the stem attached, from May to July (30 - 50 x 20 - 30 mm).

Bark
The bark is grey and smooth in young trees. In older trees it is rough and breaks into small, irregular blocks.

Spines
The spines are very prominent, especially on sterile branches where they may have 2 - 3 prongs. The fruiting branches have thinner, straight thorns. On older branches they are grey-brown.

ECOZONE SPECIALISTS
Greenthorn Torchwood

Look-alike tree
The Greenthorn Torchwood has no Look-alike tree.

Gardening
This tree can be grown from seed, and will grow in most gardens. Its abundant thorns make it unsuitable for the family garden.

Links with animals
Baboon, monkey, impala, kudu, duiker, warthog, porcupine and steenbok eat the fruit, and elephant eat young shoots.

Human uses
Although harmless to humans, the fruit can kill snails, tadpoles and fish, and has been used to control bilharzia snails. The kernels are rich in fine, colourless oil, like olive oil, and are burned for torches, thus its common English name. Bark soaked in water makes for a refreshing bath, and an extract of the bark can induce vomiting.

147

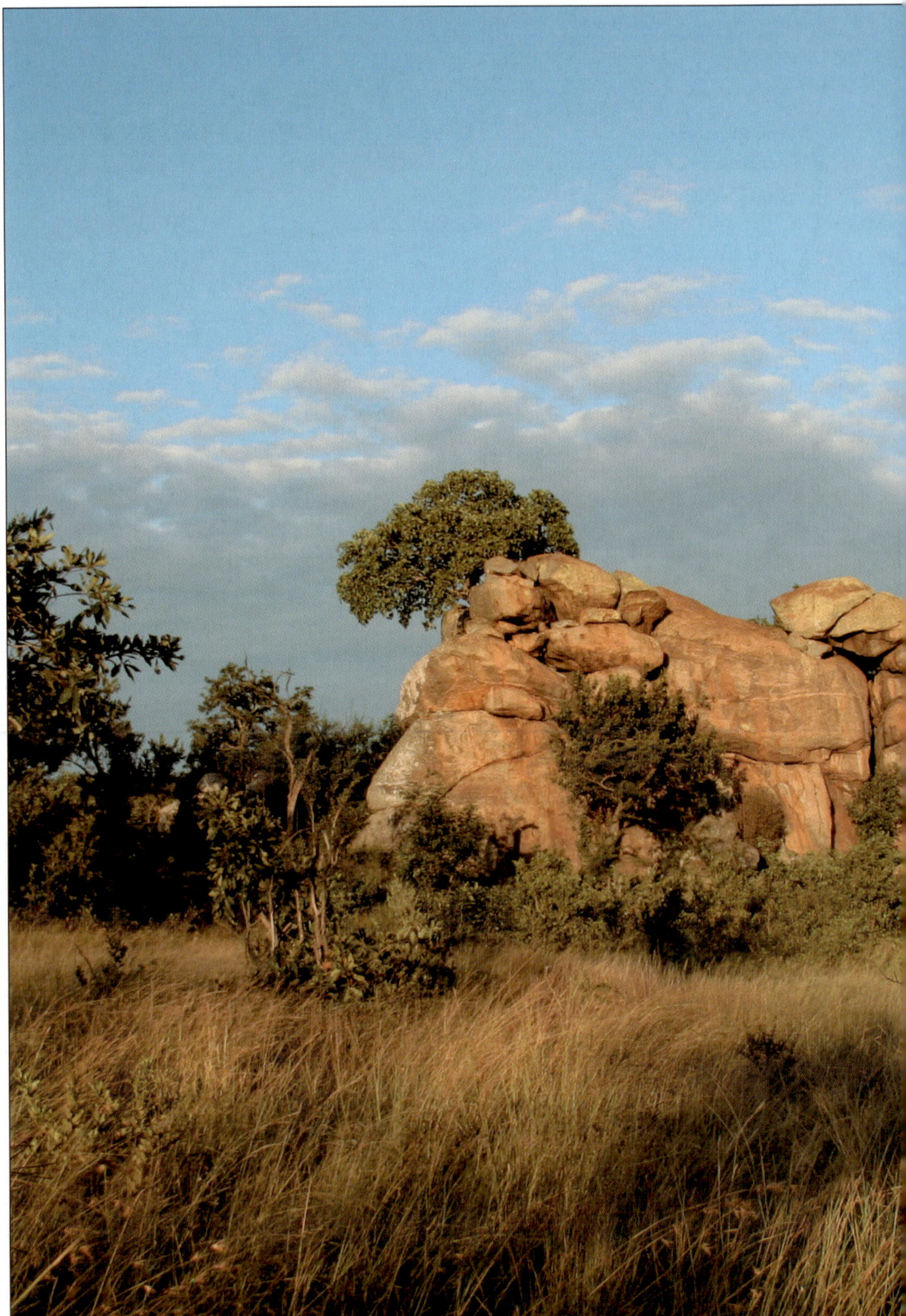

Find Trees by Easy Habitat

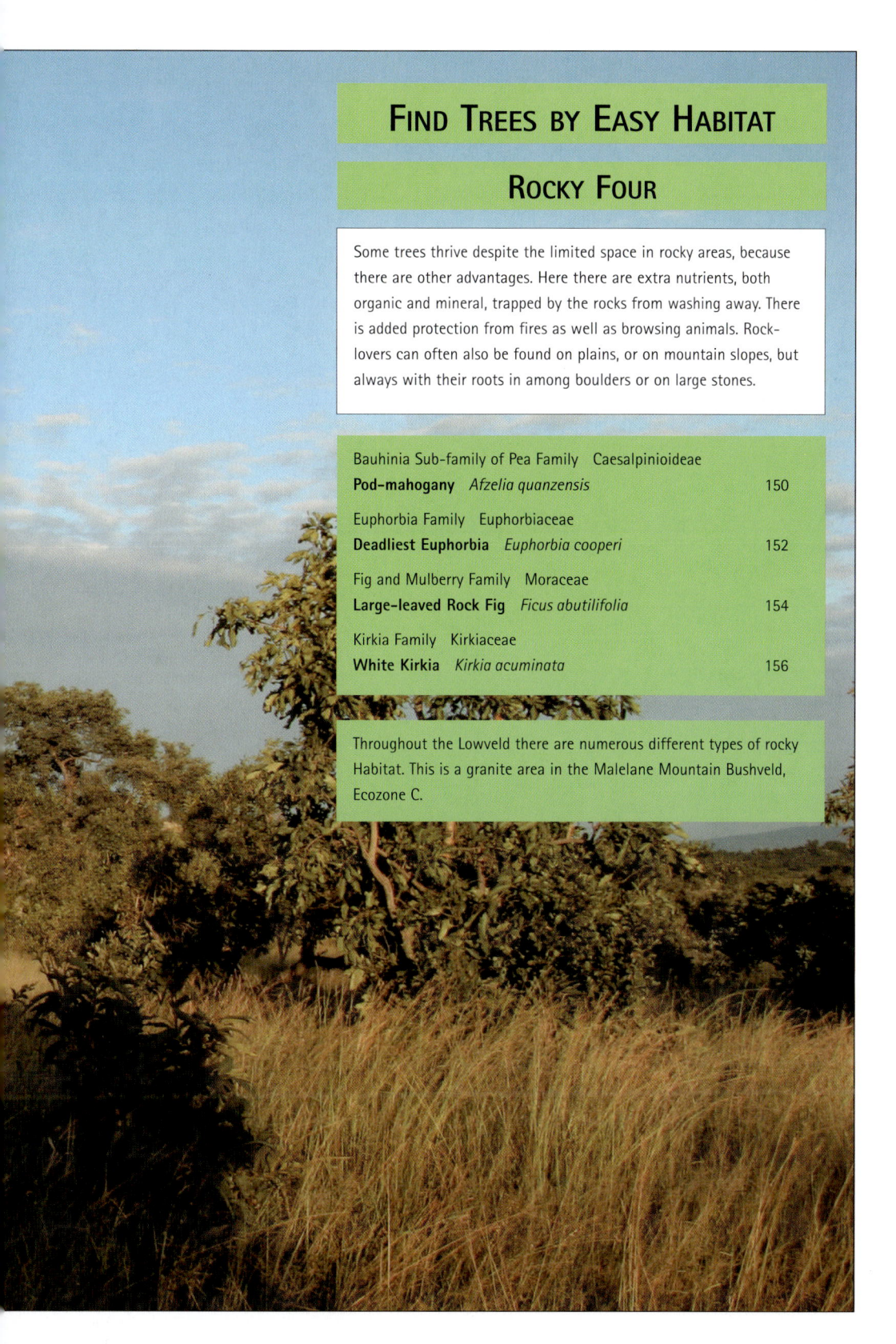

Rocky Four

Some trees thrive despite the limited space in rocky areas, because there are other advantages. Here there are extra nutrients, both organic and mineral, trapped by the rocks from washing away. There is added protection from fires as well as browsing animals. Rock-lovers can often also be found on plains, or on mountain slopes, but always with their roots in among boulders or on large stones.

Bauhinia Sub-family of Pea Family Caesalpinioideae	
Pod-mahogany *Afzelia quanzensis*	150
Euphorbia Family Euphorbiaceae	
Deadliest Euphorbia *Euphorbia cooperi*	152
Fig and Mulberry Family Moraceae	
Large-leaved Rock Fig *Ficus abutilifolia*	154
Kirkia Family Kirkiaceae	
White Kirkia *Kirkia acuminata*	156

Throughout the Lowveld there are numerous different types of rocky Habitat. This is a granite area in the Malelane Mountain Bushveld, Ecozone C.

BAUHINIA SUB-FAMILY OF PEA FAMILY   Caesalpinioideae   Tree no 207

POD-MAHOGANY   *Afzelia quanzensis*

AFRIKAANS Peulmahonie **SISWATI** umKholikholi **TSONGA** Nxenhe **VENDA** Mutokota
ZULU umHlakuva, umShamfuthi

Afzelia honours Adam Afzelius, a Swedish collector; *quanzensis* refers to the Cuanza River in Angola.

Pod

Where you'll find this tree easily

The Pod-mahogany usually grows singly, often on small rocky outcrops or in well-drained soils.

- It is easiest to find in the Sandveld (N), on sandstone ridges.
- It can also be found growing in rocky areas in Mixed Bushwillow Woodlands (A) and in both the north and south of Lebombo Mountain Bushveld (I).

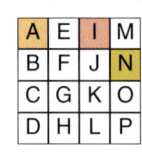

A	E	I	M
B	F	J	N
C	G	K	O
D	H	L	P

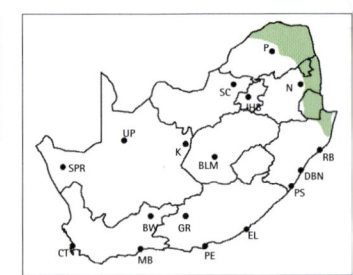

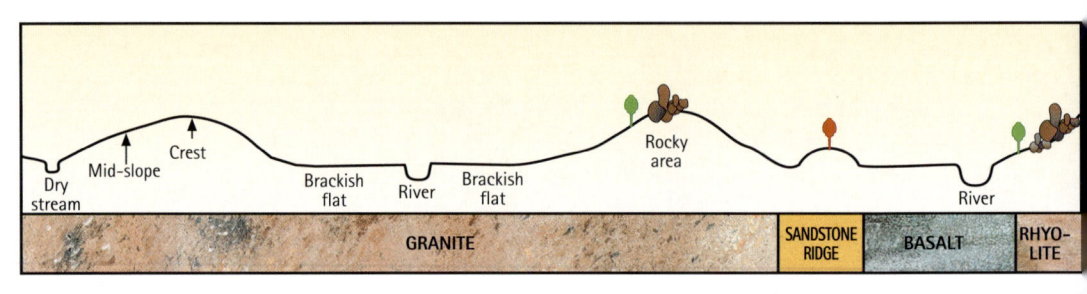

GIFF

- The Ecozone and Habitat preference of this tree helps with identification.
- **It is a large, prominent tree with a bare trunk and huge umbrella-like canopy.**
- The large, glossy leaves are Once Compound, alternate, with a pair of leaflets at the tip.
- **Black and red seeds are conspicuous when the flat, woody, broad bean pods burst open from April.**
- Conspicuous individual flowers, each have a single red petal and prominent stamens.
- The flowers grow on the ends of branches, standing upright among the drooping leaves.

In rocky areas in Ecozones A, I, and N, the Pod-mahogany is a strikingly distinctive tree.

Seasonal changes

Deciduous. In spring the copper-coloured, glossy foliage stands out amongst the other trees. In its specific Habitat, the size of the tree and the umbrella-like canopy will help with identification in winter.

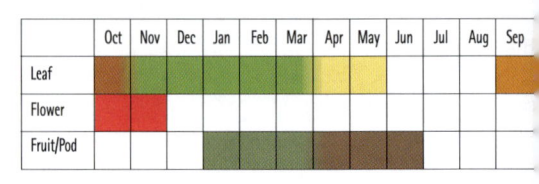

Height:
10 – 20 m
Density: Dense

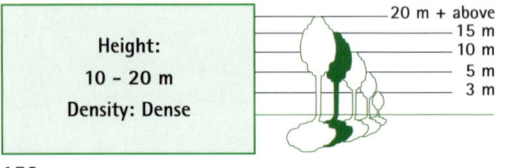

20 m + above
15 m
10 m
5 m
3 m

	Oct	Nov	Dec	Jan	Feb	Mar	Apr	May	Jun	Jul	Aug	Sep
Leaf												
Flower												
Fruit/Pod												

Growth form
The single, straight trunk is often high-branching, and branches grow horizontally.

Leaves
Leaflets are elliptic with a wavy margin. The shiny, dark green leaves are coppery-red when new in spring (Leaf: 150 - 400 mm; 4 - 7 pairs of leaflets: 55 x 30 mm).

Flowers
See GIFF. The flowers seldom form a striking display, as buds do not all open at the same time during October and November (50 mm).

Pods
Pods appear from January. They ripen to dark brown, between April and June, when the pods burst open (150 x 70 mm).

Bark
In younger trees, the bark is mostly smooth and pale grey. In older trees it is dark grey and flakes off in irregular blocks.

ROCKY FOUR — Pod-mahogany

Look-alike trees
See the comparisons of various Once Compound leaves in the Distinctive Striking Features, pages 69-70.

Gardening
This ornamental shade tree can be very attractive in the garden, preferring well-drained soils. It is fairly drought-resistant once established, but is very sensitive to frost. This tree can be grown from seed, but is slow-growing.

Links with animals
The leaves are eaten by elephant and duiker, the bark and shoots by elephant, and fallen flowers by all antelope. The caterpillars of Charaxes butterflies eat the leaves.

Human uses
The seeds are used to make necklaces, and the wood for carpentry, wagons, railway sleepers and canoes. The roots treat eye ailments, bilharzia and pneumonia.

| EUPHORBIA FAMILY | Euphorbiaceae | Tree no 346 |

DEADLIEST EUPHORBIA *Euphorbia cooperi*

AFRIKAANS Noorsdoring **N. SOTHO** Mohlotla **SISWATI** umHlonhlo, umHlohlo **TSONGA** Konde, Xihaha, Nhlohlo **VENDA** Tshikonde-ngala **ZULU** umPhapha euphorbia, umPhapha, umHlonhlo

Euphorbia honours Euphorbus, physician to King Juba of Mauritania, first century BC; **cooperi** is in honour of Thomas Cooper who collected plants in the eastern parts of South Africa between 1859 and 1862.

Flowers

Where you'll find this tree easily
The Deadliest Euphorbia grows singly in rocky areas, but there is often more than one tree in the vicinity.
- It is easiest to find this Euphorbia in the north and south of Lebombo Mountain Bushveld (I), but here it can be confused with the Lebombo Euphorbia, *Euphorbia confinalis*.
- It also occurs in the rocky hills in Pretoriuskop Sourveld (B), in Malelane Mountain Bushveld (C) and in Sabie/Crocodile Thorn Thickets (D).

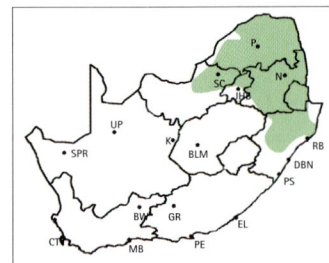

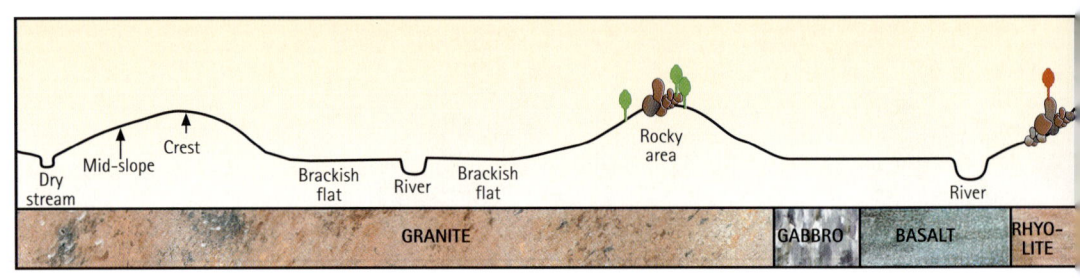

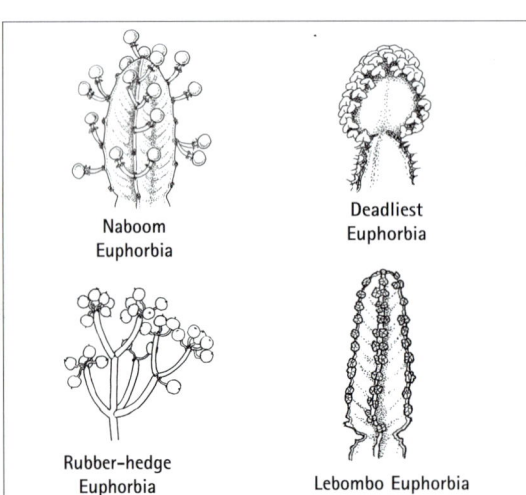

A	E	I	M
B	F	J	N
C	G	K	O
D	H	L	P

Dry stream — Mid-slope — Crest — Brackish flat — River — Brackish flat — Rocky area — River

GRANITE — GABBRO — BASALT — RHYOLITE

Naboom Euphorbia

Deadliest Euphorbia

Rubber-hedge Euphorbia

Lebombo Euphorbia

Comparisons of Euphorbias

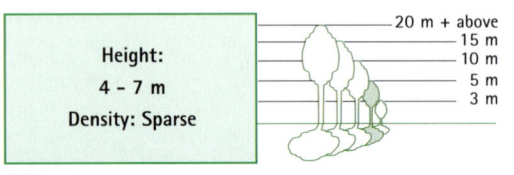

GIFF
- This is a tree with thick, succulent-looking, green branches but no obvious leaves.
- The branches leave the straight, tall, bare trunk and curl upwards to form a candelabra, wineglass shape.
- The branches create a fairly robust, but unbranching crown.
- Old, dead branches hang underneath the crown.
- Holes of previous branch attachments are visible on the trunk.
- **Branches are tightly constricted, forming a string of heart-shaped segments, that are each 4 - 6 angled.**
- **It has paired thorns along the ridges of the angles.**
- The capsule-like fruit is in rows on the ridges of the angles, and matures from green to red.

Seasonal changes
Owing to its characteristic form, this tree can be identified throughout the year, bearing in mind its look-alike tree, the Lebombo Euphorbia, *Euphorbia confinalis*.

Height: 4 - 7 m
Density: Sparse

20 m + above
15 m
10 m
5 m
3 m

	Oct	Nov	Dec	Jan	Feb	Mar	Apr	May	Jun	Jul	Aug	Sep
Leaf												
Flower												
Fruit/Pod												

Growth form
The single, straight trunk is high-branching, with the branches growing upwards.

Leave
No visible 'leaves'.

Flowers
The inconspicuous, yellow-green flowers are not true flowers. There are several male flowers and one female flower per 'flower' (cyathium). They are arranged in rows, on the ridges of the angles, on the last segment of a branch (May - Aug) (4 mm).

Fruit
The fruit bursts open on the tree, flinging the individual seeds several metres (10 mm).

Thorns
See GIFF.

Bark
See GIFF.

Look-alike trees
In Ecozone I, it is very easy to confuse this tree with the Lebombo Euphorbia, *Euphorbia confinalis*, p. 42, which occurs only in the Lebombo Mountains, and in the rhyolite of the Olifants Rugged Veld, (J). It also has heart-shaped, segmented branches, that are thinner than those of the Deadliest Euphorbia. A major difference is that the individual branches of the Lebombo Euphorbia form many side branches that originate at the same level. The Naboom Euphorbia, *Euphorbia ingens*, has thick, straight branches with slightly constricted, long, angular segments with virtually no thorns on the segments. The branches split more often than in the Deadliest Euphorbia. The other common Euphorbia, shown in the diagram on the opposite page, the Rubber-hedge Euphorbia, *Euphorbia tirucalli*, p. 39, is very different. It has long, thin, finger-like branches.

Links with animals
The soft fruit and flowers are eaten by baboons, and the seeds by doves.

Human uses
The white, milky latex is a severe irritant to humans and animals. It is claimed that this is the most toxic of the Euphorbias and skin irritation is possible simply by standing near the open sap. It is used to stupefy fish, making it possible to catch them by hand.

Gardening
This tree can be used effectively in large, rocky, well-drained gardens of the drier areas, although its spines and severely irritant latex make it unsuitable for a family garden. It is susceptible to frost but very drought-resistant. It is slow-growing and can be grown from seed or cuttings.

| Fig and Mulberry Family | Moraceae | Tree no 63 |

Large-leaved Rock Fig — *Ficus abutilifolia*

AFRIKAANS Grootblaarrotsvy   **N. SOTHO** Monokane   **TSONGA** Xirhomberhombe
TSWANA Momelantsweng   **VENDA** Tshikululu   **ZULU** imPayi

Ficus is the Latin word for a fig; **abutilifolia** refers to the fact that the leaves resemble those of the genus Abutilon.

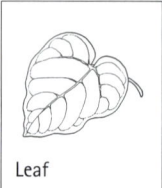

Leaf

Where you'll find this tree easily
The Large-leaved Rock Fig grows singly, only in rocky areas.
- It is easiest to find this tree on the numerous granite outcrops in Pretoriuskop Sourveld (B) and in Sabie/Crocodile Thorn Thickets (D).
- It can also be found in all other Ecozones with rocks. In the granite Ecozones this is A, C and P; and in gabbro this is Thorn Veld (E).
- It can be spotted in the rocky areas in the rhyolite, in the south of Lebombo Mountain Bushveld (I), in basalt in Olifants Rugged Veld (J), and on the sandstone ridges of Sandveld (N).

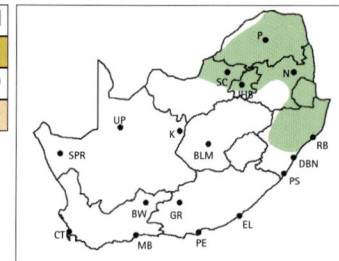

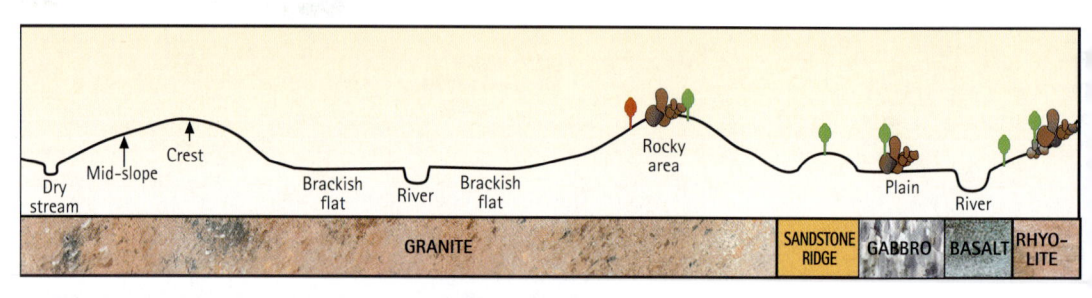

A	E	I	M
B	F	J	N
C	G	K	O
D	H	L	P

Even a small Rock Fig can start the process of splitting a huge, granite boulder.

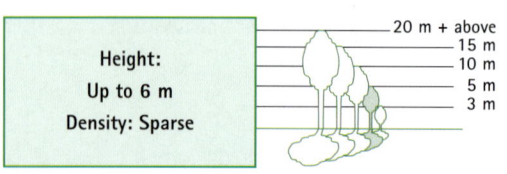

GIFF
- It has a gnarled, yellow-white, smooth trunk with papery bark that peels off.
- Conspicuous white roots are visible, spreading over the rock face.
- The large, Simple leaves are smooth and heart-shaped with prominent veins.
- All parts of the tree contain copious amounts of white latex.
- The round figs grow singly, or in small groups, on short stems, and are pale green with white spots, ripening to red.

Seasonal changes
Semi-deciduous. It can be identified throughout the year by the characteristic growth form and the colour of its bark.

Height: Up to 6 m
Density: Sparse

	Oct	Nov	Dec	Jan	Feb	Mar	Apr	May	Jun	Jul	Aug	Sep
Leaf												
Flower												
Fruit/Pod												

Growth form
The single, crooked trunk branches low down at irregular angles to form a sparse canopy.

Leaves
The leaves are spirally arranged or alternate, and the margin may be wavy. The leaves usually have a rounded tip that can, however, be pointed. The base is distinctly, deeply lobed. Leaves are dark green above and paler below. The veins are clearly visible on both surfaces and are pale red-brown to yellow. The central vein stands out underneath. The leaf-stems are long, varying from 25 to 170 mm (Leaf: 60 -160 x 80 - 250 mm).

Fruit
The figs can also grow directly on the branches in the angle formed by the leaf (Aug - Mar) (15 - 25 mm diam.).

Flowers
As in all figs the flowers are not visible as they grow inside the fig.

Bark
The bark is white to pale grey and smooth, and on older branches and trunks often flakes or peels in layers. The trunk is often twisted.

Look-alike tree
The Red-leaved Fig, *Ficus ingens*, p. 32, is also common in rocky areas. The leaves are long and thin, and new leaves are bright red (60 - 150 x 30 - 100 mm). The small figs (10 - 13 mm) are dull red when ripe.

Links with animals
Baboon, monkey, bushbuck, duiker, nyala and bushpig eat the fruit.

Human uses
The tasty fruit is a valued food. Bark extracts are taken as strengthening tonics by men.

Gardening
This tree can be used very effectively in a rocky garden. It is not frost-resistant but can withstand drought. It can be grown from cuttings and, although slow-growing, it responds well to watering in well-drained soils. It should not be planted anywhere near to buildings, driveways or ponds owing to its invasive root system.

ROCKY FOUR
Large-leaved Rock Fig

Kirkia Family — Kirkiaceae — Tree no 267

White Kirkia — *Kirkia acuminata*

AFRIKAANS Witsering **N. SOTHO** Modumela **TSONGA** Mvumayila **TSWANA** Modumela
VENDA Mubvumela **ZULU** umSila-omhlophe, umSilinga

Kirkia is named after Sir John Kirk who accompanied Livingstone on some of his travels; *acuminata* refers to the sharp, pointed leaflets.

Leaf

Where you'll find this tree easily
The White Kirkia is a common tree growing singly on sandstone ridges, and in rocky or sandy areas. However, where there is one, you will often find others growing in the vicinity.
- You will find this tree easily in Sandveld (N), growing on the sandstone ridges.
- You will also find it on the ridges of Lebombo Mountain Bushveld (I), in rocky areas in Olifants Rugged Veld (J) and in Mopane/Bushwillow Woodlands (P).

GIFF
- It has a tall, straight, single trunk and is often a handsome, well-proportioned tree, standing out proudly, on the crest of a rocky outcrop or ridge.
- **The bark is pale grey and smooth when young, and becomes flaky with corky knobs in older trees.**
- **Overall the tree has a pale green, fine-leaved and feathery-looking, spreading canopy.**
- The Once Compound leaves are bright lime-green to dark green, with a leaflet at the tip.
- They have long leaf-stems and are spirally arranged, clustered at the ends of bluntly tipped branchlets.
- Spectacular in autumn, the leaves turn brilliant gold and red.

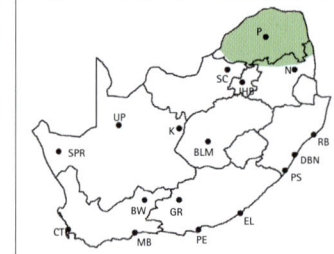

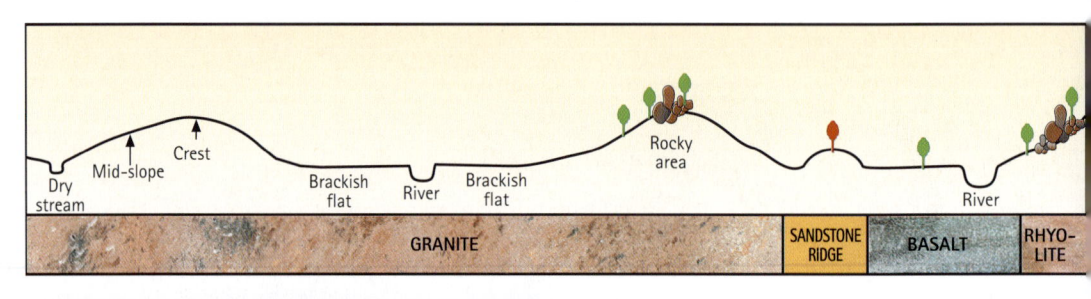

Spectacular autumn colours make this one of the most beautiful trees in the Lowveld.

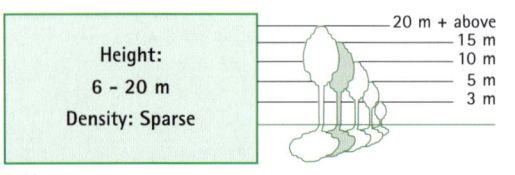

Seasonal changes
Deciduous. There is a long period without leaves in winter when it is more difficult to identify. New reddish leaves appear in spring.

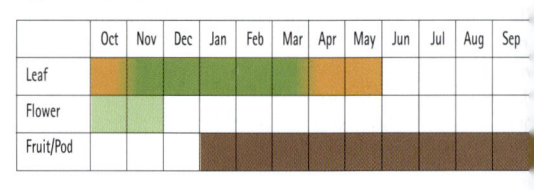

	Oct	Nov	Dec	Jan	Feb	Mar	Apr	May	Jun	Jul	Aug	Sep
Leaf												
Flower												
Fruit/Pod												

Height: 6 – 20 m **Density:** Sparse

Growth form
See GIFF.

Leaves
The leaf consists of 6 - 17 pairs of opposite or alternate leaflets. The leaflets are elliptic with finely toothed margins. They have a narrowly tapering tip and a rounded base that is asymmetrically attached to the leaflet-stem. The leaf-stalk is 50 - 100 mm long (Leaf: 200 - 450 mm; leaflet: 20 - 83 x 10 - 29 mm).

Flowers
The greenish-cream to creamy-white flowers have long stems (up to 110 mm). They grow in branched sprays at the ends of branchlets or in the angle formed by the leaves (Oct - Nov) (Spray: up to 200 mm long, including the flower-stem).

Fruit
The small, pale brown, woody capsule is divided into four sections (valves) and grows in bunches. When the capsule opens, each section contains one seed. The fruit may remain on the tree for long periods, some until the next flowering season (Jan - Sep) (15 x 5 mm).

Bark
The branchlets have visible leaf scars.

ROCKY FOUR — White Kirkia

Look-alike trees
See the comparisons of various Once Compound leaves in the Distinctive Striking Features, pages 69-70.

Gardening
This is a very attractive tree all year round, but especially in autumn and spring when the leaves are so colourful. It will only thrive in well-drained soils, such as a rocky area. It is drought-resistant but not frost-resistant. It can be grown from seeds and cuttings and is fairly fast-growing when well-watered.

Human uses
Water-laden roots may be used as a source of drinking water. The wood is used for furniture and to make household goods such as bowls.

Links with animals
Game dig up the roots in times of drought.

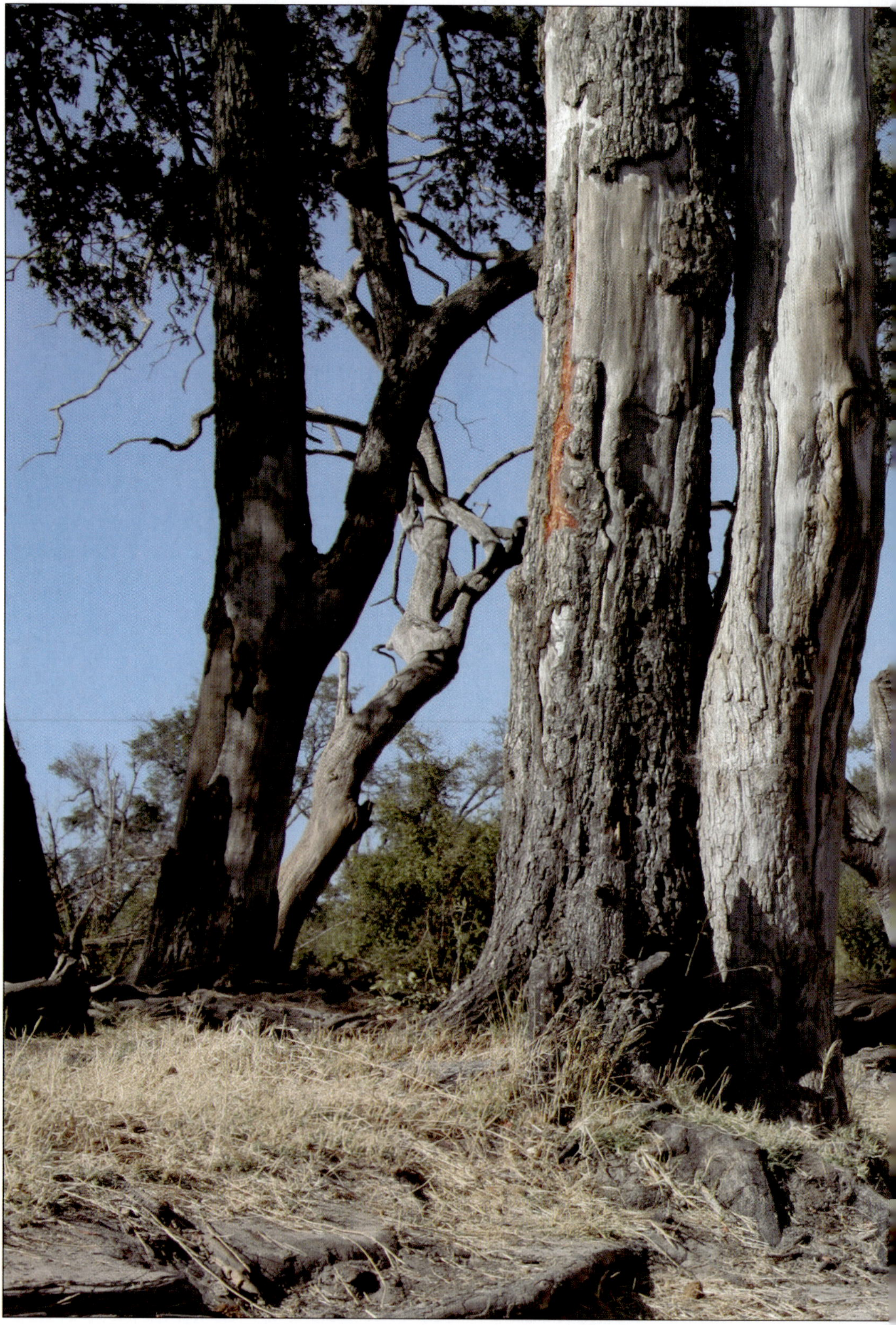

Find Trees by Easy Habitat

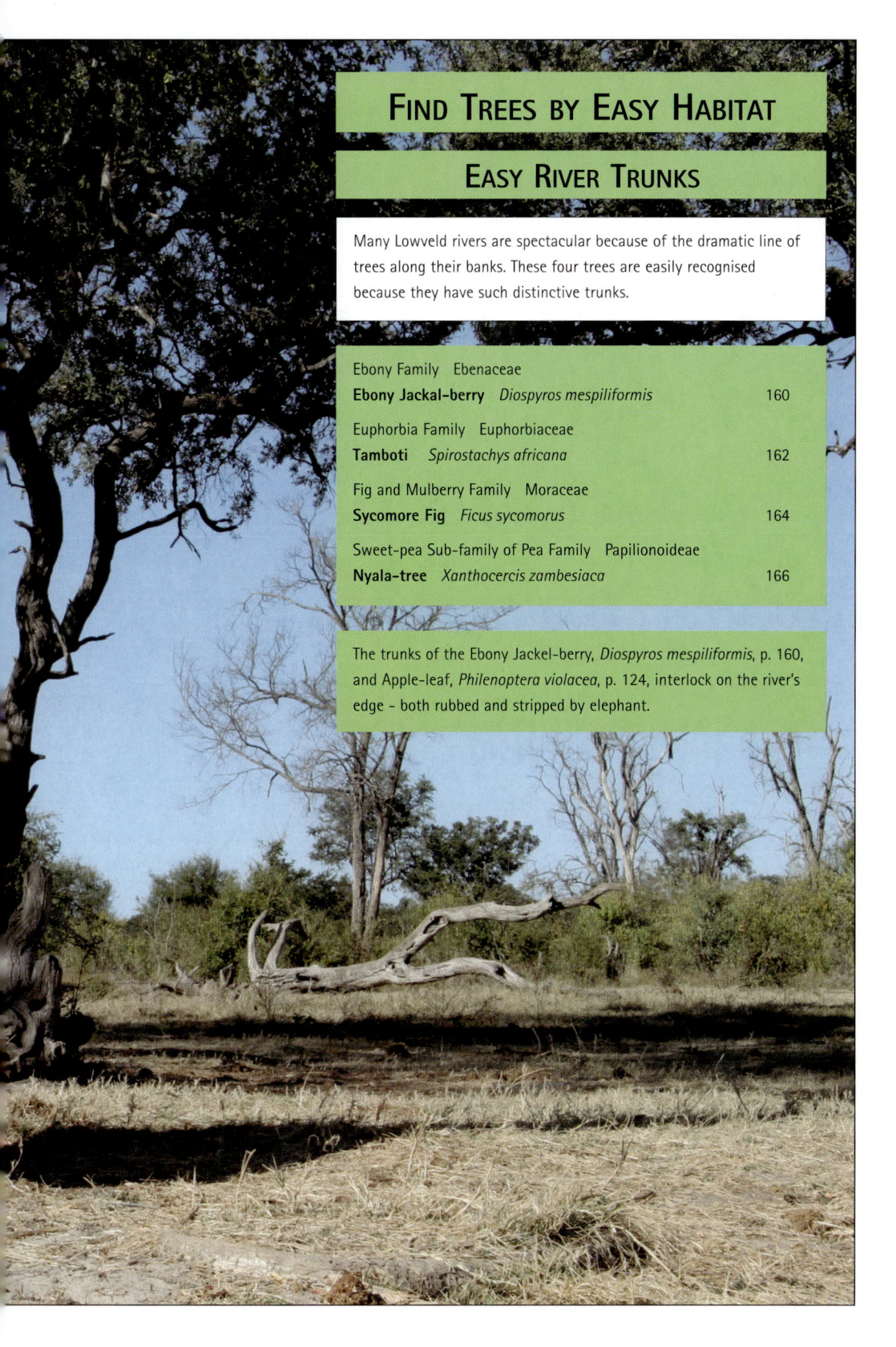

Easy River Trunks

Many Lowveld rivers are spectacular because of the dramatic line of trees along their banks. These four trees are easily recognised because they have such distinctive trunks.

Ebony Family   Ebenaceae
Ebony Jackal-berry   *Diospyros mespiliformis*   160

Euphorbia Family   Euphorbiaceae
Tamboti   *Spirostachys africana*   162

Fig and Mulberry Family   Moraceae
Sycomore Fig   *Ficus sycomorus*   164

Sweet-pea Sub-family of Pea Family   Papilionoideae
Nyala-tree   *Xanthocercis zambesiaca*   166

The trunks of the Ebony Jackel-berry, *Diospyros mespiliformis*, p. 160, and Apple-leaf, *Philenoptera violacea*, p. 124, interlock on the river's edge - both rubbed and stripped by elephant.

| EBONY FAMILY | Ebenaceae | Tree no 606 |

EBONY JACKAL-BERRY *Diospyros mespiliformis*

AFRIKAANS Jakkalsbessie   **N. SOTHO** Dithetlwa   **SISWATI** umToma   **TSONGA** Ntoma
TSWANA Mokochong   **VENDA** Muchenje   **ZULU** umThoma

Diospyros is Greek meaning 'pear of the Gods', referring to the delicious fruit of some species; *mespiliformis* means shaped like a medlar.

Leaf

Where you'll find this tree easily
The Ebony Jackal-berry grows singly along rivers and major drainage lines, as well as on termite mounds in higher rainfall areas.
- It can easily be spotted in Riverine areas (H).
- It can also be found along larger streams of all the granite Ecozones A, B, C, D and P.
- It grows along rivers in the basalt Ecozones Knob-thorn/Marula Savannah (F) and the Olifants Rugged Veld (J).
- It grows away from rivers in Pretoriuskop Sourveld (B), because the rainfall is higher.

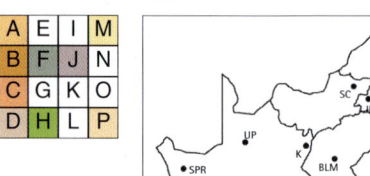

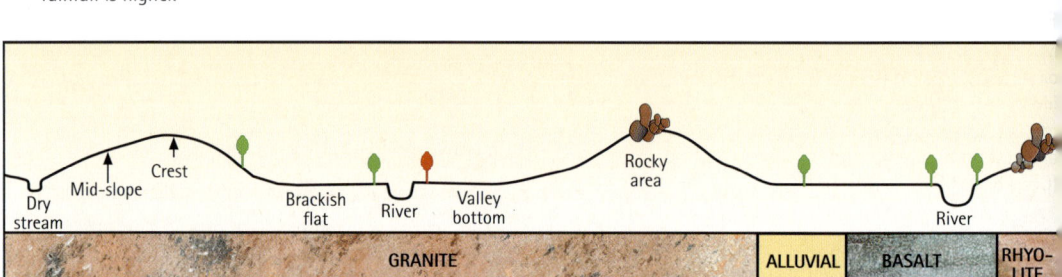

A	E	I	M
B	F	J	N
C	G	K	O
D	H	L	P

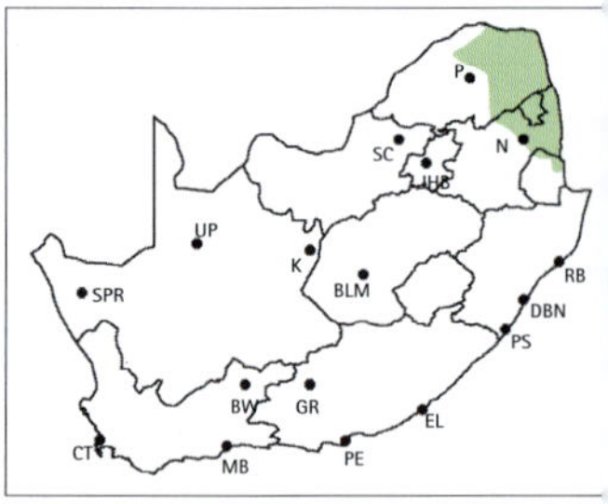

GIFF
- This is a large tree with a dense, dark green, roundish, spreading canopy.
- The single, massive trunk is usually gnarled or fluted.
- The trunk divides into a few large branches that spread out horizontally close to their origin. Each branch is itself very thick and trunk-like.
- The bark is black-grey, looking as though the tree has been burnt. It is rough and often deeply grooved.
- The leaves are Simple, alternate and elliptic with a distinctive, closely waved margin.
- Round, green berries take up to a year to ripen to yellow.

Young Ebony Jackal-berry trees are striking with old, yellow leaves, along a river in September.

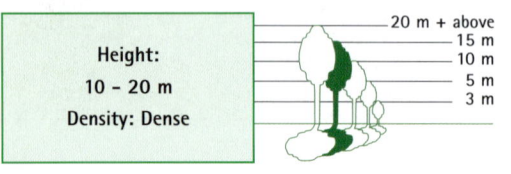

Seasonal changes
Deciduous. However, this tree is seldom without leaves, as new leaves appear at the same time as the old ones fall.

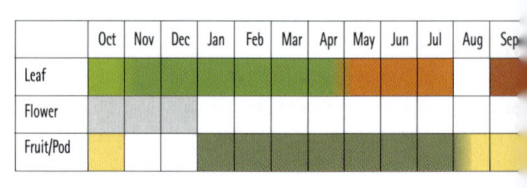

Height: 10 – 20 m
Density: Dense

	Oct	Nov	Dec	Jan	Feb	Mar	Apr	May	Jun	Jul	Aug	Sep
Leaf												
Flower												
Fruit/Pod												

160

Growth form
See GIFF.

Leaves
Young leaves are reddish, changing to dark green above and paler green below. A few old leaves turn yellow in the canopy throughout the year, and then all the leaves change and drop together as a spectacular show in late winter to spring (80 x 30 mm).

(F)

(M)

Flowers
Male and female flowers grow on different trees. They are all inconspicuous, fragrant and creamy-white, and appear after the new leaves (Oct - Dec) (12 mm).

Bark
See GIFF.

Fruit
Because of the slow ripening time, berries are sometimes present in large numbers, and most of the year you can find a few on many trees. In game reserves they tend to be eaten before they are fully ripe the following September and October (20 mm).

Look-alike tree
This tree can be confused with the Tamboti, *Spirostachys africana*, p. 162, which has dark, distinctive, very regularly blocked bark, and small, Simple leaves with toothed edges. Tambotis often grow in groups, and young trees have pale bark and spines.

Gardening
This very attractive shade tree can enhance any big garden. It will grow best in well-drained soils. It cannot take severe frost and needs to be well watered. It grows slowly but easily from seed.

Human uses
The wood is used to make furniture and household articles such as pestles for grinding maize. The fruit is edible. Fruit, leaves and roots contain tannins and have medicinal uses in the treatment of wounds and against internal parasites. Extracts of various parts of the tree have antibiotic properties.

Links with animals
Ripening fruit is eaten by African Green-pigeons, Brown-headed Parrots, African Grey Hornbills and Purple-crested Turacos. It is also eaten off the tree by monkey and baboon, and fallen fruit by kudu, impala, nyala and jackal. The leaves are browsed by elephant, kudu and eland.

EASY RIVER TRUNKS
Ebony Jackal-berry

161

EUPHORBIA FAMILY — Euphorbiaceae — Tree no 341

TAMBOTI — *Spirostachys africana*

AFRIKAANS Tambotie **N. SOTHO** Morekuri (Modiba) **SISWATI** umThombotsi, umThombothi
TSONGA Ndzopfori **TSWANA** Morukuru **VENDA** Muonze **ZULU** umThombothi, iJuqa, uvBanda

Spirostachys refers to the spiral arrangement of flowers on the spike; ***africana*** means of Africa.

Leaf

Where you'll find this tree easily

Tamboti grow singly along rivers, as well as in dense groups of smaller trees in brack areas. It is easier to find in the granites, gabbro and Ecca shale Ecozones, than in the basalts.

- It can most easily be found along rivers and drainage lines, and in Riverine areas (H), particularly in Mixed Bushwillow Woodlands (A).
- It can be spotted in drainage lines, valley bottoms and in brack areas in all other granite Ecozones, B, C, D and P.
- You can also find it on the plains of Thorn Veld (E), Delagoa Thorn Thickets (G), Alluvial Plains (M) and Tree Mopane Savannah (O).

GIFF

- This tree has a straight, upright, single, bare trunk, with a dense, narrow to rounded canopy.
- Being a member of the Euphorbia family, all parts produce white, milky, irritant latex when broken or cut.
- **The bark is characteristically dark to black, thick, rough and neatly cracked into regular rectangles.**
- Simple, elliptic leaves have finely toothed margins.
- **Old, red leaves are often visible among the mature, green leaves and on the ground, below the tree.**
- In late winter, before the new leaves appear, trees have a distinct red sheen caused by the red female portion of flower-spikes.

Seasonal changes

Deciduous to evergreen. This depends on where it grows. Leaves turn red before dropping in winter and the fresh new leaves in spring are pale green. The bark is characteristic making identification possible even when no leaves are present.

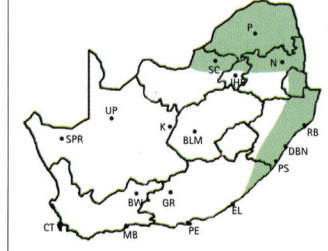

Tamboti often grow in groups along edges of smaller rivers and streams.

Height: 5 – 10 m
Density: Dense

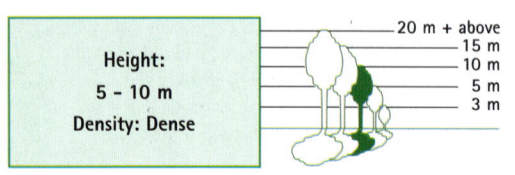

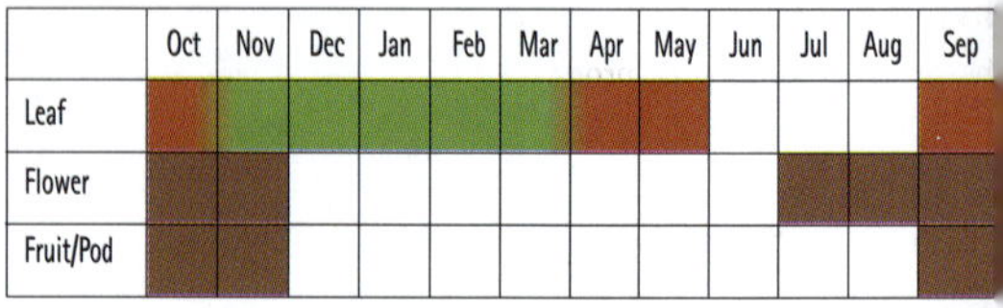

162

Growth form
It is often in groups of a few big trees growing fairly close together with spiny, pale-barked, young trees clustered densely nearby. The trunk is high-branching with branches growing upwards. Young trees may have multiple trunks and spines of up to 150 mm.

Leaves
Dull green leaves grow in a spiral along the branchlets. They have short leaf-stems. (50 x 25 mm).

Fruit
The brown capsules are three-lobed, and open with an audible explosion, that can be heard on hot summer days – see Links with animals below. They mature from September to November (10 mm).

Flowers
Both male and female flowers are on the same spikes, at the ends of branchlets and twigs. The male flowers are yellow, due to the abundance of pollen (Jul - Nov) (15 - 30 mm).

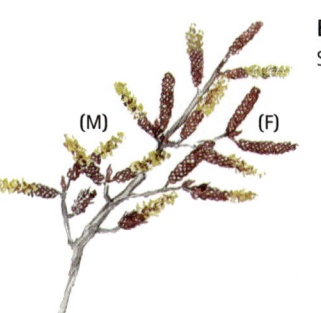

Bark
See GIFF.

(M) (F)

Look-alike tree
The bark is as dark as that of the Ebony Jackal-berry, *Diospyros mespiliformis*, p. 160. Ebony Jackal-berry bark looks burnt and is irregularly coarse. Tamboti bark has blocks that are neat, regular rectangles. The leaves are both Simple and the same size with wavy margins, but Tamboti have finely toothed edges.

Gardening
This tree can be very attractive in a large garden. It is fairly drought- and frost-resistant. It grows well from seed but slowly.

Human uses
The very valuable wood produces exceptional furniture. The poisonous latex is used to stupefy fish, making them easier to catch, but can cause severe illness if the wood is used to fuel cooking fires.

Links with animals
The fallen seeds are eaten by francolin, doves and Crested Guineafowl, and young branches by Black Rhino. Giraffe browse leaves on the tree, and dry, fallen leaves are eaten by kudu, nyala, impala and Vervet Monkey. The seeds are often infested with the catepillars of the Knotthorn Moth, *Melanobasis*, which cause the seeds to jump when they straighten themselves inside. This has led to the name 'jumping beans'.

EASY RIVER TRUNKS
Tamboti

163

FIG AND MULBERRY FAMILY | Moraceae | Tree no 66

SYCOMORE FIG | *Ficus sycomorus*

AFRIKAANS Sycomorusvy **N. SOTHO** Motoro, Magoboya **TSONGA** Nkuwa **VENDA** Muhuyu-lukuse
ZULU umNcongo, umNconjiwa, umKhiwane

Ficus is the Latin word for a fig; **sycomorus** is derived from the Greek word meaning fig-mulberry.

Fruit   Leaf

Where you'll find this tree easily
The Sycomore Fig grows singly along perennial rivers, as well as along very large rivers that, most years, have sub-surface water flow.
- It is easiest to find this tree in Riverine (H).
- It is common along rivers of Sabie/Crocodile Thorn Thickets (D), along these two major rivers, as well as along the rivers of Knob-thorn/ Marula Savannah (F) and Olifants Rugged Veld (J).
- It can also be spotted on termite mounds close to rivers in Pretoriuskop Sourveld (B).

A	E	I	M
B	F	J	N
C	G	K	O
D	H	L	P

GIFF
- The Sycomore Fig has a single, fluted, relatively short but massive trunk, that is often buttressed and gnarled.
- The tree spreads widely, low down, into thick horizontal an upright branches.
- The yellow-pinkish, smooth bark has peeling, papery sections.
- The huge canopy is wide with pale branches clearly visible between the leaves, even to the edges of the tree.
- The Simple, round leaves cluster around the branchlets and are thin, hard, hairy and rough, like a cat's tongue.
- Fruit can be seen most of the year, and grow in heavily branched masses on the trunk and main branches.

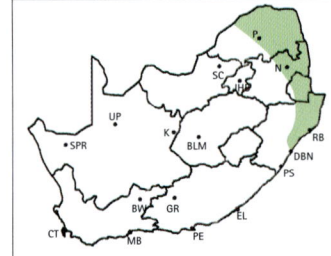

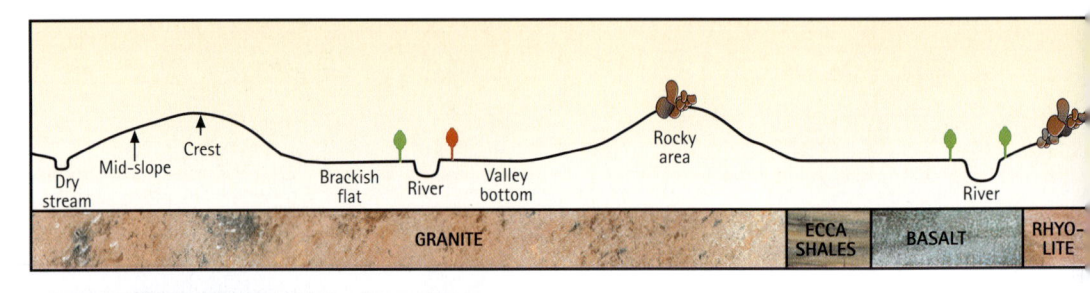

A handsome, giant Sycomore Fig grows along a river bank, with debris from a flood hooked in its branches.

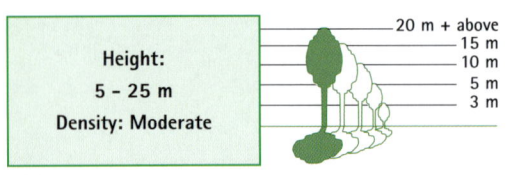

Seasonal changes
Evergreen to semi-deciduous. In years with even minimal rainfall, this tree does not lose all its leaves at once. The leaves turn yellow and fall throughout the year.

Height: 5 – 25 m
Density: Moderate

20 m + above
15 m
10 m
5 m
3 m

	Oct	Nov	Dec	Jan	Feb	Mar	Apr	May	Jun	Jul	Aug	Sep
Leaf												
Flower												
Fruit/Pod												

Growth form
It has a single trunk that branches low down. The horizontal branches form a moderately dense canopy.

Leaves
Leaves are almost round to heart-shaped and sometimes lobed, with a wavy margin. They have three distinct veins from the base (80 x 50 mm).

Flowers
Flowers grow inside the fruit and are not visible – this is a feature of all figs.

Fruit
The plum-like fruit is green to yellow-brown, turning pinkish when ripe. Fruit ripens throughout the year and trees can produce up to four crops annually (30 mm).

Bark
The peeling bark exposes a pinkish, yellowish or greenish under-surface.

Look-alike tree
All figs have similarities that can be confusing. The Sycomore Fig in the Lowveld is almost always on riverbanks, or occasionally on an old termite mound, and is often massive. The yellow-pink-green tinge to the bark is distinctive.

Links with animals
The fruit is the favourite food of hornbills, barbets, rollers, African Green-pigeons and Brown-headed Parrots. It is also eaten off the tree by baboon, monkey and bushbabies. Bushpig, warthog, rhino and many antelope 'browse' the fallen figs from the ground below.

Human uses
The trunk is used to make drums such as those seen at the Skukuza restaurant.

EASY RIVER TRUNKS
Sycomore Fig

165

SWEET-PEA SUB-FAMILY OF PEA FAMILY Papilionoideae Tree no 241

NYALA-TREE
Xanthocercis zambesiaca

AFRIKAANS Njalaboom   **TSONGA** Nhlahu   **TSWANA** Motha

Xanthocercis is from the Greek *xantho* + *cercis* meaning 'yellow' + the genus Cercis; **zambesiaca** refers to the Zambezi River.

Leaf

Where you'll find this tree easily
Nyala-trees grows singly in alluvial soils of the larger rivers as well as in deep, sandy soils. They are more common in the north. They are mostly riverine trees, but even there, they often look as though they are growing on termite mounds.

- It is easiest to find this tree growing in Riverine areas (H) of the major rivers in the north, as well as along rivers in Alluvial Plains (M).
- You can also find it along rivers and larger streams of the Sabie/Crocodile Thorn Thickets (D) as well as in Olifants Rugged Veld (J).

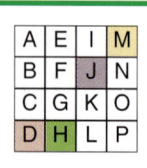

A	E	I	M
B	F	J	N
C	G	K	O
D	H	L	P

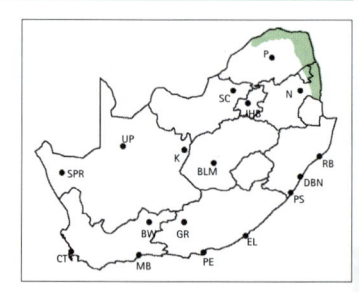

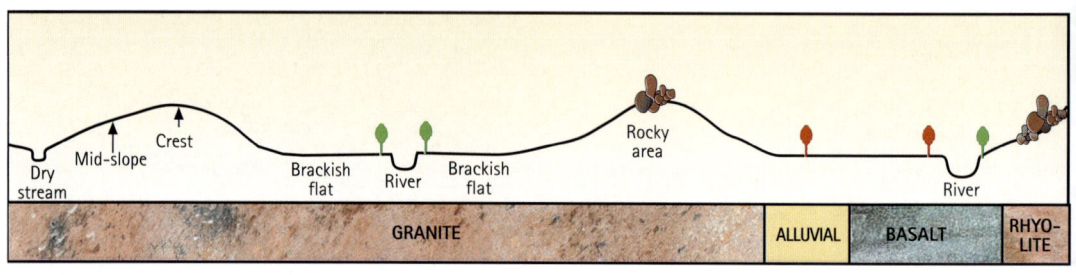

GIFF
- This is a large, dense, evergreen, riverine tree that branches low down to form a wide-spreading, round canopy.
- The massive trunk often appears to be comprised of multiple stems buttressed together.
- **The trunk is gnarled and crooked with clusters of untidy leaves growing low down, directly from the trunk.**
- Bark is dark grey tinged with yellow and tends to be rough. It does not peel, but is cracked into small, irregular squares.
- **The relatively small, Once Compound leaves are dark green and shiny, and have a single leaflet at the tip.**
- The grape-like fruit starts green and then turns dark brown from March, staying on the tree until the following spring.

The massive, dramatic skeleton of the Nyala-tree is visible through new spring leaves.

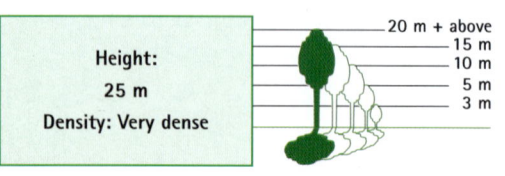

Seasonal changes
Evergreen to semi-deciduous. This tree can be recognised throughout the year.

	Oct	Nov	Dec	Jan	Feb	Mar	Apr	May	Jun	Jul	Aug	Sep
Leaf												
Flower												
Fruit/Pod												

Height: 25 m
Density: Very dense

Growth form
Branches come off horizontally and droop at the ends.

Leaves
The leaves are alternate and oval, with smooth margins. There are up to 7 pairs of leaflets that are actually not true pairs, being close to alternate. The leaves, being small, are not easily individually distinguishable from a distance of 30 metres (Leaf: 120 mm; leaflet: 55 x 20 mm).

Fruit
See GIFF.
(25 x 20 mm).

Bark
See GIFF.

Flowers
The small, inconspicuous flowers have a prominent stamen. Sweet-smelling, white to cream sprays grow at the end of the branches (Nov - Dec) (Spray: 50 - 100 mm).

Look-alike tree
The Once Compound leaf of the Nyala-tree is similar to other riverine trees, like the Sausage-tree, *Kigelia africana*, p. 178, the Natal-Mahogany, *Trichilia emetica*, p. 180, and Weeping Boer-bean, *Schotia brachypetala*, p. 170. However, it is the only reasonably common, large tree along rivers, with a Once Compound leaf that has such small leaflets, which are also not exactly opposite. The untidy leaves around the base of the trunk are also diagnostic. See the comparisons of various Once Compound leaves in the Distinctive Striking Features, pages 69-70.

Gardening
An ornamental shade tree that grows well in clay soils in large gardens, it is not frost- or drought-resistant. It can be grown from seed but is a slow grower.

Links with animals
The fruit is eaten off the tree by a wide variety of birds, as well as by monkey and baboon. Elephant and buck eat fruit that has fallen to the ground.

Human uses
The fruits are edible when fresh, and are used to make a porridge when dried.

EASY RIVER TRUNKS
Nyala-tree

167

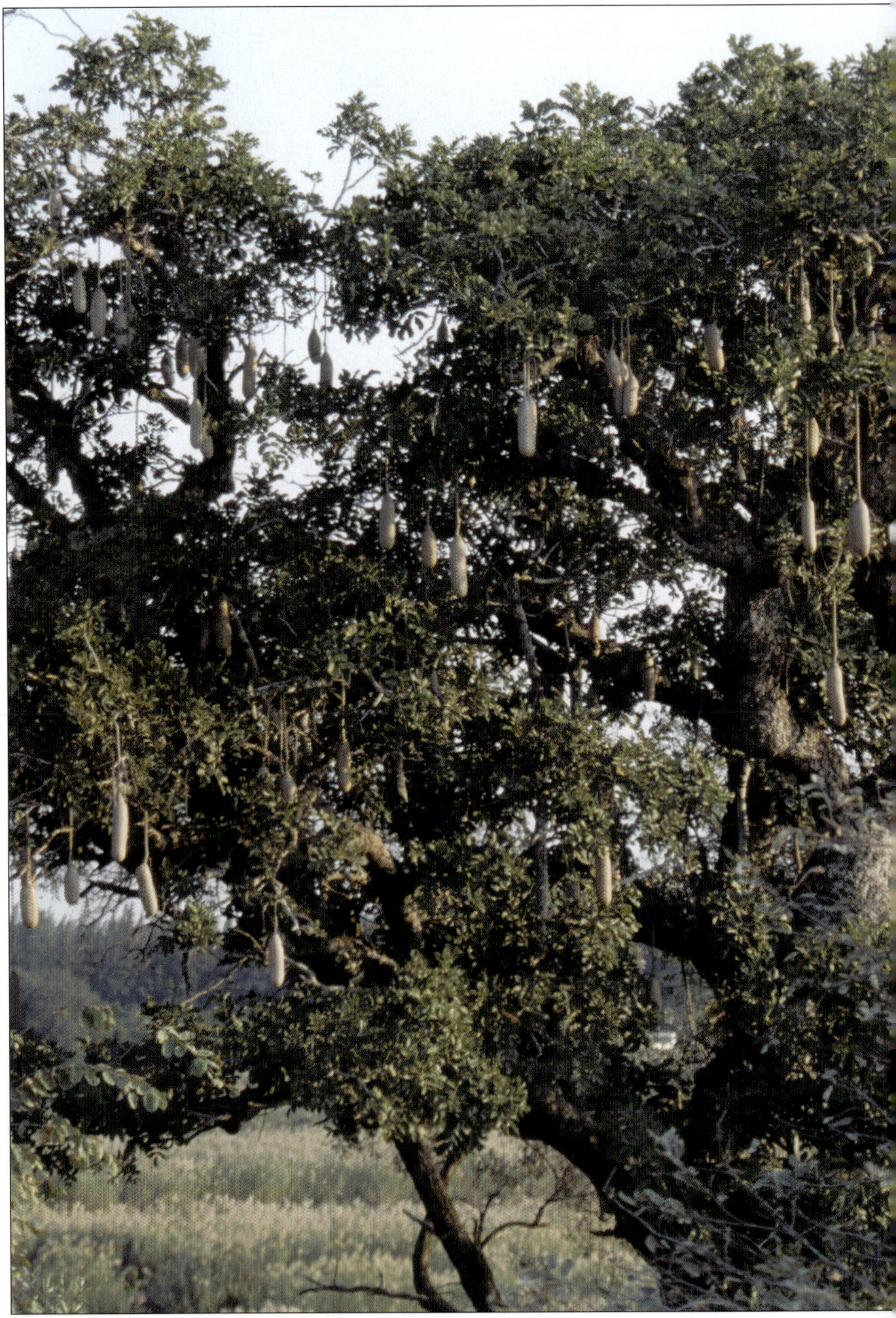

FIND TREES BY EASY HABITAT

EASY RIVER CANOPIES

The trees along Lowveld rivers grow spectacularly large, and they are often crowded together. None-the-less, the seven trees in this chapter have distinctive foliage that should make clear Search Images easy to develop. Sometimes the trees of the Big Six, pages 116-127, are also found along rivers so you could watch out for those too.

Bauhinia Sub-family of Pea Family   Caesalpinioideae
Weeping Boer-bean   *Schotia brachypetala*   170

Buddleja Family   Buddlejaceae
Water Nuxia   *Nuxia oppositifolia*   172

Bushwillow Family   Combretaceae
River Bushwillow   *Combretum erythrophyllum*   174

Coffee and Gardenia Family   Rubiaceae
Matumi   *Breonadia salicina*   176

Jacaranda Family   Bignoniaceae
Sausage-tree   *Kigelia africana*   178

Mahogany Family   Meliaceae
Natal-mahogany   *Trichilia emetica*   180

Thorn-tree Sub-family of Pea Family   Mimosoideae
River Acacia   *Acacia robusta*   182

This Sausage-tree, *Kigelia africana*, p. 178, along the Sabie River, cannot be mistaken for any other tree because of the presence of the distinctive fruit, and the stiff Once Compound leaves.

BAUHINIA SUB-FAMILY OF PEA FAMILY   Caesalpinioideae   Tree no 202

WEEPING BOER-BEAN   *Schotia brachypetala*

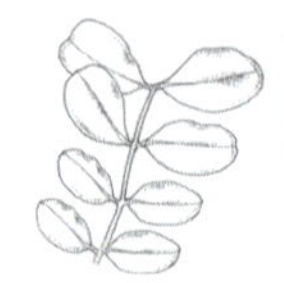

AFRIKAANS Huilboerboon   **N. SOTHO** Molope   **SISWATI** uVovovo   **TSONGA** N'wavulombe
ZULU uVovovo, umGxamu

Leaf

Schotia is named after Richard van der Schot, the head gardener at Schonbrunn, Vienna; **brachypetala** means with short petals.

Where you'll find this tree easily

The Weeping Boer-bean grows singly along larger rivers and in higher rainfall areas, often on termite mounds.

A	E	I	M
B	F	J	N
C	G	K	O
D	H	L	P

- It occurs in Riverine areas (H) virtually throughout the Lowveld.
- The easiest places to find it, however, are on major rivers running through the granite Ecozones, Mixed Bushwillow Woodlands (A), Pretoriuskop Sourveld (B), Malelane Mountain Bushveld (C) and Sabie/Crocodile Thorn Thickets (D).
- It can also be found on termite mounds in these same Ecozones A, B, C and D, as well as in Olifants Rugged Veld (J).

Dry stream — Mid-slope — Crest — Brackish flat — River — Valley bottom — Rocky area — River

GRANITE | ECCA SHALES | BASALT | RHYOLITE

GIFF

- It has a single, straight trunk that branches low down, to form a round, very dense, dark green canopy.
- On the canopy edge, branchlets and twigs tend to curve downwards, giving it its common English name. In game reserves these are often bare from browsing.
- **The Once Compound leaves have no terminal leaflet, which can help to differentiate this tree from other common, riverine species.**
- Conspicuous, dark crimson flowers make identification easy from mid-August to October.
- It has large broad, brown, bean-like pods that burst open on the tree from March to September.

Seasonal changes

Deciduous to semi-deciduous. This tree loses its leaves very late, and often over a very short period, just before the flowers appear. It is therefore easy to identify, except for a short leafless period in early spring.

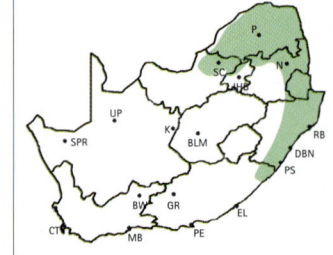

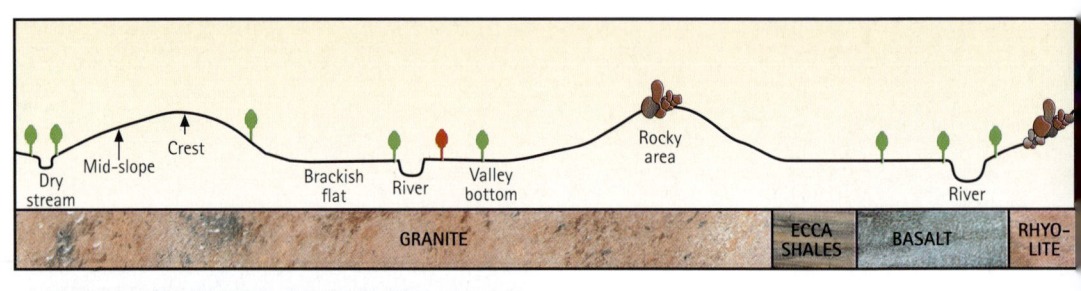

These Weeping Boer-bean flowers overhang N'wanetsi Dam, in Kruger Park in spring.

Height: 15 – 25 m
Density: Very dense

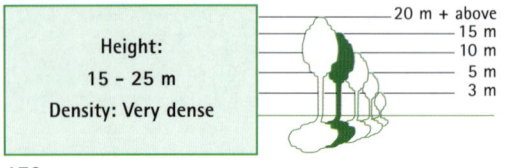

20 m + above / 15 m / 10 m / 5 m / 3 m

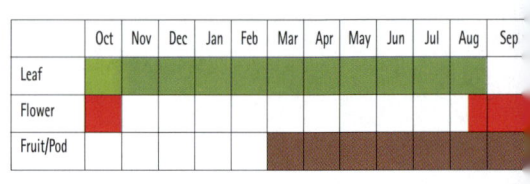

	Oct	Nov	Dec	Jan	Feb	Mar	Apr	May	Jun	Jul	Aug	Sep
Leaf												
Flower												
Fruit/Pod												

Growth form
See GIFF.

Leaves
The leaves have 4 - 7 pairs of leaflets with a pair at the tip. They are opposite to almost opposite, and broadly elliptic with a smooth margin. The central vein of each leaflet tends to be off-centre at the base. The leaves fall just before spring and are quickly replaced by new young leaves (Leaf: 180 mm; Leaflet: 65 x 40 mm).

Flowers
Flowers with prominent stamens grow at the end of the older branches (Spray: 60 - 130 mm).

Pods
Large, flat, slightly curved bean pods may hang for many months before dropping (160 x 40 mm).

Bark
The bark of younger trees is smooth and pale brown. As the tree ages, the bark becomes darker and rougher, breaking up into small, nondescript blocks.

EASY RIVER CANOPIES — Weeping Boer-bean

Look-alike tree
The Once Compound leaf of the Weeping Boer-bean is similar to other riverine trees, like the Sausage-tree, *Kigelia africana*, p. 178, the Natal-mahogany, *Trichilia emetica*, p. 180, and Nyala-tree, *Xanthocercis zambesiaca*, p. 166. However, it is the only commonly found, large tree along rivers, with a Once Compound leaf with a pair of leaflets at the tip. See the comparisons of various Once Compound leaves in the Distinctive Striking Features, pages 69-70.

Gardening
This decorative tree will grow in most gardens. It is sensitive to severe frost, but drought-resistant once established. It can be grown from seed and is fast-growing when planted in fertile soils and watered well.

Links with animals
Mature leaves are eaten by baboon, while young leaves are eaten by kudu, giraffe, impala and Black Rhino. The bark is also eaten by Black Rhino. Baboon, monkey, birds and insects drink the very sweet nectar.

Human uses
The roasted seeds are edible. Extracts of the bark are used for treating heartburn and hangovers.

171

Buddleja Family	Buddlejaceae	Tree no 635

Water Nuxia
Nuxia oppositifolia

AFRIKAANS Watervlier   **ZULU** iNkhweza

Leaves

Nuxia is in honour of the French Botanist, M de la Nux; **oppositifolia** means opposite leaves.

Where you'll find this tree easily
The Water Nuxia grows in groups along the perennial rivers.
- This tree can most easily be found growing in Riverine areas (H).
- It can also be found along larger rivers and streams of Sabie/Crocodile Thorn Thickets (D) and Alluvial Plains (M).

A	E	I	**M**
B	F	J	N
C	G	K	O
D	**H**	L	P

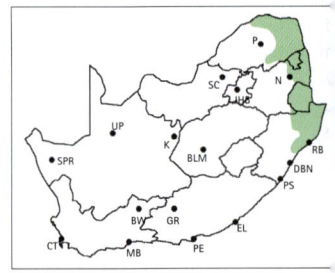

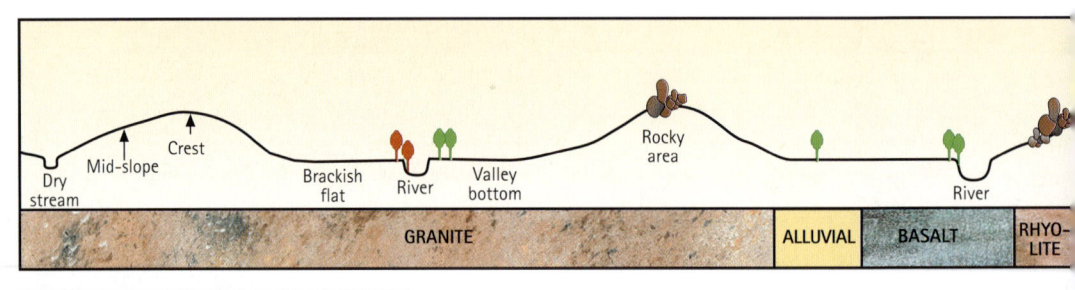

GIFF
- This is a dense, pale-green, extremely fine-leaved tree, only growing right on the edges of rivers and in riverbeds.
- It is a multi-stemmed, low-branching tree with stems that are fairly upright and slender.
- Simple leaves are thin, elliptic, opposite and long, and tend to stand upright.
- The branches, however, form downward curves.
- The bark is pale to dark brown with many distinct, lengthways fissures.

Water Nuxia are fine-leaved and beautiful along riverbanks.

Seasonal changes
Evergreen. This tree can be identified throughout the year.

	Oct	Nov	Dec	Jan	Feb	Mar	Apr	May	Jun	Jul	Aug	Se
Leaf												
Flower												
Fruit/Pod												

Height: 2 - 8 m
Density: Moderate

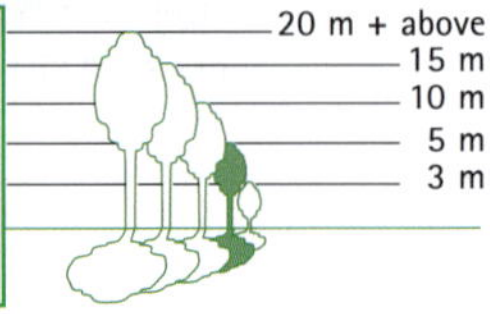

Growth form
The branches are long and thin, and older trees tend to have a V-shaped canopy.

Leaves
Leaves are narrow at the base and rounded at the tip. They are slightly closed, pale green and glossy above and dull below. Young leaves are covered by minute hairs and are slightly sticky. The veins are prominent and stand out underneath. The top third of the margin is toothed and wavy (80 x 100 mm).

Flowers
Inconspicuous, white, trumpet-like flowers grow in sprays at the end of the branches (Oct - Feb).

Fruit
Small, inconspicuous fruit capsules turn brown when ripe and stay on the tree for long periods (Jan - May) (5 mm).

Bark
The bark breaks up in longitudinal strips that peel. Old branches are grey to grey-brown. Young branches are almost angular owing to four distinct ridges.

EASY RIVER CANOPIES
Water Nuxia

Look-alike tree
The preferred Habitat of this tree overlaps with that of the River Bushwillow, *Combretum erythrophyllum*, p. 174, which has much broader leaves and four-winged pods.

Gardening
Very little is known about growing this tree from seed but it is probably a slow grower. It needs to be grown very near to permanent water.

Links with animals
Leaves are eaten by kudu, bushbuck and elephant and the bark and leaves by Black Rhino. Branches leaning over the river make ideal perches for smaller water-loving birds like Malachite and Pied Kingfisher.

Human uses
The wood is attractive and occasionally used for furniture.

173

BUSHWILLOW FAMILY
Combretaceae
Tree no 536

RIVER BUSHWILLOW
Combretum erythrophyllum

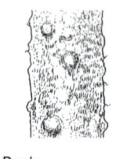

AFRIKAANS Riviervaderlandswilg **N. SOTHO** Modibo **TSWANA** Modubunoka, Mokhukhu
VENDA Muvuvhu, Mugwiti **XHOSA** umDubu **ZULU** umBondwe, umDubu

Combretum is derived from the classical Latin name for the genus used by Pliny, 23-79 AD; **erythrophyllum** refers to the red colour of the leaf in autumn.

Bark

Where you'll find this tree easily
The River Bushwillow grows in groups along the perennial rivers.
- It is easiest to find this tree growing in Riverine areas (H).
- It is most common in the riverine areas of Sabie/Crocodile Thorn Thickets (D).

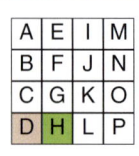

A	E	I	M
B	F	J	N
C	G	K	O
D	H	L	P

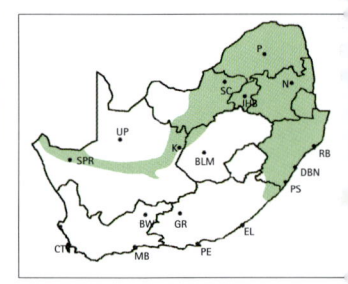

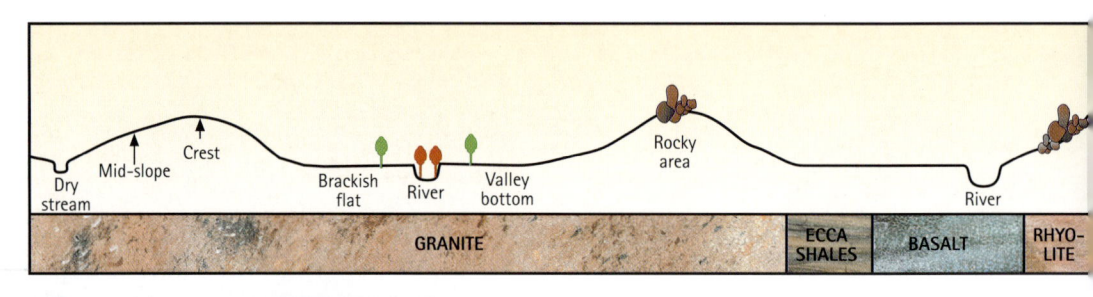

GIFF
- It is usually a multi-stemmed tree with several thick, often crooked stems growing upright, or spreading.
- **The trunk and larger branches tend to meander, and old stems are often bumpy with irregular swellings, like cellulite.**
- The bark is smooth, pale yellowish and grey-brown, and flakes in irregular patches to expose rich, apricot-coloured under-bark.
- **It has typical, four-winged, Bushwillow pods.**
- In the outer canopy new shoots are perpendicular carrying pairs of leaves growing upright in a tight V-shape.
- Simple, opposite, narrow, elliptic leaves grow towards the ends of new branches, and may form clusters.

The lumpy trunk of an older, bigger River Bushwillow looks like cellulite on fat thighs!

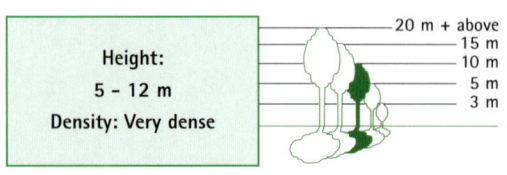

Seasonal changes
Deciduous. These trees only grow along rivers. Therefore it should be possible to identify them by their unusual bark.

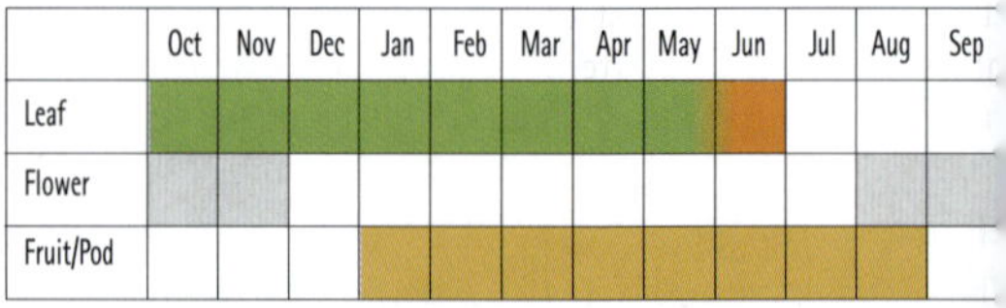

	Oct	Nov	Dec	Jan	Feb	Mar	Apr	May	Jun	Jul	Aug	Sep
Leaf												
Flower												
Fruit/Pod												

Height:
5 - 12 m
Density: Very dense

20 m + above
15 m
10 m
5 m
3 m

Growth form
The branches start from low down and form a very dense, irregular canopy of long, drooping branches, often covering the stem and hanging over the water.

Leaves
New leaves are shiny, yellow-green that deepens to darker shiny-green as the leaf matures. The leaves have a sharp tip and the margins are smooth. They are slightly hairy underneath and they turn red in autumn (50 - 100 x 20 - 50 mm).

Flowers
Roundish spikes of small, inconspicuous, cream to yellow-green, sweet-scented flowers appear just after the new leaves (Aug - Nov) (20 x 10 mm).

Pods
Abundant, small pods turn pale brown when ripe from January, and often stay on the tree until the next flowers appear in August (10 - 15 mm).

Bark
The stems are often covered by foliage in smaller trees, and then not clearly visible.

EASY RIVER CANOPIES
River Bushwillow

Look-alike tree
The Water Nuxia, *Nuxia oppositifolia*, p. 172, has simple elliptic leaves, but they are narrower, and the top one third is toothed and wavy.

Gardening
It is a very attractive, fast-growing garden plant that grows well from seed. After about two years it becomes fairly frost-resistant.

Links with animals
This is not a very palatable tree, but leaves are eaten by giraffe and elephant. Acacia Pied Barbets seem to be one of the few bird species that eat the seeds.

Human uses
The wood is used for timber. The seeds are poisonous.

175

| COFFEE AND GARDENIA FAMILY | Rubiaceae | Tree no 684 |

Matumi
Breonadia salicina

AFRIKAANS Mingerhout **SISWATI** umHlume **TSONGA** Mhlume **VENDA** Mut u-lume
ZULU umFala, umHlume

Breonadia is thought to be in honour of Jean Nicolas Breon, a French horticulturist; *salicina* means having leaves like a willow.

Leaves

Where you'll find this tree easily
The Matumi grows in rocky areas in and along rivers.
- It is easiest to find this tree in Riverine areas (H).
- It can also be found growing near or in the larger streams of Sabie/Crocodile Thorn Thickets (D), along the Olifants River in the Olifants Rugged Veld (J), and on Alluvial Plains (M).

A	E	I	M
B	F	J	N
C	G	K	O
D	H	L	P

GIFF
- This single-trunked tree overhangs large, flowing rivers and is easy to identify whether small or huge.
- It has an irregular canopy of fresh, shiny, green Simple leaves.
- Leaves are narrowly elliptic, and are crowded at the end of the branches, in a rosette.
- The leaves tend to grow upwards like the leaves of a pineapple.

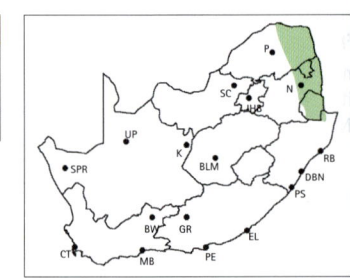

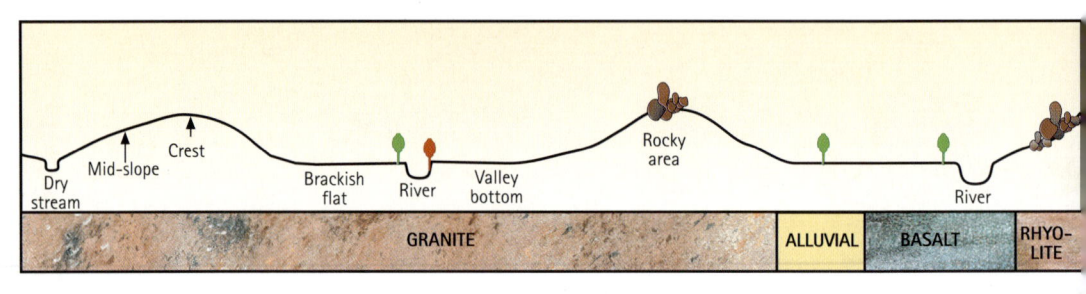

Matumis are conspicuous growing right on the edges of, or in rivers, This is a small tree, probably resprouting after a flood.

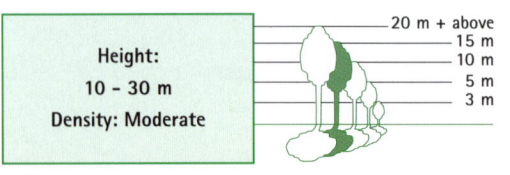

Height: 10 - 30 m
Density: Moderate

Seasonal changes
Evergreen. This tree does not lose its leaves in winter and can be identified throughout the year.

	Oct	Nov	Dec	Jan	Feb	Mar	Apr	May	Jun	Jul	Aug	Sep
Leaf												
Flower												
Fruit/Pod												

Growth form
The straight trunk often branches high up – the branches tend to grow upwards to form a moderately dense canopy. The tree may also branch low down to form a wide-spreading canopy.

Leaves
Leaves have a smooth margin and are leathery. They are green above and pale green below while new leaves are pale yellow-green (175 x 35 mm).

Flowers
Inconspicuous, small, pale yellow balls of little flowers grow in the leaf origin (Nov - Mar) (20 mm).

Fruit
The fruit consists of small capsules, each with two lobes. The capsules are densely clustered into round, red-brown, warty heads, which grow in the leaf origin (Jan - Feb) (2 - 3 mm).

Bark
The bark is grey-brown and rough, with grooves that run lengthways. Beacuse of its close proximity to water, there are often patches of green lichen on it.

EASY RIVER CANOPIES
Matumi

Look-alike tree
The Matumi is very easily confused with the Quinine-tree, *Rauvolfia caffra*, p. ii, but the Matumi is far more common in the Lowveld. Their growth form and Habitat along rivers are very similar, and the leaves are also strikingly alike. The Quinine-tree leaves are broader and longer, with marked herringbone veins. All parts of this tree have milky latex.

Gardening
The ornamental Matumi needs very well-watered soils as it only occurs along large ponds or streams. It is not frost- or drought-resistant. It can be grown from seed in coarse sandy soils, and will grow fairly fast.

Human uses
The bark is used medicinally for stomach complaints, and the wood for flooring, boats, canoes and furniture, as well as for building huts and cattle kraals.

| JACARANDA FAMILY | Bignoniaceae | Tree no 678 |

SAUSAGE-TREE *Kigelia africana*

AFRIKAANS Worsboom **N. SOTHO** Pidiso **SISWATI** umVongotsi, umVongoti **TSONGA** Mpfungurhu **TSWANA** Moporota **ZULU** umBongothi, uVunguti, umBele-le-wendlovu

Kigelia is the traditional Mozambican name for the tree *Kigeli-kei*; *africana* means of Africa.

Leaf

Where you'll find this tree easily

The Sausage-tree grows singly along perennial rivers, and may also be found away from rivers in the higher rainfall areas.

- It is easiest to find this tree in major Riverine areas (H) of literally all the Ecozones in the Lowveld.
- You can also spot it along fairly large rivers and drainage lines that are not big enough to be classified as Ecozone H, in Mixed Bushwillow Woodlands (A), Pretoriuskop Sourveld (B), Sabie/Crocodile Thorn Thickets (D), Knob-thorn/Marula Savannah (F) as well as Alluvial Plains (M).

A	E	I	M
B	F	J	N
C	G	K	O
D	H	L	P

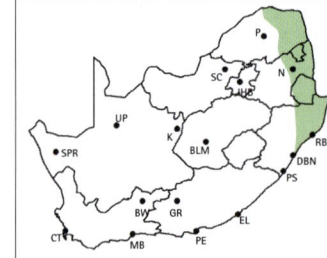

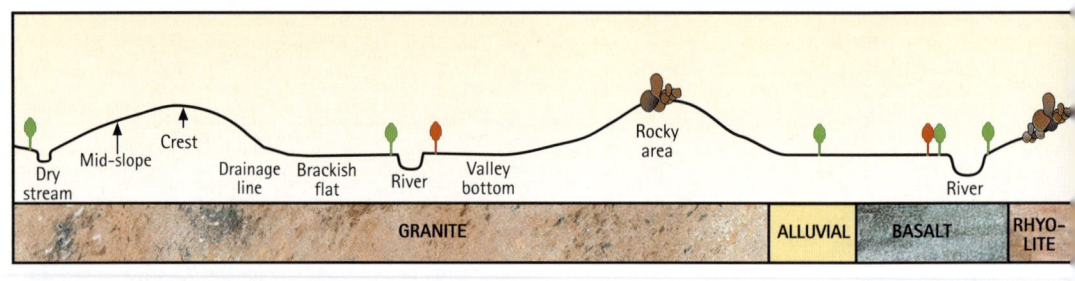

GIFF

- This is a large, riverine tree with a huge, low-branching single trunk.
- The bark is relatively smoother and paler than most of the other riverine trees along the major rivers.
- Once Compound leaves are lime-green, large, leathery and stiff, with a single, very rigid leaf at the tip.
- The leaflets tend to be separate, not overlapping one another.
- **The very prominent red-maroon flowers, that appear between July and October, make this tree easy to identify.**
- Unique sausage-like fruit is visible most of the year, although not all trees carry fruit.
- There are often empty fruit stems hanging in the canopy after the fruit has dropped.

Seasonal changes

Semi-deciduous. The leaves drop late in winter. In spring the fresh green foliage is very conspicuous. The short period without leaves, and the presence of the characteristic fruit, makes identification easy for most of the year.

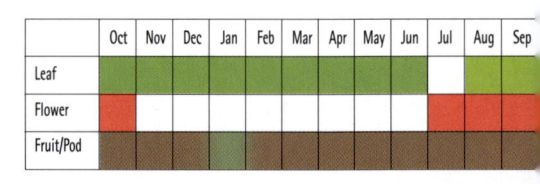

This is an unusually prolific crop of Sausage-tree pods!

Height: 6 - 20 m
Density: Very dense

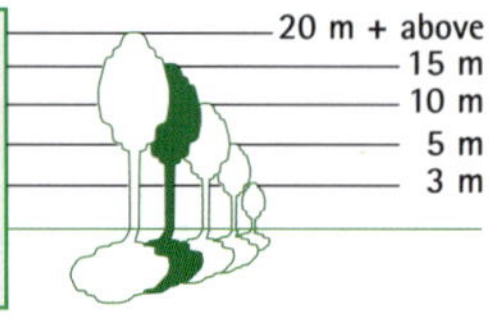

	Oct	Nov	Dec	Jan	Feb	Mar	Apr	May	Jun	Jul	Aug	Sep
Leaf												
Flower												
Fruit/Pod												

Growth form
It has a gnarled, grooved trunk. The main branches are very solid and split close to their origin from the trunk. Branches spread horizontally to form a round, very dense canopy. Branchlets end in thick twigs.

Leaves
The leaves are characteristically thick, with 2 - 5 pairs of leaflets and a single leaflet at the tip. They are opposite and elliptic with a rounded tip and a smooth, wavy margin. Most end leaflets have serrated tips. The leaves are crowded near the ends of the branches (Leaf: 250 mm; leaflets: 70 - 150 mm).

Flowers
Large cup-like flowers grow in a very unusual way, hanging in groups, like lights from a candelabra. They appear before the leaves in early spring. Flowers drop to form a red carpet on the ground (140 x 140 mm).

Bark
The bark is smooth and peels in irregular blocks.

Pods
The huge, solid, sausage-like fruit gives the tree its common English name. The long, hanging stems that carry the flowers in such an unusual way are the same stems that carry the fruit. You can sometimes see more than one sausage hanging, as the flowers did, from one main stalk. Ripe fruit falls from May through to April the following year (500 x 100 mm).

Look-alike tree
The Once Compound leaf of the Sausage-tree is similar to other riverine trees, like the Weeping Boer-bean, *Schotia brachypetala*, p. 170, the Natal-mahogany, *Trichilia emetica*, p. 180, and Nyala-tree, *Xanthocercis zambesiaca*, p. 166. However, the Sausage-tree is the only commonly found, large tree along rivers, that has such a stiff, pale green leaf, with large leaflets that do not overlap, and a rigid single leaf at the tip. See the comparisons of various Once Compound leaves in the Distinctive Striking Features, pages 69-70.

Gardening
This is a lovely, ornamental shade tree for the larger garden. It is very susceptible to frost, especially when young, and is not drought-resistant. It is fast-growing and can be grown from seed.

Human uses
The fruit is poisonous and inedible when green, but is used to brew beer when ripe. The seeds are fried and eaten. The wood is used for making canoes.

Links with animals
Ripe fruit is eaten by baboon, monkey, porcupine and bushpig. The leaves are sometimes eaten by elephant and kudu. The flowers are very palatable and many buck species, such as nyala, impala and kudu, feed on fallen flowers. The nectar is drunk by baboon, monkey, sunbirds and insects. The caterpillars of the Charaxes butterflies feed on the trees.

EASY RIVER CANOPIES — Sausage-tree

| MAHOGANY FAMILY | Meliaceae | Tree no 301 |

NATAL-MAHOGANY *Trichilia emetica*

AFRIKAANS Rooiessenhout **N. SOTHO** Mmaba **SISWATI** umKhuhlu **TSONGA** Nkuhlu
TSWANA Mosikiri **VENDA** Mutshikili, Mutuhu **ZULU** umKhuhlu, uMathunzini, iGwolo

Trichilia is from the Greek *tricha* meaning in threes, and is thought to refer to the three-lobed fruit; *emetica* refers to the bark being used to induce vomiting.

Leaves

Where you'll find this tree easily
The Natal-mahogany grows singly along the larger rivers.
- This tree can most commonly be found in Riverine areas (H) along major rivers, throughout the Lowveld.
- It can also be found along smaller rivers and larger streams of Sabie/Crocodile Thorn Thickets (D), Knob-thorn/Marula Savannah (F), Olifants Rugged Veld (J), and on Alluvial Plains (M), and along rivers in the north.

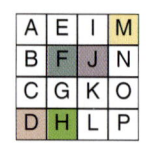

A	E	I	M
B	F	J	N
C	G	K	O
D	H	L	P

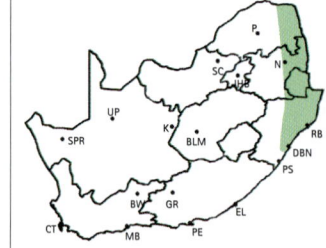

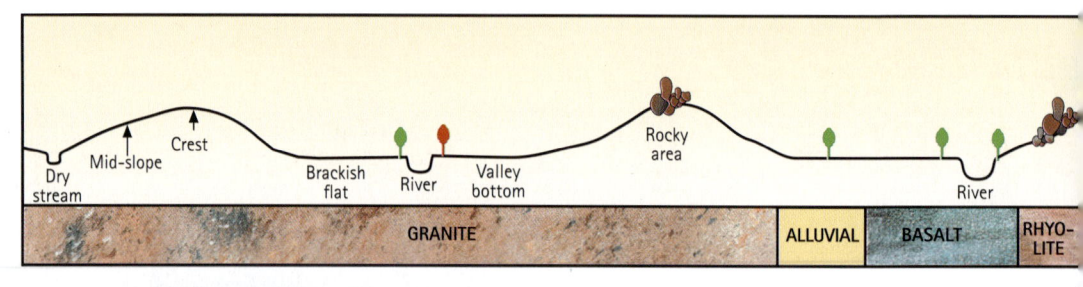

Dry stream — Mid-slope — Crest — Brackish flat — River — Valley bottom — Rocky area — River
GRANITE — ALLUVIAL — BASALT — RHYOLITE

GIFF
- This large tree is striking even from afar, because its exceptionally dense, deep green, glossy canopy shows virtually no branching, nor sky, through the leaves.
- It is sturdy, single-trunked and low-branching with a dense rounded canopy.
- **The large, alternate, Once Compound leaves have 3 - 5 pairs of leaflets, each pair growing larger towards the single leaflet at the tip.**
- Small, green, sweet-smelling, trumpet-shaped flowers appear in dense rounded heads at the ends of branches.
- Dry, grey-green, capsules grow in bunches, and when mature burst open to show striking black seeds wrapped in bright red pulp.

The exceptionally dark, dense and evenly round canopy makes the Natal-mahogany easy to spot along rivers.

Seasonal changes
Evergreen. Owing to the intense green of the leaves, and the density of the foliage, this tree stands out among other riverine trees all year round.

Height: 8 - 20 m
Density: Very dense

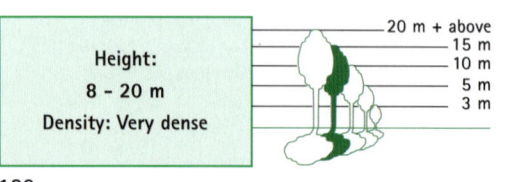

20 m + above / 15 m / 10 m / 5 m / 3 m

	Oct	Nov	Dec	Jan	Feb	Mar	Apr	May	Jun	Jul	Aug	Sep
Leaf												
Flower												
Fruit/Pod												

Growth form
See GIFF.

Leaves
The leaves are crowded towards the ends of branchlets and twigs. The leaflets are dark green above and slightly paler below with brownish hairs, particularly along the 13 - 16 side veins. Leaflets are elliptic with a tapering, rounded tip and base. They are opposite or nearly opposite and they tend to overlap one another, especially near the tip. New leaves are shiny, red-brown, and turn very bright lime-green before darkening (Leaf: 350 - 500 mm; end leaflet: 150 - 160 x 55 mm).

Flowers
See GIFF (Aug - Oct) (16 mm).

Fruit
See GIFF (Nov - Apr) (45 x 30 mm).

Bark
The bark is dark brown, fairly smooth, but becoming slightly grooved in older trees.

EASY RIVER CANOPIES Natal-mahogany

Look-alike tree
The Once Compound leaf of the Natal-mahogany is similar to other riverine trees, like the Weeping Boer-bean, *Schotia brachypetala*, p. 170, the Sausage-tree, *Kigelia africana*, p. 178, and Nyala-tree, *Xanthocercis zambesiaca*, p. 166. However, the Natal-mahogany is the only commonly found, large tree, along rivers, with such dense, dark green foliage that no sky can be seen thorugh the branches. It also has the only leaf where the leaflets get markedly larger towards the tip, and overlap one another. See the Comparisons of various Once Compound leaves in the Distinctive Striking Features, pages 69-70.

Gardening
This dense, evergreen, ornamental tree provides good shade in a garden. It will grow best in fertile soils, and is not frost- or drought-resistant. It can be grown easily from seed or cuttings, and will grow fast when well-watered. If seeds are used, plant while still fresh.

Human uses
The wood is used to make furniture, fish-floats, dugout canoes and musical instruments, and the bark for medicinal purposes. The seeds are poisonous, and an oil that can make soap, is extracted from them.

Links with animals
Young leaf shoots are browsed by kudu and giraffe. The fruit is eaten by baboon, monkey and nyala, and the seeds by Crowned, Grey and Trumpeter Hornbills. Seeds that fall into the water are eaten by fish such as barbel, and the caterpillars of several species of butterfly eat the leaves.

181

THORN-TREE SUB-FAMILY OF PEA FAMILY   Mimosoideae   Tree no 183.1

River Acacia *Acacia robusta*

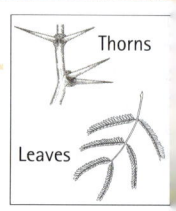

AFRIKAANS Brakdoring   **N. SOTHO** Moku   **TSONGA** Munga, Mungamazi   **TSWANA** Moga   **ZULU** umNgamanzi

Acacia is taken from the Greek *akis* meaning a 'sharp point', referring to the thorns of all African Acacia species; **robusta** refers to the robust growth form of the tree.

Thorns

Leaves

Where you'll find this tree easily

The River Acacia grows singly, usually along rivers or in areas with increased ground moisture.

- It is easiest to find in Riverine areas (H), especially in the southern granite Ecozones A, B, C and D.
- It can also be found along larger rivers and major drainage lines in Knob-thorn/Marula Savannah (F), Olifants Rugged Veld (J) and Alluvial Plains (M).

A	E	I	M
B	F	J	N
C	G	K	O
D	H	L	P

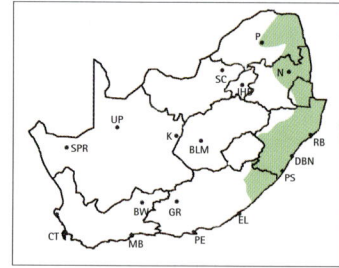

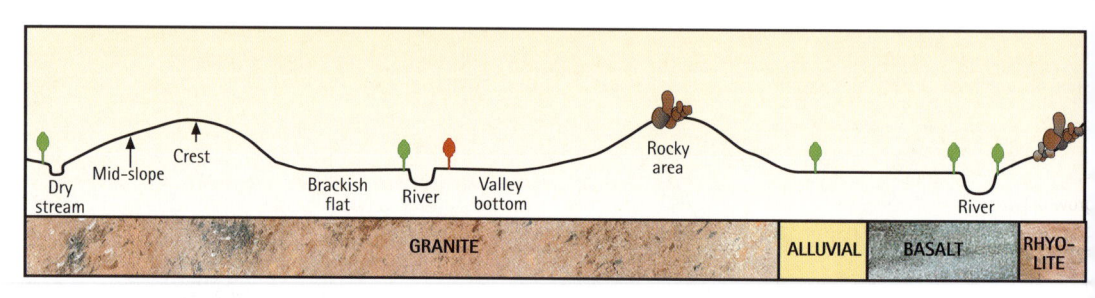

Crest — Mid-slope — Dry stream — Brackish flat — River — Valley bottom — Rocky area — River

GRANITE   ALLUVIAL   BASALT   RHYOLITE

GIFF

- This is a large, upright Acacia, with dense, dark green, feathery foliage, forming a spreading canopy.
- The branches stay robust and thick, even towards their ends.
- **The Twice Compound leaves are relatively long and droopy for an Acacia.**
- **Both the leaves (which are in tight clumps) and the paired thorns, grow from dark, prickly 'cushions'.**
- **The 'cushions' are at intervals along the twigs, which give the twigs a zigzag appearance.**
- The flower-balls are creamy-white and can be seen very early in spring.
- The pods are thick and hang from the tree in prominent bunches.

Later in summer the foliage colour deepens, from this bright, pale green of spring.

Seasonal changes

Deciduous. The dark cushions remain on the branches even after the leaves have dropped and make identification easy.

Height: 20 m
Density: Very dense

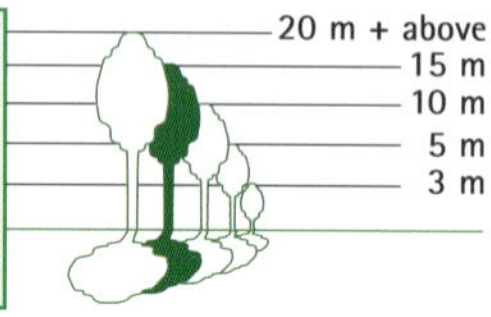

20 m + above
15 m
10 m
5 m
3 m

	Oct	Nov	Dec	Jan	Feb	Mar	Apr	May	Jun	Jul	Aug	Sep
Leaf												
Flower												
Fruit/Pod												

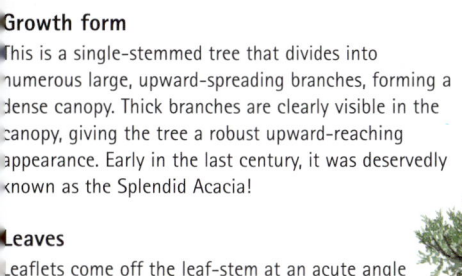

Growth form
This is a single-stemmed tree that divides into numerous large, upward-spreading branches, forming a dense canopy. Thick branches are clearly visible in the canopy, giving the tree a robust upward-reaching appearance. Early in the last century, it was deservedly known as the Splendid Acacia!

Leaves
Leaflets come off the leaf-stem at an acute angle and tend to look half-closed. Leaves consist of 2 - 6 feathers, each with 10 - 25 pairs of leaflets (Leaf: 130 mm x 70 mm; leaflet: 12 x 3 mm).

Flowers
Up to 25 ball-like flowers grow in groups, on green stems, on raised 'cushions'. The flowers grow between the leaves and the origin of the thorns. They may flower as early as July, but normally August to September (20 mm).

Thorns
The straight, white, paired thorns are joined at the base. They may be underdeveloped (70 - 110 mm).

Pods
The slender, slightly sickle-shaped pods are rounded at the tip. They are dark brown and burst open on the tree when ripe (Oct - Feb) (130 x 20 mm).

Bark
The bark is dark grey and closely grooved lengthways.

EASY RIVER CANOPIES
River Acacia

Look-alike tree
This tree can be confused with other Acacias. See pages 74-76 for comparisons.

Gardening
This tree can be very attractive in a well-watered, warm garden. It will grow very fast from seed.

Links with animals
The leaves are browsed by kudu, and flowers attract bees and butterflies.

Human uses
The under-bark is used to make twine, and the bark itself for tanning. Edible wood borer beetles are found in the wood.

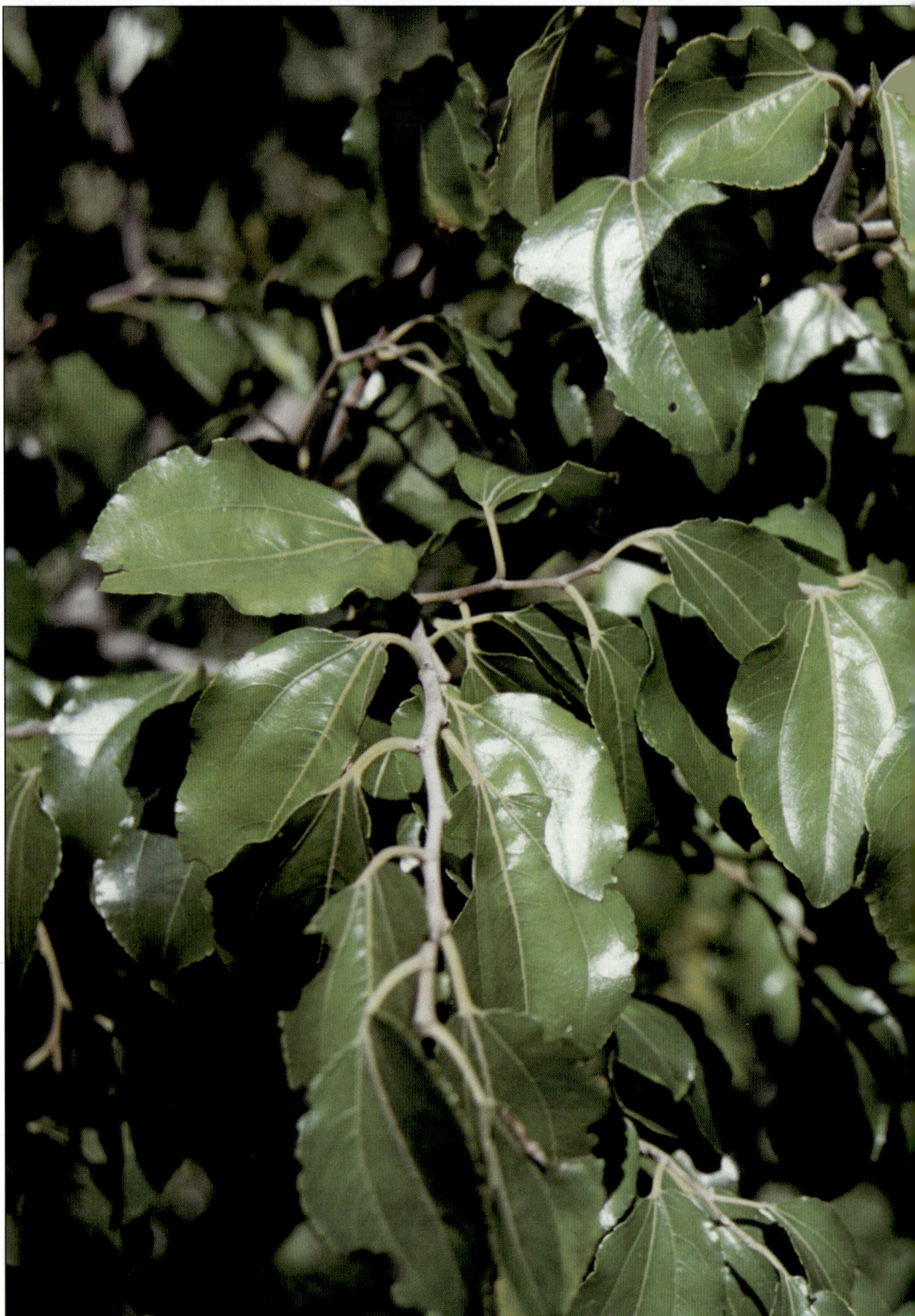

FIND MORE DIFFICULT TREES

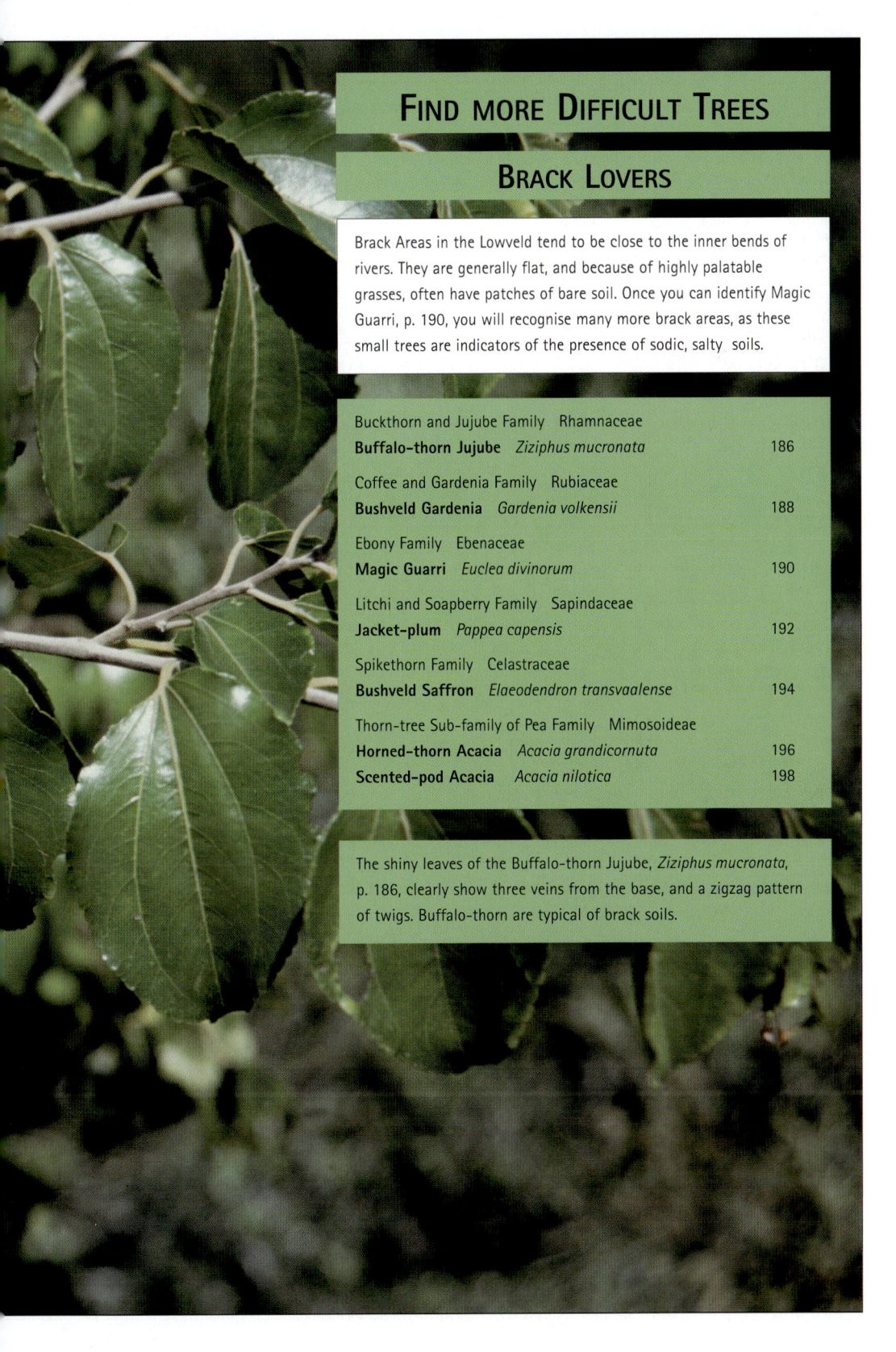

BRACK LOVERS

Brack Areas in the Lowveld tend to be close to the inner bends of rivers. They are generally flat, and because of highly palatable grasses, often have patches of bare soil. Once you can identify Magic Guarri, p. 190, you will recognise many more brack areas, as these small trees are indicators of the presence of sodic, salty soils.

Buckthorn and Jujube Family   Rhamnaceae
Buffalo-thorn Jujube   *Ziziphus mucronata*   186

Coffee and Gardenia Family   Rubiaceae
Bushveld Gardenia   *Gardenia volkensii*   188

Ebony Family   Ebenaceae
Magic Guarri   *Euclea divinorum*   190

Litchi and Soapberry Family   Sapindaceae
Jacket-plum   *Pappea capensis*   192

Spikethorn Family   Celastraceae
Bushveld Saffron   *Elaeodendron transvaalense*   194

Thorn-tree Sub-family of Pea Family   Mimosoideae
Horned-thorn Acacia   *Acacia grandicornuta*   196
Scented-pod Acacia   *Acacia nilotica*   198

The shiny leaves of the Buffalo-thorn Jujube, *Ziziphus mucronata*, p. 186, clearly show three veins from the base, and a zigzag pattern of twigs. Buffalo-thorn are typical of brack soils.

| BUCKTHORN AND JUJUBE FAMILY | Rhamnaceae | Tree no 447 |

BUFFALO-THORN JUJUBE *Ziziphus mucronata*

AFRIKAANS Blinkblaar-wag-n-bietjie **N. SOTHO** Moonaana **SISWATI** umLalhabantu
TSONGA Mphasamhala **TSWANA** Mokgalo **VENDA** Mukhalu mutshetshete **XHOSA** umPhafa
ZULU umPhafa, umLahlankosi, isiLahla, Umkhobonga

Ziziphus is derived from the Arabic word *zizouf* which is the ancient name of a member of this genus; *mucronata* refers to the pointed leaves on the tree.

Leaves

Where you'll find this tree easily

The Buffalo-thorn Jujube is very widespread and grows singly in most Habitats. It is more common on brackish flats and koppies.

A	E	I	M
B	F	J	N
C	G	K	O
D	H	L	P

- It is easy to find this tree in brack areas and drainage lines of Sabie/Crocodile Thorn Thickets (D).
- It can also be found in brack in all the other granite Ecozones A, B, C, and P.
- It can be spotted on the plains in the basalts, Knob-thorn/Marula Savannah (F) and Stunted Knob-thorn Savannah (K).

Dry stream — Mid-slope — Crest — Drainage line — Brackish flat — River — Valley bottom — Rocky area — Plain — River

GRANITE | ECCA SHALES | BASALT | RHYOLITE

GIFF

- This is a small, single-trunked tree with an irregular, spiky canopy.
- Densely branched, angular, zigzag twigs and branchlets can clearly be seen against the sky, or leaves.
- The Simple leaves are conspicuously shiny and pale green, with three veins from the base, and toothed margins.
- Pairs of brown thorns, one straight and one curved, grow on the angles of the zigzag twigs and branchlets.
- Round, berry-like fruit, also on these angles, make identification in winter possible.

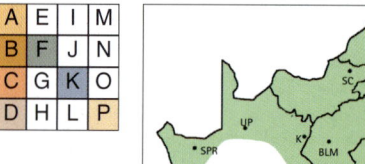

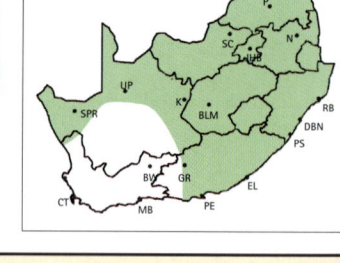

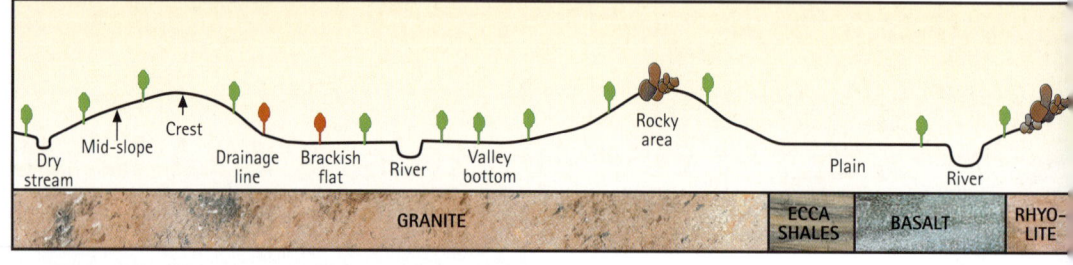

The zigzag branches and berry-like fruit make the Buffalo-thorn Jujube unmistakable.

Seasonal changes

Deciduous. This tree is without leaves for long periods as it loses them early in autumn. The zigzag shape of the branchlets and twigs and the presence of fruit make identification possible in winter.

Height: 3 - 20 m
Density: Moderate

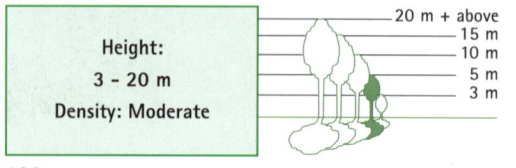

20 m + above / 15 m / 10 m / 5 m / 3 m

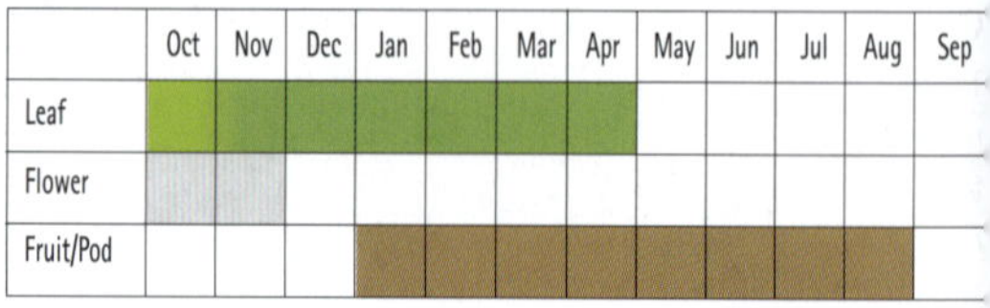

	Oct	Nov	Dec	Jan	Feb	Mar	Apr	May	Jun	Jul	Aug	Sep
Leaf												
Flower												
Fruit/Pod												

Growth form
This tree has a short, often crooked trunk that branches fairly low down to form a moderate spreading canopy. The trees often have mistletoe growing inside the canopy. Branchlets and twigs are red-brown.

Leaves
The leaves grow on the angles of the twigs and are slightly folded (40 x 30 mm).

Thorns
See GIFF.
(Straight: 20 mm; curved: 7 mm).

Flowers
Inconspicuous star-like, small, yellow-green flowers grow in clusters at the base of the leaves (Oct - Nov) (5 mm).

Fruit
The fruit is hard and dark brown, and is often still visible on trees in winter when they have lost their leaves. It ripens from January onwards (10 mm).

Bark
The bark is grey and smooth when young, becoming grooved with age.

Look-alike tree
The Buffalo-thorn Jujube has no Look-alike tree.

Links with animals
The fruit is eaten by many animals including impala, warthog, baboon, monkey, nyala and Black Rhino. The leaves are eaten by impala, nyala, kudu, giraffe and Black Rhino. Butterflies breed in the trees.

Gardening
This is a very pretty tree, but because of its thorns, it is not generally popular in a garden with small children. The tree grows fast from seed and is fairly drought- and frost-resistant.

Human uses
It is an important medicinal plant, used for stomach ailments, ulcers and chest problems. The fruit can be eaten, and is used for porridge and flour. The seeds are roasted as a coffee substitute. The wood makes fencing posts. In Zulu folklore the tree is supposed to deflect lightning and protect people sheltering under it in a thunderstorm. It is known as the burial tree of many African tribes, and branches are laid on the graves of chiefs and royalty.

BRACK LOVERS
Buffalo-thorn Jujube

| COFFEE AND GARDENIA FAMILY | Rubiaceae | Tree no 691 |

BUSHVELD GARDENIA — *Gardenia volkensii*

AFRIKAANS Bosveldkatjiepiering **SWANA** umValasangweni **TSONGA** Ntsalala **TSWANA** Morala
ZULU umGongwane, umValasangweni

Gardenia is in honour of Dr Alexander Garden, a doctor and correspondent of Linnaeus; **volkensii** is in honour of G Volkens who collected samples on Mount Kilimanjaro from 1892 to 1894.

Fruit

Where you'll find this tree easily

The Bushveld Gardenia grows singly in brack areas, in sandy soil and in some rocky conditions.

- This tree is easiest to find growing in the brack in Sabie/Crocodile Thorn Thickets (D).
- It can be spotted in rocky places in Mixed Bushwillow Woodlands (A) and in Olifants Rugged Veld (J).
- It can also be found in the deep sands of the Alluvial Plains (M).

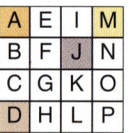

A	E	I	M
B	F	J	N
C	G	K	O
D	H	L	P

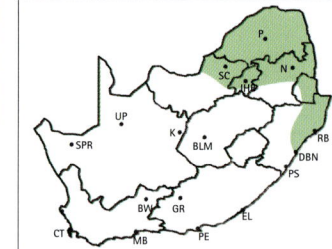

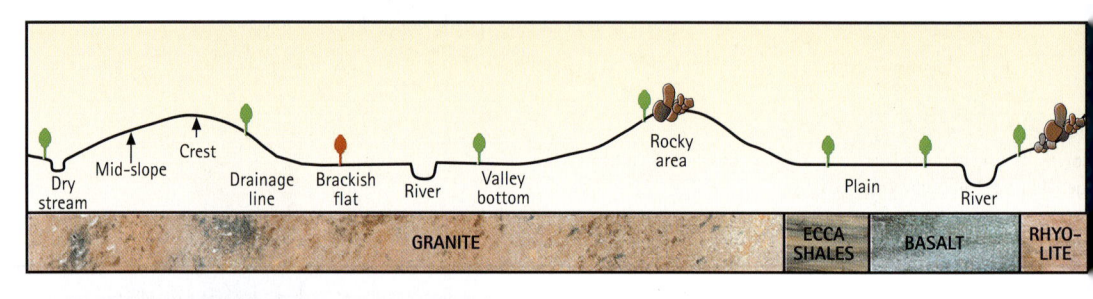

GIFF

- The tree has an irregular canopy with pale grey, densely branched, upright branches.
- **The bark of the trunk and branchlets is pale grey and smooth and flakes off, showing patches of yellow under-bark.**
- The branchlets are short and thick and often at right angles to the branches, giving the tree a spiky appearance.
- **Simple, spoon-shaped leaves are clustered at the ends of branches in whorls of three.**
- Sweet-scented, trumpet-like, white flowers grow singly at the end of the branches, often appearing before the leaves in early spring.
- The grey-green fruit looks like a rounded hen's egg, and is rough, fibrous and covered with blunt longitudinal ribs.

The presence of unique-shaped fruit helps recognition of Bushveld Gardenia.

Seasonal changes

Deciduous. The leaves turn yellow in autumn. Owing to the presence of the fruit and the particular growth form, this tree is recognisable for most of the year.

Height: 3 – 10 m
Density: Moderate

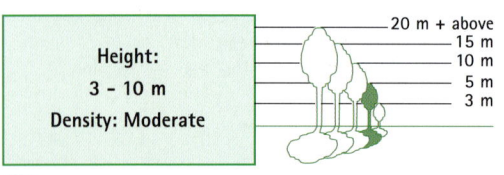

	Oct	Nov	Dec	Jan	Feb	Mar	Apr	May	Jun	Jul	Aug	Sep
Leaf												
Flower												
Fruit/Pod												

Growth form
This is a shrub or small tree with a short, sturdy stem that branches profusely low down to form a much-branched canopy. It may be single- or multi-trunked. The pale grey branchlets are clearly visible among the shiny, green leaves.

Leaves
The leaves have a broad, rounded tip with a sharp point, and a narrow pointed base. They are glossy-green, and when mature, smooth and soft. The margin is not toothed but is slightly wavy. Leaves turn yellow in autumn (30 - 50 x 25 - 40 mm).

Flowers
Flowers go creamy to yellow with age. They open at night, and each flower is very short-lived (Aug - Dec) (80 x 100 mm).

Fruit
The skin is very thick. Fruit starts growing from December to April and often remains on the tree until August (60 x 30 - 50 mm).

Bark
See GIFF.

Look-alike tree
The three pale-barked, brack-loving species can be confused with one another. The young Simple leaves of the Jacket-plum, *Pappea capensis*, p. 192, are elliptic and toothed, and form rosettes at the end of branchlets; the leaves are leathery and rough and paler underneath when mature. The Bushveld Saffron, *Elaeodendron transvaalense*, p. 194, has Simple, narrow-toothed leaves on short twigs; the branches are not as stiff as in the other species, but tend to be arching and often drooping.

Gardening
This tree is very decorative during the flowering season. It can be grown from seed and cuttings. It is slow-growing, fairly drought-resistant but not resistant to severe frost.

Human uses
The tree was believed to have magical powers and was planted at the entrance to homesteads to keep evil sprits away. Infusion of the fruits and roots was used to induce vomiting. The wood is used for fences, sticks, spoons and firewood.

Links with animals
The leaves are occasionally browsed by elephant, giraffe and kudu. Ripe fruit is eaten by baboon.

BRACK LOVERS
Bushveld Gardenia

EBONY FAMILY Ebenaceae Tree no 595

MAGIC GUARRI *Euclea divinorum*

AFRIKAANS Towerghwarrie **N. SOTHO** Mohlakola **TSONGA** Nhlangula **TSWANA** Mothakola
VENDA Mutangule **ZULU** umHlangula

Euclea is thought to be derived from the Greek, meaning 'of good report', possibly referring to the valuable wood of some species; **divinorum** refers to the use of tree parts by diviners.

Leaf

Where you'll find this tree easily
The Magic Guarri grows in groups in brack areas, which regularly occur near rivers in granites. It also thrives on the plains, in clay and sand Ecozones, and is often part of a group of trees on a termite mound.

- This tree is easily found in the granites, Mixed Bushwillow Woodlands (A) and Mopane/Bushwillow Woodlands (P), as well as in Alluvial Plains (M).
- It is also easy to find in most other Ecozones where there are brack areas, or along riverbanks.

GIFF
- This tree is characterised by usually being multi-stemmed, and by growing in groups on brackish flats.
- Bare, pale grey stems and branches grow upwards, carrying an evergreen, dense, rounded canopy.
- There is smooth bark on younger growth, and coarse, blocky, grey bark on older stems or trunks.
- The Simple, elliptic leaves have a shiny, grey-green upper-surface and paler under-surface.
- The margins of the leaves are very wavy.
- Small, round bunches of berries turn purple when ripe.

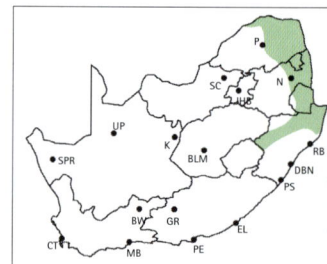

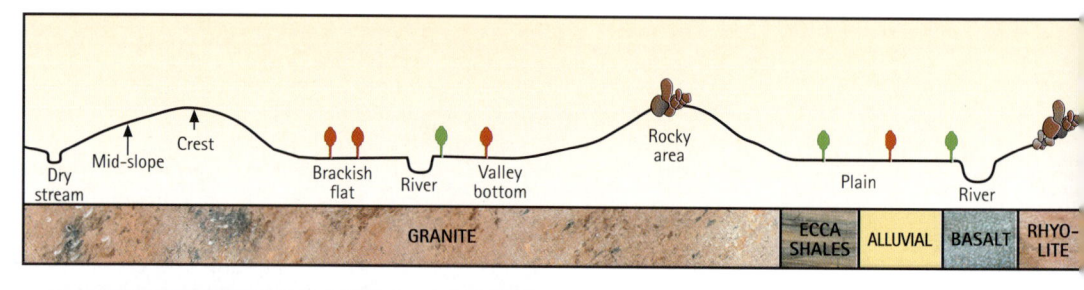

Heavily laden fruit on a branch of a Magic Guarri is attractive and distinctive.

Height: 4 – 6 m
Density: Dense

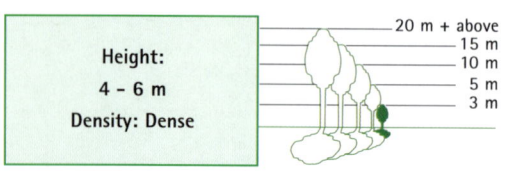

Seasonal changes
Evergreen. This is often the only green tree on the brackish flats in winter. It is therefore easily identified all year round.

	Oct	Nov	Dec	Jan	Feb	Mar	Apr	May	Jun	Jul	Aug	Sep
Leaf												
Flower												
Fruit/Pod												

Growth form
This tree branches low down, from the base, or has wide branches from the main trunk.

Leaves
The leaves are opposite and leathery (105 x 25 mm).

Flowers
Inconspicuous, sweet-scented, creamy flowers appear from August to September. Male and female flowers grow on separate plants (3 - 5 mm).

Fruit
The fruit has a thin layer of flesh around a single grooved seed (Oct – Mar) (6 mm).

Bark
See GIFF.

Look-alike tree
The Simple undulating leaf and round berries are similar to the Ebony Jackal-berry, *Diospyros mespiliformis*, p. 160, but the growth form of each species precludes confusion. The similarities are not surprising – both trees belonging to the Ebony Family. Both have fleshy round fruit with a single seed that is grooved with lines around it resembling those on a tennis ball.

Gardening
Although this tree does not seem very attractive in the field, it can be used very effectively in gardens or as windbreaks in the drier areas, as it is fairly drought- and frost-resistant. A slow-growing tree that prefers brackish soil. It can be easily grown from seed. The seeds should be sown in the locality where the trees are needed as they do not transplant well.

Human uses
The fruit is used as a purgative. Leafy branches are broken off and used to beat out veld fires. The frayed ends of the twigs are used as toothbrushes.

Links with animals
The fruit is eaten by birds such as hornbills, and the bark by Black Rhino. When other food is scarce, the leaves are browsed by rhino, giraffe, kudu, impala and Grey Duiker.

BRACK LOVERS
Magic Guarri

| LITCHI AND SOAPBERRY FAMILY | Sapindaceae | Tree no 433 |

JACKET-PLUM
Pappea capensis

Young leaf

Older leaf

AFRIKAANS Doppruim **N. SOTHO** Morôba-diêpê **TSONGA** Gulaswimbi **XHOSA** iliTye, umGqalutye **ZULU** umKhokhwane, umQhoqho, umVuma, iNdaba

Pappea is named after Carl Pappe, the first Colonial Botanist, professor of Botany at what is now the University of Cape Town, and founder of the South African Museum herbarium; **capensis** means from the Cape.

Where you'll find this tree easily
The Jacket-plum grows singly in brack areas. It can also be found on termite mounds and in rocky areas too.

- This tree can most easily be found in brack areas in the Sabie/Crocodile Thorn Thickets (D); it is also easy to spot on the plains of Mopane Shrubveld (L).
- It can be found in brack areas in granite, Mixed Bushwillow Woodlands (A), Pretoriuskop Sourveld (B) and Malelane Mountain Bushveld (C); and in gabbro, Thorn Veld (E); and basalt, Olifants Rugged Veld (J); as well as in the south of Lebombo Mountain Bushveld (I).

A	E	I	M
B	F	J	N
C	G	K	O
D	H	L	P

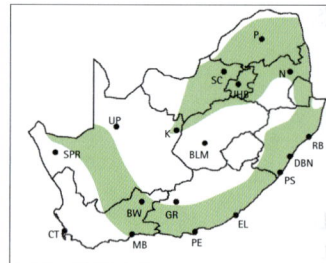

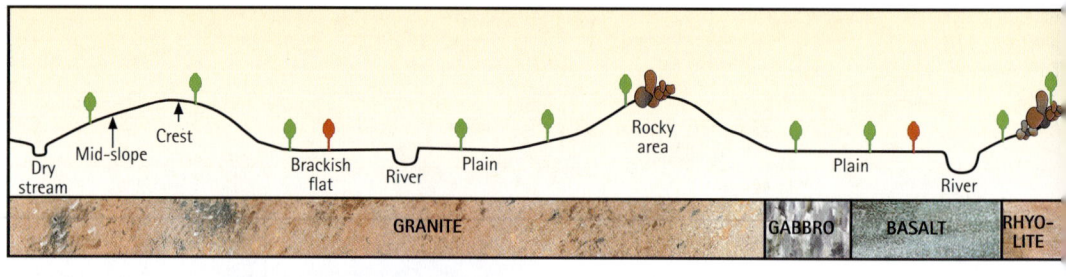

GIFF
- Jacket-plum usually has a single trunk and highly visible short branches that all tend to be very pale grey, but are mottled and marked with darker patches.
- The dull-green, rounded canopy is formed by an intense tangle of branchlets and twigs that are also pale grey.
- The Simple, elliptic leaves appear to form rosettes at the ends of the drooping branchlets.
- Leaves are unusually rigid and leathery, and are rough, with a prominent, sunken, pale central vein.
- **The margins are smooth when mature, but sharply toothed in young leaves and on coppice shoots.**
- The velvety-green, berry-like fruit that bursts open to show a bright red jelly-like flesh, is characteristic from December to July.

Seasonal changes
Deciduous to evergreen. As this tree has leaves for most of the year, it is normally easy to recognise.

The pale grey bark and rigid, leathery leaves with yellowish central veins make this tree easy to find.

Height: 4 – 10 m
Density: Moderate

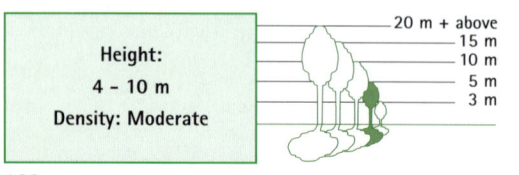

20 m + above
15 m
10 m
5 m
3 m

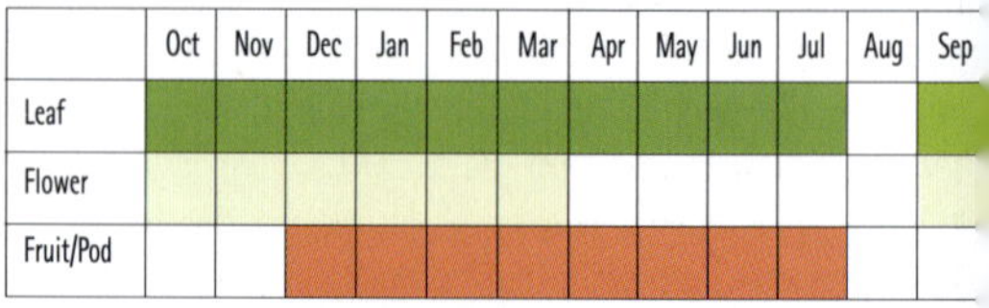

	Oct	Nov	Dec	Jan	Feb	Mar	Apr	May	Jun	Jul	Aug	Sep
Leaf												
Flower												
Fruit/Pod												

Growth form
Even within the Lowveld the growth form and the leaf size of this tree are highly variable. Under well-watered conditions it is a tall tree with a dense canopy and larger leaves. In relatively drier areas it is a tree with a short trunk that branches low down with smaller leaves.

Flowers
Small, pale creamy-green, scented flowers grow in spikes between the leaves. Male and female flowers grow on separate trees (Sep - Mar) (Spike: 25 - 160 mm).

Leaves
Leaves are alternate in the older growth and crowded towards the end of the twigs. Dependent on the rainfall, they are exrememly variable in size, but usually have a rounded base and tip. The leaves are dark olive-green above and pale underneath, with a central vein that is visible from both sides (5 - 10 x 80 - 160 mm).

Bark
The bark of young branches is smooth and may be broken into small blocks. The bark of older trees and branches is darker and rough with irregular patches of pale and dark bark. It is often covered in lichen.

Fruit
The fruit grows in bunches. The dark shells may be seen long after the fruit has dropped (20 mm).

Look-alike tree
There are three pale-barked, brack-loving species that can be confused. The Simple leaves of the Jacket-plum are leathery and rough and paler underneath when mature, and young leaves are tooth-edged. The short brachlets are not spiky. The Bushveld Gardenia, *Gardenia volkensii*, p. 188, has spiky branchlets that support clusters of spoon-shaped leaves; characteristic fruit is often present. The Bushveld Saffron *Elaeodendron transvaalense*, p. 194, has simple, narrow-toothed leaves on short twigs; the branches are not as stiff as in the other species, but tend to be arching and often drooping.

Gardening
This is an attractive tree that will flourish in most gardens. It grows well from seed but extremely slowly, and is fairly drought-resistant.

Links with animals
The fruit is eaten by a wide variety of animals and birds. The leaves are not palatable and are seldom eaten.

Human uses
The wood is white and easy to work with, heavy and tough and may be used for poles, yokes, furniture and spoons. The fruit is edible and tasty. Vinegar and jelly are made from the fruit. The seeds contain oil that is used for various purposes. The tree is still important in traditional medicine today.

| SPIKETHORN FAMILY | Celastraceae | Tree no 416 |

BUSHVELD SAFFRON (TRANSVAAL SAFFRON)   *Elaeodendron transvaalense*

AFRIKAANS Bosveldsaffraan   **TSONGA** Shimapana   **ZULU** Ngwavuma

Leaves

Elaeodendron is derived from the Greek words for 'olive' + 'tree', and the name refers to the olive-like fruits; **transvaalense** refers to the old Transvaal province.

Where you'll find this tree easily
The Bushveld Saffron tree grows singly, preferring brackish and rocky areas.

A	E	I	M
B	F	J	N
C	G	K	O
D	H	L	P

- It is easiest to find this tree in the brack of the Sabie/Crocodile Thorn Thickets (D).
- It can also be spotted in both brack and rocky areas in Mixed Bushwillow Woodlands (A), Pretoriuskop Sourveld (B) and in Thorn Veld (E).

GIFF
- This tree has a densely branched, untidy, roundish canopy.
- **It has long, thin, arching and drooping, pale grey branchlets showing clearly between the leaves.**
- The bark of younger trees and branches is pale and fairly smooth, with darker, rougher patches on the older branches and stems, and on older trees.
- **The Simple, elliptic leaves are dark glossy green above, paler below, and are arranged in groups on very short twigs.**
- The twigs come off the branchlets at right angles.
- The yellow to brown, berry-like fruit grows in bunches on the ends of the side branches, or on long whip-like twigs, through the winter months.

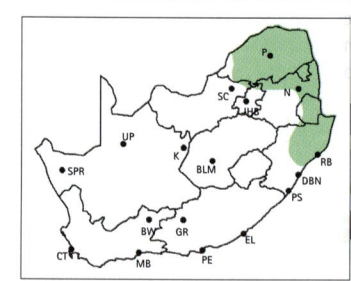

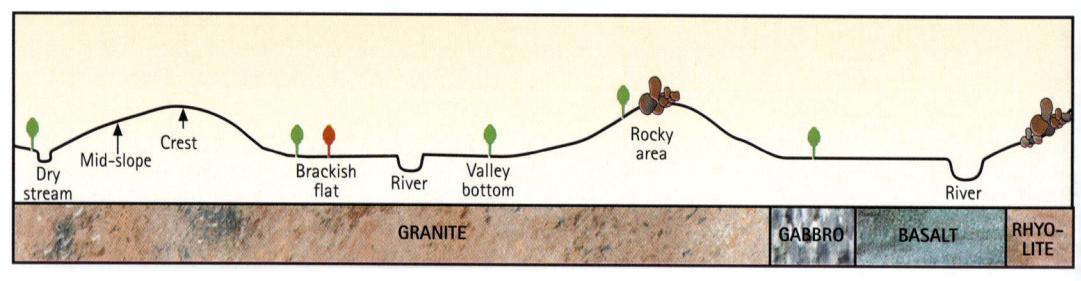

Pale, angular branchlets and very short twigs are typical of the Bushveld Saffron.

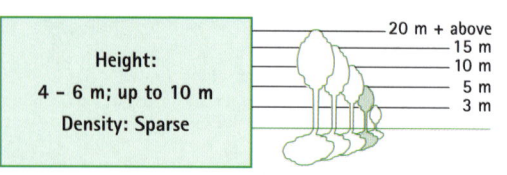

Height:
4 – 6 m; up to 10 m
Density: Sparse

Seasonal changes
Deciduous or semi-deciduous. As this tree is without leaves only for a short period, it can be identified for most of the year.

	Oct	Nov	Dec	Jan	Feb	Mar	Apr	May	Jun	Jul	Aug	Sep
Leaf	■	■	■	■	■	■	■	■	■			
Flower		■	■	■								
Fruit/Pod								■	■	■	■	

Growth form
This is a single-stemmed tree with a thick stem that branches low down.

Leaves
Leathery leaves may be alternate, and the margins are smooth or slightly toothed (20 – 70 x 10 – 30 mm).

Flowers
The inconspicuous, very small, greenish-yellow flowers are three-petalled. They grow in clusters between the leaves (Nov – Feb) (spray: 20 mm).

Fruit
See GIFF.
(Jul - Sep) (20 x 16 mm).

Bark
See GIFF.

Look-alike tree
There are three pale-barked, brack-loving species that can be confused with one another. The elliptic, Simple, young leaves of the Jacket-plum, *Pappea capensis*, p. 192, are larger than those of the Bushveld Saffron, and are tooth-edged; mature leaves are leathery and rough and paler underneath. The short, stiff Jacket-plum branchlets look nothing like the thin, arching, drooping branches of the Saffron. The Bushveld Gardenia, *Gardenia volkensii*, p. 188, has spike-like branchlets that support clusters of spoon-shaped leaves, and the characteristic fruit is often present.

Gardening
This is a decorative tree and will grow in most gardens. It is difficult to grow from seed. It is slow-growing and probably susceptible to frost.

Links with animals
The fruit is eaten by birds like the Purple-crested Turaco. The leaves and young shoots are eaten by elephant, giraffe, kudu and impala.

Human uses
The wood is used for household utensils, spoons, pipes and cattle troughs. The bark is used for tanning and to make tea. It is reputedly an excellent treatment for stomach ailments.

BRACK LOVERS
Bushveld Saffron

195

THORN-TREE SUB-FAMILY OF PEA FAMILY — Mimosoideae — Tree no 168.1

HORNED-THORN ACACIA — *Acacia grandicornuta*

AFRIKAANS Horingdoring   **ZULU** umDongola, umNgampondo

Acacia is taken from the Greek *akis* meaning a 'sharp point', referring to the thorns on all African species; **grandicornuta** means 'great-horned'.

Leaves

Where you'll find this tree easily

The Horned-thorn Acacia prefers brackish and clay soils. It often grows in groups.

- It is easiest to find in groups, growing in brack areas in Mixed Bushwillow Woodland (A) and Sabie/Crocodile Thorn Thickets (D).
- It is also common in the clay soils of the Tree Mopane Savannah (O).

GIFF

- This is normally a small tree, or shrub, with a wide, irregular to V-shaped canopy.
- The huge, white, spiny thorns are paired, and often thickened at their bases, fusing across the twig – giving it some common names.
- The branchlets and twigs are characteristically zigzagged.
- Twice Compound leaves grow in bunches of 3 - 5, at the base of the joined, paired thorns.
- There are white flower-balls throughout the summer.
- The pods are thin and woody, sickle-shaped and flat.

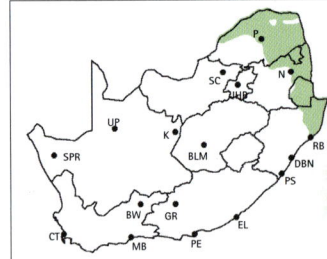

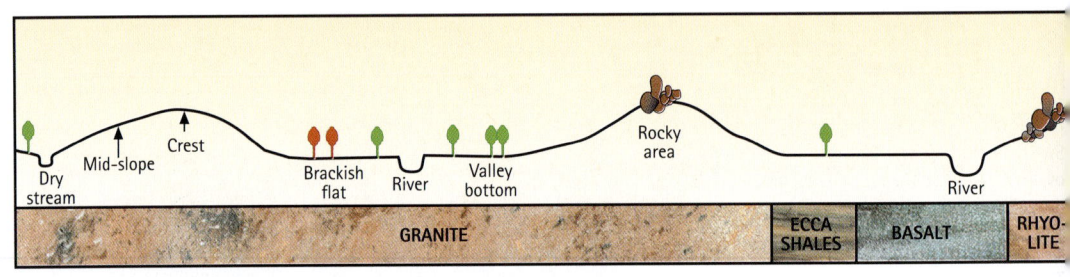

Giraffe are fond of all Acacias, using their uniquely constructed tongues and lips to feed, despite the thorns.

Seasonal changes

Deciduous. The tree will be difficult to identify without its flowers, pods and leaves.

Height: 5 - 10 m
Density: Moderate

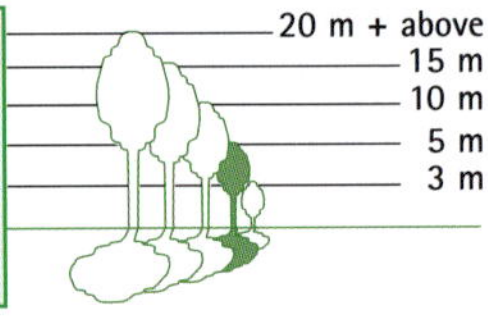

	Oct	Nov	Dec	Jan	Feb	Mar	Apr	May	Jun	Jul	Aug	Sep
Leaf												
Flower												
Fruit/Pod												

Growth form
These small, single-stemmed trees branch low down, but the branches tend to grow upwards.

Leaves
Leaves consist of 3 - 10 feather pairs, each with 8 - 16 pairs of leaflets. Leaflets are elliptic with a smooth margin (Leaf: 70 mm; leaflet: 3 x 9 mm).

Flowers
Sweet-scented flower-balls grow in tufts of 4 - 12 balls at the leaf origin on new branchlets (Oct to Mar) (10 mm).

Thorns
The long thorns are arranged spirally around the branchlets (90 mm).

Pods
Brown pods grow in bunches on the end of the twigs. They split open on the tree when ripe (Apr - Jul) (70 x 130 mm).

Bark
The bark is yellow or reddish-brown and smooth in young branches, but dark grey to black and rough with grooves in older branches and trees.

BRACK LOVERS — Horned-thorn Acacia

Look-alike tree
In its finer details the Scented-pod Acacia, *Acacia nilotica*, p. 198, can be confused with this tree. The flower-balls of the Scented-pod are bright yellow, and the Horned-thorn's are white. The pods of the Scented-pod are like a string of beads, and those of the Horned-pod are flat and sickle shaped. The Scented-pod leaflets are smaller, being 1 x 4 mm, not 3 x 9 mm. In the overall GIFF of branchlets, the River Acacia, *Acacia robusta*, p. 182, also has zigzags, but it has the distinctive 'cushions' that are lacking in the Horned-thorn Acacia.

Gardening
This tree can be used to form a hedge. It will grow fast from seed in fertile soils and when it is well watered. It is fairly drought-resistant but not frost-resistant.

Links with animals
The leaves and pods are browsed by giraffe and impala. The seeds are eaten by baboon and monkey.

Human uses
The wood is used for cooking fires.

197

Thorn-tree Sub-family of Pea Family   Mimosoideae   Tree no 179

Scented-pod Acacia   *Acacia nilotica*

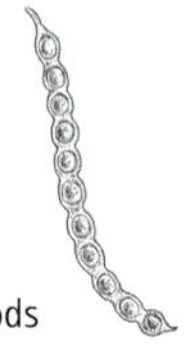

AFRIKAANS Lekkerruikpeul   **N. SOTHO** Moôka   **SISWATI** isiThwethwe, umNcawe   **TSONGA** Nxangwa
TSWANA Motabakgasi   **ZULU** umNqawe, uBobe, uBombo, umQuwe

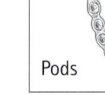

Acacia is taken from the Greek *akis* meaning a 'sharp point', referring to the thorns of all African species; **nilotica** refers to the distribution of the tree along the Nile River.

Pods

Where you'll find this tree easily
The Scented-pod Acacia prefers brackish and clay soils. It often grows in groups.

A	E	I	M
B	F	J	N
C	G	K	O
D	H	L	P

- It is easiest to find in groups, growing in brack areas and valley bottoms in the Sabie/Crocodile Thorn Thickets (D) and in the south of Knob-thorn/Marula Savannah (F).
- It is also common in valley bottoms and brack areas of Mixed Bushwillow Woodlands (A), Pretoriuskop Sourveld (B), Malelane Mountain Bushveld (C).
- It can be spotted in plains and valley bottoms of Olifants Rugged Veld (J).

GIFF
- It is usually a small Acacia tree or shrub, with a wide, V-shaped, irregular canopy.
- **The white to red-brown, paired thorns remain separate at their bases, and are usually slightly furry.**
- The thorns vary in size but can be huge and conspicuous, and they tend to curve slightly backwards.
- Twice Compound leaves grow in bunches of 3 - 4 at the base of the thorns.
- It has yellow flower-balls throughout summer.
- **The pods are swollen and enlarged over the seeds, giving them the appearance of a string of beads.**

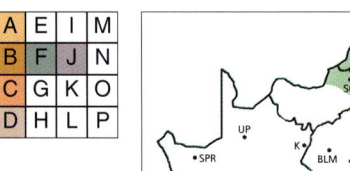

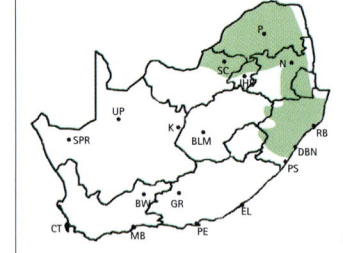

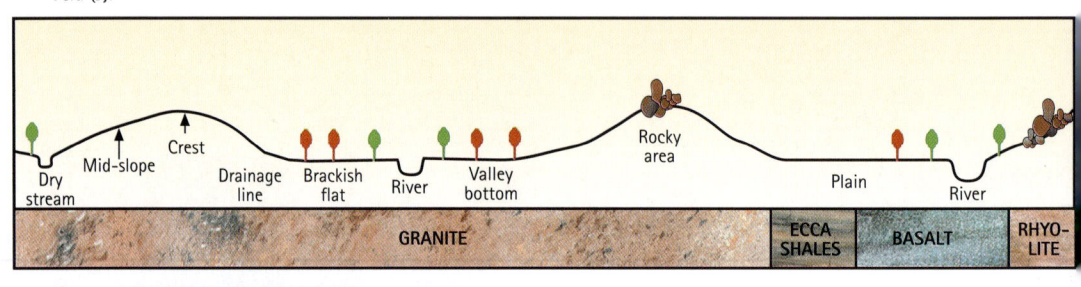

The white thorns tend to curve slightly backwards, and are surrounded by the Twice Compound leaves, that grow at their bases.

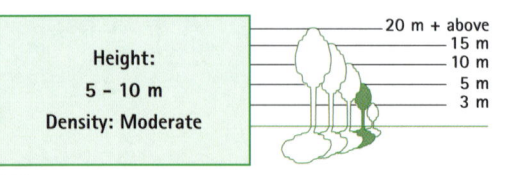

Seasonal changes
Deciduous. The tree will be difficult to identify without its flowers, pods and leaves.

	Oct	Nov	Dec	Jan	Feb	Mar	Apr	May	Jun	Jul	Aug	Sep
Leaf												
Flower												
Fruit/Pod												

Height: 5 - 10 m
Density: Moderate

Growth form
These small, single-stemmed trees branch low down.

Leaves
Leaves consist of 3 - 9 feather pairs, each with 8 - 20 pairs of leaflets. Leaflets are elliptic with a smooth margin (Leaf: 40 mm; leaflet: 1 x 4 mm).

Thorns
See GIFF (50 - 90 mm).

Flowers
Scented balls on hairy stalks grow in groups of four on the new branchlets. The tree may flower over a long period although it is never covered in flowers (Oct - Feb) (12 mm).

Pods
Young, green pods are covered with fine, reddish hairs but turn black when mature. They do not split open. Mature pods have a strong, sweet scent like fresh apples (Mar - Aug) (15 x 120 mm).

Bark
The bark is reddish-brown and smooth in young branches, but dark grey to black and rough with grooves in older branches and trees.

BRACK LOVERS — Scented-pod Acacia

Look-alike tree
The Horned-thorn Acacia, *Acacia grandicornuta*, p. 196, can be confused with this tree. The flower-balls of the Scented-pod are bright yellow, and the Horned-thorn's are white. The pods of the Scented-pod are like a string of beads, and those of the Horned-pod are flat and sickle shaped. The Horned-thorn leaflets are larger, being 3 x 9 mm, not 1 x 4 mm.

Gardening
These small trees will grow in most gardens. They can be grown from seed or root cuttings but grow slowly. They are fairly frost- and drought-resistant.

Links with animals
The pods are readily eaten by all antelope.

Human uses
The Voortrekkers used the pods to make ink. The wood was burnt for fuel, and made into mining props and fence posts. Extracts from the pods are tanning agents, and extracts from the bark treat coughs and are a sedative. Roots are used for the treatment of tuberculosis and colds, and the gum is edible.

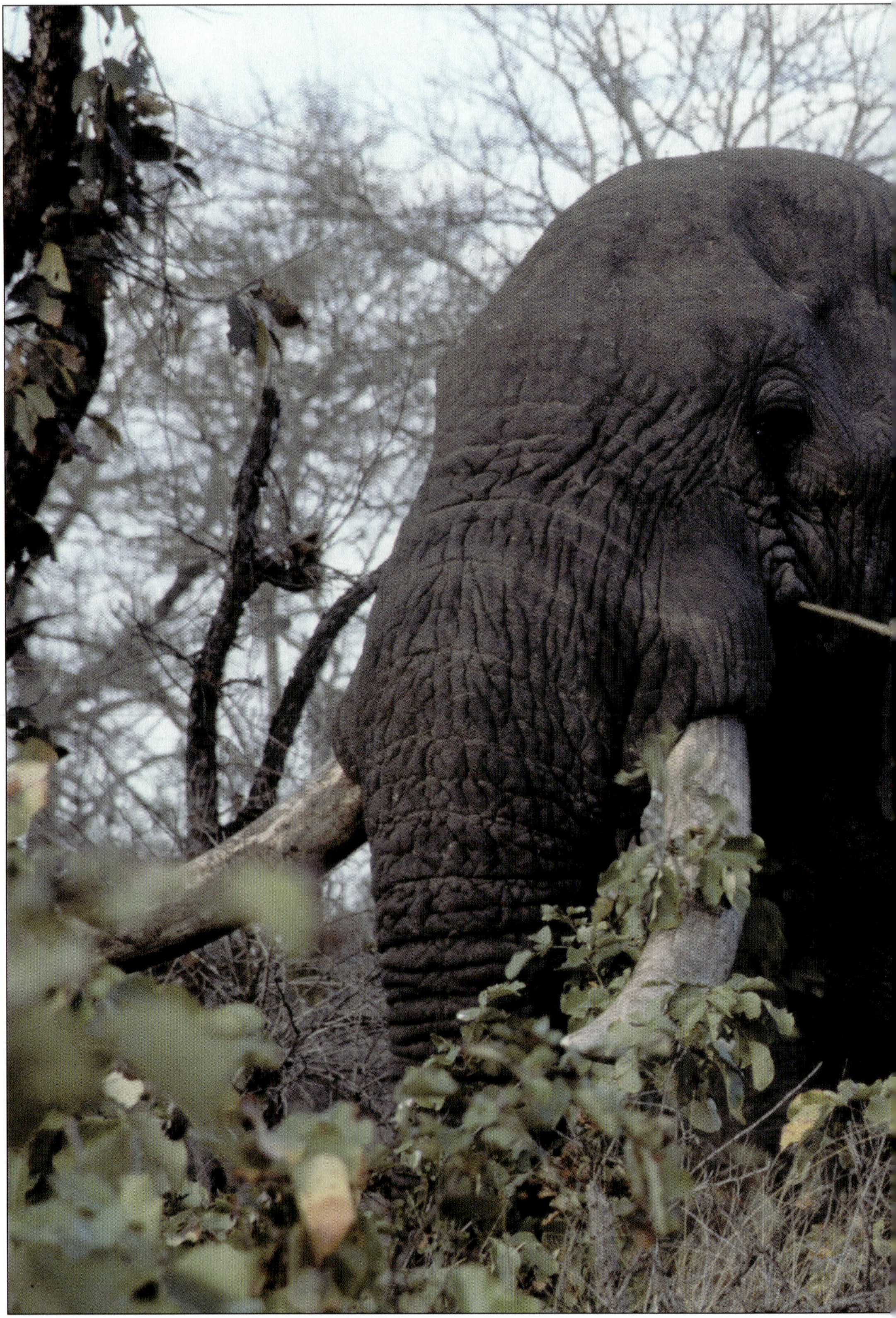

FIND MORE DIFFICULT TREES

SMALLER TREES IN GROUPS

These eight trees would be difficult to identify on their own. However, they all tend to grow in groups of their own species, with many similar-sized small trees fairly close together, making recognition very easy.

Bushwillow Family   Combretaceae
Large-fruited Bushwillow   *Combretum zeyheri*   202
Red Bushwillow   *Combretum apiculatum*   204
Russet Bushwillow   *Combretum hereroense*   206

Jute and Linden Family   Tiliaceae
Sandpaper Raisin   *Grewia flavescens*   208
White-leaved Raisin   *Grewia bicolor*   210

Sweet-pea Sub-family of Pea Family   Papilionoideae
Round-leaved Bloodwood   *Pterocarpus rotundifolius*   212

Thorn-tree Sub-family of Pea Family   Mimosoideae
Flaky-bark Acacia   *Acacia exuvialis*   214
Sickle-bush   *Dichrostachys cinerea*   216

It is a great joy ot be able to identify the long branch of a Round-leaved Bloodwood, *Pterocarpus rotundifolius*, p. 212, that the elephant is rolling through his mouth, to debark it.

| BUSHWILLOW FAMILY | Combretaceae | Tree no 546 |

LARGE-FRUITED BUSHWILLOW — *Combretum zeyheri*

AFRIKAANS Raasblaar **N. SOTHO** Moduba-tshipi **TSONGA** Mafambaborile **TSWANA** Modubana **VENDA** Mufhatela-thundu **ZULU** umBondwe-wasembudwini

Combretum is derived from the classical Latin name for the genus used by Pliny, 23-79 AD; **zeyheri** is named in honour of the German plant-collector CLP Zeyher.

Leaf/pod

Where you'll find this tree easily

The Large-fruited Bushwillow grows singly on granite crests in higher rainfall areas.

A	E	I	M
B	F	J	N
C	G	K	O
D	H	L	P

- It is easiest to find this tree on the crests in Pretoriuskop Sourveld (B), and on sandstone ridges in the Sandveld (N).
- It can also be found on crests in Mixed Bushwillow Woodlands (A), and in rocky places in the Malelane Mountain Bushveld (C).
- It can be spotted in the southern Lebombo Mountain Bushveld (I).

Dry stream · Mid-slope · Crest · Brackish flat · River · Brackish flat · Rocky area · Plain · River

GRANITE | SANDVELD | ALLUVIAL | BASALT | RHYOLITE

GIFF

- The Large-fruited Bushwillow is single- or multi-stemmed, and is usually a large shrub to small tree in the Lowveld.
- The branches are long and relatively thin, and curve downwards, sometimes hanging to the ground, especially when there are many pods present.
- The Simple, elliptic to broadly elliptic leaves are large and drooping, with wavy margins.
- They are leathery and dull, and have long, hairy leaf-stems (15 mm).
- **It has very large, conspicuous, brown, four-winged pods for most of the year.**

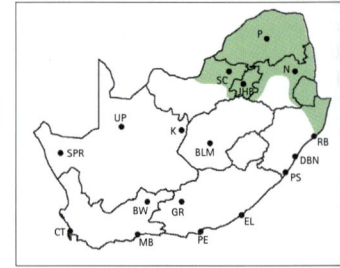

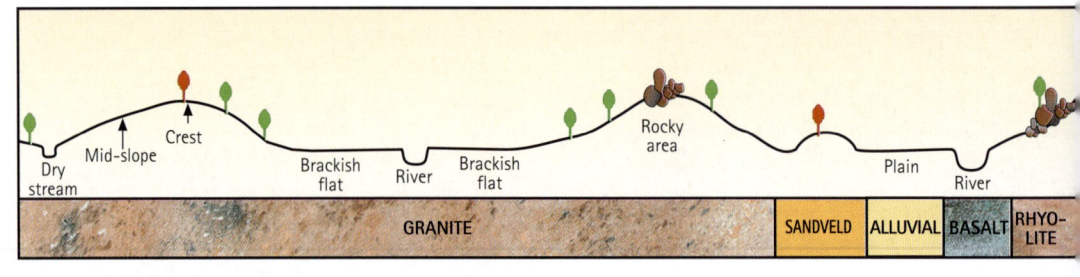

The greeny-yellow flower-spikes of the Large-fruited Bushwillow are typical of the Bushwillow Family.

Seasonal changes

Deciduous. It can be identified for most of the year while the pods are present.

Height: 5 - 15 m
Density: Moderate

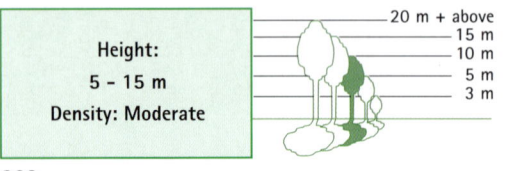

20 m + above / 15 m / 10 m / 5 m / 3 m

	Oct	Nov	Dec	Jan	Feb	Mar	Apr	May	Jun	Jul	Aug	Sep
Leaf												
Flower												
Fruit/Pod												

Growth form
This tree branches low down to form a moderately dense, irregular, roundish canopy.

Leaves
The leaves are opposite, with prominent veins especially on the under-surface. They are covered with soft hair when young, but are hairless and leathery when mature. They have a rounded tip which may be pointed or notched, and a rounded to broadly tapering base. They are yellow-green to dark green above and paler below, and turn brilliant yellow in autumn (25 - 140 x 30 - 85 mm).

Flowers
The small, yellow-green to yellow flowers grow singly in dense spikes, in the angle formed by the leaf. They appear just before or with the new leaves and may be pleasantly or unpleasantly scented (Aug - Nov) (Flower-spike: up to 75 x 25 mm).

Pods
The pods are the largest of the Bushwillow family. They are found in bunches and are produced in such abundance that they weigh down the branches and branchlets. They are initially green, turning pale brown when ripe, and may stay on the tree from February until October (Individual pod: 50 - 100 mm diam.).

Bark
The bark is smooth and pale. In older trees it becomes greyish-brown with patches of rougher bark that may peel off in small blocks, to show a red or orangy tinge in the under-bark.

Look-alike tree
This tree can be confused with other Bushwillows. See pages 71-73, in Distinctive Striking Features, for comparisons.

Gardening
This tree can be a very decorative addition to the garden. It can be grown from seed, grows slowly and is not very resistant to cold.

Links with animals
This tree is not very palatable. The leaves are eaten by giraffe and elephant, and baboons enjoy the seeds of the ripe fruit.

Human uses
The wood makes good timber and is also used for yokes. Baskets and fishing traps are made from part of the roots. Leaf extracts are used to treat backache and eye ailments, and the bark to treat gallstones. Root extracts are taken to treat bloody diarrhoea. Powdered bark is said to arrest menstrual flow and is a soothing and healing lotion when washed into the eye.

SMALLER TREES IN GROUPS
Large-fruited Bushwillow

203

| BUSHWILLOW FAMILY | Combretaceae | Tree no 532 |

RED BUSHWILLOW — *Combretum apiculatum*

AFRIKAANS Rooiboswilg   **N. SOTHO** Mohwelere-Tshipi   **TSONGA** Xikukutsu   **TSWANA** Mogodiri
ZULU umBondwe, umBondwe-omnyama

Combretum is derived from the classical Latin name for the genus used by Pliny, 23-79 AD; **apiculatum** refers to the sharp tip of the leaf.

Leaf/pod

Where you'll find this tree easily

The Red Bushwillow is most common in large groups on granite crests and in rocky places.

A	E	I	M
B	F	J	N
C	G	K	O
D	H	L	P

- It is easiest to find this tree on the crests in Mixed Bushwillow Woodlands (A), Pretoriuskop Sourveld, (B), and Mopane/ Bushwillow Woodlands (P), as well as on sandstone ridges in the Sandveld Ecozone (N).
- It is also easy to spot on the midslopes of Sabie/Crocodile Thorn Thickets (D), as well as the plains of Olifants Rugged Veld (J).
- It can also be found in rocky areas in all other granite and gabbro Ecozones B, C, D, P and E, and rhyolite and basalt Ecozones I and J.

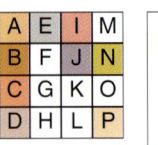

GIFF

- This small tree has a spreading, generally formless, canopy.
- **It is easiest to recognise by its Habitat, and because it grows in groups, rather than by any individual feature of the overall tree shape.**
- It has a short, often curved stem and is usually multi-stemmed.
- The Simple, broadly elliptic leaves are shiny green but yellow leaves are seen among them for most of the year.
- It is easy to spot that the tip of the leaf is characteristically twisted, and points upwards – the scientific name *apiculatum* refers to this.
- **The medium-sized, red-brown, four-winged Bushwillow pods have a smooth, slightly shiny centre, and are visible most of the year.**

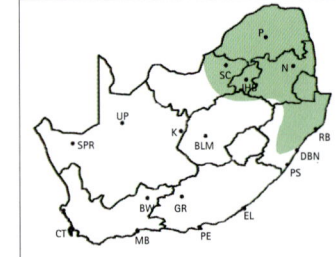

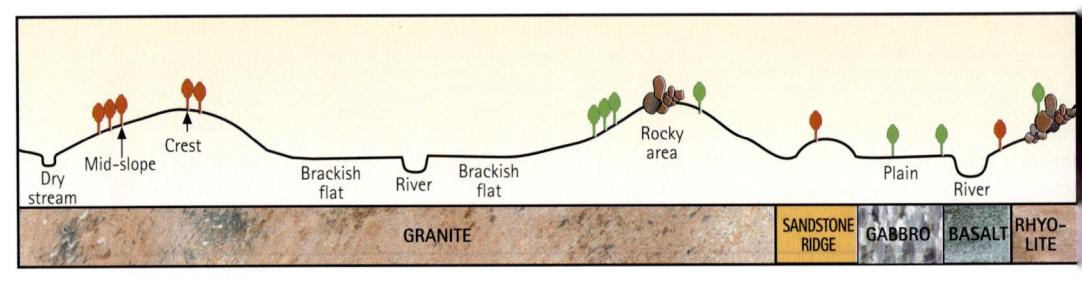

Relatively formless, and inconsistently-shaped trees, Red Bushwillows are distinctive in groups.

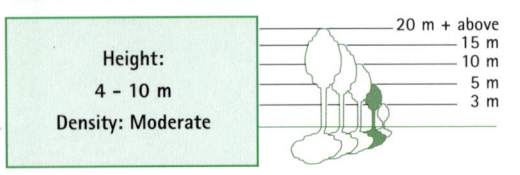

Seasonal changes

Deciduous. The beautiful autumn colours range from reddish-yellow to yellow-green and dark brown. Some fruit is present most of the year.

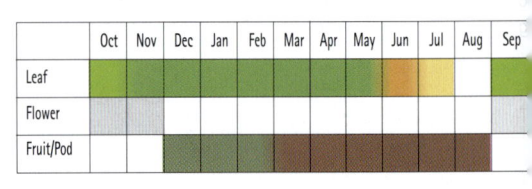

Height: 4 - 10 m
Density: Moderate

	Oct	Nov	Dec	Jan	Feb	Mar	Apr	May	Jun	Jul	Aug	Sep
Leaf												
Flower												
Fruit/Pod												

Growth form
Smaller, younger branchlets are green to pale brown, while older branchlets are grey-brown.

Leaves
The leaves are opposite, with a smooth margin. (65 x 35 mm).

Pods
The characteristic pods, with a single seed in the centre, hang in bunches which ripen in late summer and autumn (25 x 20 mm).

Flowers
The sweet-smelling, cylindrical spikes are not very conspicuous and arise from red buds with the new leaves in spring. The smell of the flowers in areas where Red Bushwillows are common is very characteristic (Sep - Nov) (Spike: 70 x 20 mm).

Bark
The bark is grey to red-brown and breaks off in flat, uneven pieces.

Look-alike tree
This tree can be confused with other Bushwillows. See pages 71-73, in Distinctive Striking Features, for comparisons.

Links with animals
Only young and fallen leaves are eaten regularly, but kudu, bushbuck, eland, giraffe and elephant also eat the mature green leaves. The fruit is eaten by Brown-headed Parrots.

Human uses
The very heavy wood is used to make furniture.

Gardening
This tree will grow in most gardens, preferring sandy soil or rocky areas with clay soil. It can be pruned into a small to medium-sized shade tree. Fairly drought-resistant, it cannot take severe frost. It is slow-growing and can be grown easily from seed.

SMALLER TREES IN GROUPS
Red Bushwillow

| BUSHWILLOW FAMILY | Combretaceae | Tree no 538 |

RUSSET BUSHWILLOW — *Combretum hereroense*

AFRIKAANS Kierieklapper **N. SOTHO** Mokabi **TSONGA** Mpotsa **TSWANA** Mokabi **VENDA** Mugavhi **ZULU** umHlalavane

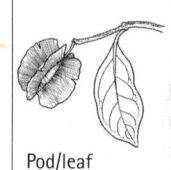

Combretum is derived from the classical Latin name for the genus used by Pliny, 23–79 AD; **hereroense** refers to the Herero people of Namibia.

Pod/leaf

Where you'll find this tree easily
The Russet Bushwillow grows in loose groups often around pans, on rocky areas and sometimes along smaller drainage lines.
- It is easiest to find throughout the Mixed Bushwillow Woodlands (A), on crests, termite mounds and in particular in valley bottoms; as well as in Mopane Shrubveld (L) around pans and vleis.
- It is common along drainage lines and valley bottoms in the other granite Ecozones B, C, D and P.
- It can also be spotted along drainage lines in Ecozones E, F, M and O, and in rocky places in J.

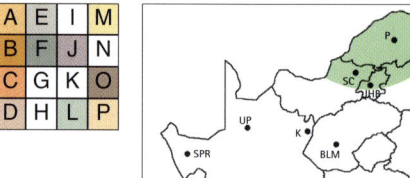

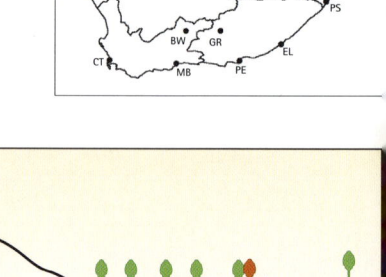

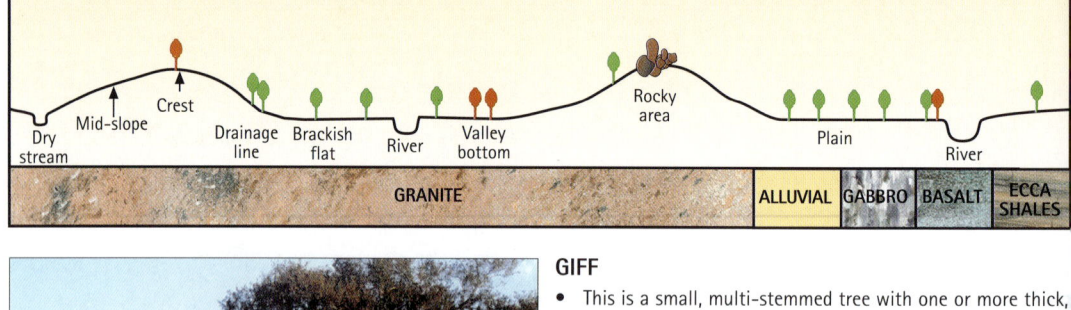

A	E	I	M
B	F	J	N
C	G	K	O
D	H	L	P

Dry stream — Mid-slope — Crest — Drainage line — Brackish flat — River — Valley bottom — Rocky area — Plain — River

GRANITE | ALLUVIAL | GABBRO | BASALT | ECCA SHALES

This is a particularly large, distinctive Russet Bushwillow, laden with pods in late May.

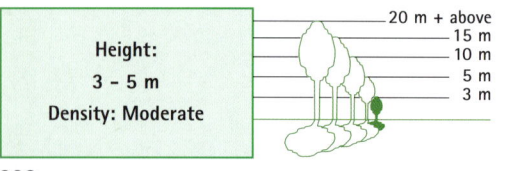

GIFF
- This is a small, multi-stemmed tree with one or more thick, crooked, often curved, stems.
- It is densely branched, with new young branches forming very straight, upward shoots.
- **The trees have an overall coppery appearance from March to July, owing to the presence of the large numbers of red-brown pods.**
- The Simple leaves are small, opposite, with smooth margins
- They vary in shape, from broadly elliptic to heart-shaped.
- They have a rounded tip, that often ends in a small, sharp point, and the under-surface is covered in rusty-brown hair
- **The pods are characteristically the four-winged Bushwillow shape, but are smaller and darker than those of similar-sized Bushwillow trees.**

Seasonal changes
Deciduous. Leaves and fruit fall in late autumn, after which identification is difficult. This is not an easy tree for beginners to find unless it has pods or flowers.

Height: 3 – 5 m **Density:** Moderate

20 m + above / 15 m / 10 m / 5 m / 3 m

	Oct	Nov	Dec	Jan	Feb	Mar	Apr	May	Jun	Jul	Aug	Sep
Leaf												
Flower												
Fruit/Pod												

Growth form
See GIFF.

Leaves
The Simple leaves have a broadly tapering base. They are dark green above and pale yellow-green below (20 - 70 x 10 - 45 mm).

Pods
The pods are brilliant russet-red from mid- to late-summer, changing to pale coppery-brown later in the season. They grow abundantly in prominent bunches, and remain on the tree for long periods, often until July (Approx. 23 x 20 mm).

Flowers
The sweet-smelling flowers are white to cream-coloured to yellow, and are found in dense spikes that grow in the angle made by the leaves, or on the tips of twigs. The flowers appear before or with the new leaves (Aug - Nov) (Flower spike: up to 60 x 15 mm).

Bark
The young bark is covered in hairs, peels in strips, and changes colour from green to red-brown to grey. Older bark is rough and fissured lengthways, and is pale grey to dark grey-brown.

Look-alike tree
This tree can be confused with other Bushwillows. See pages 71-73, in Distinctive Striking Features, for comparisons.

Gardening
This could be trimmed to be an attractive garden plant, particularly in autumn when it is covered by coppery pods. It should grow well in most gardens, as it is drought-resistant and can take fairly sharp frost. It can be grown from seed and will grow quite fast in well-watered gardens. The seeds are thought to be poisonous.

Links with animals
The leaves are eaten by kudu, impala, steenbok, elephant and giraffe.

Human uses
The wood is used as supports in mines, and for pick and hoe handles. Straight branches are ideal for making kieries (walking sticks), hence the Afrikaans name 'Kierieklapper'. Root extracts treat stomach complaints, and are mixed into enemas for venereal diseases and pains in the body. Heart disease and heartburn are treated with bark extracts, and dried young shoots are used for tonsillitis and coughs.

SMALLER TREES IN GROUPS
Russet Bushwillow

207

| Jute and Linden Family | Tiliaceae | Tree no 459.2 |

Sandpaper Raisin

Grewia flavescens

AFRIKAANS Skurwerosyntjie

Grewia is named after Nehemia Grew, a 17th Century plant anatomist; **flavescens** means 'becoming yellow' or 'yellowish', referring to the flowers.

Stem

Where you'll find this tree easily

The Sandpaper Raisin is often found in large stands growing where there is increased moisture or nutrients such as along the side of the road, in brack areas, on termite mounds, on koppies or near to river edges.

- It is easiest to find in all the above Habitats in the Sabie/Crocodile Thorn Thickets (D) and in Mopane/Bushwillow Woodlands (P).
- It can also be spotted in the Lebombo Mountain Bushveld (I), and Olifants Rugged Veld (J), which are both very rocky.

A	E	I	M
B	F	J	N
C	G	K	O
D	H	L	P

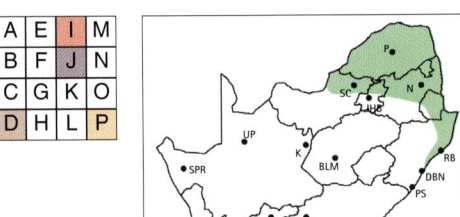

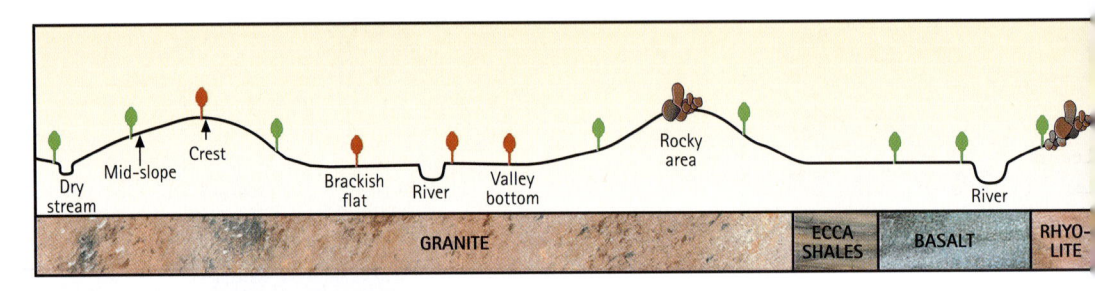

GIFF

- This scrambling shrub is multi-stemmed and densely branched, forming a very irregular, leafy canopy.
- Simple alternate leaves are broad and hairy, and the leaf-tips are pointed.
- Leaves have three distinctive veins from the base which is virtually symmetric.
- Leaf margins are irregularly toothed.
- The square-sided, fluted or grooved branchlets and stems are characteristic.
- Yellow, star-like flowers grow at the base of the leaves in mid- to late-summer.
- The hard fruit is normally two-lobed and berry-like.

These leaves, with three veins from the base, are typical of all Raisins; the fluted/grooved twig is more specific to Sandpaper Raisin.

Seasonal changes

Deciduous. This is easy to identify in winter because of the berries and square stems.

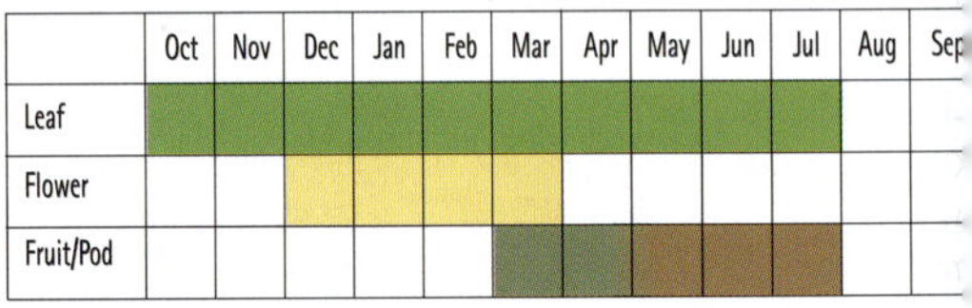

Height: 1 – 5 m
Density: Moderate

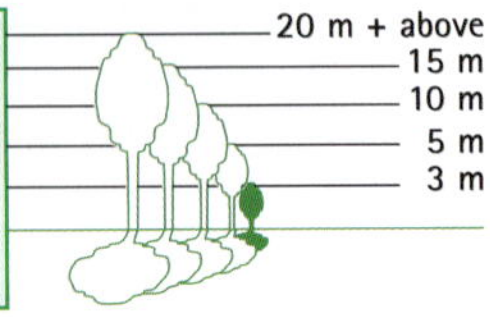

	Oct	Nov	Dec	Jan	Feb	Mar	Apr	May	Jun	Jul	Aug	Sep
Leaf												
Flower												
Fruit/Pod												

Growth form
The branchlets are covered with coarse hairs.

Leaves
Leaves are pale green on both sides. The stalk is short and velvety (30 x 70 mm).

Flowers
The flowers are sometimes sweet-scented. The outer sepals are yellow-pink and the stamens are also yellow (Dec - Mar) (10 mm).

Fruit
The fruit may be one- to four-lobed, slightly grooved and covered by whitish hair. It ripens to yellow-brown (Mar - Jul) (Each lobe: 8 - 14 mm).

Stems
The stems are square and fluted, especially the mature branches, which have four distinct angles.

Look-alike tree
The White-leaved Raisin, *Grewia bicolor*, p. 210, is often confused with this species, but it does not have square, grooved stems. In the White-leaved Raisin the tips of the leaves are round, compared with the pointed tips shown above. Its fruit is most often 1 - 2 lobed, whereas the Sandpaper Raisin's can be 1 - 4 lobed (although also usually 2). The White-leaved Raisin's flowers are also yellow but appear earlier, from October to January, while the Sandpaper is December to March.

Gardening
These small shrubs, with their colourful flowers and interesting fruit can be a feature in indigenous gardens.

Links with animals
Klipspringer and impala eat the leaves. The fruit is eaten by birds, especially hornbills, and also by baboon and monkey.

Human uses
The fruit is edible, and after soaking in water for 48 hours can make a refreshing drink. The wood is used for sticks and knobkieries. The young branchlets are used to weave baskets.

SMALLER TREES IN GROUPS
Sandpaper Raisin

| JUTE AND LINDEN FAMILY | Tiliaceae | Tree no 458 |

WHITE-LEAVED RAISIN *Grewia bicolor*

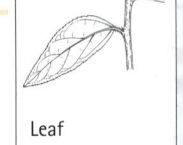

AFRIKAANS Witrosyntjie

Leaf

Grewia is named after Nehemia Grew, a 17th Century plant anatomist; **bicolor** means 'of two colours', referring to the leaves.

Where you'll find this tree easily
The White-leaved Raisin grows in groups, often in large stands along the side of the road, where the land has been disturbed and there is extra moisture from water running off the tar.
- It is easiest to find this tree in the Sabie/Crocodile Thorn Thickets (D).
- It is also found in most other Ecozones.

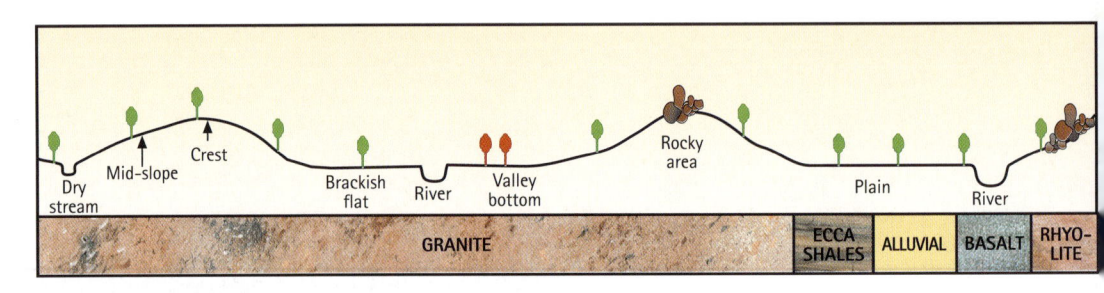

A	E	I	M
B	F	J	N
C	G	K	O
D	H	L	P

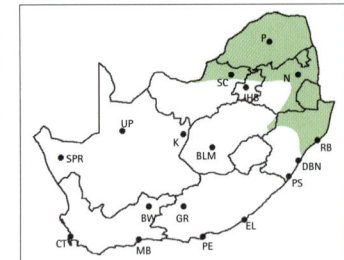

Dry stream — Mid-slope — Crest — Brackish flat — River — Valley bottom — Rocky area — Plain — River

GRANITE — ECCA SHALES — ALLUVIAL — BASALT — RHYOLITE

GIFF
- This shrub often has relatively long, twisted branches and is recognisable where it grows in large, uniform groups.
- It is multi-stemmed and densely branched, forming an irregular, leafy canopy.
- Simple, alternate leaves are broadly elliptic and finely toothed to smooth.
- **Leaves have three distinct veins from the base which can be slightly asymmetric, and leaf-tips are rounded.**
- **The under-surface of the leaves is always distinctly paler and covered with velvety-grey hairs.**
- Yellow, star-like flowers grow at the base of the leaves.
- The reddish-brown fruit is berry-like and hard, and is normally one- to two-lobed.

The bi-coloured leaves help separate this shrub from the other Raisins that have yellow flowers and similar-shaped leaves.

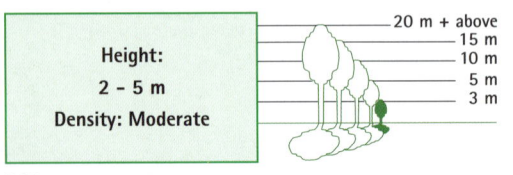

Seasonal changes
Deciduous. They are hard to recognise without leaves, flowers or fruit during August and September.

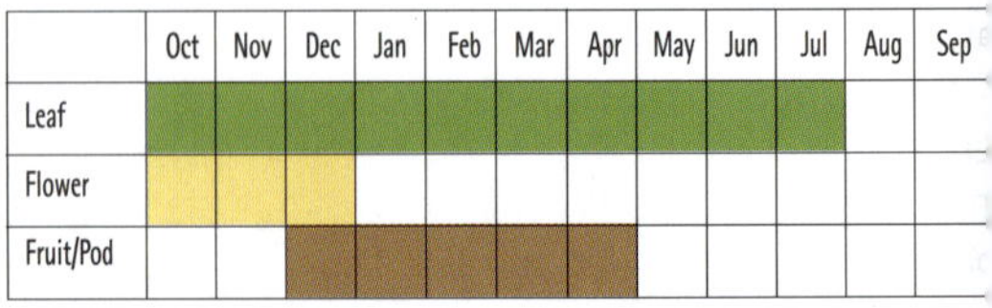

	Oct	Nov	Dec	Jan	Feb	Mar	Apr	May	Jun	Jul	Aug	Sep
Leaf												
Flower												
Fruit/Pod												

Height: 2 – 5 m
Density: Moderate

20 m + above / 15 m / 10 m / 5 m / 3 m

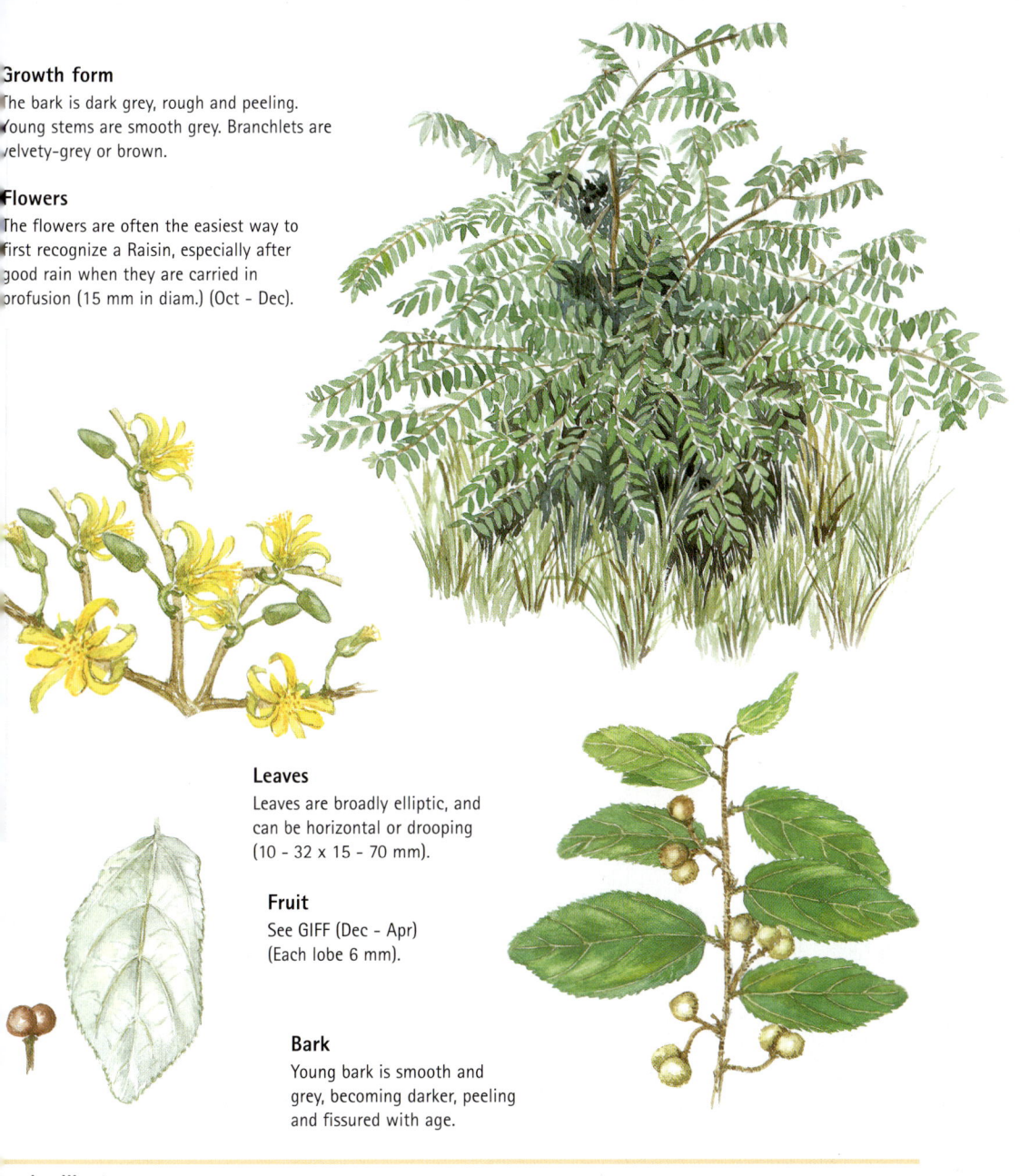

Growth form
The bark is dark grey, rough and peeling. Young stems are smooth grey. Branchlets are velvety-grey or brown.

Flowers
The flowers are often the easiest way to first recognize a Raisin, especially after good rain when they are carried in profusion (15 mm in diam.) (Oct - Dec).

Leaves
Leaves are broadly elliptic, and can be horizontal or drooping (10 - 32 x 15 - 70 mm).

Fruit
See GIFF (Dec - Apr) (Each lobe 6 mm).

Bark
Young bark is smooth and grey, becoming darker, peeling and fissured with age.

Look-alike tree
The Sandpaper Raisin, *Grewia flavescens*, p. 208, is often confused with this species, but it doesn't have the pale, hairy-leafed under-surface shown above. It also has very distinctive four-angled, grooved, mature stems. The leaves are similar in shape but the tips of the Sandpaper are pointed not round, and tend to be more symmetric. The fruit of the Sandpaper can be 1 - 4 lobed (although usually 2), and its flowers are also yellow, appearing from December to March, not October to January.

Gardening
These small shrubs, with attractive flowers and interesting fruit can be a feature in indigenous gardens, particularly attracting birds.

Human uses
The fruit is edible. The wood is used for sticks and knobkieries. Roots are stripped to make twine and rope, and used medicinally to treat coughs.

Links with animals
The fruit is eaten by birds, especially hornbills, and also by baboon and monkey

SMALLER TREES IN GROUPS
White-leaved Raisin

211

SWEET-PEA SUB-FAMILY OF PEA FAMILY | Papilionoideae | Tree no 237

ROUND-LEAVED BLOODWOOD
Pterocarpus rotundifolius

Leaf
Pod

AFRIKAANS Dopperkiaat **SWAZI** inDlebezindlovu **TSONGA** Muyataha, Ncelele
VENDA Mushusha-phombwe **ZULU** iNdlandlovu

Pterocarpus is from the Greek *pteros* meaning 'wing' + *karpon* meaning 'fruit', referring to the conspicuously winged pod; **rotundifolius** refers to the 'round' leaflets.

Where you'll find this tree easily
The Round-leaved Bloodwood grows in groups, often colonising a large area, in wooded grassland.

- This tree is most easily found in Mixed Bushwillow Woodlands (A) and on the plains of Mopane Shrubveld (L).
- It can also be found in Sabie/Crocodile Thorn Thickets (D), in Thorn Veld (E), in Knob-thorn/Marula Savannah (F) as well as in the Lebombo Mountain Bushveld (I).

A	E	I	M
B	F	J	N
C	G	K	O
D	H	L	P

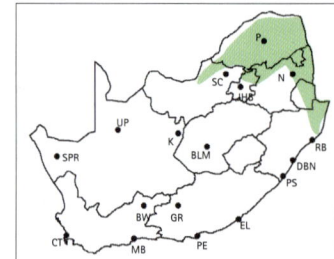

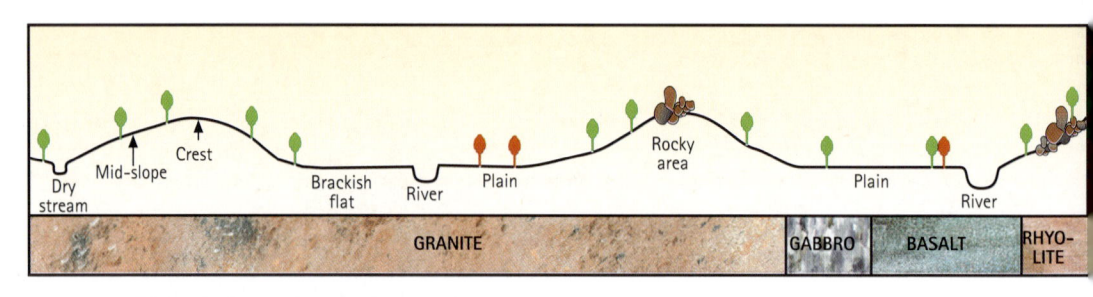

Dry stream — Mid-slope — Crest — Brackish flat — River — Plain — Rocky area — Plain — River

GRANITE | GABBRO | BASALT | RHYOLITE

GIFF
- This is usually a multi-stemmed shrub with an irregular or round canopy, often with many dead branches sticking out after veld fires.
- It can be a tall tree with bare trunk and rounded canopy.
- Large Once Compound leaves are characteristically very glossy, with firm, round leaflets on a long leaf-stalk.
- The herringbone pattern of the veins is conspicuous.
- The pea-shaped, yellow flowers grow in sprays on the ends of mature stems.
- The flowers are sweet-scented and have crinkled petals.
- The pods hang in small bunches, and consist of a central hard core surrounded by a thin, hard, very wavy membrane.

Seasonal changes
Deciduous. This tree may be without leaves from June to October, but will be recognisable as long as the fruit is present.

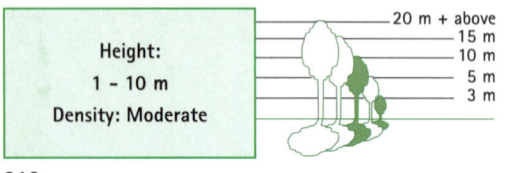

Whatever your interests, it adds to your pleasure to know that elephant enjoy eating the shiny leaves of Round-leaved Bloodwood!

Height: 1 - 10 m
Density: Moderate

20 m + above
15 m
10 m
5 m
3 m

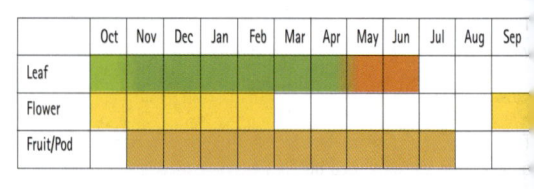

	Oct	Nov	Dec	Jan	Feb	Mar	Apr	May	Jun	Jul	Aug	Sep
Leaf												
Flower												
Fruit/Pod												

Growth form
This tree is very susceptible to veld fires, and because of regular burning, large trees are seldom seen.

Leaves
Leaves have 1 or 2 pairs of alternate leaflets with a larger terminal leaflet. Leaflets are dark green above and much paler below, and turn yellow and brown in autumn. They have smooth margins (Leaf: 100 - 300 mm; leaflet: 35 - 110 mm, and almost as broad).

Tall tree

Pods
The pods are yellow-green to dark brown and ripen in autumn. They may remain on the tree through winter (Nov - Jul) (60 x 35 mm).

Flowers
This tree normally flowers only after good rains, but may flower more than once in a season. The flowers last for 2 - 3 weeks (Sep - Feb) (Spray: 150 - 300 mm).

Shrub

Bark
Bark is grey to pale brown, and smooth when young. In older trees it is rough and breaks up into irregular blocks that peel off.

Look-alike tree
The combined GIFF features of the Round-leaved Bloodwood, plus its habit of growing in groups, makes it very distinctive. However, Apple-leaf, *Philenoptera violacea*, p. 124, has a similar-shaped leaf, but they are a very different colour, being grey-green, leathery and dull.

Human uses
The wood is durable and insect-proof and is used for wagon wheels, furniture and household articles.

Links with animals
Elephant find the leaves and young twigs very palatable, and they often break the trees and branches when eating. The leaves are also browsed by kudu and impala.

Gardening
This can be a very attractive tree for the small garden. It is quick-growing from seed but not frost-resistant.

SMALLER TREES IN GROUPS
Round-leaved Bloodwood

213

THORN-TREE SUB-FAMILY OF PEA FAMILY — Mimosoideae — Tree no 164.1

FLAKY-BARK ACACIA — *Acacia exuvialis*

AFRIKAANS Skilferdoring **TSONGA** Risavana **ZULU** umSabane

Leaf/pod/thorn

Acacia is taken from the Greek *akis* meaning a 'sharp point'. It refers to the thorns of all African species; **exuvialis** refers to the bark flaking off the tree.

Where you'll find this tree easily

The Flaky-bark Acacia grows in fairly dense groups, in a wide variety of Habitats, but particularly in sandy soils and rocky areas.

- It is easiest to find on the edges of roads in Sabie/Crocodile Thorn Thickets (D), and the plains of Mopane Shrubveld (L).
- It also grows in sandy soils of the crests, and in drainage lines and valley bottoms in Mixed Bushwillow Woodlands (A), Malelane Mountain Bushveld (C), in southern Lebombo Mountain Bushveld (I) and in Mopane/Bushwillow Woodlands (P).
- It can be spotted on the plains of Olifants Rugged Veld (J).

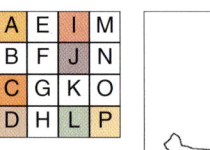

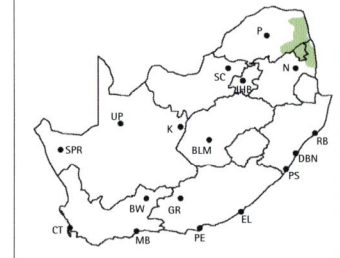

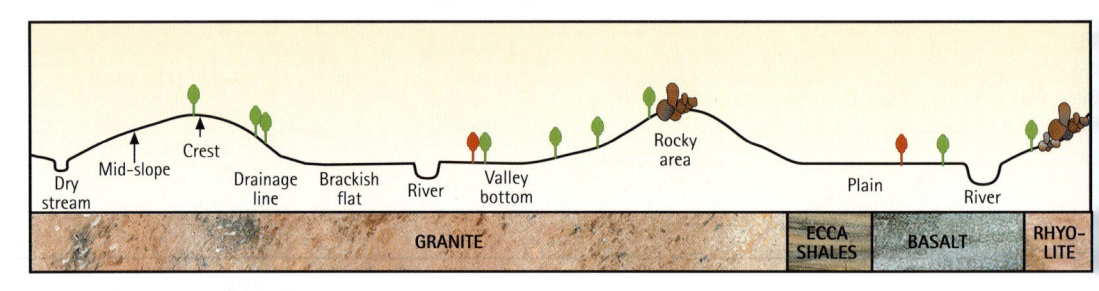

The fresh spring leaves, white thorns and flaky, orange bark of the Flaky-bark Acacia make it easy to spot.

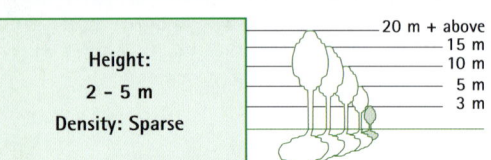

Height: 2 - 5 m
Density: Sparse

GIFF

- This is a small, often multi-stemmed, low-branching tree or shrub with a sparse, V-shaped canopy.
- **The bark is smooth and peels in large, orange-brown flakes leaving smooth, yellow-brown under-bark.**
- Twice Compound leaves have 1 - 6 pairs of feathers, each with 3 - 6 pairs of opposite leaflets, and are fine and feathery.
- **The straight, paired thorns can be very long, and are white and thickened at the base.**
- It has a few yellow flower-balls for most of the summer.
- Sickle-shaped, segmented, brown to reddish-brown pods are covered by glands that secrete a slightly sticky fluid.

Seasonal changes

Deciduous. The presence of the flaky bark and obvious white thorns makes identification possible throughout the year.

	Oct	Nov	Dec	Jan	Feb	Mar	Apr	May	Jun	Jul	Aug	Sep
Leaf		●	●	●	●	●	●	●				
Flower		●	●	●	●	●	●					●
Fruit/Pod					●	●	●					

Growth form
See GIFF.

Leaves
The leaflets are elliptic with a rounded end, a sharp tip and a smooth margin (Leaflet: 3 - 10 x 1,5 - 4,5 mm).

Flowers
The flowers on long, slender stalks may be seen sporadically from September to February. They are never abundant but the tree may flower for long periods (10 mm).

Thorns
The thorns grow from a single base and do not move apart as the branch grows. They are very conspicuous in winter and early summer when the tree is without leaves (70 - 100 mm).

Pods
The small pods are relatively flat, despite the seeds that segment it. They are sometimes sticky Feb - May) (10 x 65 mm).

Bark
Grey to dark grey bark has an under-surface that tends to have an oily/shiny appearance owing to the presence of resin.

Look-alike tree
This tree can be confused with other Acacias. See pages 74-76, for Acacia comparisons.

Gardening
This tree is small and untidy and seldom used in the garden.

Human uses
Roots are cooked like vegetables in the same way as Sweet Potatoes.

Links with animals
Leaves and pods are eaten by impala and duiker.

SMALLER TREES IN GROUPS
Flaky-bark Acacia

| THORN-TREE SUB-FAMILY OF PEA FAMILY | Mimosoideae | Tree no 190 |

SICKLE-BUSH
Dichrostachys cinerea

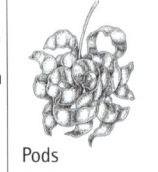

AFRIKAANS Sekelbos **PEDI** Moretshe, Mongana, Moselesele **SISWATI** umSilazembe **TSONGA** Ndzenga
TSWANA Mosêlêsêlê **VENDA** Murenzhe **ZULU** uGagane, umZilazembe, umThezane, uMnukelambiba

Dichrostachys comes from the Greek *dis + chroos + stachys* meaning 'two + colour + spike', referring to the pink and yellow, spike-like flowers; *cinerea* refers to the ashy colour of the bark.

Pods

Where you'll find this tree easily
The Sickle-bush grows in dense groups and prefers clay soils. It often colonises areas of disturbed soils such as roadsides, as well as overgrazed areas near old waterholes and unused cattle troughs.

- This tree can easily be found growing in Sabie/Crocodile Thorn Thickets (D) and Stunted Knob-thorn Savannah (K).
- This tree can also be found in most other Ecozones.

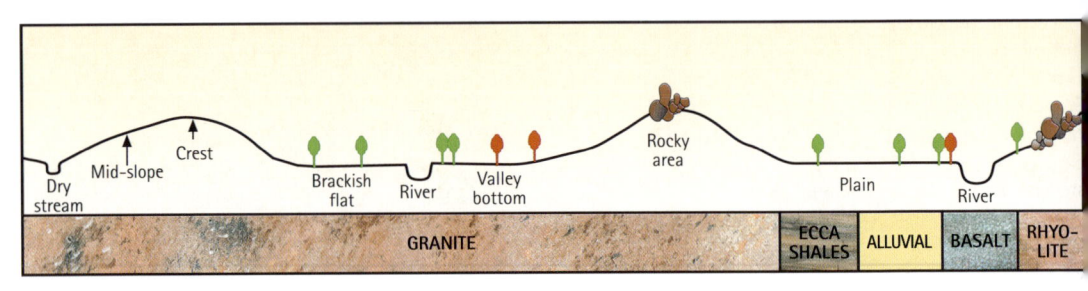

A	E	I	M
B	F	J	N
C	G	K	O
D	H	L	P

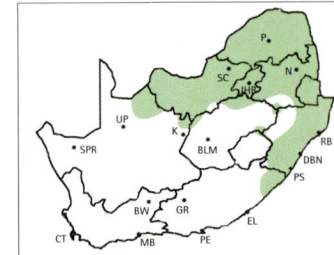

GIFF
- This smallish, multi-stemmed, low-branching shrub (or occasionally tree), has a heavily intertwined or matted canopy with fine feathery foliage.
- The branches and twigs have long, pale grey, straight spines, that are tough enough to puncture tractor tyres.
- **The long, Twice Compound, olive-green leaves are alternate, with small, delicate leaflets.**
- The fluffy, mauve-pink and yellow flower-spikes grow on long stalks towards the ends of the branchlets and twigs.
- The flowers resemble Chinese lanterns.
- **Tightly coiled dark brown pods are very distinctive.**

Search the Sickle-bush shapes in mist, and find the Pearl-spotted Owlet!

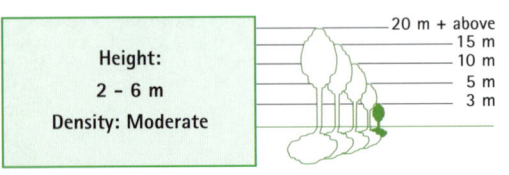

Seasonal changes
Deciduous. This tree can be identified in winter by its growth form, spines and pods.

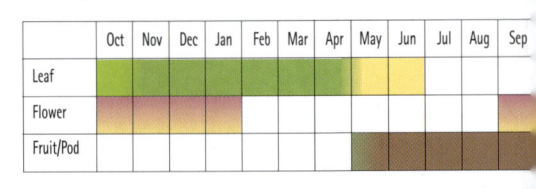

Height: 2 - 6 m
Density: Moderate

	Oct	Nov	Dec	Jan	Feb	Mar	Apr	May	Jun	Jul	Aug	Sep
Leaf												
Flower												
Fruit/Pod												

Growth form
See GIFF.

Leaves
The leaflets are elliptic with a smooth margin. There are 8 - 12 pairs of feathers and 15 - 30 pairs of leaflets
Leaf: 30 - 200 mm; leaflet: 3 x 0,5 mm).

Flowers
The mauve-pink filaments at the base of the flower-spikes are sterile. The yellow tip consists of minute, fertile flowers closely packed together (Oct - Jan) (40 - 60 mm).

Spines
The spines are modified side branchlets. Sometimes they have leaves growing on them (20 - 40 mm).

Pods
The closely packed, fertilised flowers mature to form pods growing bunched together from each flower-spike. The clusters of pods ripen to dark brown and do not split open on the tree. Pods may remain on the tree even after the leaves have dropped (May - Sep) (Cluster: 70 -100 mm diam.).

Bark
As the scientific name, *cinerea*, indicates, the bark is pale brown to ash-grey with shallow lengthways grooves.

Look-alike tree
This tree can be confused with the Acacias and Albizias. See pages 74-77, for comparisons.

Gardening
With its very attractive flowers, sharp spines and tendency to encroach, the Sickle-bush can make an attractive, impenetrable hedge for the indigenous garden. It is fairly drought- and frost-resistant. It grows slowly but can be grown from seed easily.

Human uses
Roots, bark, pods and leaves are used for medicinal purposes including the treatment of toothache, snakebite and skin diseases. The leaves are said to have local anaesthetic properties. The wood is used for fence poles. Fresh bark is used to make fibre.

Links with animals
The pods are very nutritious and are eaten by a wide variety of animals including rhino, monkey, giraffe, bushpig and buffalo.

SMALLER TREES IN GROUPS
Sickle-bush

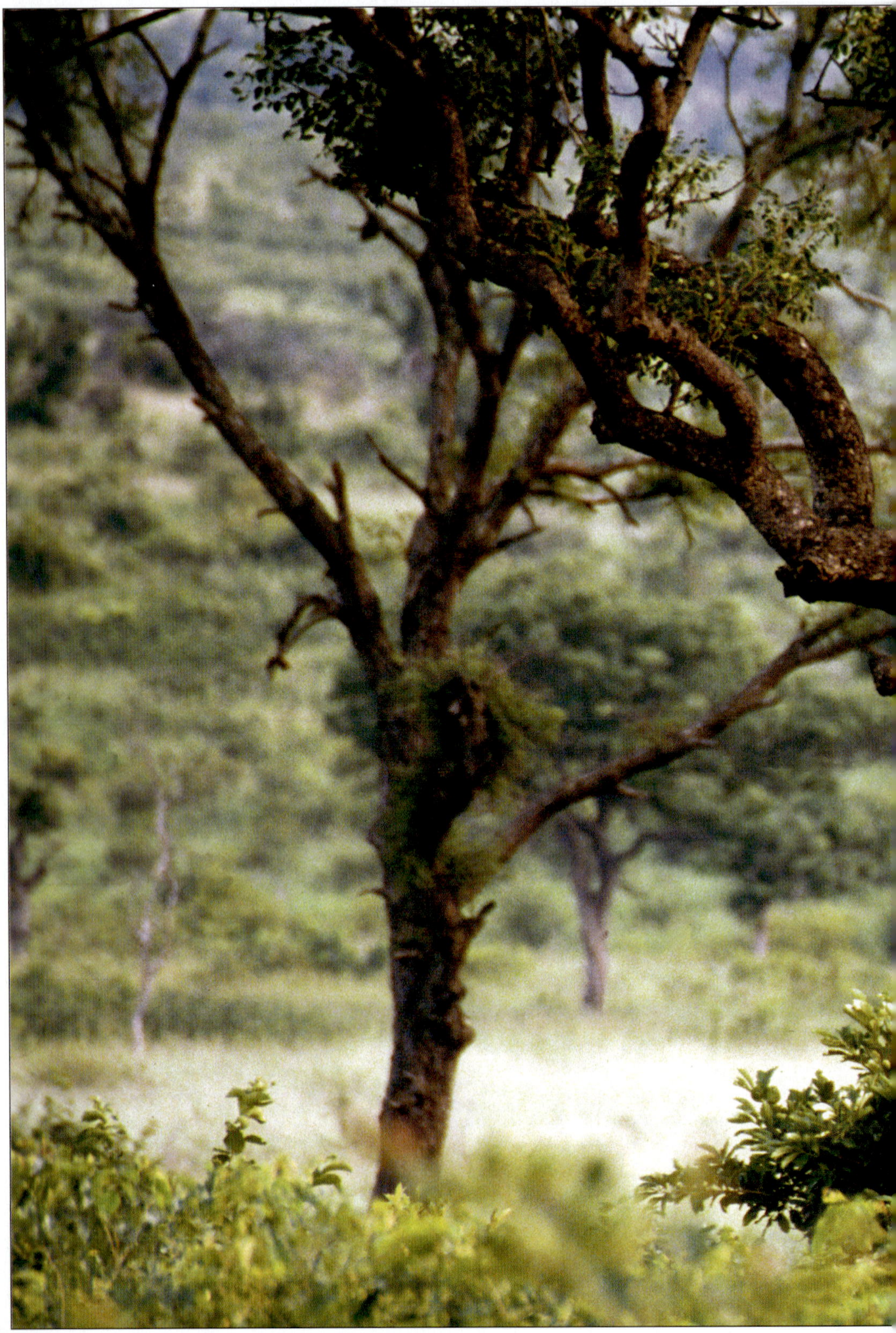

REFERENCES

This section contains reference material which will add to your knowledge base rapidly and easily and enable you to make Tree Spotting an enjoyable and rewarding pastime.

Family Features	220
Lowveld Maps	224
Tree Index	238
References	243

In summer when the grass is high, it is more difficult for predators to look out for prey. Although lions seldom climb trees, this lioness has taken advantage of the conveniently placed branches of a Marula, *Sclerocarya birrea*, p.122, to get a higher viewpoint.

FAMILY FEATURES

All living things have relatives that share certain distinctive features. In plants this can be similar growth form, seed dispersal mechanism, or leaf, flower, fruit or pod structure. Scientists classify plants by their flower features that can be minute details, hardly visible to the naked eye.

As a pleasure-seeking Tree Spotter you will find that knowing some visible similarities between family members will help you build up methods of recognising new trees wherever you go in Africa or further afield.

The scientific classifications tend to change quite regularly, so these statistics of world and South African distribution are simply there to give you an idea of the family size and distribution.

The information includes the Ecozones where you are most likely to find each family member. This is shown by the letter A to P in brackets. With this information you can look for related trees in one area. Remember to check their Habitat distribution on the Ecozone Tree Lists, pages 50-58.

BAUHINIA Caesalpinioideae

Worldwide - 162 genera, 2 000 species, mainly tropics;
South Africa - 50 species; one of the largest woody families.

Family Features
- Leaves - Compound, alternate, paired leaflets at tip, swelling at base of leaf-stalk
- Flowers - large, showy, 5 symmetrical petals
- Seeds - usually more pod-encased, usually more than one seed

Trees in this book
African Weeping-wattle (A,B,C,D,E,F,I,J,K,L,P) p. 96;
Long-tail Cassia (A,B,D,F,I,P) p. 98;
Mopane (I,L,M,O,P) p. 116;
Pod-mahogany (A,I,N) p. 150;
Pride-of-de-Kaap Bauhinia (B,H,N,) p. 100;
Small False Mopane (N,P) p. 49;
Weeping Boer-bean (A,B,C,D,H,J) p. 170

BUCKTHORN AND JUJUBE Rhamnaceae

Worldwide - 52 genera, 600 species;
South Africa - 7 genera, 20 tree species.

Family Features
- Leaves - shiny, Simple, alternate
- Flowers - small, inconspicuous, nectar-rich

Tree in this book
Buffalo-thorn Jujube (A,B,C,D,F,K,P) p. 186

BUDDLEJA Buddlejaceae

Worldwide - in Africa, eastern Asia and the Americas;
South Africa - 12 species.

Family Features
- Leaves - opposite or in whorls of 3
- Flowers - in dense, heavily scented heads

Tree in this book
Water Nuxia (D,H,M) p. 172

BUSHWILLOW Combretaceae

Worldwide - 60 genera, 400 species;
South Africa - well represented with 5 genera, 41 tree species.

Family Features
- Leaves - Simple
- Flowers - spiked
- Seeds - four-winged

Trees in this book
Flame Climbing Bushwillow (B,D,H,J,M) p. 102;
Forest Bushwillow (C,F,G,I) p. 71;
Large-fruited Bushwillow (A,B,C,I,N) p. 202;
Leadwood Bushwillow (A,B,C,F,H,J,M,O,P) p. 118;
Red Bushwillow (A,B,C,D,E,I,J,N,P) p. 204;
River Bushwillow (D,H) p. 174;
Russet Bushwillow (A,B,C,D,E,F,J,L,M,O,P) p. 206;
Velvet Bushwillow (I,J,K,L,N) p. 72;
Weeping Bushwillow (A,B,C,J,N) p. 35;
Purple-pod Cluster-leaf (C,D,I,J,L,P) p. 104;
Silver Cluster-leaf (A,B,C,D,N,P) p. 120
Stink-bushwillow (N) p. 73

CAPER Capparaceae

Worldwide - 46 genera and about 700 species;
South Africa - 40 species.

Family Features
- Leaves - variable
- Flowers - 4 free petals, numerous long stamens

Trees in this book
Bushveld Bead-bean (F,G,J,K,L,O) p. 48;
Shepherds-tree (I,J,M,O,P) p. 43

Flaky-bark Acacia
Acacia exuvialis
p. 214

220

COFFEE AND GARDENIA Rubiaceae
Worldwide - 400 genera, 5 000 - 6 000 species, warmer parts of the world;
South Africa - 47 genera.
Family Features
- Leaves - hairy pits in axils of veins (under-surface), untoothed margin, opposite or whorled

Trees in this book
Bushveld Gardenia (A,D,J,M) p. 188;
Matumi (D,H,J,M) p. 176

EBONY Ebenaceae
Worldwide - 2 genera, 485 species, mostly tropical regions;
South Africa - 2 genera, 35 tree species;
wood traded by ancient merchants.
Family Features
- Very variable
- Leaves - Simple, smooth margin

Trees in this book
Ebony Jackal-berry (A,B,C,D,F,H,J,M,P) p. 160;
Magic Guarri (A,B,C,D,F,G,M,O,P) p. 190

EUPHORBIA Euphorbiaceae
Worldwide - 2 000 species;
South Africa - 100 species; 2nd largest woody family.
Family Features
- Latex - milky or watery, often poisonous
- Leaves - Simple, usually alternate, toothed margin
- Fruit - small, 3-lobed capsule

Trees in this book
Deadliest Euphorbia (B,C,D,I) p. 152;
Lebombo Euphorbia (I,J) p. 42;
Naboom Euphorbia (A,B,C,D,I) p. 152;
Rubber-hedge Euphorbia (D,E) p. 39;
Feverberry Croton (F,H,L,P) p. 46;
Lebombo-ironwood (I,N) p. 130;
Tamboti (B,C,D,E,G,H,M,O,P) p. 162

FIG AND MULBERRY Moraceae
Worldwide - tropical and sub-tropical area, 1 000 species;
South Africa - Ficus genus, 35 species.
Family Features
- Leaves - alternate, rounded leaf-buds
- Latex - milky

Trees in this book
Large-leaved Rock Fig (A,B,C,D,E,I,J,N,P) p. 154;
Red-leaved Fig (A,B,C,D,E,I,J,N,P) p. 32;
Sycomore Fig (A,B,D,F,H,J) p. 164

JACARANDA Bignoniaceae
South Africa - 11 native species.
Family Features
- Leaves - Once Compound, opposite or whorled and without stipules
- Flowers - large, bell- or funnel-shaped and very showy
- Fruit - the fruit bursts open while still on the tree and resembles a long, narrow pod, usually with winged seeds

Tree in this book
Sausage-tree (A,B,D,F,H,M) p. 178

JUTE AND LINDEN Tiliaceae
Worldwide - 44 genera, 500 species;
South Africa - 30 tree and shrub species.
Family Features
- Leaves - Simple, alternate, 3-veined from base, toothed margin, star-shaped hairs

Trees in this book
Sandpaper Raisin (D,I,J,P) p. 208;
White-leaved Raisin (A,B,C,D,F,G,H,I,J,K,L,M,O,P) p. 210

KAPOK Bombacaceae
Worldwide - about 21 genera, 150 species;
only tree of this family in Africa.
Family Features
- Trunks - swollen, bottle-shaped or barrel-shaped
- Leaves - alternate, often Hand-shaped Compound
- Flowers - large with 5 free petals and numerous stamens
- Fruit - capsule or nut

Tree in this book
Baobab (I,L,M,N,P) p. 84

KIRKIA Kirkiaceae
Worldwide - 30 genera and over 100 species;
South Africa - 4 tree species.
Family Features
- Leaves - Once Compound, alternate leaves with a leaflet at the tip, and toothed margins
- Flowers - some have separate male and female flowers
- Fruit - may be dry and woody, or fleshy

Trees in this book
Mountain Kirkia (B,C) p. 37;
White Kirkia (I,J,N,P) p. 156

Sickle-bush
Dichrostachys cinerea
p. 216

Litchi and Soapberry Sapindaceae
Worldwide - 120 genera, about 1 000 species;
South Africa - about 30 species.
Family Features
- Leaves - variable
- Flowers - small and inconspicuous in local species
- Fruit - small, fleshy parts (arils) of many species are edible

Tree in this book
Jacket-plum (A,B,C,D,E,I,J,L) p. 192

Mahogany Meliaceae
Worldwide - in Asia a well known Seringa;
South Africa - 6 genera, 20 tree and shrub species.
Family Features
- Leaves - Once Compound, alternate, crowded towards end of branchlets
- Flowers - stamens fused into a tube, 5 free petals

Tree in this book
Natal-mahogany (D,F,H,J,M) p. 180

Mango Anacardiaceae
Worldwide - 60 genera;
South Africa - 10 genera, 80 species.
Family Features
- Trees have watery latex
- Leaves - variable
- Flowers - separate male and female flowers, on separate trees
- Fruit - edible in most species
- Bark - rich in resin

Trees in this book
Bushveld Resin-tree (F,J,K,L,I) p. 40;
Drooping Resin-tree (F,I,L) p. 40;
False-marula Lannea (A,B,D,E,F,H,I,L) p. 38;
Marula (A,B,D,E,F,H,I,J) p. 122

Monkey-orange Strychnaceae
Worldwide - 3 genera, 220 species;
South Africa - 10 species.
Family Features
- Very varied
- Leaves - opposite pairs, 3 - 7 veined
- Flowers - 4 - 5 lobed
- Fruit - small to large berry with leathery rind

Tree in this book
Black Monkey-orange (A,B,C,N,P) p. 132

Mustard-tree Salvadoraceae
Family Features
- Leaves - Simple, opposite, elliptic to round, with smooth margins

Tree in this book
Narrow-leaved Mustard-tree (M) p. 134

Myrrh Burseraceae
Worldwide - 200 species, mainly Africa and Arabia;
South Africa - 26 species; linked to biblical times; produced frankincense and myrrh from resin.
Family Features
- Latex - milky
- Leaves - variable, aromatic
- Bark - thin, papery, flaky (in some species)

Trees in this book
Firethorn Corkwood (F,I,J,L,N) p. 2;
Tall Firethorn Corkwood (F,I,J,L,M,N,P) p. 136;
Zebra-bark Corkwood (L) p. 47

Myrtle Myrtaceae
Worldwide – large tropical and sub tropical family, 2 000 species;
South Africa - 25 species.
Family Features
- Leaves - Simple, opposite, smooth margin
- Flowers – many stamens
- Fruit – tipped with remains of flower

Tree in this book
Umdoni Waterberry (A,B,D,H) p. 30

Oleander Apocynaceae
Worldwide - large family;
South Africa - 14 genera, 40 tree species.
Some species have medicinal properties, others extremely poisonous.
Family Features
- Flowers - attractive
- Latex - milky or watery

Tree in this book
Quinine-tree (C,N) p. ii

Many-stemmed Albizia
Albizia petersiana
p. 142

PALM Arecaceae
Worldwide - 140 genera, 100 species;
South Africa - 7 shrub or tree species;
strongly associated with humans.
Family Features
- Flowers - small spray enclosed in sheath
- Fruit - berry-like
Trees in this book
Northern Lala-palm (H,M,P) p. 86;
Southern Lala-palm (F,H,M,P) p. 86;
Wild Date-palm (H) p. 88

SOURPLUM Olacaceae
Worldwide - 25 genera, 250 species;
South Africa - 2 genera, 3 species;
some plants hemiparasitic;
family of woody shrubs or trees.
Family Features
- Leaves - alternate
- Fruit - fleshy drupe, some edible
Tree in this book
Large Sourplum (A,D,P) p. 3

SPIKETHORN Celastraceae
Worldwide - 60-70 genera;
South Africa - 60 tree species, widely distributed.
Family Features
- Very variable
Trees in this book
Bushveld Saffron (A,B,D,E) p. 194;
Pioneer Spikethorn (A,F,H) p. 33;
Red Spikethorn (D,F,H,J,L,M) p. 106

STAR-CHESTNUT Sterculiaceae
Worldwide - 50 genera, 1 000 species;
South Africa - 3 genera, Cocoa Family member.
Family Features
- Leaves - star-shaped clumps of hairs
  (visible only with magnifying glass)
Tree in this book
Wild-pear Dombeya (A,B,C,N) p. 36

SWEET-PEA Papilionoideae
Worldwide - 437 genera, 11 300 species;
South Africa - 2 genera, 35 tree species.
Family Features
- Flowers - pea-like, broad, erect upper petal,
  2 narrower wings on both sides, 2 lowest petals joined
  (boat-like keel)
- Seeds - encased in pods usually covering more than
  one seed
Trees in this book
Apple-leaf (A,B,C,D,F,G,H,J,L,M,P) p. 124;
Kiaat Bloodwood (B,C) p. 138;
Nyala-tree (D,H,J,M) p. 166;
Round-leaved Bloodwood (A,D,E,F,I,L) p. 212;
Tree Wistaria (A,B,E,F,G) p. 108;
Zebrawood Flat-bean (A,E,F,M,O,P) p. 110

THORN-TREE Mimosoideae
Worldwide - 58 genera, 3 100 species,
mainly tropical regions;
South Africa - 8 genera, 100 tree species
(3rd largest woody family).
Family Features
- Leaves - Twice Compound, the leaves of certain species
  fold up at night
- Flowers - balls or spikes, protruding stamens
- Seeds - protected by palatable bean-like pods
Trees in this book
Black-monkey Acacia (A,B,D,G,H,I,P) p. 41;
Delagoa Acacia (G) p. 140;
Fever-tree Acacia (F,L,M) p. 90;
Flaky-bark Acacia (A,C,D,I,J,L,P) p. 214;
Horned-thorn Acacia (A,D,O) p. 196;
Knob-thorn Acacia (A,B,C,D,E,F,G,H,J,K,L,O,P) p. 126;
Red Acacia (A,B,C,D,F,G,I,P) p. 144;
River Acacia (A,B,C,D,F,H,J,M) p. 182;
Scented-pod Acacia (A,B,C,D,F,J) p. 198;
Umbrella Acacia (A,B,C,D,E,F,G,K,L,M,O,P) p. 92;
Broad-pod Albizia (D,F,H) p. 112;
Bushveld Albizia (A,E,F,G,I,J,K,L,N,O,P) p. 45;
Large-leaved Albizia (B,C,N) p. 77;
Many-stemmed Albizia (G) p. 142;
Sickle-bush (A,B,C,D,F,G,I,J,K,L,M,O,P) p. 216

TORCHWOOD Balanitaceae
Family Features
- Leaves - Two-leaflet Compound
Tree in this book
Greenthorn Torchwood (A,D,E) p. 146

Matumi
Breonadia salicina
p. 176

223

MAP 1

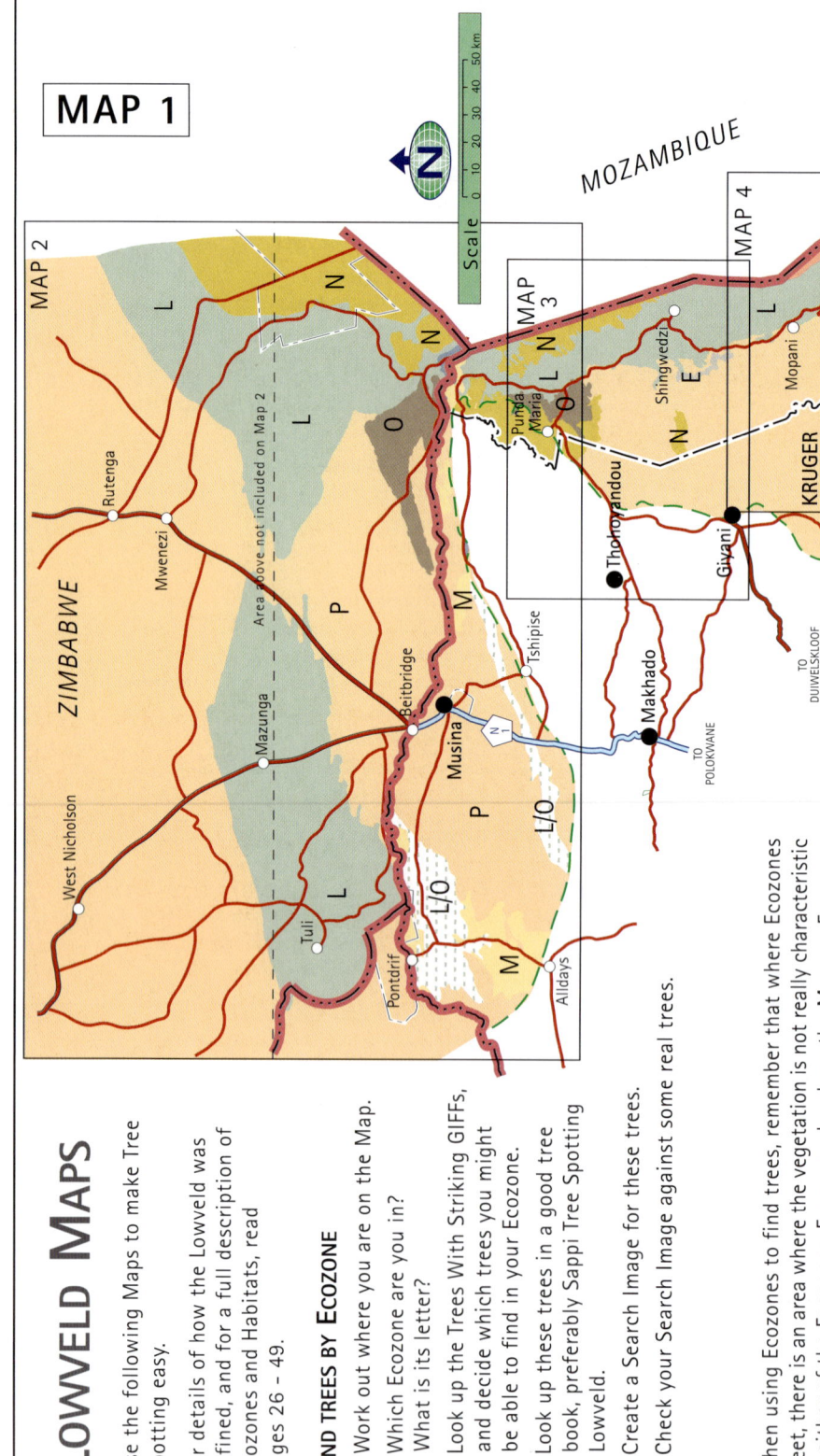

LOWVELD MAPS

Use the following Maps to make Tree Spotting easy.

For details of how the Lowveld was defined, and for a full description of Ecozones and Habitats, read pages 26 - 49.

FIND TREES BY ECOZONE

1. Work out where you are on the Map.
2. Which Ecozone are you in? What is its letter?
3. Look up the Trees With Striking GIFFs, and decide which trees you might be able to find in your Ecozone.
4. Look up these trees in a good tree book, preferably Sappi Tree Spotting Lowveld.
5. Create a Search Image for these trees.
6. Check your Search Image against some real trees.

When using Ecozones to find trees, remember that where Ecozones meet, there is an area where the vegetation is not really characteristic of either of the Ecozones. For example where the Mopane Ecozones (L and P) meet the Mixed Bushwillow Woodlands (Ecozone A), there is no sudden change. Pockets of Mopane trees, *Colophospermum mopane*, become more and more common in Ecozones A and J as one moves north, until they become the dominant trees, in Ecozones L and P.

224 Base information obtained from official maps produced by the Chief Directorate of Surveys and Land Information

KEY

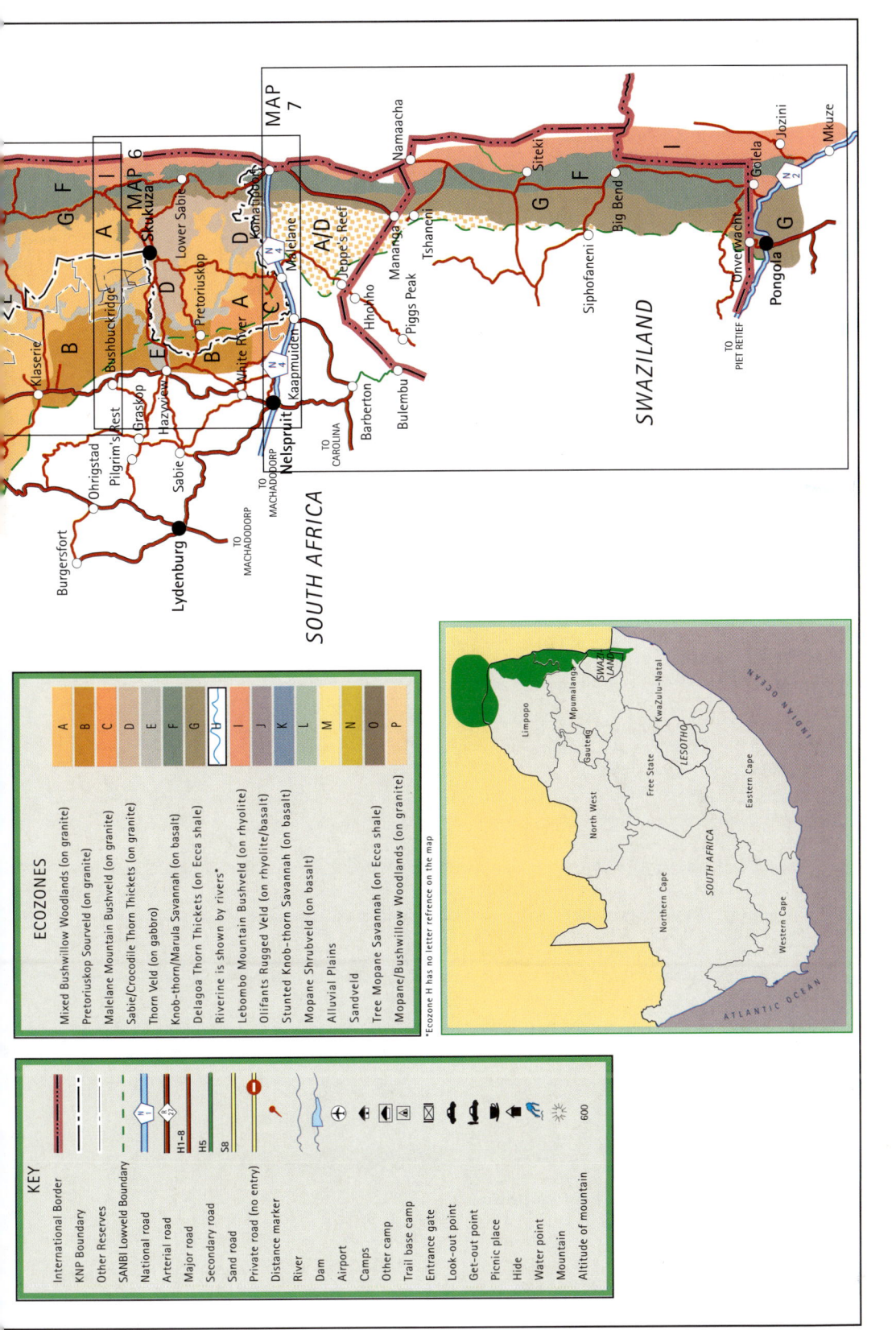

- International Border
- KNP Boundary
- Other Reserves
- SANBI Lowveld Boundary
- National road
- Arterial road
- Major road
- Secondary road
- Sand road
- Private road (no entry)
- Distance marker
- River
- Dam
- Airport
- Camps
- Other camp
- Trail base camp
- Entrance gate
- Look-out point
- Get-out point
- Picnic place
- Hide
- Water point
- Mountain
- Altitude of mountain

ECOZONES

- A. Mixed Bushwillow Woodlands (on granite)
- B. Pretoriuskop Sourveld (on granite)
- C. Malelane Mountain Bushveld (on granite)
- D. Sabie/Crocodile Thorn Thickets (on granite)
- E. Thorn Veld (on gabbro)
- F. Knob-thorn/Marula Savannah (on basalt)
- G. Delagoa Thorn Thickets (on Ecca shale)
- H. Riverine is shown by rivers*
- I. Lebombo Mountain Bushveld (on rhyolite)
- J. Olifants Rugged Veld (on rhyolite/basalt)
- K. Stunted Knob-thorn Savannah (on basalt)
- L. Mopane Shrubveld (on basalt)
- M. Alluvial Plains
- N. Sandveld
- O. Tree Mopane Savannah (on Ecca shale)
- P. Mopane/Bushwillow Woodlands (on granite)

*Ecozone H has no letter reference on the map

Base information obtained from official maps produced by the Chief Directorate of Surveys and Land Information

MAP 2

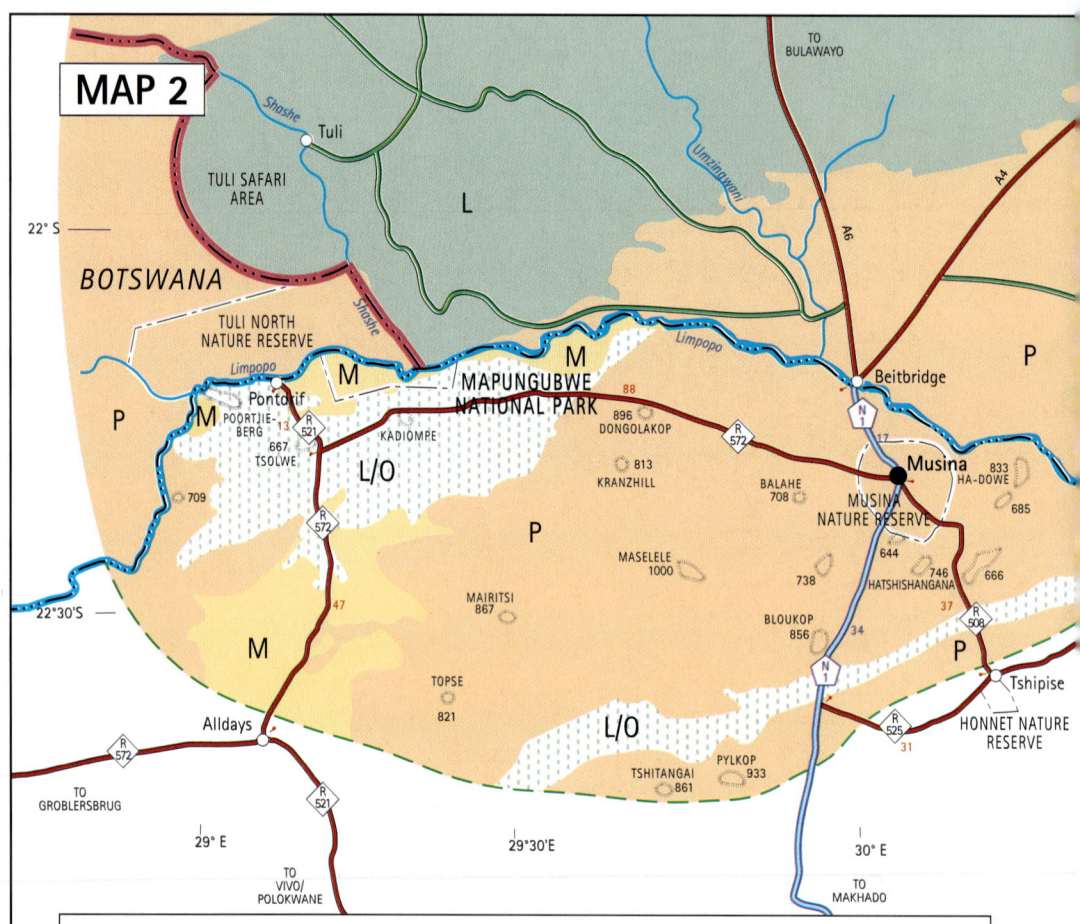

LIMPOPO AND ZIMBABWE

The Zimbabwe part of this Map was created by integrating the "Vegetation of Zimbabwe" Map with practical experience and knowledge of the area.

This whole area is dominated by Mopane trees and shrubs. In the more sandy areas, the Silver Cluster-leaf and Pod-mahogany are more numerous in the Lowveld of Zimbabwe than in similar vegetation types in Kruger.

The green dotted line indicates the Lowveld as defined by the South African National Biodiversity Institute's Vegetation Map of South Africa, Lesotho and Swaziland (1996). The area to the west of this green dotted line (which is shown in colour on this Map, between Punda Maria and Pafuri), is in fact not part of the Lowveld. It is, however, included here in colour because it is part of the Kruger National Park.

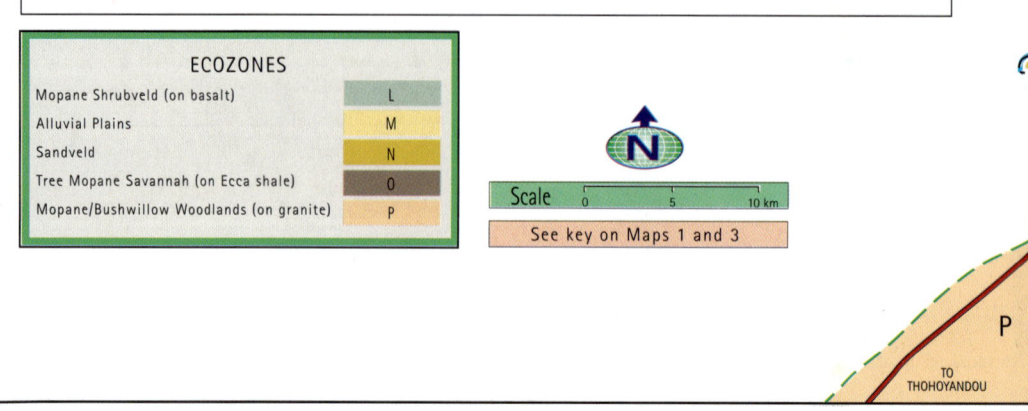

ECOZONES

Ecozone	Code
Mopane Shrubveld (on basalt)	L
Alluvial Plains	M
Sandveld	N
Tree Mopane Savannah (on Ecca shale)	O
Mopane/Bushwillow Woodlands (on granite)	P

Scale 0 — 5 — 10 km

See key on Maps 1 and 3

Base information obtained from official maps produced by the Chief Directorate of Surveys and Land Information

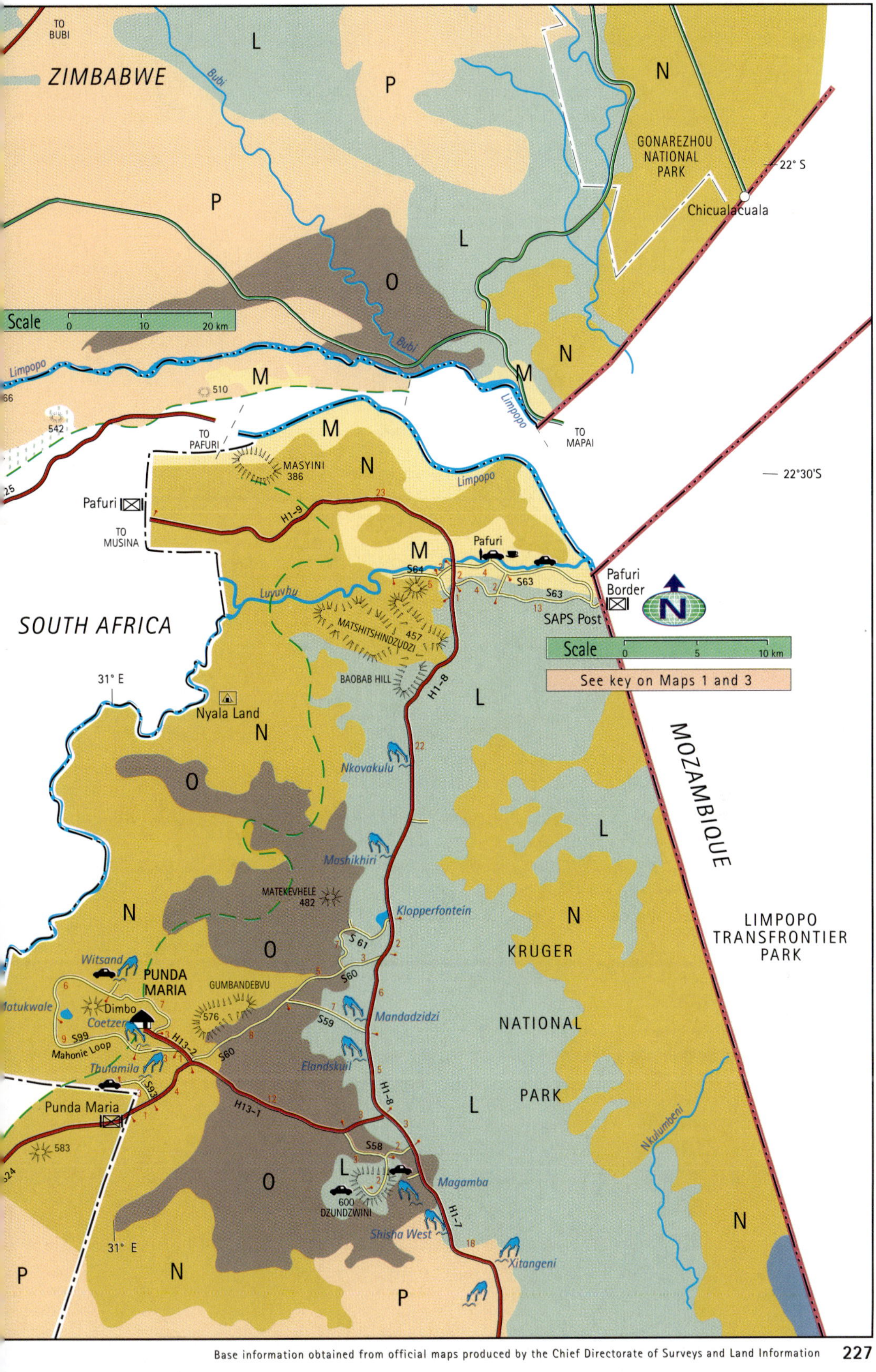
ZIMBABWE
TO BUBI
Bubi
GONAREZHOU NATIONAL PARK
22° S
Chicualacuala
Scale 0 10 20 km
Limpopo
510
542
TO PAFURI
TO MAPAI
MASYINI 386
22°30'S
Pafuri
TO MUSINA
H1-9
Pafuri
Luvuvhu
S64
S63
Pafuri Border
SAPS Post
MATSHITSHINDZUDZI 457
Scale 0 5 10 km
See key on Maps 1 and 3
SOUTH AFRICA
BAOBAB HILL
H1-8
31° E
Nyala Land
MOZAMBIQUE
Nkovakulu
Mashikhiri
MATEKEVHELE 482
Klopperfontein
LIMPOPO TRANSFRONTIER PARK
KRUGER NATIONAL PARK
S 61
S60
Witsand
PUNDA MARIA
GUMBANDEBVU
Matukwale
Dimbo
Coetzer
576
Mandadzidzi
S59
S99
Mahonie Loop
H13-2
Thulamila
Elandskuil
S93
Punda Maria
H13-1
583
S58
Nkulumbeni
600 DZUNDZWINI
Magamba
H1-7
Shisha West
31° E
Xitangeni

MAP 3

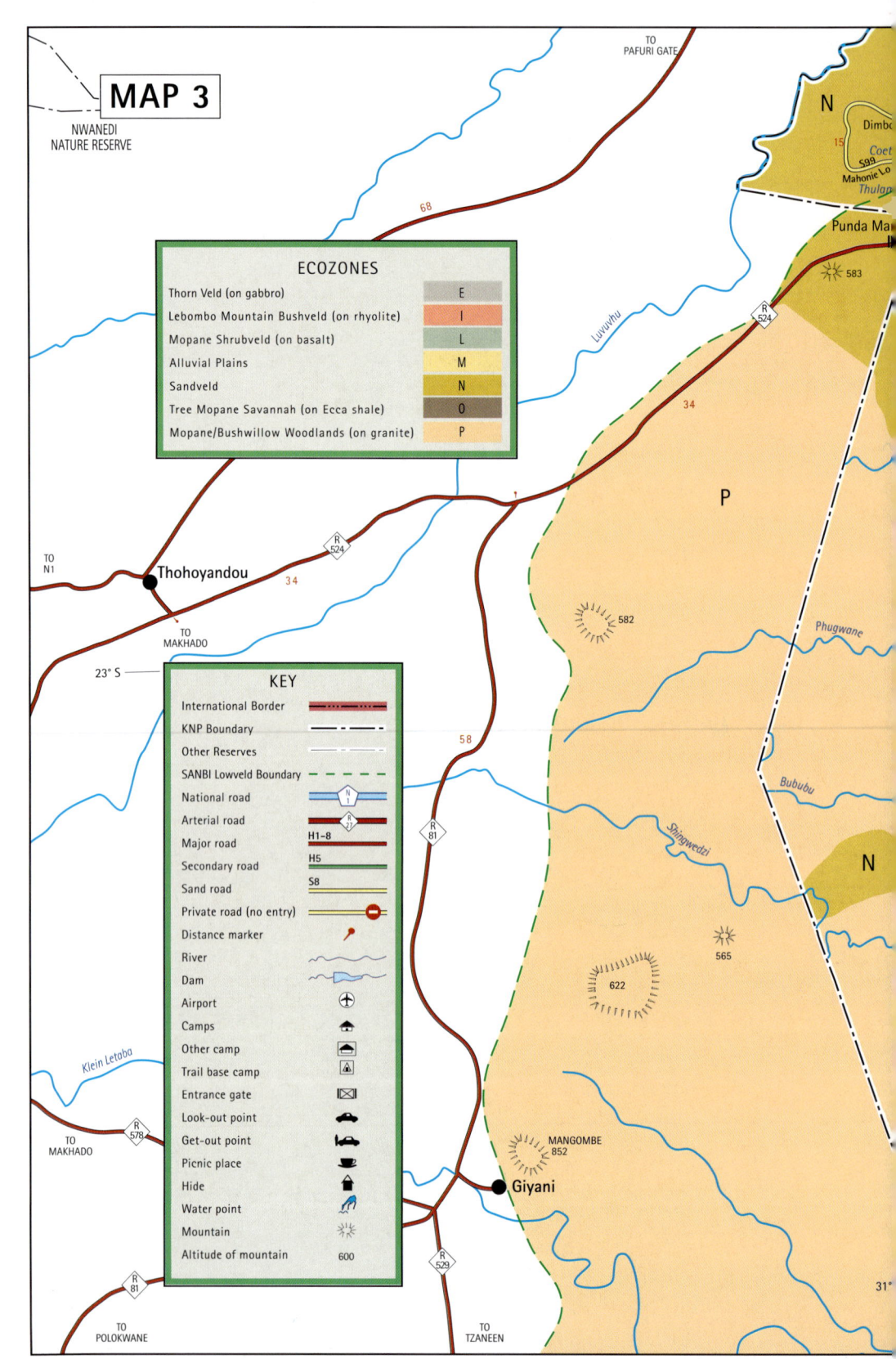

NWANEDI NATURE RESERVE

TO PAFURI GATE

ECOZONES

Thorn Veld (on gabbro)	E
Lebombo Mountain Bushveld (on rhyolite)	I
Mopane Shrubveld (on basalt)	L
Alluvial Plains	M
Sandveld	N
Tree Mopane Savannah (on Ecca shale)	O
Mopane/Bushwillow Woodlands (on granite)	P

Punda Ma...
Dimbo
Coet
Mahonie Lo
Thulap

Luvuvhu
Phugwane
Bububu
Shingwedzi

Thohoyandou
TO N1
TO MAKHADO
23° S

Klein Letaba
TO MAKHADO

MANGOMBE 852
Giyani

TO POLOKWANE
TO TZANEEN

KEY

International Border	
KNP Boundary	
Other Reserves	
SANBI Lowveld Boundary	
National road	N1
Arterial road	R71
Major road	H1–8
Secondary road	H5
Sand road	S8
Private road (no entry)	
Distance marker	
River	
Dam	
Airport	
Camps	
Other camp	
Trail base camp	
Entrance gate	
Look-out point	
Get-out point	
Picnic place	
Hide	
Water point	
Mountain	
Altitude of mountain	600

Base information obtained from official maps produced by the Chief Directorate of Surveys and Land Information

Scale
0
5
10 km
See key on Maps 1 and 3
PUNDA
MARIA
GUMBANDEBVU
576
Klopperfontein
S61
S60
S59
Mandadzidzi
Elandskuil
H13-2
H13-1
H1-8
H1-7
S58
Magamba
600
DZUNDZWINI
Shisha West
Mawawi
Shisha
Mphongolo
Babalala
SIRHENI
S56
Sirheni
S57
Boyela
N'warihlangari
Nkulumbeni
Langtoon
31°30'E
MOZAMBIQUE
427
SHINGOMENI
Mphongolo Loop
23° S
Mooigesig
Wik-en-weeg
Phugwane
S53
S56
KRUGER
NATIONAL
PARK
Lamont
S55
Mandzemba
Biesiesvlei
S135
SHINGWEDZI
Bububu
S101
Shipirivirhi
Joāo
H1-6
S134
Kanniedood
Kanniedood
Mashagadzi
404
PHONDA
HILLS
S52
Shingwedzi
S50
Red Rocks
Silwervis
BATELEUR
Nkokodzi
Mashokwe
Tshanga
Tshanga
Nkokodzi
Dzombo
West
S144
Dzombo
Ganspan
Nyawutsi
Ntshivana
Rooibosrant
Krapkuil
Buig-of-bars
Voetpad
Mahlati
S103
Olifantsbad
Pan
Grootvlei
S105
Tsendze
N'wambu
Hlamvu
Uitspan
Eendrag
S142
31°30'E

MAP 4

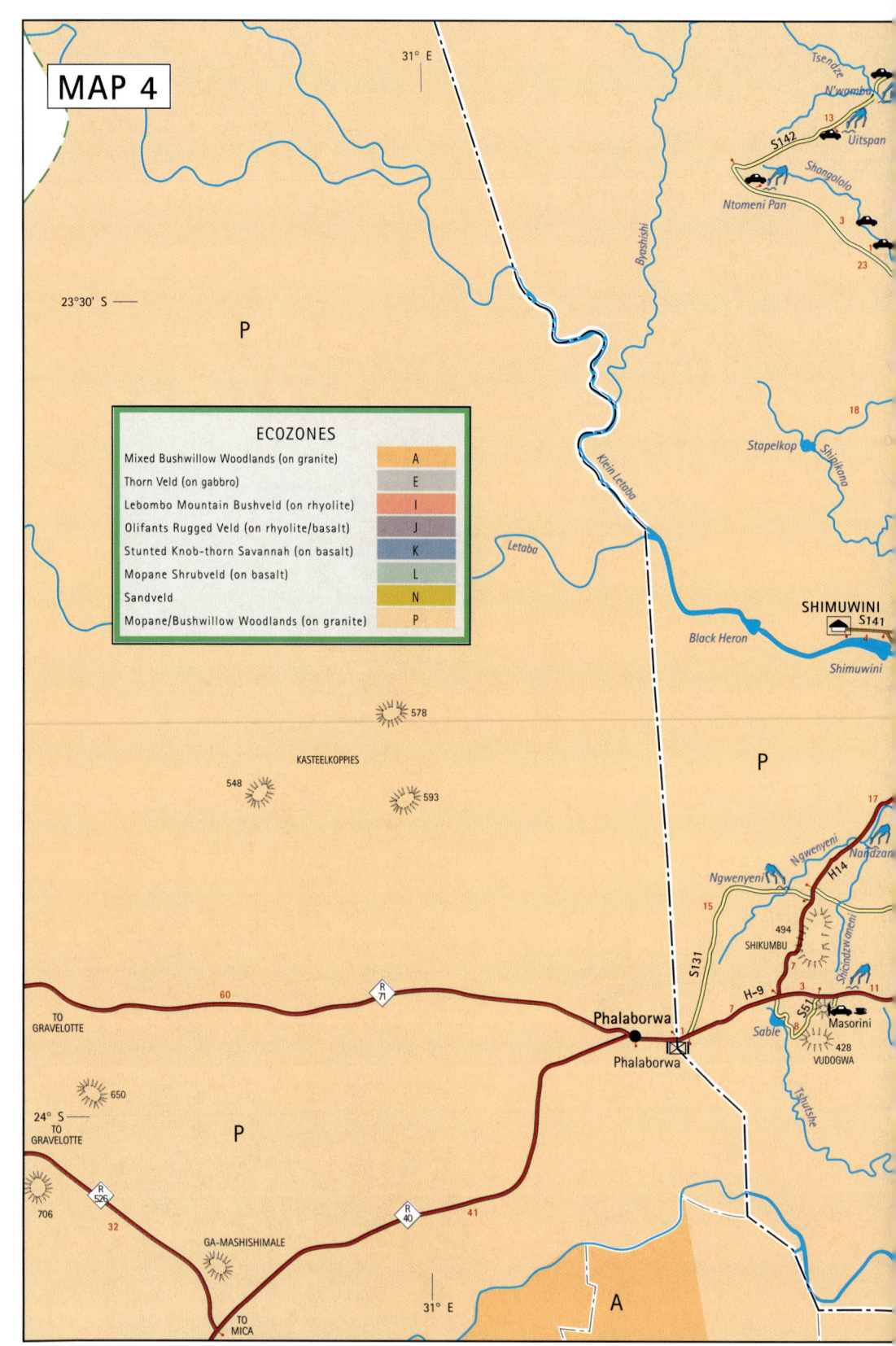

ECOZONES

Ecozone	Code
Mixed Bushwillow Woodlands (on granite)	A
Thorn Veld (on gabbro)	E
Lebombo Mountain Bushveld (on rhyolite)	I
Olifants Rugged Veld (on rhyolite/basalt)	J
Stunted Knob-thorn Savannah (on basalt)	K
Mopane Shrubveld (on basalt)	L
Sandveld	N
Mopane/Bushwillow Woodlands (on granite)	P

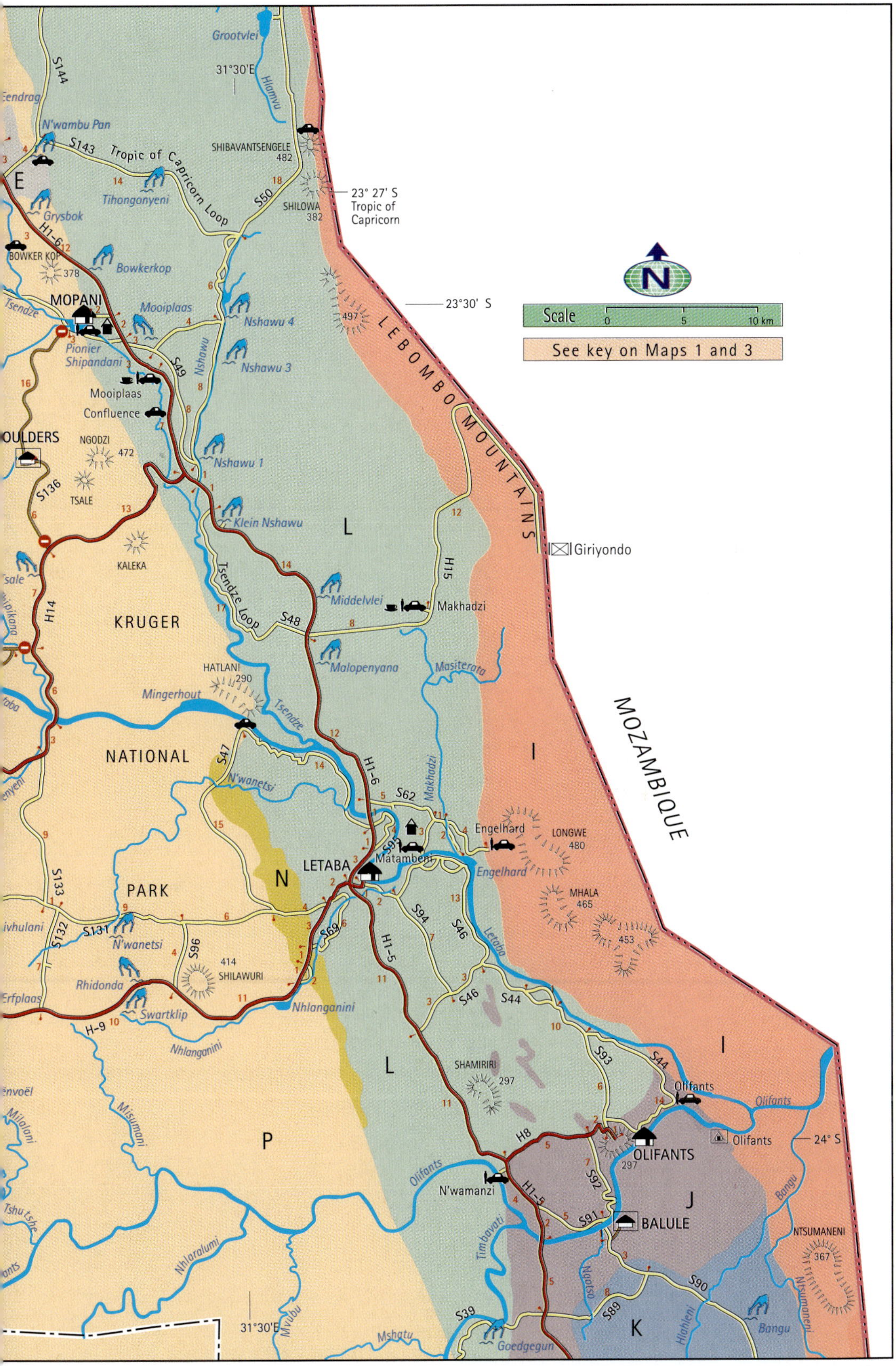
Grootvlei
31°30'E
S144
Hlamvu
N'wambu Pan
S143
Tropic of Capricorn Loop
SHIBAVANTSENGELE
482
Tihongonyeni
S50
SHILOWA
382
23° 27' S
Tropic of Capricorn
Grysbok
H1-6
BOWKER KOP
378
Bowkerkop
MOPANI
Mooiplaas
Nshawu 4
Tsendze
Pionier
Shipandani
S49
Nshawu
Nshawu 3
Mooiplaas
Confluence
497
23°30' S
LEBOMBO MOUNTAINS
Scale
0
5
10 km
See key on Maps 1 and 3
NGODZI
472
Nshawu 1
S136
TSALE
Klein Nshawu
KALEKA
Giriyondo
H15
Makhadzi
Middelvlei
Tsendze Loop
S48
H14
KRUGER
Malopenyana
Masiterata
HATLANI
290
Mingerhout
Tsendze
MOZAMBIQUE
NATIONAL
S47
H1-6
N'wanetsi
S62
Makhadzi
Engelhard
LONGWE
480
S85
Matambeni
LETABA
Engelhard
MHALA
465
S133
PARK
S94
S46
S131
N'wanetsi
S132
S69
453
S96
414
SHILAWURI
H1-5
Letaba
Rhidonda
S46
S44
Swartklip
Nhlanganini
H-9
Nhlanganini
S93
S44
SHAMIRIRI
297
Olifants
Olifants
Misumani
H8
OLIFANTS
Olifants
24° S
297
Olifants
S92
N'wamanzi
H1-5
S91
BALULE
Bangu
NTSUMANENI
367
Timbavati
Ngotso
S90
Nhlaralumi
S89
S39
Hlahleni
Bangu
Nsumaneni
31°30'E
Mvubu
Mshatu
Goedgegun

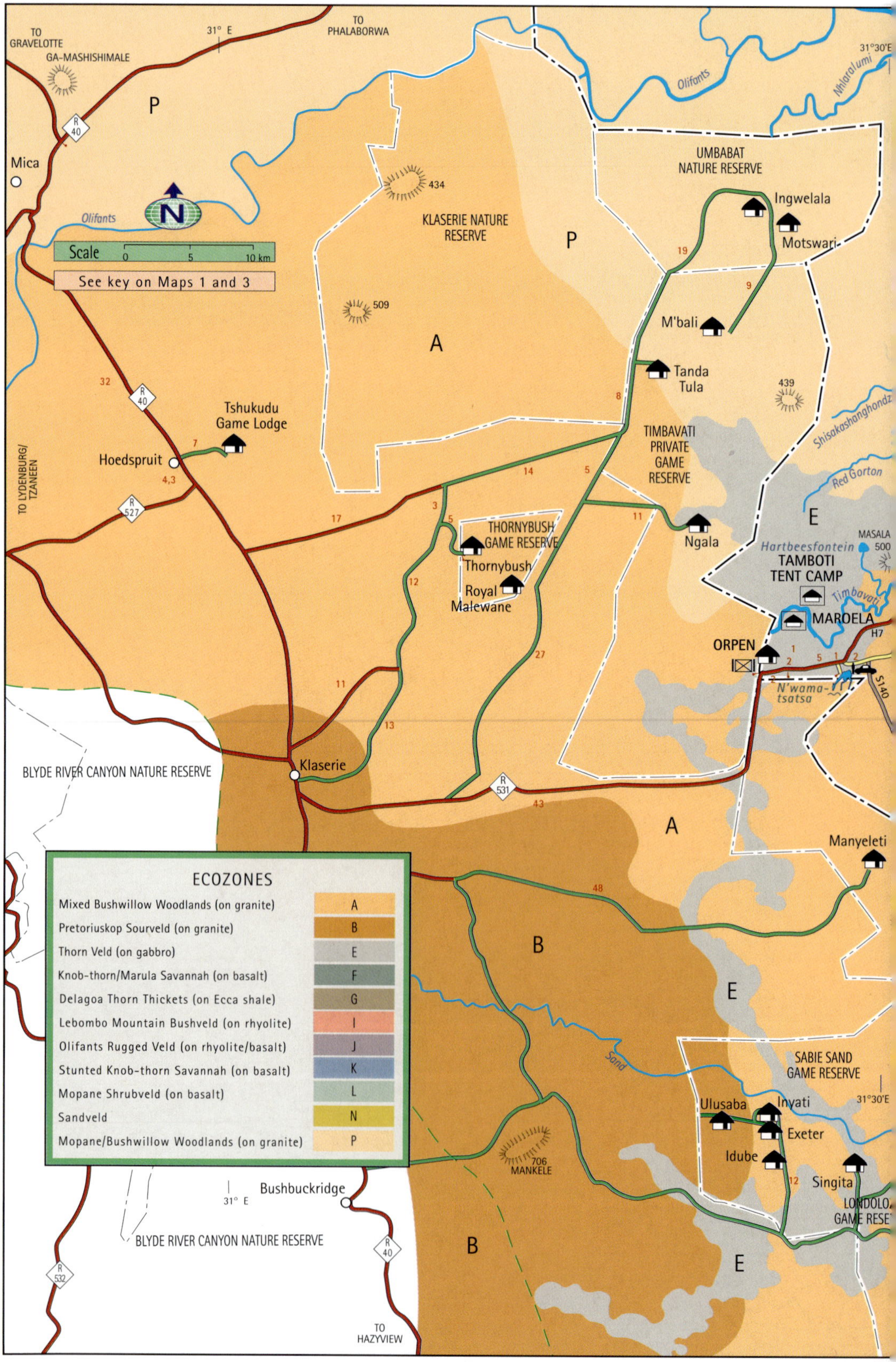

 Base information obtained from official maps produced by the Chief Directorate of Surveys and Land Information

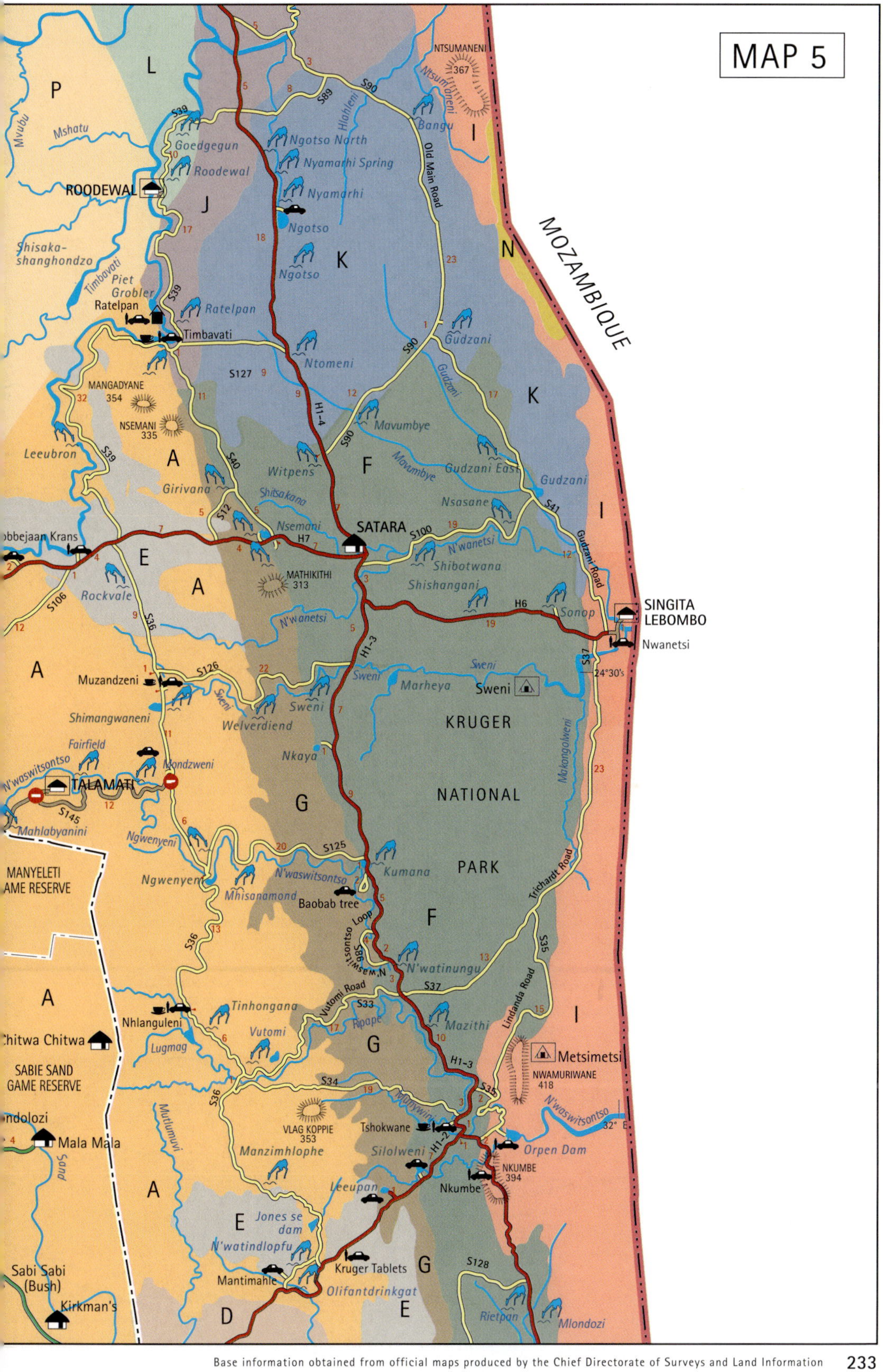
MAP 5
MOZAMBIQUE
NTSUMANENI
367
Ntsumaneni
Bangu
Hlahleni
S90
S89
Old Main Road
Ngotso North
Nyamarhi Spring
Nyamarhi
Ngotso
Ngotso
Goedgegun
Roodewal
ROODEWAL
Mshatu
Mvubu
Shisaka-
shanghondzo
Timbavati
Piet
Grobler
Ratelpan
Ratelpan
Timbavati
S39
Gudzani
Ntomeni
S127
MANGADYANE
354
NSEMANI
335
Leeubron
Mavumbye
Mavumbye
Witpens
Gudzani East
Gudzani
Girivana
Shitsakana
Nsemani
Nsasane
SATARA
S100
N'wanetsi
S41
Gudzani Road
bbejaan Krans
H7
Shibotwana
Shishangani
MATHIKITHI
313
Rockvale
S106
S40
S12
S36
N'wanetsi
H6
Sonop
SINGITA
LEBOMBO
Nwanetsi
S37
24°30's
Muzandzeni
S126
Sweni
Sweni
Sweni
Marheya
Sweni
Shimangwaneni
Welverdiend
KRUGER
NATIONAL
PARK
Fairfield
Mondzweni
N'waswitsontso
TALAMATI
S145
Mahlabyanini
Nkaya
Makongolweni
Ngwenyeni
S125
Kumana
MANYELETI
AME RESERVE
Ngwenyeni
N'waswitsontso
Mhisanamond
Baobab tree
N'waswitsontso Loop
S86
Trichardt Road
S35
N'watinungu
Vutomi Road
S37
S33
Lindanda Road
Nhlanguleni
Tinhongana
Vutomi
Lugmag
Rpape
Mazithi
Chitwa Chitwa
SABIE SAND
GAME RESERVE
H1-3
H1-4
Metsimetsi
NWAMURIWANE
418
S34
S36
Mutlumuvi
VLAG KOPPIE
353
Tshokwane
Munywini
N'waswitsontso
32° E
ndolozi
Mala Mala
Sand
Manzimhlophe
Silolweni
H1-2
Orpen Dam
NKUMBE
394
Nkumbe
Leeupan
Jones se
dam
N'watindlopfu
Kruger Tablets
S128
Sabi Sabi
(Bush)
Mantimahle
Olifantdrinkgat
Kirkman's
Rietpan
Mlondozi
P
L
I
J
K
N
K
A
F
E
A
I
A
G
F
A
G
I
A
E
G
D
E

MAP 6

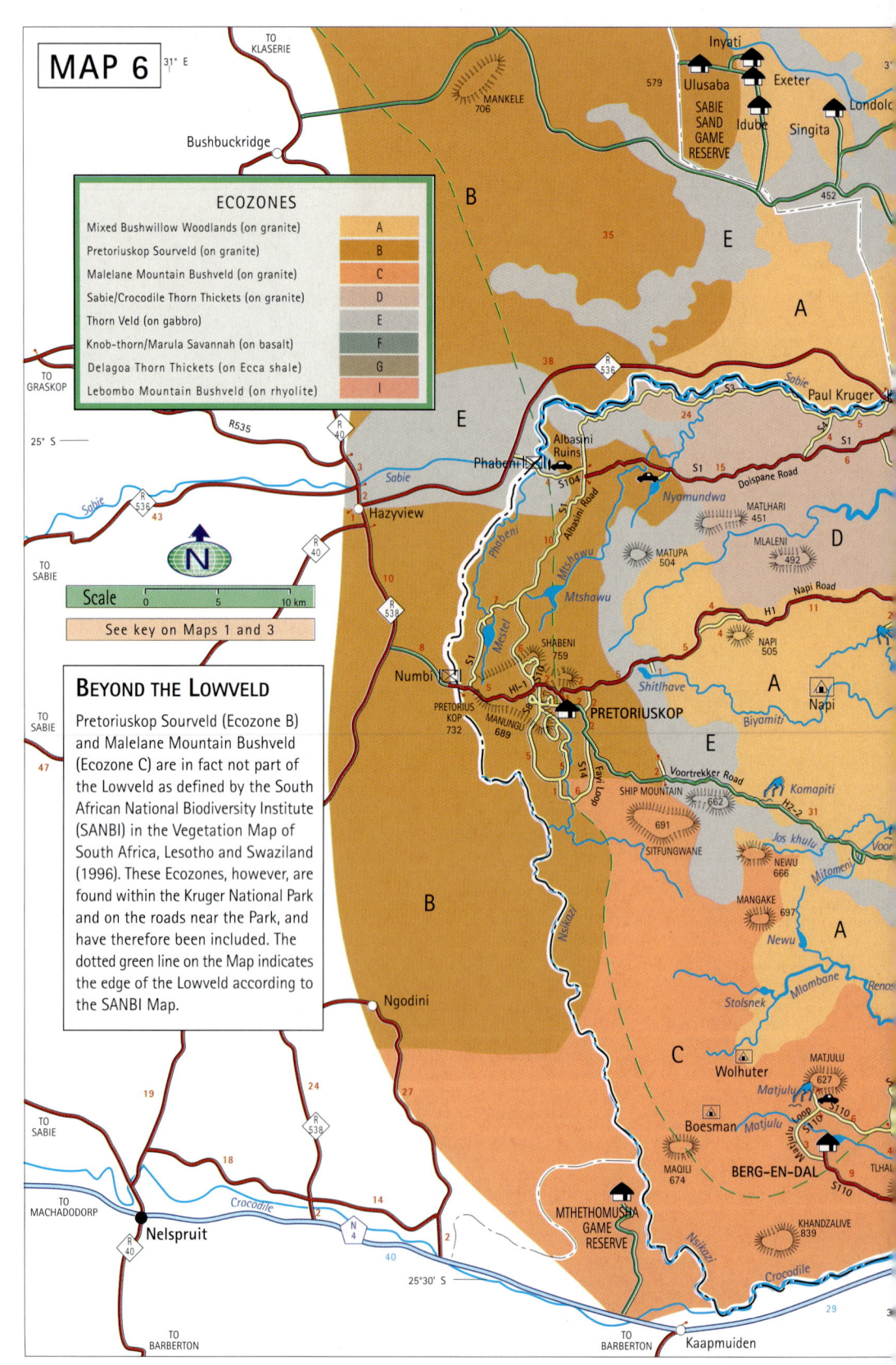

ECOZONES

Ecozone	Description	Color
A	Mixed Bushwillow Woodlands (on granite)	
B	Pretoriuskop Sourveld (on granite)	
C	Malelane Mountain Bushveld (on granite)	
D	Sabie/Crocodile Thorn Thickets (on granite)	
E	Thorn Veld (on gabbro)	
F	Knob-thorn/Marula Savannah (on basalt)	
G	Delagoa Thorn Thickets (on Ecca shale)	
I	Lebombo Mountain Bushveld (on rhyolite)	

Scale 0 — 5 — 10 km

See key on Maps 1 and 3

BEYOND THE LOWVELD

Pretoriuskop Sourveld (Ecozone B) and Malelane Mountain Bushveld (Ecozone C) are in fact not part of the Lowveld as defined by the South African National Biodiversity Institute (SANBI) in the Vegetation Map of South Africa, Lesotho and Swaziland (1996). These Ecozones, however, are found within the Kruger National Park and on the roads near the Park, and have therefore been included. The dotted green line on the Map indicates the edge of the Lowveld according to the SANBI Map.

234 Base information obtained from official maps produced by the Chief Directorate of Surveys and Land Information

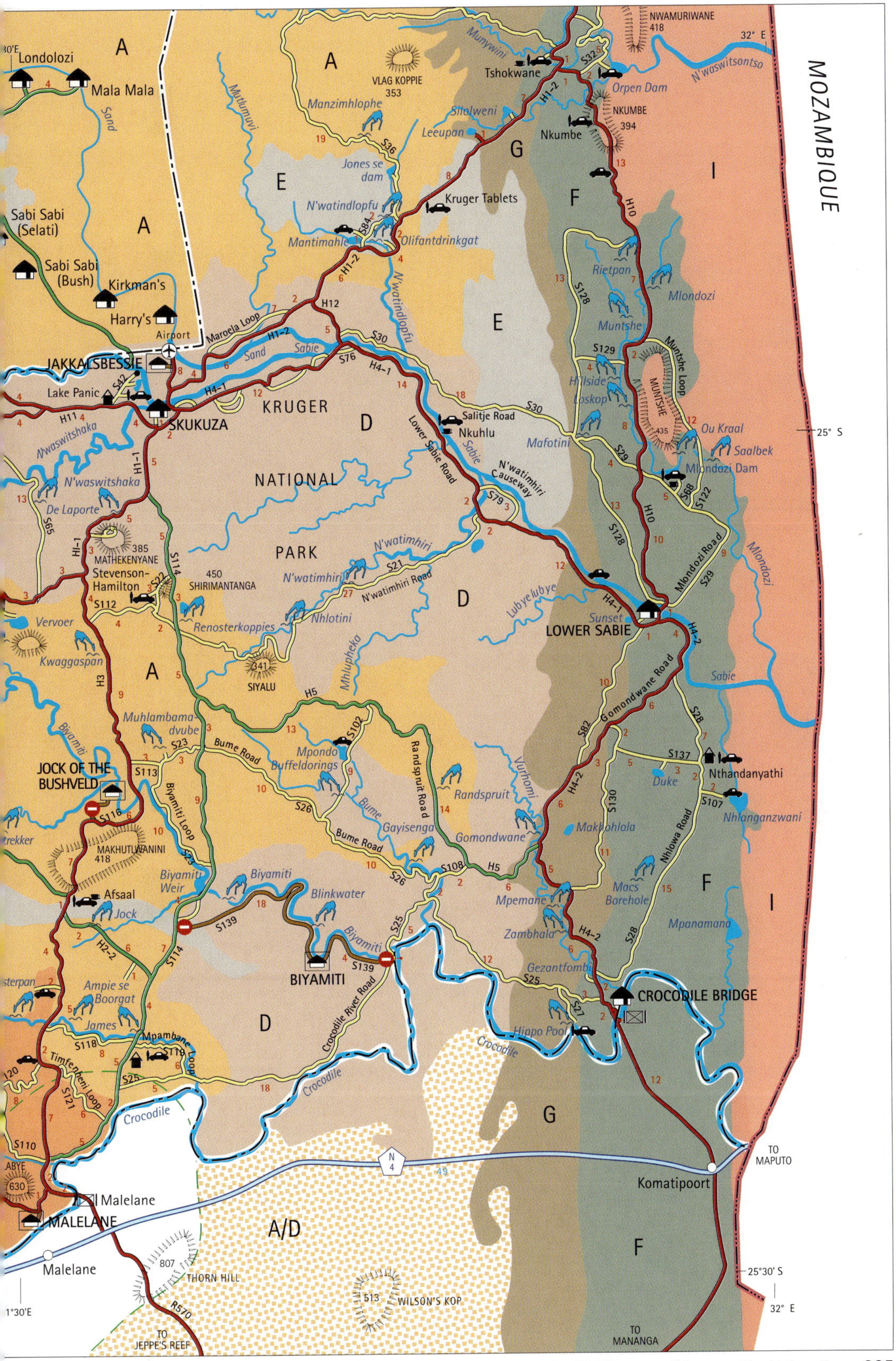
MOZAMBIQUE
Londolozi
Mala Mala
Sabi Sabi (Selati)
Sabi Sabi (Bush)
Kirkman's
Harry's
Airport
JAKKALSBESSIE
Lake Panic
SKUKUZA
KRUGER
NATIONAL
PARK
Tshokwane
Nkumbe
NKUMBE 394
NWAMURIWANE 418
Orpen Dam
N'waswitsontso
VLAG KOPPIE 353
Manzimhlophe
Silolweni
Leeupan
Jones se dam
N'watindlopfu
Kruger Tablets
Mantimahle
Olifantdrinkgat
Rietpan
Mlondozi
Muntshe
Muntshe Loop
MUNTSHE 435
Hillside
Loskop
Ou Kraal
Saalbek
Mlondozi Dam
Mlondozi Road
Salitje Road
Nkuhlu
Lower Sabie Road
Mafotini
N'watimhiri Causeway
Maroela Loop
N'waswitshaka
De Laporte
MATHEKENYANE 385
Stevenson-Hamilton
450 SHIRIMANTANGA
N'watimhiri
N'watimhiri Road
Nhlotini
Renosterkoppies
Vervoer
Kwaggaspan
341 SIYALU
Mhlupheka
Lubyelubye
Sunset
LOWER SABIE
Sabie
Gomondwane Road
Nthandanyathi
Duke
Nhlanganzwani
Muhlambamadvube
Bume Road
Mpondo
Buffeldorings
Randspruit Road
Randspruit
Vurhami
JOCK OF THE BUSHVELD
Biyamiti Loop
MAKHUTLWANINI 418
Biyamiti
Biyamiti Weir
Blinkwater
Gayisenga
Gomondwane
Makhohlola
Nhlowa Road
Macs Borehole
Mpanamana
Mpemane
Zambhala
Afsaal
Jock
BIYAMITI
Crocodile River Road
Gezantfombi
CROCODILE BRIDGE
Ampie se Boorgat
James
Mpambane Loop
Timfeneni Loop
Hippo Pool
Crocodile
Komatipoort
TO MAPUTO
Malelane
MALELANE
A/D
807 THORN HILL
513 WILSON'S KOP
TO JEPPE'S REEF
TO MANANGA
25° S
25°30' S
32° E

MAP 7

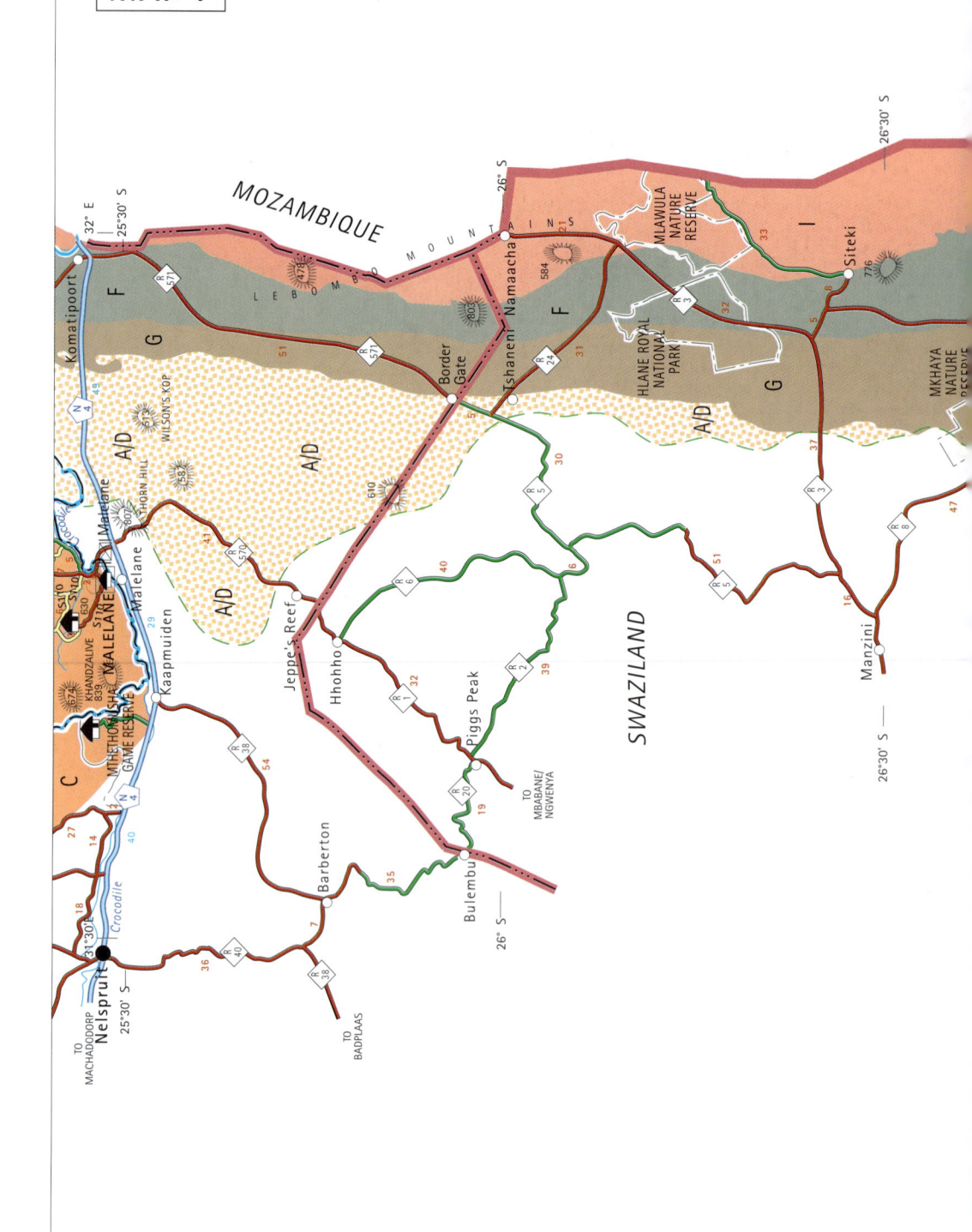

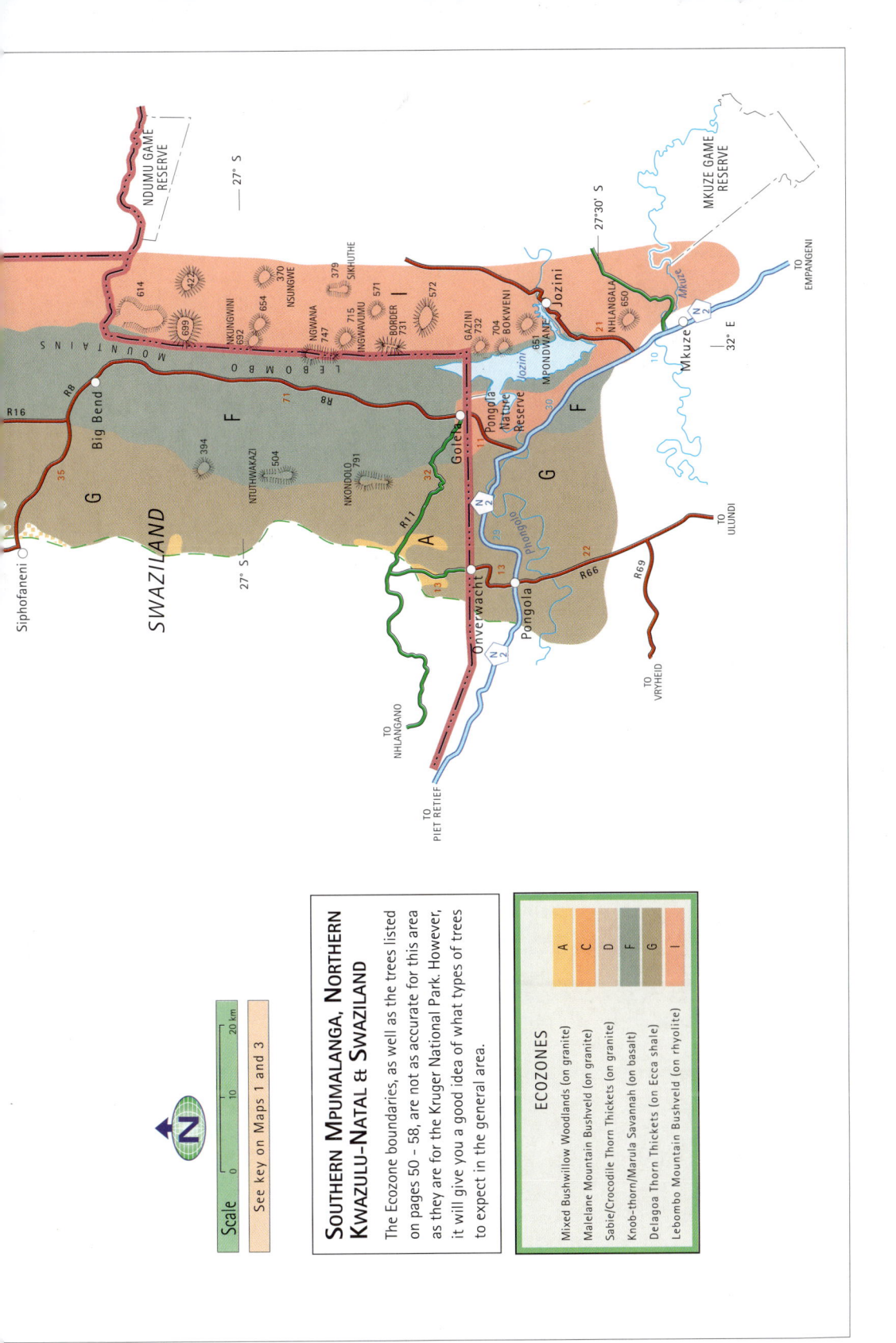

Southern Mpumalanga, Northern Kwazulu-Natal & Swaziland

The Ecozone boundaries, as well as the trees listed on pages 50 - 58, are not as accurate for this area as they are for the Kruger National Park. However, it will give you a good idea of what types of trees to expect in the general area.

ECOZONES

- A Mixed Bushwillow Woodlands (on granite)
- C Malelane Mountain Bushveld (on granite)
- D Sabie/Crocodile Thorn Thickets (on granite)
- F Knob-thorn/Marula Savannah (on basalt)
- G Delagoa Thorn Thickets (on Ecca shale)
- I Lebombo Mountain Bushveld (on rhyolite)

Scale 0 10 20 km

See key on Maps 1 and 3

Base information obtained from official maps produced by the Chief Directorate of Surveys and Land Information

Tree Index

The entries in this index are for tree names only. Those trees that are covered with detailed information, rather than simply a Look-alike picture, or name, have their page number in **bold**, for both the English common and the botanical, scientific names.

Acacia, Black-monkey 41, 74, 80
Acacia burkei **41**, 74, 80
Acacia, Delagoa **140**, 41, 74
Acacia exuvialis **214**, 74, 78
Acacia, Fever-tree **90**, 33, 40, 46, 74, 78
Acacia, Flaky-bark **214**, 74, 78
Acacia gerrardii **144**, 63, 64, 75, 80
Acacia grandicornuta **196**, 75, 80
Acacia, Horned-thorn **196**, 75, 80
Acacia, Knob-thorn **126**, 29, 35, 39, 40, 44, 63, 65, 75, 78
Acacia nigrescens **126**, 29, 35, 39, 40, 44, 63, 65, 75, 78
Acacia nilotica **198**, 29, 38, 63, 65, 76, 80
Acacia, Red **144**, 63, 64, 75, 80
Acacia, River **182**, 27, 65, 75, 80
Acacia robusta **182**, 27, 65, 75, 80
Acacia, Scented-pod **198**, 29, 38, 63, 65, 76, 80
Acacia, Small Knob-thorn 44
Acacia tortilis **92**, 64, 76, 80
Acacia, Umbrella **92**, 64, 76, 80
Acacia welwitschii **140**, 41, 74
Acacia xanthophloea **90**, 33, 40, 46, 74, 78
Adansonia digitata **84**, 26, 62, 66, 70, 81
African Weeping-wattle **96**, 63, 65, 76, 80
Afzelia quanzensis **150**, 26, 47, 62, 64, 69
Albizia, Broad-pod **112**, 63, 65, 77
Albizia, Bushveld **45**, 77
Albizia forbesii **112**, 63, 65, 77
Albizia harveyi **45**, 77
Albizia, Large-leaved 77
Albizia, Many-stemmed **142**, 41, 77
Albizia petersiana **142**, 41, 77
Albizia versicolor 77
amaNgwe-amphlophe 120
Anacardiaceae 122
Androstachys johnsonii **130**
Appelblaar 124
Apple-leaf **124**, 63, 65, 70, 78
Arecaceae 86

Balanitaceae 146
Balanites maughamii **146**, 38, 67, 69, 81

Baobab **84**, 26, 62, 66, 70, 81
Bauhinia Family 96, 98, 100, 116, 150, 170, 220
Bauhinia galpinii **100**, 62, 65, 69
Bauhinia, Pride-of-de-Kaap **100**, 62, 65, 69
Bead-bean, Bushveld **48**, 63, 65
Bignoniaceae 178
Black-monkey Acacia 41, 74, 80
Black Monkey-orange **132**, 36, 66, 68, 78
Blinkblaar-wag-n-bietjie 186
Bloodwood, Kiaat **138**, 36, 63, 64, 69, 81
Bloodwood, Round-leaved **212**, 40, 63, 64, 69
Boer-bean, Weeping **170**, 62, 64, 69, 70, 81
Bolusanthus speciosus **108**, 63, 65, 69, 80
Bombacaceae 84
Boscia albitrunca **43**, 67, 79
Bosveld Katjiepiering 188
Bosveldsaffraan 194
Botterklapper 132
Brakdoring 182
Breëpeulvalsdoring 112
Breonadia salicina **176**, 30, 68
Broad-pod Albizia **112**, 63, 65, 77
Buckthorn Family 186, 220
Buddleja Family 172, 220
Buddlejaceae 172
Buffalo-thorn Jujube **186**, 67, 68, 80
Burseraceae 136
Bushveld Albizia **45**, 77
Bushveld Bead-bean **48**, 63, 65
Bushveld Gardenia **188**, 31, 62, 66, 68, 78
Bushveld Resin-tree **40**, 67
Bushveld Saffron **194**, 31, 67, 68, 79
Bushwillow Family 102, 104, 118, 120, 174, 202, 204, 206, 220
Bushwillow, Flame Climbing **102**, 30, 63, 71, 95
Bushwillow, Forest 71
Bushwillow, Large-fruited **202**, 35, 64, 71, 78
Bushwillow, Leadwood **118**, 71, 81
Bushwillow, Red **204**, 28, 35, 49, 72, 79

Bushwillow, River **174**, 30, 68, 72, 79
Bushwillow, Russet **206**, 72
Bushwillow, Velvet 72
Bushwillow, Weeping **35**, 73

Caesalpinioideae 96, 98, 100, 116, 150, 170
Caper Family 220
Cassia abbreviata **98**, 39, 62, 65, 69
Cassia, Long-tail **98**, 39, 62, 65, 69
Celastraceae 106, 194
Cluster-leaf, Purple-pod **104**, 43, 63, 64, 73
Cluster-leaf, Silver **120**, 28, 36, 64, 68, 73, 80
Coffee Family 176, 188, 221
Colophospermum mopane **116**, 28, 45, 48, 49, 64, 69
Combretaceae 102, 104, 118, 120, 174, 202, 204
Combretum apiculatum **204**, 28, 35, 49, 72, 79
Combretum collinum **35**, 73
Combretum erythrophyllum **174**, 30, 68, 72, 79
Combretum hereroense **206**, 72
Combretum imberbe **118**, 71, 81
Combretum kraussii 71
Combretum microphyllum **102**, 30, 63, 71, 95
Combretum molle 72
Combretum zeyheri **202**, 35, 64, 71, 78
Commiphora glandulosa **136**, 66, 78
Commiphora pyracanthoides 2
Commiphora species 32, 47, 68, 136
Commiphora viminea **47**, 78
Corkwood, Firethorn 2
Corkwood species 32, 47, 68, 136
Corkwood, Tall Firethorn **136**, 66, 78
Corkwood, Zebra-bark **47**, 78
Croton, Feverberry **46**, 67, 68
Croton megalobotrys **46**, 67, 68

Dalbergia melanoxylon **110**, 63, 65, 69, 79
Date-palm, Wild **88**, 66, 69
Deadliest Euphorbia **152**, 43

238

Delagoa Acacia **140**, 41, 74
Delagoadoring 140
Dichrostachys cinerea **216**, 40, 63, 64, 76, 80
Diospyros mespiliformis **160**, 36, 67, 79
Dithetlwa 98, 160
Dombeya rotundifolia **36**, 61, 62, 66, 68, 80
Dombeya, Wild-pear **36**, 61, 62, 66, 68, 80
Dopperkiaat 212
Doppruim 192
Doringtrosblaar 104
Drooping Resin-tree 40

Ebenaceae 160, 190
Ebony Family 160, 190, 221
Ebony Jackal-berry **160**, 36, 67, 79
Elaeodendron transvaalense **194**, 31, 67, 68, 79
Euclea divinorum **190**, 31, 67, 79
Euphorbia confinalis **42**, 152
Euphorbia cooperi **152**, 43
Euphorbia, Deadliest **152**, 43
Euphorbia ingens 152
Euphorbia Family 130, 152, 162, 221
Euphorbia, Lebombo **42**, 152
Euphorbia, Naboom 152
Euphorbia, Rubber-hedge **39**, 152
Euphorbia tirucalli **39**
Euphorbiaceae 130, 152, 162

False-marula Lannea **38**, 67, 70, 79
False Mopane, Small **49**, 64, 69
Fever-tree Acacia **90**, 33, 40, 46, 74, 78
Feverberry Croton **46**, 67, 68
Ficus abutilifolia **154**, 32, 67, 81
Ficus ingens **32**, 67
Ficus sycomorus **164**, 36, 46, 67, 78
Fig Family 154, 164, 221
Fig, Large-leaved Rock **154**, 32, 67, 81
Fig, Red-leaved **32**, 67
Fig, Sycomore **164**, 36, 46, 67, 78
Firethorn Corkwood **2**
Flaky-bark Acacia **214**, 74, 78
Flame Climbing Bushwillow **102**, 30, 63, 71, 95
Flat-bean, Zebrawood **110**, 63, 65, 69, 79
Forest Bushwillow 71

Gardenia, Bushveld **188**, 31, 62, 66, 68, 78
Gardenia Family 176, 188, 221
Gardenia volkensii **188**, 31, 62, 66, 68, 78
Greenthorn Torchwood **146**, 38, 67, 69, 81
Grewia bicolor **210**, 62, 67, 68
Grewia flavescens **208**, 68
Groendoring 146
Grootblaarrotsvy 154
Grootdoringkanniedood 136
Guarri, Magic **190**, 31, 67, 79
Guibourtia conjugata **49**, 64, 69
Gulaswimbi 192
Gymnosporia buxifolia **33**, 62, 80
Gymnosporia senegalensis **106**, 33, 40

Haak-en-steek 92
Haakdoring 92
Hardekool 118
Horingdoring 196
Horned-thorn Acacia **196**, 75, 80
Huilboerboon 170
Huilboom 96
Hyphaene coriacea **86**, 33, 45, 66, 69
Hyphaene petersiana **86**, 33, 69

ILala 86
iChithamuzi 134
iGwolo 180
iJuqa 162
iliTye 192
imHlosinga 90
iMinyela 136
imPayi 154
imPondozendhlovu 118
iNdaba 192
iNdlandlovu 212
inDlebezindlovu 212
iNkhweza 172
isiBambapala 126
isiHlangu 106
isiHlangwane 106
isiHomuhomu 124
isiLahla 186
isiThwethwe 92, 198
iSundu 88
iWapha 102

Jacaranda Family 178, 221
Jackal-berry, Ebony **160**, 36, 67, 79
Jacket-plum **192**, 31, 66, 68, 79
Jakkalsbessie 160

Jujube, Buffalo-thorn **186**, 67, 68, 80
Jujube Family 186, 220
Jute Family 208, 210, 221

Kapok Family 84, 221
Kersboom 98
Kiaat 138
Kiaat Bloodwood **138**, 36, 63, 64, 69, 81
Kierieklapper 206
Kigelia africana **178**, 30, 62, 66, 70, 78
Kirkia acuminata **156**, 32, 43, 47, 70, 78
Kirkia Family 156, 221
Kirkia, Mountain **37**, 70
Kirkia, White **156**, 32, 43, 47, 70, 78
Kirkia wilmsii **37**, 70
Kirkiaceae 156
Knob-thorn Acacia **126**, 29, 35, 39, 40, 44, 63, 65, 75, 78
Knoppiesdoring 126
Konde 152
Koorsboom 90
Kremetart 84

Lala-palm **86**, 33, 45, 66, 69
Lala-palm, Northern **86**, 33, 66, 69
Lala-palm, Southern **86**, 33, 45, 66, 69
Lannea, False-marula **38**, 67, 70, 79
Lannea schweinfurthii **38**, 67, 70, 79
Large-fruited Bushwillow **202**, 35, 64, 71, 78
Large-leaved Albizia 77
Large-leaved Rock Fig **154**, 32, 67, 81
Large Sourplum 3
Leadwood Bushwillow **118**, 71, 81
Lebombo Euphorbia **42**, 152
Lebombo-ironwood **130**
Lebombo ysterhout 130
Leeubos 134

Pod–mahogany
Afzelia quanzensis
p. 150

239

Lekkerruikpeul 198
Lengana 124
liLala 88
Linden Family 208, 210, 221
liSololo 100
Litchi family 192, 222
Lonchocarpus capassa 124
Long-tail Cassia **98**, 39, 62, 65, 69

Maerua angolensis **48**, 63, 65
Mafambaborile 202
Magic Guarri **190**, 31, 67, 79
Mahogany Family 180, 222
Mango Family 122, 222
Many-stemmed Albizia **142**, 41, 77
Maroela 122
Marula **122**, 26, 39, 40, 67, 70, 79, 219
Matumi **176**, 30, 68
Maytenus senegalensis **106**
Mbandu 124
Mbhandzu 124
Meerstamvalsdoring 142
Meliaceae 180
Mimosoideae 90, 92, 112, 126, 140, 142, 144, 182, 196, 198, 214, 216
Mingerhout 176
Mmaba 180
Mmabane 90
Mmilo 138
Mochiara 104
Modiba 162
Modibo 174
Moduba-tshipi 202
Modubana 202
Modubunoka 174
Modumela 156
Mofaka 86
Moga 182
Mogaya 126
Mogodiri 204
Mogohlo 108
Mogônônô 120
Mohota 124
Mohlakola 190
Mohlaretodi 90

Umdoni Waterberry
Syzygium cordatum
p. 30

Mohlotla 152
Mohwelere-Tshipi 204
Mokabi 206
Mokala 126
Mokelete 110
Mokgalo 186
Mokhukhu 174
Moki 144
Mokôba 128
Mokochong 160
Moku 92, 182
Mokwa 138
Moletsa-nakana 120
Molope 170
Momelantsweng 154
Monang 90
Mondzo 118
Mongana 216
Monkey-orange, Black **132**, 36, 66, 68, 78
Monkey-orange Family 132, 222
Monkey-orange, Spiny **23**, 68, 79
Monokane 154
Mooka 144
Moôka 198
Mookwane 132
Moonaana 186
Mopalema 86, 88
Mopane **116**, 28, 45, 48, 49, 64, 69
Mopane, Small False **49**, 64, 69
Mopanie 116
Mophne 116
Moporota 178
Moraceae 154, 164
Morala 188
Morekuri 162
Moretshe 216
Morôba-diêpê 192
Morôka 136
Morôtô 138
Morukuru 162
Morula 122
Mosehla 96
Mosêlêsêlê 216
Mosêthla 96
Mosikiri 180
Mosu 92
Moswana 92
Motabakgasi 198
Motha 166
Mothakola 190
Mothetlwa 98
Motoro 164
Motsiyara 104
Motswere 118
Motswiri 118
Mountain Kirkia **37**, 70
Mowana 84
Mpfimbahongonyi 108

Mpfungurhu 178
Mpfunta 102
Mphasamhala 186
Mpotsa 204
Mubvumela 156
Muchenje 160
Mufhanda 124
Mufhatela-thundu 202
Mufula 122
Mugavhi 206
Mugwiti 174
Muheri 118
Muhuluri 110
Muhuyu-lukuse 164
Mukhalu mutshetshete 186
Mukumba 108
Mukwalo 126
Mulala 86
Mulberry Family 154, 164, 221
Muluma-nama 98
Munembe-nembe 98
Munga 182
Mungamazi 182
Muonze 162
Mupani 116
Murenzhe 216
Murotso 138
Murunda-gopokopo 102
Musese 96
Mushusha-phombwe 212
Mustard-tree Family 134, 222
Mustard-tree, Narrow-leaved **134**, 46, 67
Mususu 120
Muswinga-phala 108
Mut u-lume 176
Mutalu 136
Mutangule 190
Mutokota 150
Mutondo 138
Mutshema 88
Mutshikili 180
Mutswiriri 100
Muunga 144
Muvhuyu 84
Muvuvhu 174
Muyataha 212
Mvhangazi 138
Mvumayila 156
Myrrh Family 136, 222
Myrtle Family 222

Naboom Euphorbia 152
Nala 86
Narrow-leaved Mustard-tree **134**, 46, 67
Natal-mahogany **180**, 30, 62, 66, 70, 78

Ncelele 212
Ncindzu 88
Ndedze 96
Ndzenga 216
Ndzopfori 162
Ngwavuma 194
Nhlahu 166
Nhlangula 190
Nhlohlo 152
Njalaboom 166
Nkanyi 122
Nkaya 126
Nkelenga 90
Nkonono 120
Nkuhlu 180
Nkuwa 164
Nkwakwa 132
Nnala 142
Nnulu 146
Noorsdoring 152
Northern Lala-palm 86, 33, 66, 69
Nsasane 92
Nsimbitsi 130
Ntoma 160
Ntsalala 188
Numanyama 98
Nuxia oppositifolia 172, 30, 68
Nuxia, Water 172, 30, 68
N'wavulombe 170
Nxanatsi 116
Nxangwa 198
Nxenhe 150
Nyala-tree 166, 30, 67, 70, 81

Oleander Family 222
Ozoroa engleri 40
Ozoroa paniculosa 40, 67

Palm Family 86, 223
Papilionoideae 108, 110, 124, 138, 166, 212
Pappea capensis 192, 31, 66, 68, 79
Peltophorum africanum 96, 63, 65, 76, 80
Peulmahonie 150
Philenoptera violacea 124, 63, 65, 70, 78
Phoenix reclinata 88, 66, 69
Pidiso 178
Pioneer Spikethorn 33, 62, 80
Pod-mahogany 150, 26, 47, 62, 64, 69
Pride-of-de-Kaap Bauhinia 100, 62, 65, 69
Pteleopsis myrtifolia 73
Pterocarpus angolensis 138, 36, 63, 64, 69, 81

Pterocarpus rotundifolius 212, 40, 63, 64, 69
Purple-pod Cluster-leaf 104, 43, 63, 64, 73

Quinine-tree ii, 1

Raasblaar 202
Rain tree 124
Raisin, Sandpaper 208, 68
Raisin, White-leaved 210, 62, 67, 68
Rauvolfia caffra ii, 1
Red Acacia 144, 63, 64, 75, 80
Red Bushwillow 204, 28, 35, 49, 72, 79
Red-leaved Fig 32, 67
Red Spikethorn 106, 33, 40
Resin-tree, Bushveld 40, 67
Resin-tree, Drooping 40
Rhamnaceae 186
Rinyani 112
Risavana 214
River Acacia 182, 27, 65, 75, 80
River Bushwillow 174, 30, 68, 72, 79
Riviervaderlandswilg 174
Rock Fig, Large-leaved 154, 32, 67, 81
Rooiboswilg 204
Rooidoring 144
Rooiessenhout 180
Rooipendoring 106
Round-leaved Bloodwood 212, 40, 63, 64, 69
Rubber-hedge Euphorbia 39, 152
Rubiaceae 176, 188
Russet Bushwillow 206, 72

Saffron, Bushveld 194, 31, 67, 68, 79
Saffron, Transvaal 194
Salvadora australis 134, 46, 67
Salvadoraceae 134
Sambokpeul 98
Sandpaper Raisin 208, 68
Sapindaceae 192
Sausage-tree 178, 30, 62, 66, 70, 78
Scented-pod Acacia 198, 29, 38, 63, 65, 76, 80
Schotia brachypetala 170, 62, 64, 69, 70, 81
Sclerocarya birrea 122, 26, 39, 40, 67, 70, 79, 219
Seboi 84

Sebrahout 110
Sekelbos 216
Shepherds-tree 43, 67, 79
Shilutsi 110
Shimapana 194
Shipalatsi 110
Sickle-bush 216, 40, 63, 64, 76, 80
Silver Cluster-leaf 120, 28, 36, 64, 68, 73, 80
siNga 144
Sjambok pod 98
Skilferdoring 214
Skurwerosyntjie 208
Smalblaarmosterdboom 134
Small False Mopane 49, 64, 69
Small Knob-thorn Acacia 44
Soapberry Family 192, 222
Sourplum Family 223
Sourplum, Large 3
Southern Lala-palm 86, 33, 45, 66, 69
Spikethorn Family 106, 194, 223
Spikethorn, Pioneer 33, 62, 80
Spikethorn, Red 106, 33, 40
Spiny Monkey-orange 23, 68, 79
Spirostachys africana 162, 26, 31, 63, 68, 81
Star-chestnut Family 223
Sterkbos 104
Stink-bushwillow 73
Strychnaceae 132
Strychnos madagascariensis 132, 36, 66, 68, 78
Strychnos spinosa 23, 68, 79
Swartklapper 132
Sweet-pea Family 108, 110, 124, 138, 166, 212, 223
Sycomore Fig 164, 36, 46, 67, 78
Sycomorusvy 164
Syzygium cordatum 30, 63, 66, 68, 81

Tall Firethorn Corkwood 136, 66, 78
Tamboti 162, 26, 31, 63, 68, 81
Tambotie 162
Terminalia prunioides 104, 43, 63, 64, 73
Terminalia sericea 120, 28, 36, 64, 68, 73, 80

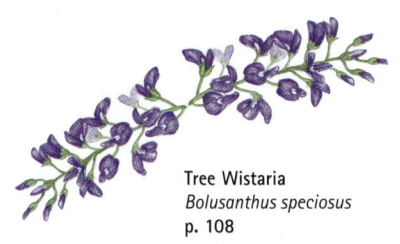

Tree Wistaria
Bolusanthus speciosus
p. 108

241

Thorn-tree Family 90, 92, 112, 126, 140, 142, 144, 182, 196, 198, 214, 216, 223
Tiliaceae 208, 210
Torchwood Family 146, 223
Torchwood, Greenthorn 146, 38, 67, 69, 81
Towerghwarrie 190
Transvaal Saffron 194
Tree Wistaria 108, 63, 65, 69, 80
Trichilia emetica 180, 30, 62, 66, 70, 78
Tshikondengala 152
Tswiriri 100

UBuhlangwe 106
uBukhunku 130
uGagane 216
uVovovo 170
uiSololo 100
umBandu 124
umBhebe 126
umBilo 138
umBitzani 130
umBondwe 174, 204
umBondwe omnyama 118, 204
umBondwe-wasembudwini 202
umBongothi 178
Umbrella Acacia 92, 64, 76, 80
umDlondlovo 100
umDlovume 90
umDongola 196
Umdoni Waterberry 30, 63, 66, 68, 81
umDubu 174
umFala 176
umGana 122
umGongwane 188
umGuluguza 132
umHlakuva 150
umHlalavane 206
umHlambamanzi 98
umHlangula 190

umHlofunga 90
umHlonhlo 108, 152
umHlume 176
umHohlo 108, 152
umHonhlo 108
umKhanyakude 90
umKhaya 126
umKhokhwane 192
umKholikholi 150
umKhuhlu 180
umLahlabantu 186
umMono 118
umNala 112, 142
umNala albizia 112
umNcongo 164
umNgamanzi 182
umNgampondo 196
umNqawe 198
umNulu 146
umNununu 146
umPhafa 186
umPhandu 124
umPhapha Euphorbia 152
umPheme 134
umPhingo 110
umPhuze 144
umSabane 214
umSasane 92
umSehle 96
umSila-omhlophe 156
umSilazembe 216
umThoma 160
umThombothi 162
umThombotsi 162
umToma 160
umValasangweni 188
umVangatane 100
umVangazi 138
umVongotsi 178
umZololo 116

Vaalboom 120
Vanwykshout 108
Velvet Bushwillow 72
Vlam-van-die-vlakte 100
Vlamklimop 102

Water Nuxia 172, 30, 68
Waterberry, Umdoni 30, 63, 66, 68, 81
Watervlier 172
Weeping Boer-bean 170, 62, 64, 69, 70, 81
Weeping Bushwillow 35, 73
Weeping-wattle, African 96, 63, 65, 76, 80
White Kirkia 156, 32, 43, 47, 70, 78
White-leaved Raisin 210, 62, 67, 68
Wild Date-palm 88, 66, 69
Wildedadelpalm 88
Wildekweper 130
Wild-pear Dombeya 36, 61, 62, 66, 68, 80
Wistaria, Tree 108, 63, 65, 69, 80
Witrosyntjie 210
Witsering 156
Worsboom 178

Xanthocercis zambesiaca 166, 30, 67, 70, 81
Xaxandzawu 104
Xicindzu 88
Xifati 136
Xikukutsu 204
Ximenia caffra 3
Ximuwu 84
Xirhomberhombe 154

Zebra-bark Corkwood 47, 78
Zebrawood Flat-bean 110, 63, 65, 69, 79
Ziziphus mucronata 186, 67, 68, 80

Sausage-tree
Kigelia africana
p. 178